HOW WE HOLIDAY

WHAT IS LOVE DURING THE HOLIDAY SEASON? How about jam-stuffed brioche French toast with crisp edges and a custardy center? Or just-from-the-oven buttery, garlicky caraway rolls—tops glistening with melted herb butter? Sometimes love is unapologetically retro clam dip, spinach-artichoke dip, onion dip, or cheese balls, or almond crescents dusted with powdered sugar on the kitchen counter. Or it's the triumphant turkey or bleeding, rare slices of beef rib roast napped with a creamy caper gravy. It most certainly is a juniper-scented roast duck served with a cherry jus infused with flambéed kirsch. Love is a nightly helping of oysters, morale-boosting cook's snacks slurped over the sink, plus one proper shrimp cocktail with pink tails arched and fanned around a bowl of fancy cocktail sauce like two dozen synchronized swimmers. It's a slab of coconut cake and letterpress cookies for later. And warming mulled red wine, sparkling cocktails and conversation, an abundance of good spirits. There's plenty to go around.

This is how the weeks from Thanksgiving through New Year's unspool at my kitchen island—and in the home kitchens of all of us at *Food & Wine*. Cooking becomes a way we celebrate the holidays and our love for one another, with recipes cooked faithfully, and joyfully, through the years.

This collection of more than 300 recipes is your go-to resource for this holiday season—and in the years to come, too. It's a reminder that the most important prep work we can all do is make sure everyone at our tables feels welcome.

A lot of butter, sugar, and chicken stock went into the making of this book, by the by pound and by the gallon. A whole lot of love, too.

HUNTER LEWIS
@NOTESFROMACOOK
HUNTER@FOODANDWINE.COM

CONTENTS

THE ULTIMATE HOLIDAY PARTY PLANNING GUIDE

Whether you're hosting a formal feast for family, a casual dinner get-together with friends, or a festive cocktail party, a bit of advance prep will help your holiday gathering go off without a hitch. Making an impression with delicious food, wine, and cocktails doesn't need to be complicated, nor should it break the bank. And don't be afraid to lean on store-bought shortcuts like phyllo cups for a retro party spread, order sides from your favorite restaurant so you can focus your time on a mouthwatering main dish, or divvy up the cooking and ask guests to bring a dish or beverage.

DINNER PARTIES

The holidays are hectic enough without playing host, so no one would blame you if you outsource your dinner party prep—there will still be plenty of things on your entertaining to-do list. After all, the heart of holiday celebrations isn't the logistics, but the people we bring together. Make-ahead recipes are key so you're not trapped in the kitchen during a party. Shoot for cooking no more than two courses on the day of the party. Here's how to keep relaxed so you can be fully present at your party.

TIME LINE

Three to four weeks out:

- Choose your main course and order any special roasts or cuts of meat to ensure they'll be available when you need them.

- Make and freeze cookie dough for any last minute dessert needs and to bake as you need gifts throughout the month.

- Buy games, small gifts if you want to host a grab bag, or anything else to up the festive quotient.

- Buy paper and ribbons for ornaments: Ask guests to send a photo of a favorite moment from the past year, then turn them into ornaments to decorate with or use as favors or seating cards for guests.

Two weeks out:

- Prepare anything else—pie doughs, soups, and appetizers—that can be made ahead and frozen. If you're baking pies for dessert, make the dough for the crust, roll it out, lay it into pie plates, and freeze right in the pie plate.

- Take a quick inventory to determine if you need to buy any additional serving pieces, glasses, etc.

- Visit your local wine store to inquire about case discounts or any other specials, select your wines, and arrange to have them delivered.

About one week out:

- Shop for all nonperishables, including extra cocktail snacks like nuts and breadsticks, just in case.

- Buy extra plastic containers or Chinese takeout-style food boxes to send leftovers home with guests.

- Buy a stain-remover pen for the guest bathroom.

One to two days out:

- Buy salad greens, seafood, and other perishable ingredients.

PREPPING AND COOKING

Make-ahead recipes are key so you're not trapped in the kitchen during a party. Shoot for cooking no more than two courses on the day of the party.

**Smoky Mezcal-Fig
Sour,** RECIPE P. 45

FOOD & WINE® MAGAZINE
EDITOR IN CHIEF **Hunter Lewis**
EXECUTIVE DIRECTOR, CONTENT STRATEGY **Miles Stiverson**
DEPUTY EDITOR **Melanie Hansche**
EXECUTIVE EDITOR **Karen Shimizu**
EXECUTIVE WINE EDITOR **Ray Isle**
DIGITAL EXECUTIVE EDITOR **Ryan Grim**
MANAGING EDITOR **Caitlin Murphree Miller**

FOOD & EDITORIAL
SENIOR FOOD EDITOR **Mary-Frances Heck**
FOOD EDITOR **Josh Miller**
ASSOCIATE FOOD EDITOR **Kelsey Youngman**
RESTAURANT EDITOR **Khushbu Shah**
ASSOCIATE RESTAURANT EDITOR **Oset Babur**
ASSISTANT EDITOR **Nina Friend**
BUSINESS MANAGER **Alice Eldridge Summerville**

COPY & RESEARCH
COPY EDITOR **Erin Clyburn**
ASSOCIATE COPY EDITOR **Winn Duvall**

ART
CREATIVE DIRECTOR **Winslow Taft**
ART FELLOW **Rachel Carney**

PHOTO
PHOTO DIRECTOR **Tori Katherman**
PHOTO EDITOR **Dan Bailey**

PRODUCTION
PRODUCTION DIRECTOR **Liz Rhoades**

DIGITAL
SENIOR ENGAGEMENT EDITOR **Meg Clark**
DIGITAL DEPUTY EDITOR **Adina Steiman**
SENIOR EDITOR **Kat Kinsman**
SENIOR EDITOR **Margaret Eby**
AUDIENCE ENGAGEMENT EDITOR **Caroline Schnapp**
RESTAURANT EDITOR **Maria Yagoda**
ASSOCIATE NEWS EDITOR **Adam Campbell-Schmitt**
DIGITAL REPORTER **Bridget Hallinan**
DIGITAL PHOTO EDITOR **Sarah Crowder**
DIGITAL OPERATIONS EDITOR **Elsa Säätelä**
ASSOCIATE DIGITAL EDITOR **Megan Soll**

CONTRIBUTORS
CULINARY DIRECTOR AT LARGE **Justin Chapple**

MEREDITH CORPORATION CONSUMER MARKETING
CONSUMER MARKETING PRODUCT DIRECTOR **Daniel Fagan**
CONSUMER MARKETING PRODUCT MANAGER **Max Daily**
CONSUMER PRODUCTS MARKETING MANAGER **Kylie Dazzo**
CONSUMER MARKETING CONTENT MANAGER **Julie Doll**
SENIOR PRODUCTION MANAGER **Liza Ward**

WATERBURY PUBLICATIONS, INC.
EDITORIAL DIRECTOR **Lisa Kingsley**
CREATIVE DIRECTOR **Ken Carlson**
ASSOCIATE EDITOR **Tricia Bergman**
ASSOCIATE DESIGN DIRECTOR **Doug Samuelson**
PRODUCTION ASSISTANT **Mindy Samuelson**
ASSISTANT EDITOR **Will Bortz**
CONTRIBUTING COPY EDITOR **Michael Olivo**
CONTRIBUTING PROOFREADER **Carrie Truesdell**
CONTRIBUTING INDEXER **Mary Williams**

MEREDITH CORPORATION
PRESIDENT AND CEO **Tom Harty**
CHAIRMAN **Stephen M. Lacy**

FOOD & WINE
Holiday Recipes

BY THE EDITORS OF *FOOD & WINE*

FOOD & WINE
BOOKS

Cheddar Rillettes,
RECIPE P. 20

CREAM IT

The correct ratio of cheese, mayonnaise, and bacon fat yields a softer, creamier dip that's ideal for scooping up with crudités, toast, and crackers.

Shrimp Toasts with Scallion-Chile Sauce,
RECIPE P. 20

Smoked Trout-Caraway Rillettes

TOTAL 15 MIN; MAKES 2½ CUPS

Labneh is yogurt that's been strained to remove all the whey, resulting in a thick, creamy fresh cheese. Here, it provides the base for a light and tangy smoked trout spread.

- 1½ cups labneh
- 2 Tbsp. minced shallot
- 3 Tbsp. extra-virgin olive oil
- 2 tsp. caraway seeds
- 3 thinly sliced scallions, plus more for garnish
- Kosher salt and black pepper
- 4 smoked trout fillets (12 oz.), skinned, meat flaked into large pieces
- Spicy Quick-Pickled Radishes (recipe follows) and rye crackers, for serving

Combine labneh, shallot, oil, caraway seeds, and 3 sliced scallions in a medium bowl; season with salt and pepper and mix well. Gently fold in flaked trout. Garnish rillettes with scallions and serve at room temperature with Spicy Quick-Pickled Radishes and rye crackers. —KAY CHUN

MAKE AHEAD The rillettes can be refrigerated for 2 to 3 days and brought to room temperature before serving.

♦ ♦ ♦

Duck Liver Pâté with Blackberry Conserva

TOTAL 1 HR 20 MIN, PLUS 6 HR REFRIGERATION; SERVES 8

The tartness and texture of the blackberry conserva is a nice contrast to the rich, silky pâté. Spoon leftover blackberry conserva on pancakes, waffles, or ice cream.

DUCK LIVER PÂTÉ

- 14 oz. duck livers (about 1¼ cups)
- 1 Tbsp. plus ¼ tsp. kosher salt, divided
- ½ cup plus 2 Tbsp. unsalted butter (5 oz.)
- 1 medium yellow onion, thinly sliced
- 10 fresh sage leaves
- ⅓ cup Champagne or dry white wine
- ⅓ cup duck fat, melted

BLACKBERRY CONSERVA

- 2 lb. fresh or frozen blackberries

- 5 Tbsp. granulated sugar
- 2 Tbsp. water
- 4 fresh thyme sprigs
- 3 whole cloves
- ⅛ tsp. kosher salt
- Pinch of black pepper
- Grilled bread slices and whole-grain mustard, for serving

1. Make duck liver pâté Stir together livers and ¼ teaspoon salt in a medium bowl. Set aside.

2. Melt butter in a large skillet over medium. Add onion, and cook, stirring occasionally, until softened and translucent but not browned, about 10 minutes. Transfer onion mixture to bowl of a food processor. Add livers to skillet, and cook over medium until bright pink all the way through, 1 minute to 1 minute and 30 seconds per side. Add sage, and cook until fragrant, about 15 seconds. Remove skillet from heat; stir in Champagne. Let stand 5 minutes.

3. Transfer liver mixture to food processor with onion mixture. Process until smooth and silky, about 2 minutes, stopping to scrape down sides as needed. Add remaining 1 tablespoon salt. Process until incorporated, about 10 seconds. Using a rubber spatula, press liver mixture through a fine wire-mesh strainer into a bowl; discard solids. Transfer pureed liver mixture to a large (20- to 24-ounce) terrine mold or ramekin or 2 smaller (10- to 12-ounce) ramekins. Smooth top, and tap ramekin on counter a few times to remove any air bubbles. Cover pâté with melted duck fat (about ¼ inch thick), and chill, uncovered, until set, at least 6 hours or up to 2 days.

4. Make the blackberry conserva Combine blackberries, sugar, and 2 tablespoons water in a large saucepan. Wrap thyme and cloves in cheesecloth, and tie ends to make a sachet. Add sachet to blackberry mixture. Bring to a boil over medium-high, stirring often. Reduce heat to medium-low; cook, stirring often, until blackberries break down and mixture has thickened and reduced to about 2 cups, 30 to 40 minutes.

5. Remove from heat. Remove and discard sachet. Stir in salt and pepper. Transfer blackberry mixture to a shallow bowl, and spread out to cool. Immediately transfer to refrigerator, and chill, uncovered, 2 hours to preserve vibrant color. Transfer blackberry conserva to an airtight container, and chill at least 2 hours or up to 3 days.

6. Remove pâté from refrigerator 30 minutes before serving. Serve pâté with blackberry conserva, grilled crusty bread, and whole-grain mustard. —ANGIE MAR

MAKE AHEAD Duck liver pâté can be made up to 2 days in advance; blackberry conserva can be made 3 days in advance.

WINE Pair with a robust but elegant rosé Champagne.

♦ ♦ ♦

Spicy Quick-Pickled Radishes

TOTAL 15 MIN, PLUS COOLING; MAKES 1 QUART

Pickling with dill, garlic, and chiles tones down the radishes' harshness while making them nicely herbal and aromatic.

- 1 lb. radishes with fresh leafy greens, halved lengthwise
- 12 dill sprigs
- 1½ cups distilled white vinegar
- 5 garlic cloves, crushed
- 5 chiles de árbol, halved
- 3 Tbsp. kosher salt
- 1 Tbsp. granulated sugar

1. Pack radishes and dill into a heatproof 1-quart jar.

2. Combine vinegar, garlic, chiles, salt, sugar, and ½ cup water in a small saucepan. Bring to a boil, stirring to dissolve sugar. Pour hot brine over radishes and let cool to room temperature. Serve at room temperature or chilled. —KAY CHUN

MAKE AHEAD The pickled radishes can be refrigerated in the brine for 3 days.

Green Cocktail Sauce

ACTIVE 10 MIN; TOTAL 40 MIN;
MAKES 2 CUPS

F&W's Justin Chapple puts a spin on traditional cocktail sauce, making it with tangy green tomatillos and cilantro, horseradish, and spicy green bottled hot sauce.

- 1 lb. tomatillos
- 1 cup fresh cilantro, lightly packed
- 2 Tbsp. horseradish, drained
- 1 Tbsp. green hot sauce

Combine tomatillos, cilantro, horseradish, and hot sauce in a food processor. Cover; puree until nearly smooth. Scrape into a bowl and season with salt and black pepper. Cover and refrigerate until chilled, about 30 minutes. — JUSTIN CHAPPLE

MAKE AHEAD The sauce can be refrigerated in an airtight container for up to 1 week.

Guajillo Mayonnaise

ACTIVE 15 MIN; TOTAL 45 MIN;
MAKES 1⅓ CUPS

Consider using this rich sauce for dipping shrimp and lobster (and french fries, too).

- ½ cup extra-virgin olive oil
- 2 guajillo chiles, stemmed, seeded, and chopped
- 1 cup mayonnaise

Heat olive oil in a medium skillet over medium until shimmering. Add guajillo chiles, and fry, stirring, until fragrant, 30 seconds. Remove from heat; let cool. Combine chiles and oil with mayonnaise in a food processor, and puree until nearly smooth. Scrape into a bowl and season with salt and black pepper. — JUSTIN CHAPPLE

MAKE AHEAD The mayonnaise can be refrigerated for up to 2 weeks.

Apple-Cucumber Mignonette

ACTIVE 15 MIN; TOTAL 45 MIN;
MAKES 1½ CUPS

Mignonette sauce is traditionally served with raw oysters.

- ¾ cup Champagne vinegar
- ¼ Pink Lady or Honey Crisp apple, cored and minced
- 1 Persian cucumber, minced
- 2 Tbsp. minced fresh chives
- 1 tsp. white pepper
  Kosher salt

Whisk together vinegar, apple, cucumber, minced, and chives in a large bowl. Season mignonette with white pepper and kosher salt. Cover and refrigerate until chilled, about 30 minutes. — JUSTIN CHAPPLE

MAKE AHEAD The mignonette can be refrigerated for up to 3 days.

Deviled Eggs with Crab and Caviar

ACTIVE 35 MIN; TOTAL 1 HR; MAKES 24

These upgraded deviled eggs with crabmeat and caviar are an easy make-ahead: Hard-boil your eggs the day before and even separate your whites and yolks to make your filling for easy next-day assembly. Store the prepared filling with a sheet of plastic wrap pressed on the surface to prevent it from drying out in the refrigerator.

- 1 dozen large eggs
- ¾ cup mayonnaise
- 2 Tbsp. Dijon mustard
- 2 Tbsp. minced shallot
- 2 Tbsp. thinly sliced fresh chives, plus more for garnish
- 1 Tbsp. finely chopped fresh parsley
- 1 Tbsp. rinsed and finely chopped capers
- 1 tsp. finely chopped fresh thyme
- 1 tsp. sherry vinegar
- ¼ tsp. hot sauce
  Kosher salt
- 3 oz. crabmeat, picked over
  Caviar, for garnish

1. Fill a large bowl with ice water. Place eggs in a large saucepan and cover with water by 1 inch; bring to a boil. Cover and remove pan from heat. Let stand for 10 minutes. Drain eggs and transfer to ice water bath to cool completely.

2. Peel and halve eggs lengthwise. Transfer yolks to a medium bowl and mash with back of a spoon. Arrange egg whites on a platter. To the bowl with egg yolks add mayonnaise, mustard, shallot, 2 tablespoons chives, parsley, capers, thyme, vinegar, and hot sauce, and whisk until smooth. Season with salt. Transfer mixture to a piping bag and fill egg whites (or use a small spoon). Top each deviled egg with some crab and garnish with caviar and chives. — JOHN BESH & CHRIS LUSK

MAKE AHEAD The cooked eggs can be refrigerated overnight.

Chicken Liver Pâté with Green Peppercorns

TOTAL 40 MIN, PLUS OVERNIGHT SOAKING; MAKES 2½ CUPS

The richness of this silky pâté is balanced by tart green peppercorns. It's even better made a day ahead, making it a convenient Thanksgiving Day starter.

- 1 lb. chicken livers, well trimmed
- 2 cups whole milk
- 3 Tbsp. extra-virgin olive oil, divided
- 1 small onion, thinly sliced
  Small fresh sage leaves
- 2 garlic cloves, thinly sliced
  Kosher salt and black pepper
- 2 Tbsp. bourbon
- 3 Tbsp. fresh lemon juice
- 2 sticks unsalted butter, at room temperature
- 2 Tbsp. chopped brined green peppercorns, plus 1 Tbsp. brine from the jar
  Rye crackers, for serving

1. Combine livers and milk in a bowl and refrigerate overnight.

2. Drain and rinse livers; pat dry. Heat 2 tablespoons oil in a large nonstick skillet over medium. Add onion and 5 sage leaves, and cook until deep golden, about 8 minutes. Stir in garlic, and cook for 1 minute. Scrape mixture into a food processor.

3. Heat remaining 1 tablespoon oil in same skillet over medium. Season livers with salt and pepper, and cook, turning once, until golden, 2 minutes. Add bourbon, and cook until almost evaporated and the livers are barely pink inside, 1 minute.

4. Add livers and lemon juice to a food processor; pulse to finely chop. With machine running, add butter, 1 tablespoon at a time, until pâté is very smooth. Stir in green peppercorns and brine. Season with salt and pepper.

5. Transfer pâté to 2 bowls. Cover and refrigerate until chilled. Garnish with sage and serve with rye crackers. — KAY CHUN

Chile-Toasted Marcona Almonds, RECIPE P. 29

Marinated Olives with Orange, RECIPE P. 29

Duck Liver Pâté with
Blackberry Conserva

Guajillo Mayonnaise

Green Cocktail Sauce

Apple-Cucumber
Mignonette

Small Bites

Popcorn with Sesame-Glazed Pistachios,
RECIPE P. 29

Spiced Pickled Beets,
RECIPE P. 29

In early December, make and freeze cookie dough for any last-minute dessert needs and to bake as you need gifts throughout the month. About two weeks before your party, prepare anything else—pie doughs, soups, appetizers—that can be made ahead and frozen. If you're baking pies for dessert, make the dough for the crust, roll it out, lay it into pie plates, and freeze right in the plate.

ENTERTAINING TIPS

Studies show that people remember the beginning and end of an experience most. But with last-minute food prep and logistics to figure out, that's not usually where a host's attention is. Think about ways to make a guest's arrival and departure special. Maybe that's a brief welcome toast or ice-breaker game before dinner, and a favor for guests to take when they leave.

Lighting creates a vibe, so spend some time to get it right. Candles are the easiest way to create soft lighting and illuminate different areas. Scatter a combination of votives and pillars around, or fill a large tray with all different sizes of candles and place it in a corner. String lights also provide a warm glow. Try tucking them inside a lantern or under a glass dome.

COCKTAIL PARTIES

There's no reason to let hosting a cocktail party consume you. This season, reconsider your approach to service, and take your cues from fine-dining restaurants. Set your mise en place and focus on the art of gathering ingredients, glassware, and dishes for serving, such as punch bowls and pitchers.

PREPARE AHEAD

A few days before the event, collect your ingredients, start making syrups and special ice, and figure out what space you'll need for beverages and glassware. Batch cocktails like the Earl Grey-Aquavit Spritz (recipe, page 42) can be made the night before so on the day of, you can just set out your garnishes, and let guests assemble their own drinks.

SERVE THYSELF

If you don't want to work a bartending shift in your own home, have self-serve options, like beer, wine, and sparkling water, plus batch cocktails and mocktails in a pitcher or punch bowl. This frees you up and allows guests to take ownership of their drinking. The key is making sure not to put everything out at once. Set out some of the beer and wine along with half of the cocktails, and refill throughout the night.

RENT THE DISHES

If you're entertaining a crowd, don't go out and buy festive glassware—rent it. Racks for glassware generally come in sets of 15 to 25, starting at 40 cents a glass, and you don't have to worry about cleaning them afterward. Punch bowls are fragile and bound to break if you are putting them to good use. Rent them, or buy them inexpensively at thrift stores, estate sales, eBay, and discount stores.

WINE FOR A CROWD

GLASSES 101

For parties of 20 people or more, renting makes sense. It will cost up to $1 per stem or so, and there's no cleanup involved. Contact a party rental company. If you throw frequent parties, consider buying glasses.

Providing a different glass for red wine, white wine, water, and Champagne and sparkling wine cocktails can seem a bit daunting, so look for stemware that works well for both red and white wines and can serve as a water glass, too. Champagne and sparkling wine cocktails are the exceptions and deserves their own fluted glasses so you can enjoy all of those lovely bubbles.

WINE CALCULATOR

To figure out how much wine you need for your party, know that a standard bottle of wine is 750 milliliters, which is about 25 ounces. That translates to five 5-ounce pours, which is considered the correct amount, no matter the size of the glass.

For a four-hour dinner party, plan on five glasses of wine per person (or one bottle per person). For a two-hour cocktail party, plan on three glasses of wine per person (for 20 people this means 12 bottles of wine). Choose inexpensive and versatile wines for your gathering.

PROPER SERVING TEMPERATURE

White Wine (serve at 55°F)
In a refrigerator: 1½ hours
In a freezer: 40 minutes
In ice & water: 20 minutes
If it's been stored in a refrigerator, keep it at room temperature for 20 minutes
Red Wine (serve at 65°F)
In a refrigerator: 20 minutes

COPING WITH RED WINE STAINS

Don't let a spill spoil the party. Red wine stains aren't as difficult to get out as you might think. One foolproof way to get stains out of carpets and upholstery is to use a spray made of fruit and vegetable extracts created for wine spills. Or blot up as much of the stain as possible with a paper towel or clean cloth, saturate the area with cold water, blot that up, then apply a paste of 3 parts baking soda to 1 part water. Let the paste dry, then vacuum it up.

Mini Wedge Salads with Anchovy Dressing, RECIPE P. 20

WEDGE IT

Instead of chopped or torn lettuces, serve tiny wedges of Little Gem brushed with Caesar-style dressing and dredged in lemony herbed bread crumbs.

CASUAL, MASTERED

We've all been to that party. The hors d'oeuvres look amazing but require a fork and plate, and you have a glass in your hand. What do you do? Juggle everything and try not to spill? Set down the glass? These appetizers each require one hand—and only one hand—to eat.

SMEAR IT

A quick shrimp mousse, after just 3 minutes in a hot skillet, clings to classic sandwich bread, forming a crisp one-handed toast that's perfect for dipping.

CASUAL, MASTERED MENU

Mini Wedge Salads with Anchovy Dressing

TOTAL 35 MIN; MAKES 2 DOZEN SALADS

These mini wedges are coated in a creamy, anchovy-packed dressing and dredged in crunchy panko, making them easy to eat with your hands. Alternatively, you can serve the dressing and bread crumbs alongside the lettuce wedges, for easy dipping.

- 1 cup mayonnaise
- 1 (2-oz.) can flat anchovy fillets in oil, drained
- 1 oz. Parmigiano-Reggiano cheese, finely grated (about ¼ cup)
- 1½ Tbsp. red wine vinegar
- 1 Tbsp. Dijon mustard
- 1 small garlic clove, peeled
- Kosher salt, to taste
- Finely ground black pepper, to taste
- 2 Tbsp. extra-virgin olive oil
- 1 cup panko
- ¼ cup finely chopped fresh chives
- 2 tsp. lemon zest
- 4 (4-oz.) heads Little Gem lettuce, stems trimmed, outer leaves removed, and heads cut lengthwise into 6 wedges each

1. Combine mayonnaise, anchovies, cheese, vinegar, mustard, and garlic in a food processor. Process until smooth, about 45 seconds, stopping to scrape down sides as needed. Transfer mixture to a bowl; season generously with salt and pepper. Refrigerate, uncovered, until ready to use.

2. Heat oil in a medium skillet over medium until shimmering, about 2 minutes and 30 seconds. Add panko; cook, stirring occasionally, until lightly browned, about 5 minutes. Season with salt and pepper. Transfer to a small baking sheet; let cool 10 minutes. Stir in chives and lemon zest.

3. Using a small offset spatula, spread anchovy dressing over cut sides of lettuce. Dredge in panko mixture. Transfer to a platter or board, and serve. — JUSTIN CHAPPLE

MAKE AHEAD Store dressing in an airtight container in refrigerator up to 5 days.

WINE Pair this menu with a citrusy Prosecco.

Shrimp Toasts with Scallion-Chile Sauce

TOTAL 35 MIN; MAKES 4 DOZEN TOASTS

The secret to this semitraditional dim sum favorite is a butter-studded shrimp mousse that comes together quickly in a food processor with just five ingredients.

- 8 oz. peeled and deveined raw large shrimp
- 1 large egg
- 1 tsp. kosher salt
- 2 Tbsp. cold unsalted butter, cubed
- 3½ tsp. toasted sesame seeds, divided
- 6 (¾-oz.) white bread slices, crusts removed
- Canola oil, for frying
- ½ scallion, finely chopped
- 1 Tbsp. soy sauce
- 1 Tbsp. rice vinegar
- 1½ tsp. sambal oelek
- Thinly sliced scallion, for garnish

1. Combine shrimp, egg, and salt in a food processor; process until smooth, about 15 seconds, stopping to scrape down sides as needed. Add butter and 2 teaspoons sesame seeds, and pulse until smooth with flecks of butter remaining, about 7 times. Spread ¼ cup shrimp mousse on each bread slice.

2. Pour oil to a depth of ⅛ inch in a large nonstick skillet; heat over medium until shimmering, about 3 minutes and 30 seconds. Working in batches, add bread slices, mousse-side down, and cook until lightly browned, about 2 minutes. Flip toasts; cook until browned and mousse is firm to touch, about 1 minute. Transfer to a paper towel-lined plate to drain.

3. Stir together 1½ teaspoons scallion, soy sauce, vinegar, sambal oelek, and remaining 1½ teaspoons sesame seeds in a small bowl. Cut each toast into

8 triangles; transfer to a platter or board. Serve soy sauce mixture with toasts. Garnish toasts with sliced scallion, and serve. — JUSTIN CHAPPLE

MAKE AHEAD Store uncooked shrimp mousse in an airtight container up to 2 days. Let stand at room temperature 30 minutes before spreading on bread slices in Step 1.

Cheddar Rillettes

TOTAL 20 MIN; MAKES ABOUT 1½ CUPS

Unlike traditional rillettes, such as pork or duck, which rely on fat to preserve and flavor the meat, this pimento cheese-inspired version made with cheddar incorporates rendered bacon fat to create the perfect texture and lend a pleasant, smoky flavor. Sprinkle the crisp bacon on top for crunchy contrast.

- 2 Tbsp. extra-virgin olive oil
- 4 center-cut bacon slices (about 5 oz.), finely chopped (about 1 cup)
- ½ cup mayonnaise
- 1½ tsp. finely grated shallot or white onion
- ½ tsp. hot sauce
- 8 oz. sharp white cheddar cheese, shredded (about 2 cups)
- Kosher salt, to taste

1. Heat oil in a large skillet over medium-low. Add bacon, and cook, stirring occasionally, until rendered and crisp, about 7 minutes. Using a slotted spoon, transfer bacon to a paper towel-lined plate to drain. Transfer 2 tablespoons rendered bacon drippings to a small bowl; discard remaining drippings.

2. Whisk together mayonnaise, shallot, and hot sauce in a medium bowl. Slowly drizzle in reserved bacon drippings, whisking constantly, until blended. Combine mayonnaise mixture and cheese in a food processor, and pulse until cheese is very finely chopped, about 4 times. Scrape into a serving bowl, and season with salt. Sprinkle with bacon. Serve with crudités, toasted bread, or crackers. — JUSTIN CHAPPLE

Four-Layer Caviar Dip

ACTIVE 15 MIN; TOTAL 2 HR 15 MIN; SERVES 12

Layers of creamy egg salad; crisp red onion; herbed cream cheese; and salty, briny caviar come together in a beautiful molded dip that serves up an entire caviar platter in one dish.

- Nonstick cooking spray
- 6 large hard-cooked eggs, chopped
- 2 Tbsp. sour cream
- 2 Tbsp. mayonnaise
- ½ tsp. salt
- 1 cup rinsed and dried finely chopped red onion
- 8 oz. softened cream cheese
- ⅓ cup thinly sliced fresh chives
- 2 oz. black caviar
- Crackers

Lightly grease a 6-inch ring mold with cooking spray. Stir together eggs, sour cream, mayonnaise, and salt in a medium bowl. Spoon egg mixture evenly on bottom of prepared ring mold. Top evenly with red onion. Stir together cream cheese and chives in a bowl, and gently spread over onion; top with caviar. Refrigerate 2 hours. Unmold onto a serving plate or platter, and serve with crackers. — BETSY ANDREWS

Warm Spinach-Artichoke Dip

ACTIVE 10 MIN; TOTAL 40 MIN; SERVES 10

Filled with four kinds of cheese and plenty of tender artichoke hearts, this dip is creamy with a crisp, golden top. Be sure to drain the thawed frozen spinach well to avoid excess water, which can break the cheese sauce.

- 6 oz. softened cream cheese
- 1 cup thawed and drained frozen spinach
- ¾ cup thawed frozen artichoke hearts
- ¾ cup grated Gouda
- ½ cup mozzarella
- ¼ cup chopped scallions
- ¼ cup mayonnaise
- 1 tsp. finely chopped garlic
- ½ tsp. kosher salt
- ¼ tsp. cayenne pepper
- ¼ cup Parmesan
- Crostini and/or tortilla chips

Preheat oven to 400°F. Stir together cream cheese, spinach, artichoke hearts, Gouda, mozzarella, scallions, mayonnaise, garlic, salt, and cayenne in a medium bowl until smooth. Spoon into a 1-quart baking dish; sprinkle top evenly with Parmesan. Bake in preheated oven until browned and bubbly, about 25 minutes. Serve with crostini or tortilla chips. — BETSY ANDREWS

Herbed Potato Chips

TOTAL 45 MIN; SERVES 10 TO 12

Chef, author, and TV host Tyler Florence fries fresh herbs in hot oil until crispy, infusing it with great flavor before he adds the potatoes.

- 3 large baking potatoes, scrubbed and patted dry, sliced very thinly crosswise on a mandoline
- Grapeseed oil, for frying
- 4 sage sprigs
- 3 fresh rosemary sprigs
- 3 fresh thyme sprigs
- 2 fresh parsley sprigs
- Kosher salt

1. Place potatoes into a bowl, and cover with cold water and swish to rinse off starch; drain. Repeat rinsing until water is clear. Transfer potato slices to a paper towel-lined baking sheet and pat thoroughly dry.

2. Heat 3 inches grapeseed oil in a large pot to 360°F. Add sage, rosemary, thyme, and parsley sprigs to hot oil and fry, stirring, until crisp, 1 to 2 minutes. Using a slotted spoon, transfer herbs to paper towels to drain.

3. Working in small batches, fry potato slices at 350°F, stirring occasionally, until golden, 3 to 5 minutes. Using a slotted spoon, transfer potato chips to paper towels to drain. Generously sprinkle chips and herbs with salt and serve. — TYLER FLORENCE

MAKE AHEAD The chips and herbs can be made early in the day and stored uncovered at room temperature.

Roasted Onion Dip

ACTIVE 45 MIN; TOTAL 2 HR 45 MIN; SERVES 10 TO 12

Chef and restaurateur Tyler Florence makes smart use of whole onions for this extremely tasty recipe. He roasts them, scoops out the tender centers to mix into the dip, and turns the onion shells into serving bowls.

- 2 medium unpeeled red onions
- 2 medium unpeeled Spanish onions
- 2 medium unpeeled sweet onions
- ½ cup mayonnaise
- ½ cup sour cream
- ½ tsp. onion powder
- Kosher salt and black pepper
- Salmon, trout, and sturgeon caviar, for serving
- Fennel fronds, for garnish
- Herbed Potato Chips (recipe precedes), for serving

1. Preheat oven to 350°F. Using a paring knife, trim bottoms of onions and stand them in a baking dish. Bake for about 1 hour and 30 minutes, until very soft. Let cool.

2. Using a paring knife, carefully cut ½ inch off top of onions. Using a small spoon, scoop out all but 2 or 3 layers of the roasted onions to form cups; you should have 2½ cups of pulp. Finely chop onion pulp and transfer to a medium bowl. Stir in mayonnaise, sour cream, and onion powder, and season dip generously with salt and pepper. Cover and refrigerate until chilled, about 30 minutes. Keep onion cups at room temperature.

3. Spoon onion dip into onion cups and transfer to a platter. Top dip with salmon, trout, and sturgeon caviar, and garnish with fennel fronds. Serve with Herbed Potato Chips. — TYLER FLORENCE

MAKE AHEAD The onion cups and onion dip can be refrigerated separately overnight. Let the onion cups return to room temperature before filling them.

Sweet Potato and Feta Bourekas

ACTIVE 1 HR; TOTAL 1 HR 40 MIN; SERVES 8

Bourekas are crisp, savory little parcels filled with anything from vegetables and cheese to ground meat. Inspired by his grandmother's recipe, Israeli chef Michael Solomonov's version is stuffed with sweet potato, Bulgarian feta, dill, and olives.

- 1 small sweet potato (about 8 oz.), peeled and cut into 1-inch cubes
- ⅓ cup crumbled Bulgarian feta cheese
- ¼ cup roughly chopped fresh dill
- 1 Tbsp. finely chopped Kalamata olives
- ½ tsp. kosher salt
- 1 large egg, lightly beaten, divided
- 1 (17.3-oz.) pkg. frozen puff pastry sheets, thawed
- 2 tsp. water
- Sesame seeds

1. Place sweet potato cubes in a small saucepan, and add cold water to cover by 2 inches. Bring to a boil over high; reduce heat to medium-low, and simmer until potatoes are fork-tender, about 10 minutes. Drain; transfer to a medium bowl. Let cool completely, about 30 minutes. Add feta, dill, olives, salt, and 2 tablespoons of egg; mash mixture with a fork until almost creamy (some lumps are okay).

2. Preheat oven to 400°F. On a lightly floured surface, roll 1 pastry sheet into a 12-inch square. Cut sheet into 16 (3-inch) squares. Transfer squares to a parchment paper-lined baking sheet. Whisk together 2 teaspoons water and remaining beaten egg in a small bowl. Spoon a scant 2 teaspoons sweet potato mixture onto center of each square; brush edges lightly with egg wash. Fold each square over to make a triangle. Using tines of a fork, crimp edges to seal. Transfer to a second parchment paper-lined baking sheet. Repeat rolling and filling procedures with remaining puff pastry sheet and remaining sweet potato mixture. Lightly brush tops with remaining egg wash; sprinkle with sesame seeds. Refrigerate on baking sheets 15 minutes.

3. Bake on same oven rack in preheated oven until golden brown, about 25 minutes, rotating baking sheets (front to back) halfway through baking. (If pans don't fit on same rack, bake separately.)
— MICHAEL SOLOMONOV

Khinkali (Meat-Filled Dumplings)

ACTIVE 1 HR; TOTAL 1 HR 10 MIN; SERVES 8

These chewy dumplings are one of the most popular foods in the country of Georgia. The dough is the right strength to contain the juicy filling and is easy to work with as long as there isn't too much flour on the work surface. The dough should grip the table in order to stretch properly and not spring back.

DOUGH

- 2 cups all-purpose flour (about 8½ oz.), plus more for work surface
- ½ tsp. fine sea salt
- 1 large egg, beaten
- Extra-virgin olive oil, for greasing

MEAT FILLING

- 4 oz. 80% lean ground beef
- 4 oz. ground pork
- ⅓ cup finely chopped yellow onion
- 2 Tbsp. finely chopped fresh cilantro
- 2 Tbsp. unsalted butter, melted
- 1 tsp. fine sea salt
- ¼ tsp. dried kondari (summer savory) or mild thyme
- ¼ tsp. coriander seeds, crushed
- ¼ tsp. caraway seeds, finely chopped
- ¼ tsp. freshly ground black pepper, plus more for serving
- ¼ tsp. crushed red pepper, or to taste
- ⅛ tsp. ground cumin
- 1 garlic clove, finely chopped

ADDITIONAL INGREDIENTS

- 2 fresh bay leaves

1. Make the dough Stir together flour and salt in a medium bowl. Make a well in center; add ½ cup water and egg. Stir with a wooden spoon until a shaggy dough forms. Turn dough out onto a lightly floured surface, and knead until smooth and elastic, 4 to 5 minutes. Place dough in a lightly oiled bowl, and cover loosely with plastic wrap. Set aside.

2. Make the meat filling Using a fork or your hands, stir together ground beef, ground pork, ¾ cup water, onion, cilantro, butter, sea salt, kondari, coriander seeds, caraway seeds, black pepper, red pepper, cumin, and garlic in a large bowl until ground meat is completely broken up and mixture is well blended.

3. Divide dough into thirds. Shape 1 dough portion into a ball, and roll out to about ¼-inch thickness on a lightly floured work surface. (Keep remaining dough portions covered with plastic wrap while you work.) Using a 2½-inch round cutter, cut out 8 dough circles, rerolling dough scraps as necessary.

4. Roll each dough circle into a larger 4-inch circle. Place about 1 tablespoon (about ½ ounce) meat filling in center of each dough circle, and pleat dough edge, gathering top like a pouch to enclose filling. When you have pleated all the way around, pinch top edges together firmly, and give the dough a little twist to make a stem and to make sure the khinkali is well sealed. (If you don't want the stems, lightly press the twisted stem down into the dumpling with your finger.) Place finished dumplings on a piece of lightly floured parchment paper; cover loosely with plastic wrap, and repeat process with remaining dough portions and filling.

5. Bring a large pot of salted water and bay leaves to a boil over high. Carefully add half of dumplings to water, and stir gently with a wooden spoon (without piercing dumplings) to make sure they don't stick to bottom of pot. Boil until dough is tender and meat is cooked through, 8 to 10 minutes. Remove khinkali with a spider, and drain on paper towels. Repeat with remaining half of dumplings. Sprinkle khinkali with black pepper, and serve hot.
— CARLA CAPALBO

NOTE Khinkali are designed to be eaten by hand. Hold each dumpling by its stem (like an open umbrella) and take a small bite from the side of the cushiony top, sucking out the hot broth before digging into the filling. Discard the stem.

Sweet Potato and
Feta Bourekas

Mushroom Toasts with Delice de Bourgogne

Mushroom Toasts with Délice de Bourgogne

TOTAL 45 MIN; SERVES 12

Triple-crème cheese, an ultra-rich version of Brie, is topped with pan-roasted mushrooms and herbs in this elevated appetizer.

- 6 Tbsp. olive oil, divided
- 1 lb. mixed fresh wild mushrooms, cut into 1-inch pieces, divided
- 9 fresh thyme sprigs, divided
- 6 large garlic cloves, crushed, divided
- 1¼ tsp. kosher salt, divided
- 1 tsp. black pepper, divided
- 5 Tbsp. unsalted butter, softened, divided
- 3 Tbsp. finely chopped fresh flat-leaf parsley, divided, plus more for garnish
- 1 Tbsp. sherry vinegar, divided
- 6 (½-inch-thick) brioche slices, halved
- 8 oz. Délice de Bourgogne or other triple-crème cheese, at room temperature
  Pickled pearl onions, thinly sliced
  Chopped frisée, white and light green parts only, for garnish
  Snipped fresh chives, for garnish
  Fresh lemon juice, for drizzling
  Extra-virgin olive oil, for drizzling

1. Heat 2 tablespoons oil in a large cast-iron skillet over high just until smoking. Add one-third of the mushrooms in a single layer, and cook, without stirring, until golden brown, about 3 minutes. Stir in 3 thyme sprigs, 2 crushed garlic cloves, ¼ teaspoon salt, and ¼ teaspoon pepper. Reduce heat to medium-high, and cook, stirring occasionally, until mushrooms are tender and browned all over, about 3 minutes. Add 1 tablespoon butter, 1 tablespoon parsley, and 1 teaspoon vinegar. Cook, stirring occasionally, until mushrooms are coated in butter, about 1 minute. Transfer mushroom mixture to paper towels to drain; discard cooked garlic and thyme.

2. Wipe skillet clean, and repeat process 2 times with remaining oil, remaining mushrooms, remaining thyme, remaining garlic, ½ teaspoon salt, ½ teaspoon pepper, 2 tablespoons butter, remaining parsley, and remaining vinegar. Place all mushrooms in a large bowl, and season with remaining ½ teaspoon salt and remaining ¼ teaspoon pepper. Keep warm or let cool to room temperature.

3. Preheat oven to 350°F. Place brioche slices in a single layer on a wire rack set inside a baking sheet. Bake in preheated oven until lightly toasted, about 8 minutes per side. Brush with remaining 2 tablespoons softened butter.

4. Spread cheese evenly over brioche toasts. Spoon mushroom mixture evenly over toasts; garnish with parsley, pickled onion slices, frisée, and chives. Drizzle with lemon juice and extra-virgin olive oil. — KRISTEN KISH

WINE Pair with a crisp sparkling rosé.

Brussels Sprout Baba Ghanoush

ACTIVE 15 MIN; TOTAL 30 MIN; SERVES 8

Michael Solomonov serves this brilliant riff on baba ghanoush at Zahav in Philadelphia. After a whirl in the food processor, Brussels sprouts and tahini come together to form a creamy dip. Solomonov serves it topped with more roasted Brussels sprouts and hazelnuts, and with warm pita for dipping.

- ½ lb. Brussels sprouts, trimmed and halved lengthwise
- 1 Tbsp. extra-virgin olive oil, plus more for drizzling
- 1 tsp. kosher salt, divided, plus more to taste
- ½ cup hazelnuts
- 1 cup tahini
- ¼ cup fresh lemon juice (from 2 lemons)
- ½ tsp. ground cumin
- 1 ice cube
- ½ cup cold water
- ¼ cup chopped fresh flat-leaf parsley

1. Preheat oven to 500°F. Toss together Brussels sprouts, oil, and ¼ teaspoon salt on a large rimmed baking sheet. Spread in a single layer, and roast in preheated oven until tender and lightly charred, about 12 minutes. Transfer to a plate to cool. Reduce oven temperature to 300°F.

2. Spread hazelnuts on a large rimmed baking sheet, and bake at 300°F until golden and skins wrinkle, about 8 minutes.

Transfer to a clean kitchen towel, and rub off skins. Let stand until cool enough to handle; coarsely chop.

3. Place tahini, lemon juice, cumin, ice cube, half the cooled Brussels sprouts, and remaining ¾ teaspoon salt in a food processor. Process until ice melts and a chunky paste forms. With processor running, add ½ cup cold water in a slow, steady stream, processing until mixture is emulsified and resembles the texture of hummus. Season to taste with salt.

4. To serve, spread tahini mixture on a platter, and top with remaining Brussels sprouts. Garnish with hazelnuts, chopped parsley, and a generous drizzle of oil. — MICHAEL SOLOMONOV

Fancy Clam Dip

ACTIVE 10 MIN; TOTAL 1 HR 10 MIN; SERVES 6

This classic white clam dip, filled with cream cheese, crème fraîche, and—of course—canned clams, is salty, cheesy, and craveable. Some generous splashes of hot sauce and plenty of fresh dill add brightness and cut through the rich, indulgent dip.

- 2 (6.5-oz.) cans clams
- 4 oz. softened cream cheese
- ½ cup crème fraîche
- 1½ Tbsp. grated shallot
- 1 tsp. lemon zest
- 1 Tbsp. fresh lemon juice
- 1 tsp. Worcestershire sauce
- ½ tsp. kosher salt
- 1 tsp. reserved clam liquor
  Hot sauce, for garnishing
  Fresh dill, for garnishing
  Potato chips, for serving

Drain clams, reserving clam liquor. Stir together clams and cream cheese in a medium bowl until smooth. Gently stir in crème fraîche, shallot, lemon zest, lemon juice, Worcestershire sauce, and kosher salt. Stir in 1 tsp. reserved clam liquor. Refrigerate at least 1 hour or up to 8 hours. Garnish with hot sauce and dill; serve with potato chips. — BETSY ANDREWS

Stilton-Stuffed Pickled Peppers, RECIPE P. 28

SHOP IT

Bring together two high-impact ingredients, like funky Stilton cheese and pickled sweet or spicy peppers, for the ultimate one-bite snack.

POST-WORK & PERFECT

In just over an hour and with a little help from secret weapons—hello, pickled peppers and marinated artichokes!—you can proudly host guests any day of the week this holiday season.

'Nduja Toasts with Quick-Pickled Celery, RECIPE P. 28

SPREAD IT

Serve creamy foods like meat spreads or soft cheeses on lightly toasted bread, topped with either store-bought condiments or quick homemade pickles.

Marinated Artichoke Hummus, RECIPE P. 28

SCOOP IT

For the perfect scoopable dip—and boost of flavor—upgrade your everyday homemade hummus using tangy marinated artichoke hearts.

POST-WORK & PERFECT MENU

Stilton-Stuffed Pickled Peppers

TOTAL 25 MIN; MAKES 60 PEPPERS

Two high-impact ingredients—funky Stilton cheese and pickled sweet or spicy peppers—come together to form the ultimate one-bite snack.

- 1 (16-oz.) jar whole pickled pepperoncini, drained and patted dry
- 8 oz. Stilton cheese
- 1 (14-oz.) jar mild whole Peppadew peppers, drained and patted dry

1. Using a paring knife, cut off and discard pepperoncini stems; scoop out and discard seeds with a small spoon. (Dip spoon into a small bowl of water to wash away seeds as needed.)

2. Remove and discard cheese rind. Cut into about 60 (½-inch) pieces. Stuff 1 cheese piece into each pepperoncini and Peppadew pepper. Transfer to a platter and serve. — JUSTIN CHAPPLE

'Nduja Toasts with Quick-Pickled Celery

TOTAL 30 MIN; MAKES 20 TOASTS

Store-bought 'nduja, the spicy, spreadable sausage, is transformed into a special canapé when served on toasted baguette and topped with a quick-pickled celery.

- ½ cup finely chopped inner celery stalks
- ¼ cup Champagne vinegar
- 1 Tbsp. granulated sugar
- 1 tsp. kosher salt
- 20 (¼-inch-thick) baguette slices
- 8 oz. 'nduja, at room temperature
- Extra-virgin olive oil, for serving
- Flaky sea salt, for serving
- Celery leaves, for garnish

1. Toss together celery, vinegar, sugar, and kosher salt in a medium bowl until salt and sugar dissolve. Let stand 15 minutes. Meanwhile, lightly toast or grill baguette slices.

2. Drain pickled celery. Spread 'nduja evenly on toasts using a small offset spatula. Arrange toasts on a platter or board. Sprinkle pickled celery evenly over toasts. Drizzle with oil; sprinkle with sea salt. Garnish with celery leaves. — JUSTIN CHAPPLE

MAKE AHEAD Prepare and drain the celery mixture; refrigerate overnight.

Marinated Artichoke Hummus

TOTAL 10 MIN; MAKES 2 CUPS

When pureed with chickpeas, marinated artichoke hearts (plus some of their liquid) come together to form a perfectly textured dip. Their vinegary flavor adds brightness and tang to an otherwise classic recipe.

- 1 (15.5-oz.) can chickpeas, rinsed and drained
- 1 (12-oz.) jar marinated artichoke hearts, marinating liquid drained and reserved
- 1 small garlic clove, crushed
- ¼ cup extra-virgin olive oil, plus more for drizzling
- Kosher salt, to taste
- Freshly ground black pepper, to taste
- Crudités, pita chips, toasted bread, and/or crackers, for serving

Combine chickpeas, artichoke hearts, garlic, and 2 tablespoons artichoke marinating liquid in a food processor. Discard remaining marinating liquid. Process until smooth, about 1 minute and 30 seconds, stopping to scrape down sides as needed. With processor running, slowly pour oil through food chute until incorporated, about 20 seconds. Scrape mixture into a medium bowl, and season with salt and pepper; drizzle with oil. Serve hummus with crudités, pita chips, toasted bread, or crackers. — JUSTIN CHAPPLE

WINE Pair this menu with a sparkling brut rosé.

Marinated Olives with Orange

PHOTO P. 13

TOTAL 15 MIN; MAKES 1 QUART

Olives marinated in citrus juice, garlic, and spicy crushed red pepper become a sensational cocktail-party snack.

- 2 Tbsp. extra-virgin olive oil
- 1 Tbsp. thinly sliced garlic
- 1½ tsp. finely grated orange zest
- 1 tsp. crushed red pepper
- 1 qt. mixed olives
- ⅓ cup fresh orange juice

Heat oil in a large skillet over medium Add garlic, orange zest, and crushed red pepper, and cook, stirring, until garlic is softened, about 2 minutes. Add olives and cook, stirring, until hot, about 5 minutes. Remove from heat and stir in orange juice. Let cool completely, stirring occasionally. Serve at room temperature. — MARTHA WIGGINS

Spiced Pickled Beets

PHOTO P. 12

ACTIVE 30 MIN; TOTAL 2 HR, PLUS OVERNIGHT PICKLING; MAKES 6 CUPS

Pickled beets spiced with cinnamon, bay leaves, allspice, and cloves are the perfect cocktail snack.

- 3 lb. medium beets
- 2½ cups water, divided
- 2 tsp. kosher salt, plus more
- 1½ cups apple cider vinegar
- 1½ cups granulated sugar
- 3 bay leaves
- 1 (2-inch) cinnamon stick
- 2 tsp. whole allspice berries
- 2 tsp. black peppercorns
- ¾ tsp. whole cloves

1. Preheat oven to 375°F. Place beets in a large baking dish. Add 1 cup water and a generous pinch of salt. Cover tightly with foil and bake until beets are tender, about 1 hour. Uncover and let cool. Peel beets and cut into ¾-inch wedges. Transfer to a large heatproof bowl.

2. In a medium saucepan, combine 1½ cups water, vinegar, sugar, bay leaves, cinnamon stick, allspice, peppercorns, cloves, and 2 teaspoons salt. Bring to a boil over high, then simmer over medium-low until reduced to 3 cups, about 12 minutes. Pour liquid over beets and let cool; refrigerate overnight. Drain following day, before serving. — MARTHA WIGGINS

MAKE AHEAD The drained pickled beets can be refrigerated for up to 5 days.

Chile-Toasted Marcona Almonds

PHOTO P. 13

TOTAL 15 MIN, PLUS COOLING; MAKES 3 CUPS

These cocktail almonds from New Orleans chef Martha Wiggins get plenty of heat from crushed red pepper.

- 2 Tbsp. unsalted butter
- 3 garlic cloves, minced
- 1 tsp. crushed red pepper
- 3 cups roasted marcona almonds
  Kosher salt and black pepper
- 1 Tbsp. minced fresh chives

Melt butter in a large skillet over medium. Add garlic and red pepper, and cook, stirring, until garlic is softened, about 2 minutes. Add almonds and cook, stirring occasionally, until coated and hot, about 2 minutes. Season with salt and pepper. Let cool completely; stir in chives. — MARTHA WIGGINS

MAKE AHEAD The almonds can be stored at room temperature overnight; stir in the chives before serving.

WINE Pair with a full-bodied sparkling rosé.

Popcorn with Sesame-Glazed Pistachios

PHOTO P. 12

ACTIVE 15 MIN; TOTAL 30 MIN; MAKES 18 CUPS

Mixing popcorn with glazed pistachios creates a sweet-salty snack that's fantastic with cocktails.

- ⅓ cup vegetable oil
- ½ cup popping corn
- 2 tsp. kosher salt, plus more
- 3 Tbsp. extra-virgin olive oil
- 2 Tbsp. granulated sugar
- 2 Tbsp. toasted sesame seeds
- 2 tsp. soy sauce
- ½ tsp. garlic powder
- 2 cups shelled unsalted pistachios (8 oz.)

1. Preheat oven to 350°F. Line a baking sheet with parchment paper. Heat oil in a large saucepan over medium. Add popcorn, cover, and cook, until corn starts to pop. Cook, shaking pan until popping stops, 3 to 5 minutes. Transfer popcorn to a large bowl and season lightly with salt.

2. Wipe out saucepan. Add olive oil, sugar, sesame seeds, soy sauce, garlic powder, and 2 teaspoons salt, and cook over medium, stirring, until sugar dissolves, about 3 minutes. Add pistachios and cook, stirring, 1 minute. Scrape pistachios onto prepared baking sheet and bake until bubbling, about 10 minutes. Scrape pistachio mixture into popcorn and toss well. Let cool before serving. — MARTHA WIGGINS

MAKE AHEAD The mix can be made early in the day and stored in an airtight container at room temperature.

Potato Pancakes

Potato Pancakes

ACTIVE 40 MIN; TOTAL 1 HR 10 MIN;
SERVES 8

Hanukkah at the home of chef and television host Andrew Zimmern always includes a night with friends and neighbors making and eating these hot, crispy little beauties. Mixing cooked mashed Yukon Golds with raw shredded russet potatoes before frying makes the texture uniquely cakey-crunchy.

- 1¼ lb. Yukon Gold potatoes, peeled and cubed
- 2 tsp. kosher salt, plus more
- 1½ lb. russet potatoes, peeled
- 1 large onion, grated
- 2 large eggs, lightly beaten
- ½ cup matzo meal
- ½ tsp. freshly ground white pepper
- Vegetable oil, for frying
- Applesauce, crème fraîche, smoked fish, and fresh dill sprigs, for serving

1. Place potatoes in a medium saucepan, and add cold water to cover; season generously with salt and bring to a boil. Cook until tender, about 15 minutes. Drain and pass through a ricer into a large bowl.

2. Shred russets on large holes of a box grater into a colander. Rinse under cold water, then pat dry with a clean kitchen towel. Add half to riced potatoes.

3. Place remaining shredded potatoes and onion in a food processor, and pulse until pasty, about 20 times. Transfer to a fine wire-mesh strainer and press dry. Add to riced potatoes. Stir in eggs, matzo meal, white pepper, and 2 teaspoons salt.

4. Line a baking sheet with paper towels. Heat ¼ inch oil in a large, heavy skillet over medium to 350°F. Working in batches, spoon 2 tablespoons batter into oil for each pancake and press to flatten. Fry, turning once, until golden and crisp on both sides, about 7 minutes. Transfer to prepared baking sheet and sprinkle lightly with salt. Serve with applesauce, crème fraîche, smoked fish, and dill.
— ANDREW ZIMMERN

MAKE AHEAD The latkes can be refrigerated overnight. Reheat in a 375°F oven for 5 minutes.

WINE Pair with a rich Israeli Chardonnay.

Cheese Croustades

TOTAL 25 MIN; SERVES 15

A dollop of sweet-tart cranberry relish hides at the center of the goat cheese and ricotta mousse for a burst of flavor. Garnish with fresh, oniony chives or tart lemon zest for some color and brightness.

- 24 phyllo cups
- 8 oz. softened goat cheese
- ½ cup salted European-style butter (4 oz.), softened
- ½ cup whole-milk ricotta (4 oz.)
- 1 tsp. lemon zest
- ½ tsp. herbes de Provence
- ¼ tsp. white pepper
- Pinch finely ground sea salt
- ¼ tsp. cranberry jam or currant jam
- Chive batons
- Lemon zest curls

Bake 24 store-bought phyllo cups according to package directions; let cool on a wire rack. Stir together goat cheese, butter, ricotta, lemon zest, herbes de Provence, white pepper, and salt in a medium bowl. Spoon mixture into a pastry bag fitted with a star tip. Dollop jam into each phyllo cup; pipe cheese mixture on top of jam in phyllo cups. Garnish with chive batons and lemon zest curls.
— MATT AND TED LEE

◆ ━━━ ◆ ━━━ ◆

Pimento Cheese with Salt-and-Pepper Butter Crackers

ACTIVE 1 HR; TOTAL 2 HR 45 MIN; SERVES 12

For TV chef Carla Hall and her family, pimento cheese is a holiday must. She prefers to make her own crackers during this special time of year.

CRACKERS

- 2 cups all-purpose flour, plus more for dusting
- 2 cups whole-wheat pastry flour
- 2 Tbsp. baking powder
- 2 Tbsp. sugar
- 1½ tsp. kosher salt
- ¼ tsp. black pepper, plus more for sprinkling
- 10 Tbsp. unsalted butter, cubed and chilled, plus 3 Tbsp. melted butter
- 6 Tbsp. canola oil
- ⅔ cup plus 2 Tbsp. cold water

PIMENTO CHEESE

- 2 garlic cloves, crushed
- 1 jarred roasted red bell pepper, chopped
- 8 oz. sharp cheddar cheese, shredded (2 cups)
- 8 oz. Monterey Jack cheese, shredded (2 cups)
- 4 oz. cream cheese, at room temperature
- ½ cup mayonnaise
- 1 tsp. cayenne pepper
- 1 tsp. kosher salt

1. Make the crackers Combine all-purpose flour, whole-wheat flour, baking powder, sugar, salt, and ¼ teaspoon pepper in a food processor; pulse. Add cubed butter and canola oil, and pulse until mixture resembles coarse meal. Add water and pulse just until dough comes together. Transfer to a lightly-floured work surface and knead several times. Divide dough in half and form into two 1-inch-thick squares. Wrap in plastic and refrigerate 1 hour.

2. Line 2 baking sheets with parchment paper. On a lightly floured work surface, using a lightly floured rolling pin, roll out one piece of dough to a ⅛-inch-thick square. Using a fluted pastry cutter, cut dough into 24 (2½-inch) squares. Arrange crackers on prepared baking sheets, spaced ½ inch apart. Poke 4 rows of holes in center of each cracker. Freeze crackers until firm, 30 minutes.

3. Preheat oven to 400°F. Brush crackers with half the melted butter; sprinkle with pepper. Bake 12 to 15 minutes, shifting pans halfway through. Transfer crackers to a wire rack to cool. Repeat Steps 2 and 3 with remaining dough.

4. Make the pimento cheese Place garlic in a food processor, and pulse until finely chopped. Add bell pepper, cheddar, Monterey Jack, cream cheese, mayonnaise, cayenne, and salt, and pulse until well blended. Scrape pimento cheese into a large bowl and refrigerate for at least 1 hour before serving with crackers.
— CARLA HALL

A GRAND FÊTE

When you're feeling fancy, up your hosting game with these thoughtful, luxe, one-handed bites.

WAFFLE IT

Instead of serving blini alongside a tin of caviar, make handheld snacks: Cut waffles into batons, and fill the pockets with caviar and traditional accompaniments.

Caviar Waffle Bites,
RECIPE P. 34

SKEWER IT

Rather than arranging thin slices of rare roast beef on a platter, skewer them with roasted mushrooms to form elegant one-bite appetizers.

Peppered Beef and Hen-of-the-Woods Bundles, RECIPE P. 34

PIPE IT

Make deviled eggs less awkward to eat—and more modern than ever. Puree hard-boiled eggs with the usual suspects, then pipe or spread on crackers.

Deviled-Egg Crisps, RECIPE P. 35

A GRAND FÊTE MENU

Peppered Beef and Hen-of-the-Woods Bundles

ACTIVE 45 MIN; TOTAL 1 HR 20 MIN;
MAKES 32 BUNDLES

Garlic oil-basted mushrooms and beef tenderloin make for a satisfying bite.

- 1 (1-lb.) center-cut beef tenderloin, tied
- 4 tsp. black pepper, divided
- 1 Tbsp. kosher salt, divided
- 5 Tbsp. extra-virgin olive oil, divided
- 2 garlic cloves, finely grated
- 1½ lb. fresh hen-of-the-woods mushrooms, stems removed, cut into 1-inch pieces
- Finely chopped fresh flat-leaf parsley, for garnish

1. Preheat oven to 400°F. Rub beef all over with 1 tablespoon pepper and 2 teaspoons salt. Heat 1 tablespoon olive oil in a large cast-iron skillet over medium-high until shimmering. Add beef and cook, turning occasionally, until browned all over, 6 to 8 minutes. Transfer skillet to preheated oven, and roast until an instant-read thermometer inserted in thickest portion registers 120°F, 12 to 15 minutes. Transfer to a carving board, and let rest 20 minutes.

2. Meanwhile, whisk together garlic and remaining ¼ cup olive oil in a small bowl. Arrange mushrooms in an even layer on a large rimmed baking sheet, and spoon garlic oil evenly over mushrooms. Sprinkle with remaining 1 teaspoon pepper and remaining 1 teaspoon salt. Bake at 400°F until lightly browned and just tender, 12 to 15 minutes. Let mixture cool.

3. Cut off and discard twine around beef. Cut beef into 16 thin slices; cut slices in half. Spoon mushroom mixture evenly onto center of beef pieces; gather edges and secure each with a cocktail pick, forming little bundles. Transfer bundles to a platter or board. Garnish with parsley, and serve warm or at room temperature.
— JUSTIN CHAPPLE

MAKE AHEAD Refrigerate whole cooked beef tenderloin, covered, overnight. Bring to room temperature before slicing.

Caviar Waffle Bites

TOTAL 25 MIN; MAKES 2 DOZEN PIECES

Instead of serving blini alongside a tin of caviar, Justin Chapple makes these adorable handheld snacks. Waffles are cut into strips, and the pockets are filled with caviar, crème fraîche, and snipped chives to form the perfect pop-in-your-mouth morsel.

- ½ cup all-purpose flour (about 2⅛ oz.)
- 2 tsp. granulated sugar
- ¾ tsp. kosher salt
- ½ tsp. baking powder
- ½ cup buttermilk
- 1 large egg
- 2 Tbsp. unsalted butter, melted, plus more for greasing
- 3 Tbsp. crème fraîche
- 1 (1.1-oz.) jar paddlefish caviar
- Chopped fresh chives, for garnish

1. Grease a round waffle iron with butter; preheat to high. Whisk together flour, sugar, salt, and baking powder in a bowl. Whisk together buttermilk, egg, and melted butter in a small bowl until well combined. Add buttermilk mixture to flour mixture; whisk just until incorporated.

2. Pour half of waffle batter (about ½ cup) onto preheated waffle iron; spread gently over iron grid with a small spatula. Close iron; cook until browned and slightly crisp, about 3 minutes. Transfer to a wire rack; cool slightly, about 5 minutes. Repeat with remaining batter.

3. Following the waffle grid marks as a guide, cut each waffle into 4 wedges, then cut 3 long rectangular pieces from each wedge to yield 12 pieces per waffle. (Discard scraps, or reserve for another use.)

4. Spoon crème fraîche into a small zip-top plastic bag; snip the tip off one corner of bag to form a ¼-inch opening. Spoon caviar evenly into outermost square of each rectangular waffle piece; pipe a small dollop of crème fraîche into squares directly next to caviar. Garnish with chives. Transfer to a platter and serve.
— JUSTIN CHAPPLE

MAKE AHEAD Store cooled waffles, separated by wax paper, in zip-top bags; freeze up to 3 months. To reheat, bake at 350°F until warmed through, about 5 minutes. Let cool 5 minutes, and serve.

Deviled-Egg Crisps

ACTIVE 20 MIN; TOTAL 40 MIN; MAKES 2 DOZEN CRISPS

Missy Robbins, chef at Lilia in Brooklyn, makes a deviled-egg toast that's topped with bottarga (salted, cured fish roe). This riff, served on crisp artisan crackers, is topped with smoky-sweet Urfa biber, shaved jalapeño, and lime zest.

- 6 **large eggs**
- ½ **cup mayonnaise**
- 1 **Tbsp. Dijon mustard**
   Kosher salt, to taste
   Ground white pepper, to taste
- 24 **thin sourdough or rye crackers**
   Very thinly sliced seeded jalapeños, Urfa biber (see Note), and lime zest, for serving

1. Fill a medium bowl with ice water. Place eggs in a medium saucepan; add water to cover by 1 inch. Bring to a boil over high. Reduce heat to medium; simmer 8 minutes. Using a slotted spoon, remove eggs from water; plunge into ice water. Let cool completely, about 10 minutes. Remove from water, and peel eggs.

2. Place peeled eggs, mayonnaise, and mustard in a food processor; process until very smooth, about 1 minute, stopping to scrape down sides as needed. Season with salt and white pepper. Transfer mixture to a large zip-top plastic bag. Snip the tip off one corner of bag to form a ¼-inch opening. Pipe mixture in a zigzag design onto crackers (about 1 tablespoon per cracker). Top with jalapeño slices, Urfa biber, and lime zest. Transfer to a platter or board, and serve. — JUSTIN CHAPPLE

MAKE AHEAD Store in an airtight container in refrigerator up to 1 day.

NOTE Urfa biber (commonly referred to as Urfa pepper) is a Turkish chile that's distinctive for its dark burgundy color, irregularly sized flakes, and intriguing, salty-sweet-smoky-sour flavor. If you cannot find Urfa biber, you can substitute Aleppo pepper or even smoked paprika.

WINE Pair this menu with a creamy Champagne.

Cocktails

Citrus-Champagne **Punch,** RECIPE P. 38

Clementine 75

ACTIVE 15 MIN; TOTAL 1 HR 15 MIN;
MAKES 8 COCKTAILS

This cocktail is a riff on a classic French 75, but instead of using lemon juice, F&W's Justin Chapple swaps in clementine juice. It also makes an excellent mocktail: Use apple cider vinegar and chilled seltzer instead of the gin and Champagne.

- ½ cup granulated sugar
- 1 (3-inch) piece of fresh ginger, thinly sliced
- ¼ cup juniper berries, crushed
- ¼ cup dried cranberries
- 2 cinnamon sticks
  Ice
- 6 oz. fresh clementine juice
- 4 oz. gin
  Chilled brut Champagne or Prosecco, for topping

1. Combine sugar, ginger, juniper berries, cranberries, cinnamon sticks, and ½ cup water in a small saucepan, and bring to a boil, stirring to dissolve sugar. Remove from heat and let steep for 1 hour. Pour juniper syrup through a fine wire-mesh strainer into a small bowl, pressing on solids; discard solids.

2. Fill a cocktail shaker with ice. Add clementine juice, gin, and juniper syrup, and shake well. Pour into 8 Champagne flutes and top with Champagne.
— JUSTIN CHAPPLE

MAKE AHEAD The juniper syrup can be refrigerated for up to 2 weeks.

Anjou Punch

TOTAL 40 MIN; SERVES 12

Leo Robitschek of the NoMad bar in New York City makes his perfect holiday punch with warming flavors of pear, cinnamon, and citrus.

- 3 (3-inch) cinnamon sticks, broken into pieces, plus whole cinnamon sticks for garnish
- ½ cup granulated sugar
  Crushed ice
  Orange and lemon wheels
- 12 oz. Cognac
- 12 oz. Belle de Brillet (pear liqueur)
- 9 oz. fresh lemon juice
- 6 oz. triple sec
- 12 oz. chilled Champagne

1. Combine cinnamon sticks and 2 cups water in a small saucepan; bring to a boil. Simmer over medium-low until reduced by half. Stir in sugar until dissolved. Let cool, then pour liquid through a fine wire-mesh strainer into a bowl; refrigerate until chilled.

2. Mound crushed ice in middle of a large punch bowl. Using a long stirrer or spoon, slide orange and lemon wheels against inside of punch bowl, then push crushed ice back to keep fruit in place.

3. In a cocktail shaker, combine one-fourth each of cinnamon syrup, Cognac, Belle de Brillet, lemon juice, and triple sec; shake well. Add one-fourth of Champagne and shake once, then add to punch bowl. Repeat shaking 3 more times with remaining ingredients. Serve punch in crushed-ice-filled glasses, garnished with cinnamon sticks and orange and lemon wheels. — DANA COWIN

Citrus-Champagne Punch

PHOTO P. 36

ACTIVE 20 MIN; TOTAL 30 MIN, PLUS 5 HR FREEZING; SERVES 12

Spicy-sweet fig-ginger syrup, bright lemon juice, and freshly grated nutmeg round out the intensely smoky mezcal in this refreshing, balanced cocktail while still letting the bold liquor shine.

- 3 pints lemon sorbet, divided
- 2 lemons, thinly sliced, seeds removed
- 2 limes, thinly sliced, seeds removed
- 16 oz. London Dry gin
- 2 (750-ml.) bottles chilled Champagne
  Maraschino cherries

Let 2 pints of the lemon sorbet stand at room temperature 10 minutes. Arrange lemon and lime slices in an 8-cup metal tube pan. Top with softened sorbet, packing citrus slices against sides of pan and smoothing top. Cover with plastic wrap; freeze until firm, about 5 hours. To serve, pour gin into a large chilled punch bowl; stir in remaining 1 pint sorbet. Add frozen citrus ring to bowl. Gently pour Champagne around inside of bowl; stir gently to combine. Garnish with maraschino cherries.

PUNCH BOWL BASICS

No matter what you're celebrating, coming together over a cup of cheer is one of the universal pleasures of the holiday season. To mix up a perfect punch, remember "one of sour, two of sweet, three of strong, four of weak"— the rhyme most punch connoisseurs defer to as the rule for proportions. Sour usually means citrus (usually lime, lemon, or grapefruit juice). Sweet could be simple syrup or a low-alcohol liqueur or aperitif, like Cointreau or Aperol. Strong is, of course, spirits: bourbon, rye, brandy, and the like. Traditionally, the "weak" is water or tea, but fresh-pressed juices and ciders can be another delicious way to add layers of flavor.

Morrison Mule

Skyliner

Palmer Park Swizzle

Daiq on a Hot
Tin Roof

Brandy Sazerac

Big-Batch Rye Sours

ACTIVE 10 MIN; TOTAL 35 MIN; SERVES 15

Hibiscus flowers, curaçao, and lemon juice bring bright and refreshing floral notes to this rye-base cocktail.

- ½ cup granulated sugar
- ¼ cup boiling water
- 1 Tbsp. dried hibiscus flowers
- 1 (750-ml.) bottle 100-proof rye whiskey
- 2 cups dry curaçao
- 1½ cups fresh lemon juice
- 4 cups ice
- Lemon peel strips, for garnish

1. Combine sugar, ¼ cup boiling water, and hibiscus in a heatproof mug. Stir until sugar is dissolved; let stand until cooled. Cover and chill hibiscus syrup until ready to use.

2. Combine whiskey, curaçao, lemon juice, and ½ cup hibiscus syrup in a pitcher. Add ice, and stir until ice is melted. Serve chilled; garnish with lemon peel strips.

— SOTHER TEAGUE

MAKE AHEAD Batched drink may be made one day ahead; keep chilled until ready to serve.

Palmer Park Swizzle

ACTIVE 10 MIN; TOTAL 2 HR 10 MIN; MAKES 1 COCKTAIL

The ultimate southern refresher, this cocktail combines tea-infused bourbon, lime juice, and mint for a boozy take on iced tea.

- 2 cups bourbon
- 1 black tea bag
- Ice
- 1 oz. fresh lime juice
- ¾ oz. Simple Syrup (recipe, p. 42)
- 8 mint leaves
- Mint sprig

In a 1-quart jar, steep the bourbon with black tea bag for 2 hours; discard tea bag. Fill a shaker with ice and add lime juice, simple syrup, mint leaves, and 2 ounces of tea-infused bourbon; shake well. Strain into an ice-filled collins glass and garnish with a mint sprig; serve immediately.

— BENTON BOURGEOIS

Skyliner

TOTAL 10 MIN; MAKES 1 COCKTAIL

The subtle spice on the finish of this cocktail from New Orleans bar manager Benton Bourgeois brings complexity and interest to a grapefruit-tinged vodka collins.

- Ice
- 1½ oz. vodka
- 1 oz. fresh grapefruit juice
- ½ oz. fresh lime juice
- ½ oz. Campari
- ½ oz. Simple Syrup (recipe, p. 42)
- 8 drops habanero bitters
- 1 oz. club soda
- Lime wheel

Fill a shaker with ice and add vodka, grapefruit juice, lime juice, Campari, simple syrup, and habanero bitters; shake well. Strain into an ice-filled collins glass and top with club soda. Garnish with a lime wheel; serve immediately.

— BENTON BOURGEOIS

Morrison Mule

TOTAL 10 MIN; MAKES 1 COCKTAIL

In memory of Jim Morrison's stay at the historic Pontchartrain Hotel in New Orleans (and his affinity for whiskey), Benton Bourgeois created this take on a classic Moscow Mule with bourbon and local Peychaud's Aperitivo.

- Ice
- 4 oz. ginger beer
- 1½ oz. bourbon
- ½ oz. Peychaud's Aperitivo or Aperol
- ½ oz. fresh lime juice
- 1 3-inch strip orange zest

Fill a copper mug with ice, then add ginger beer, bourbon, Peychaud's Aperitivo, and lime juice; stir well. Garnish with orange strip; serve immediately. — BENTON BOURGEOIS

Brandy Sazerac

TOTAL 10 MIN; MAKES 1 COCKTAIL

This take on the New Orleans classic from Yon Davis at CaterZoo harkens back to the original incarnation of the drink. After a Cognac shortage in France in the 1870s, bartenders began to use American rye whiskey as a substitute.

- ¼ oz. Legendre Herbsaint
- Ice
- 2 oz. Rémy Martin 1738 Accord Royal Cognac
- ¼ to ½ oz. Simple Syrup (recipe, p. 42)
- 4 to 5 dashes Peychaud's bitters
- Lemon twist

Fill a rocks glass with ice and add Legendre Herbsaint. Fill a pint glass with ice and add Rémy Martin 1738 Accord Royal Cognac, simple syrup, and Peychaud's bitters; stir well. Discard ice and Herbsaint from rocks glass, then strain drink into it. Garnish with a lemon twist and serve immediately.

— YON DAVIS

Daiq on a Hot Tin Roof

TOTAL 10 MIN; MAKES 1 COCKTAIL

This refreshing daiquiri uses passion fruit for a tiki twist on the classic. The Smith & Cross rum is highly recommended, as it adds a spiced tropical note to the drink.

- Ice
- 1½ oz. Papa's Pilar blonde rum
- 1 oz. fresh lime juice
- 1 oz. passion fruit nectar
- ½ oz. Smith & Cross Jamaican rum
- ½ oz. Simple Syrup (recipe, p. 42)
- Lime wheel

Fill a shaker with ice. Add Papa's Pilar blonde rum, lime juice, passion fruit nectar, Jamaican rum, and simple syrup; shake well. Strain into a chilled coupe glass and garnish with a lime wheel; serve immediately. — BENTON BOURGEOIS

Tourmaline

TOTAL 5 MIN; SERVES 1

Julia Child wasn't the only recipe writer in her household. Paul Child delighted in inventing cocktail recipes, which he prepared for Julia and for the couple's lucky guests. Named for the gemstone, this cocktail by Paul Child gets its ruby color from beet juice. Use fresh or bottled beet juice to impart color and a faintly earthy-sweet aroma.

- ¼ cup (2 oz.) London dry gin
- 1 Tbsp. beet juice
- 1 Tbsp. sweetened lime juice, or more to taste
- Ice
- 1 lime wheel

Pour gin, beet juice, and sweetened lime juice in a mixing glass, and fill with ice. Using a bar spoon, stir until outside of glass is frosty, about 30 seconds; strain into a cocktail glass. Garnish with a lime wheel. — PAUL CHILD

Earl Grey-Aquavit Spritz

ACTIVE 15 MIN; TOTAL 2 HR 35 MIN, INCLUDING 2 HR CHILLING; SERVES 12

Honey simple syrup is even easier to prepare than standard simple syrup; just vigorously stir together honey and water until well combined. The mellow, floral sweetness of the honey syrup pairs perfectly with a touch of lemon in this tea-infused cocktail.

- 1 (750-ml.) bottle aquavit
- 1 (3-inch) lemon peel strip (from 1 lemon)
- 2 Tbsp. Earl Grey tea leaves
- ¾ cup fresh lemon juice
- ¾ cup honey simple syrup
- ½ cup water
- 8 dashes pear bitters
- 1 (750-ml.) bottle sparkling wine (such as brut Cava or Champagne) or club soda
- Crushed ice
- Lemon and pear slices

1. Stir together aquavit, lemon peel strip, and tea leaves in bowl or large glass measuring cup. Let stand, uncovered, at room temperature 20 minutes. Pour mixture through a fine wire-mesh strainer into another large measuring cup or bowl; discard solids. Repeat straining procedure. Store in airtight container at room temperature up to 3 months.

2. Add 2 cups Earl Grey-infused aquavit to a pitcher. (Reserve remaining infused aquavit for another use). Stir in lemon juice, honey simple syrup, ½ cup water, and bitters. Refrigerate until chilled, 2 hours or up to overnight. Just before serving, stir in sparkling wine or club soda. Serve over crushed ice in rocks glasses. Garnish servings with lemon and pear slices. — ASHTIN BERRY

MAKE AHEAD Earl Grey-infused aquavit can be made 3 months in advance.

NOTE Aquavit is a Scandinavian liquor flavored with caraway seeds.

Far From the Tree

TOTAL 10 MIN; SERVES 12

Bartender Ivy Mix, the award-winning co-owner of Leyenda in Brooklyn, created this cardamom-scented holiday punch. Layers of apple flavor, from cold-pressed juice, brandy, hard cider, and fresh apple slices, give the not-too-boozy punch an autumnal feel.

- 3 cardamom pods
- ¼ tsp. kosher salt
- 1½ cups French Sauvignon Blanc or similar dry white wine
- 1 cup cold-pressed apple juice or apple cider
- ¾ cup white verjus
- ½ cup amontillado sherry
- ½ cup Calvados or other apple brandy
- ½ cup Simple Syrup (recipe follows)
- 1 (1-lb.) ice block
- 1 cup dry Spanish-style hard cider
- 1 crisp, red-skin apple, thinly cut crosswise into 12 rounds

Muddle cardamom pods and salt in bottom of a punch bowl. Stir in wine, apple juice, verjus, sherry, Calvados, and simple syrup. Add a 1-pound ice block or ice ring; stir gently until punch is chilled, about 30 seconds. Top with hard cider, and garnish with apple slices. — IVY MIX

SIMPLE SYRUP Bring 1 cup water and 1 cup granulated sugar to a boil in a small saucepan. Simmer over medium, stirring, until sugar dissolves, about 3 minutes. Let cool, then refrigerate for up to 1 month. Makes 1½ cups.

Carioca Quencher

TOTAL 5 MIN; SERVES 1

While the late, great Julia Child was cooking in the kitchen, her husband, Paul Child, put his mind to creating cocktails behind the bar. Falling between a tiki drink and a Rum Collins, this highball Paul created originally called for Tom Collins mix, a sweet-and-sour carbonated mixer popular in midcentury cocktails. We've updated it with contemporary ingredients.

- ¼ cup (2 oz.) dark rum
- 2 Tbsp. fresh lemon juice
- 1 Tbsp. sweetened lime juice
- 1 Tbsp. (½ oz.) apricot liqueur
- Crushed ice
- Club soda
- 3 drops Angostura bitters

Pour rum, lemon juice, sweetened lime juice, and apricot liqueur into a mixing glass; fill with ice. Using a bar spoon, stir until outside of glass is frosty, about 30 seconds; strain into a chilled highball glass filled with crushed ice. Top with a splash of club soda and bitters. — PAUL CHILD

Butterfly's Breath

TOTAL 5 MIN; SERVES 1

The late Julia and Paul Child often entertained friends with cocktails, many of them invented by Paul Child, who delighted in creating custom drinks. A small collection of Paul's recipes, written on 3-by-5 index cards, was recently discovered in Julia Child's archives. Among them is this sweet, apricot brandy-laced riff on the gimlet.

- 3¾ tsp. sweetened lime juice
- ½ tsp. granulated sugar
- ¼ cup (2 oz.) London dry gin
- 2 Tbsp. (1 oz.) apricot brandy
- Ice
- Lemon peel twist or lime peel twist

Stir together lime juice, 1 tablespoon water, and sugar in a mixing glass until sugar is dissolved. Pour gin and apricot brandy into glass, and fill glass with ice. Using a bar spoon, stir until outside of glass is frosty, about 30 seconds. Strain into a cocktail glass. Garnish with a lemon peel twist. — PAUL CHILD

Carioca Quencher

Tourmaline

Butterfly's Breath

Spiced Maple Gimlets

Spiced Maple Gimlets

TOTAL 5 MIN; SERVES 15

With warm, rounded flavors like maple syrup and sarsaparilla, this gin cocktail is comforting and deeply flavored.

- 1 (750-ml.) bottle juniper-forward gin
- 1½ cups pure maple syrup
- 1 cup fresh lime juice
- 6 dashes Angostura bitters or ½ tsp. sarsaparilla
- 4 cups ice, plus more for serving
- 15 star anise, for garnish

Combine gin, maple syrup, lime juice, and bitters in a pitcher. Add 4 cups ice, and stir until ice is melted. Serve in rocks glasses over fresh ice; garnish with star anise. — PAUL FINN

MAKE AHEAD Batched drink may be made one day ahead; keep chilled until ready to serve.

◆ ◆ ◆

Walker's Mulled Wine

ACTIVE 30 MIN; TOTAL 1 HR; SERVES 12

Over-boiled mulled wines, made with headache-inducing quantities of sugar, have long given this holiday classic a dire reputation. This version, from sommelier Danielle Johnson Walker of Walkers Maine restaurant in Cape Neddick, Maine, is gently infused with nutmeg, vanilla, and star anise, then lightly sweetened with honey and maple syrup. The result is a concoction you'll want to sip all winter long.

- 20 whole cloves
- 8 whole star anise
- 6 cinnamon sticks
- 1 whole nutmeg, smashed
- 2 (750-ml.) bottles dry red wine (such as Blaufränkisch, Zweigelt, or Pinot Noir)
- 4 (6- × 1-inch) orange peel strips (from 2 large oranges)
- 2 vanilla bean pods, halved lengthwise
- 2 oz. pure maple syrup
- 2 oz. honey
- ¾ cup (6 oz.) applejack brandy (optional)

1. Heat cloves, star anise, cinnamon sticks, and nutmeg in a small skillet over low, stirring often, until toasted and fragrant, about 5 minutes.

2. Transfer spice mixture to a large saucepan over medium-low; stir in wine, orange peel strips, vanilla bean pods, maple syrup, and honey. Slowly bring wine mixture to just below a simmer, stirring occasionally, 15 to 20 minutes. Remove from heat, and let steep until spices bloom and infuse into wine, about 30 minutes.

3. Return saucepan to medium-low; stir in applejack brandy, if desired, and continue to cook, stirring occasionally, until warmed through, about 5 minutes. Pour mixture (through a fine wire-mesh strainer, if desired) into a large heatproof bowl. Ladle mulled wine into glasses. — MADDY SWEITZER-LAMME

◆ ◆ ◆

Smoky Mezcal-Fig Sour

PHOTO P. 10

ACTIVE 20 MIN; TOTAL 8 HR 50 MIN, INCLUDING 8 HR CHILLING; SERVES 12

Spicy-sweet fig-ginger syrup, bright lemon juice, and freshly grated nutmeg round out the intensely smoky mezcal in this refreshing, balanced cocktail.

- 1⅓ cups Simple Syrup (recipe, p. 42)
- 10 dried figs, halved
- 1 (4-inch) piece fresh ginger, peeled and thinly sliced (about ⅓ cup)
- 1 (750-ml.) bottle mezcal
- 1¼ cups fresh lemon juice (from 8 large lemons)
- ¾ cup water
  Whole nutmeg

1. Combine simple syrup, figs, and ginger in a small saucepan. Bring to a boil over medium. Reduce heat to low, and simmer until figs are softened, about 5 minutes. Remove from heat, and let cool 30 minutes. Refrigerate mixture, covered, 8 hours or overnight. Pour mixture through a fine wire-mesh strainer into a bowl; discard solids. Store in an airtight container up to 1 week.

2. Place mezcal in a pitcher. Pour 1¼ cups fig-ginger syrup through a fine-mesh sieve into pitcher, followed by lemon juice and ¾ cup water. Refrigerate until chilled, 2 hours or up to overnight. Stir before serving. Pour over large ice cubes into rocks glasses. Garnish servings with freshly grated nutmeg. — ASHTIN BERRY

MAKE AHEAD Fig-ginger syrup can be made up to 1 week ahead of time.

Cucumber-and-Mint "Fauxjito"

TOTAL 5 MIN; SERVES 1

This virgin riff on a classic mojito from F&W's Justin Chapple gets a hint of sweetness from agave.

- 6 thin slices of English cucumber, plus 1 long, thin slice for garnish
- 6 large fresh mint leaves, plus 1 sprig for garnish
- 2 oz. fresh lime juice
- ½ oz. agave
  Ice
- 4 oz. cold club soda

In a cocktail shaker, muddle the cucumber with the mint leaves. Add the lime juice and agave and fill with ice; shake well. Pour mixture through a fine wire-mesh strainer into an ice-filled collins glass. Add the club soda; stir once. Garnish with the cucumber slice and mint sprig. — JUSTIN CHAPPLE

◆ ◆ ◆

Wise Guy Mocktail

TOTAL 5 MIN; SERVES 1

Verjus, the juice of unripened grapes, gives this julep-style mocktail a nuanced tanginess.

- 4 fresh sage leaves, plus 1 sprig for garnish
- ¼ oz. Jalapeño Agave Syrup (see Note)
- 1½ oz. fresh pineapple juice
- 1 oz. verjus (available at specialty food stores)
- ½ oz. fresh lime juice
  Pinch of kosher salt
  Ice cubes, plus crushed ice for serving
  Pinch of Aleppo pepper, for garnish

In a cocktail shaker, lightly muddle the 4 sage leaves with the Jalapeño Agave Syrup. Add the pineapple juice, verjus, lime juice, and salt. Fill the shaker with ice cubes and shake well. Pour mixture through a fine wire-mesh strainer into a chilled, crushed-ice-filled julep cup, and garnish with the sage sprig and Aleppo pepper. — LACY HAWKINS

NOTE In a heatproof measuring cup, stir 4 ounces agave syrup into 2 ounces hot water until combined. Stir in ½ chopped unseeded jalapeño and let steep for 5 minutes. Strain the syrup into a heatproof jar, let cool, and refrigerate for up to 2 weeks. Makes about 5 ounces.

Breakfast
& Brunch

Hanukkah Doughnuts,
RECIPE P. 55

Tater Tot Waffles with Truffled Eggs

TOTAL 40 MIN; MAKES 4 (8-INCH) WAFFLES

Jen Pelka Bililies of The Riddler in San Francisco and New York City makes super crunchy and delicious waffles using Tater Tots, then tops them with poached eggs and truffles, making them ideal for brunch.

Nonstick cooking spray

8 cups thawed frozen Tater Tots (32 oz.), divided

Flaky sea salt

Truffled Egg (recipe follows)

Heat an 8-inch waffle iron; preheat oven to 200°F. Grease waffle iron with nonstick spray. Spread 2 cups of tots on it; sprinkle with salt. Close and cook on medium-high until nearly crisp, about 5 minutes. Open waffle iron and fill in any holes with more tots, then close and cook until golden and crispy, 2 to 3 minutes. Transfer to a baking sheet; keep warm in the oven. Repeat with remaining tots. Top with a Truffled Egg and serve. — JEN PELKA

TRUFFLED EGG Bring a large, deep skillet of water to a simmer. Crack 4 eggs into skillet and simmer over medium-low until whites are set and yolks are runny, about 4 minutes. Using a slotted spoon, transfer poached eggs to a plate; blot dry with paper towels and season with salt. Top each warm waffle with a poached egg, then shave fresh black truffle on top and serve. — JEN PELKA

Open-Face Egg and Griddled Ham Breakfast Sandwiches

TOTAL 30 MIN; MAKES 12

F&W's Justin Chapple poaches a dozen eggs at once in a muffin pan in the oven, making his cute and tasty breakfast sliders extraordinarily easy to prepare for entertaining.

1 dozen large eggs

Kosher salt and black pepper

6 oz. thinly sliced baked ham

1 cup mixed chopped fresh herbs, such as parsley, tarragon, and chives

1 Tbsp. fresh lemon juice

6 slider buns, split and lightly toasted

1. Preheat oven to 350°F. Pour 1 tablespoon water into each cup of a 12-cup muffin tin. Crack an egg into each cup and season with salt and pepper. Bake until the whites are just firm and the yolks are still runny, 13 to 15 minutes. Using a slotted spoon, immediately transfer eggs to a plate.

2. Meanwhile, in a medium skillet, cook ham over medium, turning, until hot, about 2 minutes. In a small bowl, toss herbs with lemon juice and season with salt and pepper.

3. Arrange split buns cut-side up on a platter. Top with the ham, eggs, and herbs. Serve open-face. — JUSTIN CHAPPLE

Jam-Stuffed Brioche French Toast

TOTAL 45 MIN; SERVES 4

Jessica Koslow started making jam in Los Angeles and soon developed such a huge following that she had to expand her business, and her beloved brunch-and-lunch restaurant, Sqirl, was born. This is just one of the showcases for jam you'll find there. No matter what time of day you have breakfast, have fun with it.

4 (1½-inch-thick) slices brioche

¼ cup strawberry jam, plus more for serving

3 large eggs

¼ cup heavy cream

1½ tsp. granulated sugar

½ tsp. fleur de sel, plus more for serving

4 Tbsp. unsalted butter, divided

Confectioners' sugar

Crème fraîche, for serving

½ lemon

1. Preheat oven to 350°F. Cut a 2-inch pocket in the side of each brioche slice; spoon 1 tablespoon jam in each one.

2. Whisk eggs, cream, sugar, and ½ teaspoon fleur de sel in a shallow bowl.

3. Melt 2 tablespoons butter in a large skillet over medium. Dip 2 slices of the stuffed brioche in the egg mixture and soak until saturated. Add to the skillet and cook, until nicely browned on both sides, about 2 minutes. Transfer the French toast to a baking sheet. Repeat with the remaining butter, brioche, and egg mixture.

4. Bake French toast in preheated oven until cooked through, about 5 minutes. Transfer to plates and sift confectioners' sugar evenly over top, and add a dollop of crème fraîche and strawberry jam. Squeeze a little lemon juice over each slice and sprinkle with fleur de sel. Serve right away. — JESSICA KOSLOW

Lemony Crêpe Casserole

ACTIVE 40 MIN; TOTAL 55 MIN; SERVES 8

Reminiscent of a classic bread pudding, this sweet-tart crêpe casserole has a beautiful lacy top and tender-but-sliceable center.

2 (8-oz.) pkg. cream cheese, at room temperature

¾ cup purchased lemon curd

¼ tsp. kosher salt, divided

¼ cup unsalted butter, plus more for greasing

24 (10-inch) purchased crêpes

1 medium Meyer lemon, very thinly sliced and seeded

¼ cup pure maple syrup

1 Tbsp. powdered sugar

1. Preheat oven to 350°F. Beat cream cheese, lemon curd, and ⅛ teaspoon salt in a medium bowl with an electric mixer on medium speed until smooth, about 3 minutes.

2. Grease a 13- × 9-inch baking dish with butter. Arrange 1 crêpe on a work surface. Using a small offset spatula, spread 1½ tablespoons cream cheese mixture evenly over crêpe, leaving a 1-inch border. Fold crêpe in half, and then fold in half again. Place folded crêpe in prepared baking dish. Repeat with remaining crêpes and remaining cream cheese mixture, overlapping folded crêpes in baking dish. Bake in preheated oven until crêpes are heated through and edges are golden brown, 15 to 20 minutes.

3. Meanwhile, melt ¼ cup butter in a large nonstick skillet over medium-low. Add lemon slices, sprinkle with remaining ⅛ teaspoon salt, and cook, stirring occasionally, until lemon peel is softened, about 7 minutes. Stir in maple syrup, and remove from heat. Spoon lemon sauce over casserole. Dust with powdered sugar and serve. — JUSTIN CHAPPLE

**Tater Tot Waffles
with Truffled Eggs**

Ricotta Hotcakes with
Honeycomb Toffee Butter

Ricotta Hotcakes with Honeycomb Toffee Butter

ACTIVE 35 MIN; TOTAL 2 HR 10 MIN; SERVES 4

Honeycomb toffee, honey, and salt add a sweet, crunchy bite to the butter that tops these ricotta hotcakes studded with fresh banana. Using an electric griddle helps maintain an even temperature over the cooking time, resulting in fluffy, moist pancakes.

HONEYCOMB BUTTER

- 1 cup honeycomb toffee pieces
- ½ cup unsalted butter (4 oz.), softened
- 1 Tbsp. honey
- ¼ tsp. kosher salt

HOTCAKES

- 1⅔ cups whole-milk ricotta cheese (about 13¾ oz.)
- 1 cup whole milk
- 5 large eggs, separated
- 1¼ cups all-purpose flour (about 5⅜ oz.)
- 1¼ tsp. baking powder
- 1 tsp. kosher salt
  Unsalted butter, for greasing griddle
- 2 large bananas, sliced
- 1 cup crushed honeycomb toffee

1. Make the honeycomb butter Process toffee pieces in a food processor until very finely ground, about 30 seconds. Add butter, honey, and salt. Process until blended, about 30 seconds. Transfer butter mixture to a large sheet of plastic wrap, and roll into a 5-inch-long (about 1½-inch-wide) log. Chill at least 2 hours or up to 2 weeks.

2. Make the hotcakes Whisk together ricotta, milk, and egg yolks in a medium bowl. Sift together flour, baking powder, and salt in a large bowl. Whisk ricotta mixture into flour mixture until combined. Beat egg whites on medium speed with an electric mixer until stiff peaks form, about 3 minutes. Fold beaten egg whites into ricotta mixture in 2 batches until just combined.

3. Heat an electric griddle to 375°F or a large stainless-steel skillet over medium-low. Lightly grease with butter. Working in batches, spoon ⅓ cup batter per pancake onto griddle. Cook until tops are speckled with bubbles and sides look set, 5 to 6 minutes. Flip and cook until golden brown, 5 to 6 minutes; remove pancakes. Wipe griddle; repeat with remaining batter.

4. To serve, divide hotcakes into 4 stacks; top each stack with ½ cup banana slices, 2 honeycomb butter slices, and ¼ cup crushed honeycomb toffee. — BILL GRANGER

◆ ◆ ◆

Chilaquiles Rojos with Fried Eggs and Cotija

ACTIVE 35 MIN; TOTAL 50 MIN; SERVES 4

Charring the tomato and onion before adding them to the red chile sauce is a quick way to create rich, slow-cooked flavor. Thick-cut fresh tortilla chips soak up the sauce and runny egg yolks without getting soggy.

- 1½ lb. plum tomatoes (about 8 medium), halved lengthwise
- 1 medium white onion, cut into 1-inch wedges
- 2 dried de árbol chiles, stemmed and seeded
- 5 dried guajillo chiles, stemmed and seeded
- 1 dried chipotle chile, stemmed and seeded
- 3 medium garlic cloves, unpeeled
- 1 qt. water
- 2½ Tbsp. fresh oregano leaves
- 1 Tbsp. kosher salt
- 1 bunch fresh cilantro, leaves and stems separated, divided
- 1 Tbsp. olive oil
- 4 large eggs
- 12 cups thick corn tortilla chips (such as Montes)
- 2 avocados, sliced
- 8 oz. queso fresco, crumbled (about 2 cups)
- ½ cup Mexican crema, for serving

1. Preheat broiler with oven rack in middle of oven. Place tomatoes and onion, cut-sides up, on a rimmed baking sheet, and broil in preheated oven on middle rack until charred, 16 to 22 minutes. Let cool 15 minutes, and set aside.

2. Meanwhile, heat a large cast-iron skillet over medium. Add chiles and garlic cloves, and cook, turning often, until chiles are fragrant, about 4 minutes. Remove chiles from skillet. Continue cooking garlic cloves, turning occasionally, until blackened in spots and softened, about 10 minutes total. Let garlic cloves cool 10 minutes; peel and set aside.

3. Bring 1 quart water to a boil in a small saucepan over medium-high. Add toasted chiles, and boil, stirring occasionally, until softened, about 10 minutes. Drain, reserving 1½ cups cooking liquid.

4. Combine tomatoes, onion, garlic, chiles, oregano, salt, reserved cooking liquid, and 1 cup cilantro stems in a blender. (Reserve any remaining cilantro stems for another use.) Process until smooth, about 20 seconds. Pour mixture through a fine wire-mesh strainer into a bowl; discard solids. Set red chile sauce aside.

5. Heat oil in a 12-inch nonstick skillet over medium. Crack eggs into skillet, leaving 1 inch between them. Cook until edges are set and starting to brown, about 2 minutes. Cover skillet, and cook until whites are set and yolks reach desired degree of doneness, 2 to 3 minutes for runny yolks. Transfer eggs to a plate; tent with aluminum foil to keep warm. Add red chile sauce to skillet over medium. Bring to a simmer. Pour red chile sauce over chips in a large bowl; toss to coat. Divide chilaquiles evenly among 4 plates. Top with eggs, avocado slices, queso fresco, crema, and cilantro leaves. Serve immediately. —CLAUDETTE ZEPEDA

MAKE AHEAD Red chile sauce can be chilled in an airtight container up to 3 days.

WINE Brambly, rich Zinfandel.

Za'atar-Baked Eggs

TOTAL 30 MIN; SERVES 4

During her teenage years, food writer and television personality Gail Simmons spent a summer on a kibbutz in Israel, working in her first professional kitchen. She was assigned to breakfast duty, and fell in love with scrambling, poaching, and frying eggs by the dozens. Today, one of her go-to brunches is baked eggs in a cherry tomato-pepper mix seasoned with the Mediterranean spice blend za'atar.

- 3 Tbsp. extra-virgin olive oil, plus more for drizzling
- 1 medium yellow onion, thinly sliced
- Kosher salt and black pepper
- 2 pints cherry tomatoes
- 2 red bell peppers, chopped
- ¼ cup plus 2 tsp. finely chopped fresh parsley, plus more for garnish
- 2 tsp. za'atar, divided, plus more for garnish
- 4 large eggs
- 1 cup plain yogurt
- ½ cup finely chopped and seeded English cucumber
- 1 Tbsp. fresh lemon juice, plus more for drizzling
- ½ tsp. sumac
- 2 tsp. finely chopped fresh mint

1. Preheat oven to 375°F. Heat 3 tablespoons oil in a large ovenproof skillet over medium until shimmering. Add onion, season with salt and pepper, and cook, stirring occasionally, until softened, about 5 minutes. Add tomatoes and cook, stirring occasionally, until some of them burst, 5 to 7 minutes. Add bell peppers and cook, stirring occasionally, until the peppers are softened and all of the tomatoes have burst, about 10 minutes. Remove from heat and stir in ¼ cup parsley and 1½ teaspoons za'atar. Season the tomato sauce with salt and pepper.

2. Using a spoon, make 4 wells in tomato sauce, then crack an egg into each one; season with salt and pepper. Transfer skillet to the preheated oven and bake until egg whites are just set and yolks are still runny, 10 to 12 minutes.

3. Meanwhile, mix yogurt, cucumber, 1 tablespoon lemon juice, sumac, mint, remaining 2 teaspoons parsley, and ½ teaspoon za'atar in a small bowl. Season with salt and garnish with za'atar. Drizzle eggs with oil and garnish with parsley. Drizzle tomato sauce with lemon juice. Serve with cucumber yogurt. — GAIL SIMMONS

———— ◆ ◆ ◆ ————

Glazed Cinnamon Rolls with Pecan Swirls

ACTIVE 1 HR; TOTAL 10 HR 30 MIN; MAKES 2 DOZEN ROLLS

Chef Megan Garrelts needs at least two days to make the rolls. She heats and serves them in mini cast-iron skillets. Baking these cinnamon rolls in big batches makes the effort worth it—they take time but are so satisfying.

DOUGH
- 2¼ tsp. instant dry yeast
- 2 Tbsp. warm water
- ¼ cup plus 1 tsp. granulated sugar
- 6 large eggs
- 4½ cups sifted all-purpose flour (1¼ pounds), plus more for rolling
- 1½ tsp. salt
- 3 sticks unsalted butter, cut into ½-inch cubes and chilled

FILLING
- 4 oz. pecans (1 cup)
- 1½ cups light brown sugar
- 1 Tbsp. cinnamon
- 1 cup sour cream
- 2 large eggs beaten with ¼ cup water

SUGAR GLAZE
- 1½ cups confectioners' sugar
- 4 Tbsp. unsalted butter, softened
- ¼ cup heavy cream
- 1 tsp. pure vanilla extract

1. Make the dough Combine yeast with the warm water and 1 teaspoon sugar in a medium bowl and let stand until foamy, about 5 minutes. Whisk in the 6 eggs. In the bowl of a stand mixer fitted with the dough hook, mix the 4½ cups flour with salt and remaining ¼ cup sugar. Add egg mixture and beat on medium speed until dough is just moistened and very stiff. Add chilled butter, a few cubes at a time, waiting until it is partially kneaded into dough before adding more. Continue kneading until butter is fully incorporated

and dough is silky, 8 to 10 minutes. Transfer dough to an oiled bowl, cover with plastic wrap, and refrigerate until chilled and slightly risen, at least 2 hours or overnight.

2. Make the filling Preheat oven to 350°F. Spread pecans in a pie plate and toast until fragrant and browned, about 8 minutes. Let cool, then finely chop pecans. Transfer to a medium bowl, and stir in brown sugar and cinnamon.

3. Line 2 baking sheets with parchment paper. On a floured surface, cut dough into 2 pieces. Working with 1 piece at a time (while keeping the other refrigerated), roll dough out to a 12 × 16-inch rectangle. Transfer dough to a baking sheet and refrigerate until chilled. Repeat with remaining dough.

4. Spread half of the sour cream over 1 sheet of dough, leaving a ½-inch border all around. Sprinkle with half of the pecan filling. Brush long sides with some of the egg wash. Roll up dough from a long side into a tight cylinder and pinch ends to seal. Freeze dough log until chilled, about 2 hours. Repeat with remaining dough and filling. Cover and refrigerate remaining egg wash.

5. Transfer dough to a work surface, and cut each one into 12 even slices. Set slices on the baking sheet, cut-sides up. Cover with plastic wrap and freeze until firm, at least 3 hours and preferably overnight.

6. Unwrap rolls and let stand at room temperature 1 hour.

7. Preheat the oven to 350°F. Brush tops and sides of rolls with egg wash and bake in the center of the oven until golden and risen, 35 to 40 minutes.

8. Make the sugar glaze In a medium bowl, use an electric mixer to beat confectioners' sugar with butter, heavy cream and vanilla extract until thick and smooth. Spread sugar glaze on the hot cinnamon rolls, and let cool for 20 minutes before serving. —MEGAN GARRELTS

MAKE AHEAD The unbaked cinnamon rolls and sugar glaze can be frozen separately for up to 1 month.

Za'atar-Baked Eggs

Polenta Dutch Baby
with Ham and Swiss

Polenta Dutch Baby with Ham and Swiss

ACTIVE 25 MIN; TOTAL 2 HR 55 MIN;
SERVES 4 TO 6

This Dutch baby is perfect for your holiday brunch. Preheating the pan (we love cast iron) is crucial to a successful rise. When the brown edges start to curl inward, it's finished and ready to serve.

- ½ cup all-purpose flour (about 2⅛ oz.)
- 3 Tbsp. granulated sugar
- 2 Tbsp. uncooked polenta
- ⅞ tsp. kosher salt, divided
- ½ cup whole milk
- 3 large eggs
- 3 Tbsp. unsalted butter, cut into 3 pieces
- 1 oz. thinly sliced deli ham, patted dry and cut into 2- × ½-inch strips
- 1 oz. Swiss cheese, grated (about ¼ cup)
- 1 tsp. country Dijon mustard
- 1 tsp. Champagne vinegar
- ¼ tsp. pure maple syrup or honey
- 1 Tbsp. grapeseed oil
- 1 oz. baby arugula (about 1 cup)
- 1 oz. red grapes, quartered (about ¼ cup)

1. Whisk together flour, sugar, polenta, and ¾ teaspoon salt in a medium bowl. Whisk together milk and eggs in a small bowl. Add milk mixture to flour mixture, and whisk until smooth. Cover and chill at least 2 hours or up to 8 hours.

2. Preheat oven to 425°F with oven rack in lower third of oven. Remove batter from the refrigerator; whisk until well combined, and allow to stand at room temperature while oven preheats. Place a 10-inch cast-iron skillet in preheated oven, and let heat 15 minutes. Add butter pieces to skillet, and return to oven for 1 minute. Carefully remove skillet from oven, and swirl, if needed, until butter is completely melted and beginning to brown.

3. Whisk batter again until well combined. Working quickly, pour batter into skillet. Sprinkle ham and cheese around edges of batter, leaving about a 4-inch-wide circle in center. Immediately return skillet to oven, and bake until golden brown, puffed, and center is cooked through, 16 to 20 minutes.

4. While batter bakes, whisk together mustard, vinegar, maple syrup, and remaining ⅛ teaspoon salt in a small bowl. Gradually add oil, whisking until dressing is emulsified. Toss arugula with 2 teaspoons of the dressing.

5. Carefully transfer hot Dutch baby to a serving plate. Serve immediately with dressed arugula and grapes, and drizzle with remaining dressing. — JONATHAN BROOKS

◆ ◆ ◆

Hanukkah Doughnuts

PHOTO P. 47

ACTIVE 30 MIN; TOTAL 4 HR; MAKES 24

Hebrew for doughnuts, sufganiyot are the most popular Hanukkah food in Israel. These fried treats are simply made from balls of yeast dough and filled with chocolate, creams, curd, or—as here—jam.

- ¾ cup whole milk
- 1 Tbsp. active dry yeast
- 3 cups plus 1 Tbsp. all-purpose flour
- ⅓ cup superfine sugar
- 6 Tbsp. unsalted butter, at room temperature, diced
- 1 large egg
- 4 tsp. Armagnac or apple brandy
- 1 tsp. pure vanilla extract
- ½ tsp. kosher salt
- 5 cups canola oil, plus more for brushing
- 1 cup granulated sugar
- 1 Tbsp. ground cinnamon
- 3 cups strawberry jam

1. In a small microwavable bowl, warm milk on HIGH to 110°F, about 1 minute. Sprinkle the yeast over milk and let stand until foamy, about 10 minutes.

2. In a stand mixer fitted with the dough hook, combine flour and superfine sugar. Add milk mixture, butter, egg, Armagnac, vanilla, and salt. Knead on low speed, scraping down sides of bowl, until dough starts to come together, about 4 minutes. Increase speed to medium and knead until dough is soft and pulls away from the bowl, about 10 minutes.

3. Lightly brush a large bowl with oil. Place dough in the bowl, cover with plastic wrap, and let stand in a warm spot until doubled in size, about 2 hours. Lightly brush 2 rimmed baking sheets with oil. Punch down the dough and cut in half. Roll each half into a 12-inch log. Cut each log into 12 equal pieces, roll into balls, and arrange on the prepared baking sheets, about 3 inches apart. Cover with plastic wrap and let stand until doubled in size, about 1½ hours.

4. Combine granulated sugar and cinnamon in a medium bowl.

5. Heat 5 cups canola oil in a large saucepan over medium to 325°F. Working in batches, fry the doughnuts, turning once, until golden, about 2 minutes per side. Using a slotted spoon, transfer doughnuts as they're done to the cinnamon-sugar and toss to coat. Let cool on a rack about 15 minutes.

6. Spoon jam into a pastry bag or small resealable plastic bag with 1 corner snipped. Pipe about 2 tablespoons jam into 2 opposite ends of each doughnut, and serve as soon as possible. — ANDREW ZIMMERN

MAKE AHEAD The doughnuts can be stored in an airtight container overnight.

◆ ◆ ◆

Bacon-and-Butter Sandwiches

TOTAL 15 MIN; SERVES 4

Pastry genius Dominique Ansel gives the beloved English "bacon butty" a French accent by subbing slender baguette for the standard white toast.

- 8 slices back bacon (see Note)
- 4 Tbsp. unsalted butter, softened
- 2 tsp. dry sherry
- 4 (4-inch-long) baguette pieces, split and lightly toasted

1. Cook half the bacon in a large cast-iron skillet over medium-high, turning once, until browned and the edges are crisp, 5 to 7 minutes. Transfer to a paper towel-lined plate to drain. Repeat with remaining bacon.

2. Stir together butter and sherry in a small bowl. Spread it on baguette bottoms. Top each with 2 slices of bacon, close the sandwiches, and serve. — DOMINIQUE ANSEL

NOTE Back bacon includes a portion of both the loin and the belly. It's available from British butchers and amazon.com, or try a combination of Canadian bacon and thick-cut bacon.

Apple Cider Doughnuts

ACTIVE 1 HR 45 MIN; TOTAL 7 HR 15 MIN;
MAKES ABOUT 13 DOUGHNUTS AND
DOUGHNUT HOLES, PLUS SCRAPS

*Nothing is wasted at Pennsylvania-based
Curiosity Doughnuts. Do as they do and
cut the rounds out close together, then
fry everything—including the holes and
scraps, which make a perfect mini snack.*

DOUGHNUTS

- 1¼ cups plus 2 Tbsp. fresh apple cider
- 3 Tbsp. unsalted butter
- 4½ cups plus 1 Tbsp. all-purpose flour, plus more for dusting
- 1 cup heavy cream
- 1 cup granulated sugar
- 2 large eggs
- 2 tsp. vanilla bean paste
- 1 Tbsp. baking powder
- 2 tsp. fine salt
- 1 tsp. baking soda
-    Canola oil or rice bran oil, for frying

CIDER GLAZE

- ¼ cup granulated sugar
- 1 Tbsp. water
- ¼ cup heavy cream
- ¼ cup boiled cider
- 3 Tbsp. unsalted butter
- 1 tsp. fine salt
- ¼ cup plus 2 Tbsp. buttermilk
- 2¼ cups confectioners' sugar

CINNAMON-CARDAMOM SUGAR

- 1 cup granulated sugar
- 1½ Tbsp. ground cinnamon
- 2 tsp. ground cardamom

1. Make the doughnuts Combine ¼ cup plus 2 tablespoons apple cider and the butter in a small saucepan. Bring to a boil over medium. Stir in ¼ cup plus 1 tablespoon flour and cook, stirring constantly, until a paste forms and pulls away from the pan, 1 to 2 minutes. Scrape paste into a small bowl and let cool, then refrigerate until well chilled, about 2 hours.

2. Place cider paste, cream, granulated sugar, eggs, vanilla bean paste, and remaining 1 cup cider in a blender; purée until smooth. Sift together remaining 4¼ cups of flour, baking powder, salt, and baking soda in a large bowl. Add wet ingredients and, using a rubber spatula, stir until a sticky dough forms.

3. Scrape dough out onto a plastic-lined large baking sheet. Cover with a large sheet of plastic wrap, and roll out or pat dough to 1-inch thickness. Refrigerate until well chilled, at least 4 hours.

4. Make the cider glaze Combine granulated sugar and 1 tablespoon water in a small saucepan. Cook over medium-high, swirling occasionally, until an amber caramel forms, 5 to 7 minutes. Remove from heat and carefully add cream and boiled cider; the caramel will seize. Cook over medium, stirring with a wooden spoon, until caramel dissolves, about 2 minutes. Gradually add butter and cook until thickened slightly, about 2 minutes. Stir in salt. Scrape mixture into a medium bowl, and let cool completely. Whisk in buttermilk and confectioners' sugar until the glaze is smooth.

5. Make the cinnamon-cardamom sugar Whisk sugar, cinnamon, and cardamom in a medium bowl.

6. Remove the top sheet of plastic wrap and invert the dough onto a floured work surface. Peel off the plastic wrap and dust dough with flour. Roll out dough to ½-inch thickness. Using a 3-inch round biscuit cutter, stamp out 13 rounds. Using a 1-inch round cutter, stamp out the center from each round. Cut the scraps into 2-inch pieces. Transfer doughnuts, holes, and scraps to 2 baking sheets and refrigerate until chilled, about 30 minutes.

7. Heat 3 inches canola oil in a large saucepan to 375°F and top 2 baking sheets with racks. Keep doughnuts chilled. Add one-third of the scraps at a time to the hot oil and fry, turning once, until browned, about 2 minutes per batch. Using a slotted spoon, transfer the scraps to a rack.

8. Return the oil to 375°F. Add doughnut holes and fry until browned all over, 1 to 2 minutes. Using a slotted spoon, transfer to a rack. Toss doughnut scraps and holes in the cinnamon-cardamom sugar until coated and transfer to a platter.

9. Return the oil to 375°F. In batches, fry doughnuts, turning once, until browned, about 3 minutes per batch. Using a slotted spoon, transfer the doughnuts to a rack to cool for 10 minutes.

10. Stir glaze. Dip one side of each doughnut in glaze, and let stand until set before serving. — ALEX TALBOT & AKI KAMOZAWA

MAKE AHEAD The recipe can be prepared through Step 5; refrigerate the doughnut dough and glaze overnight.

STEP-BY-STEP

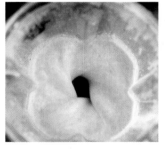

1. MAKE A CIDER PASTE Boil fresh apple cider with butter, then add flour and cook until a thick paste forms. Let cool, then chill.

2. GET OUT YOUR BLENDER Add the chilled cider paste, cream, sugar, eggs, vanilla, and remaining cider, and blend until smooth.

3. MAKE THE DOUGH Mix the wet ingredients into the flour mixture until a tacky dough forms. Pat out on a baking sheet and chill.

4. ROLL IT OUT Unwrap the chilled dough on a floured work surface, and roll it out about ½ inch thick.

5. GO AROUND IN CIRCLES Using 3-inch and 1-inch round cutters, stamp out doughnuts and holes. Cut scraps into 2-inch pieces.

6. FRY AND TOSS Fry the scraps and holes–in separate batches–and toss to coat in cinnamon-cardamom sugar while warm.

7. KEEP ON FRYING Cook the doughnuts in batches, turning once, until browned. Let cool on a rack for 10 minutes.

8. GET YOUR GLAZE ON Hold each doughnut and dip it in cider glaze to coat; transfer to a rack and let stand until set.

Rye and Crème Fraîche Strata with Smoked Salmon

Ginger-Molasses Scones

ACTIVE 20 MIN; TOTAL 45 MIN; MAKES 8

Baker Claire Ptak, owner of Violet in London, adds whole-wheat flour and molasses to these scones to give them a rich and hearty flavor.

- 2 cups all-purpose flour (about 8½ oz.)
- 1½ cups whole-wheat flour
- 1 Tbsp. baking powder
- 1 tsp. ground ginger
- ½ tsp. ground cinnamon
- ¼ tsp. ground cloves
- ¼ tsp. kosher salt
- 1 stick plus 6 Tbsp. cold unsalted butter, cut into small cubes
- ¾ cup crème fraîche
- 5 Tbsp. unsulfured molasses
- 1 Tbsp. honey, plus more for serving
- 1 tsp. finely grated orange zest
- ¼ cup turbinado sugar, plus more for sprinkling
- 1 cup candied ginger (4 oz.), finely chopped
- 1 large egg, lightly beaten
- Softened unsalted butter, for serving

1. Preheat oven to 400°F. Combine all-purpose flour, whole-wheat flour, baking powder, ground ginger, cinnamon, cloves, and salt in a food processor; pulse to combine. Add the butter and pulse until pea-size crumbs form.

2. Whisk the crème fraîche, molasses, 1 tablespoon honey, orange zest, and ¼ cup sugar in a bowl. Add molasses mixture to the food processor along with candied ginger. Pulse until dough just comes together, about 30 seconds. Transfer to a lightly floured work surface and pat into a 12- × 4-inch rectangle, about 1 inch thick. Divide scone dough into 4 equal rectangles, then cut each rectangle into 2 triangles.

3. Arrange scones on a parchment paper-lined baking sheet and brush generously with beaten egg; sprinkle with sugar. Bake scones until golden brown and slightly firm, 20 to 25 minutes. Serve warm with butter and honey. — CLAIRE PTAK

MAKE AHEAD The unbaked scones can be wrapped in plastic and frozen for up to 1 month. Bake from frozen, allowing a little extra baking time.

Christmas-Morning Casserole

ACTIVE 40 MIN; TOTAL 1 HR 40 MIN, PLUS OVERNIGHT SOAKING; SERVES 8

Chef Bryan Voltaggio loves this make-ahead dish: a classic baked bread-and-egg casserole with bites of pepperoni, mushrooms, and gooey cheese. It's as good for dinner as it is for breakfast.

- Butter, for greasing
- 2 Tbsp. extra-virgin olive oil
- ½ cup finely diced pepperoni (2 oz.)
- ½ lb. shiitake mushrooms, stems discarded and caps cut into ¾-inch pieces
- 1 medium onion, minced
- 1 red bell pepper, cut into ½-inch pieces
- 2 tsp. kosher salt, plus more for seasoning
- 8 large eggs
- 3 cups whole milk
- 1 Tbsp. Dijon mustard
- 1 Tbsp. soy sauce
- ½ tsp. black pepper
- ¾ lb. day-old challah, sliced 1 inch thick and cut into 1-inch cubes (10 cups)
- 6 oz. Black Forest ham, finely diced (1¼ cups)
- 1 cup shredded Monterey Jack cheese (¼ lb.)
- 1 cup shredded aged white cheddar cheese (¼ lb.)
- ½ cup finely chopped scallions, plus thinly sliced scallions for garnish
- Hot sauce, for serving

1. Butter a 13- × 9-inch baking dish. Heat oil in a large skillet over medium. Add pepperoni, and cook until the fat is rendered, about 3 minutes. Add mushrooms, and cook until lightly browned and tender, about 5 minutes. Add onion, bell pepper, and a generous pinch of salt, and cook, stirring occasionally, until softened and browned, about 7 minutes; let cool completely.

2. Beat eggs, milk, mustard, soy sauce, pepper, and 2 teaspoons salt in a large bowl. Add cooled vegetable mixture, challah, ham, Monterey Jack cheese, white cheddar cheese, and chopped scallions, and mix well. Scrape mixture into prepared baking dish, cover with plastic wrap, and refrigerate overnight.

3. Preheat oven to 350°F. Uncover casserole and bake, until it's just set and the top is browned, about 50 minutes. Let stand 10 minutes, then top with thinly sliced scallions and serve with hot sauce. — BRYAN VOLTAGGIO

Rye and Crème Fraîche Strata with Smoked Salmon

ACTIVE 25 MIN; TOTAL 2 HR 25 MIN; SERVES 6 TO 8

In this playful riff on a bagel with cream cheese and lox, F&W's Justin Chapple makes a custardy rye bread pudding with capers, then tops it with smoked salmon and red onion. It's warm, comforting, and a guaranteed crowd-pleaser.

- 8 oz. crème fraîche
- 6 large eggs, at room temperature
- 2½ cups half-and-half
- 2 tsp. kosher salt
- 1 tsp. black pepper
- 1 lb. rustic rye bread with crust, cut into 1-inch pieces
- 4 scallions, thinly sliced
- ¼ cup drained capers, plus more for garnish
- Thinly sliced smoked salmon and sliced red onion, for serving

1. Whisk crème fraîche, eggs, half-and-half, salt, and pepper in a large bowl. Add bread, scallions, and ¼ cup capers, and mix well. Scrape into a 13- × 9-inch baking dish, cover with plastic wrap, and let soak for 1 hour.

2. Preheat oven to 375°F. Bake until puffed and the top is golden, 45 to 50 minutes. Let stand for 10 minutes. Scatter some salmon on top and garnish with red onion and capers. Serve, passing more salmon at the table. — JUSTIN CHAPPLE

MAKE AHEAD The unbaked strata can be covered and refrigerated overnight. Bring to room temperature before baking.

Buttermilk Pancakes with Quince-and-Cranberry Compote

TOTAL 1 HR; SERVES 4

Chef Amanda Freitag, a judge on Chopped *and co-host of the show* American Diner Revival, *sometimes eats these tender pancakes for dessert, topped with a scoop of ice cream.*

COMPOTE

- 1 quince, peeled, cored, and cut into ¼-inch dice
- ⅓ cup granulated sugar
- ½ tsp. kosher salt
- 1 cinnamon stick
- 2 Gala apples, peeled and cut into ¼-inch dice
- ⅓ cup fresh or thawed frozen cranberries
- 2 tsp. honey
- Finely grated zest and juice of ½ lemon

PANCAKES

- 1½ cups all-purpose flour
- 1½ Tbsp. baking powder
- ½ tsp. kosher salt
- 2 large eggs
- 1½ cups buttermilk
- 3 Tbsp. unsalted butter, melted, plus 4 Tbsp. cold unsalted butter, divided
- ¼ cup confectioners' sugar
- Pure maple syrup, for serving

1. Make the compote Combine quince, sugar, salt, cinnamon stick, and ⅓ cup water in a saucepan over medium. Bring to a simmer and cook 5 minutes. Stir in apples, cranberries, honey, and lemon zest and juice, and cook, stirring, until the fruit is tender but not broken down, 5 minutes. Let cool.

2. Make the pancakes In a bowl, whisk the flour, baking powder, and salt. In another bowl, beat the eggs with an electric mixer until pale yellow and doubled in volume, about 4 minutes. Beat in buttermilk, then beat in melted butter. Using a rubber spatula, fold in dry ingredients.

3. Melt 1 tablespoon cold butter in a large nonstick skillet over medium. Using a small measuring cup, scoop three 4-inch pancakes into the skillet, and cook, until golden brown on bottom and bubbles appear on the surface, 1 to 2 minutes. Flip pancakes and cook until golden on

bottom, 1 to 2 minutes more. Transfer to a baking sheet and keep warm. Repeat with remaining butter and batter.

4. Stack pancakes on plates and top with compote. Dust with confectioners' sugar and serve with maple syrup.
— AMANDA FREITAG

◆　　◆　　◆

Eggs Benedict Salad

TOTAL 30 MIN; SERVES 4

Instead of starting his day with traditional eggs Benedict, F&W's Justin Chapple opts for this healthier salad. To mimic hollandaise, he makes a richly flavored yogurt dressing, and he tosses that with greens, torn ham, and crunchy English muffin croutons. It's a deeply satisfying and healthy alternative to heavier brunch options.

- 2 English muffins, split and torn into bite-size pieces
- 8 large eggs
- ¼ cup yogurt
- 3 Tbsp. extra-virgin olive oil
- 1½ Tbsp. Dijon mustard
- ⅛ tsp. finely grated lemon zest plus 1½ Tbsp. fresh lemon juice
- Kosher salt and black pepper
- 5 oz. mixed baby greens
- ½ head radicchio, torn into bite-size pieces
- 4 oz. thinly sliced ham, torn into bite-size pieces
- ⅓ cup snipped fresh chives

1. Preheat oven to 350°F. Spread English muffins on a baking sheet and toast until golden, about 7 minutes. Let cool.

2. Meanwhile, bring a large, deep skillet of water to a simmer. One at a time, crack eggs into a small bowl, then gently slide them into skillet. Poach over medium-low until whites are set and yolks are runny, 4 to 5 minutes. Using a slotted spoon, transfer poached eggs to a plate.

3. In a large bowl, whisk yogurt, oil, mustard, lemon zest, and lemon juice. Season the dressing with salt and pepper. Add mixed greens, radicchio, ham, chives, and croutons, and toss to coat. Transfer to plates and top with poached eggs. Sprinkle with pepper, and serve right away.
— JUSTIN CHAPPLE

French Rolled Omelet

TOTAL 10 MIN; SERVES 1

Perhaps better than anyone, chef Jacques Pépin understands the satisfaction of improving a familiar food through technique—an ethereal, delicate entrée worthy of pairing with a chilled glass of Champagne. Here's how to make it in just a few minutes.

- 3 large eggs
- 1 Tbsp. chopped fresh herbs, such as chives, tarragon, and flat-leaf parsley
- Kosher salt
- Freshly ground black pepper
- 1 Tbsp. unsalted butter, plus more for serving
- 2 Tbsp. shredded Gruyère or cheddar cheese (optional)

1. Crack eggs into a bowl, add herbs, and season lightly with salt and pepper. Using chopsticks, beat until well blended.

2. Heat an 8-inch nonstick or seasoned carbon-steel pan over high. Add butter, and cook until foamy but not browned, tipping pan to coat bottom evenly with melted butter.

3. Pour eggs into pan; immediately swirl pan clockwise while stirring eggs vigorously counterclockwise to keep curds small and creamy.

4. When a soft scramble forms, stop stirring eggs. Drag chopsticks around outside edge of omelet to turn wispy edges into scrambled eggs. Once a thin sheet of cooked egg (egg crêpe) forms on surface of pan, quickly sprinkle with cheese, if desired.

5. Using an underhanded grip on handle, tilt pan away and begin rolling egg crêpe filled with soft scrambled eggs toward edge of pan opposite the handle. Using chopsticks, tuck edge into omelet. Turn out omelet onto plate, seam-side-down.
— MARY-FRANCES HECK

WINE Pair with an elegant, focused blanc de blancs Champagne.

French Rolled Omelet

Caraway Rolls with Garlic-Parsley Butter, RECIPE P. 67

Breads

Halvah-Stuffed Challah

ACTIVE 1 HR; TOTAL 3 HR 45 MIN;
MAKES 2 LOAVES

Blogger Molly Yeh fills this braided bread with a mix of halvah (the confection made with crushed sesame seeds and honey) and tahini. Yeh recommends using an extra-smooth, pourable tahini (Whole Foods' 365 brand is a good bet), but if your tahini is cakey and thick, she advises mixing it with warm water until spreadable.

DOUGH

- 1½ cups warm water
- 1½ Tbsp. active dry yeast
- ½ cup plus 1 tsp. granulated sugar
- 4 large eggs
- ⅔ cup canola oil
- 1 Tbsp. pure vanilla extract
- 8¼ cups all-purpose flour
- 2 tsp. ground cinnamon
- ⅛ tsp. ground cardamom

FILLING AND TOPPING

- 1 cup tahini
- ⅓ cup plus 1 Tbsp. honey
- 1½ tsp. pure vanilla extract
- ½ tsp. ground cinnamon
- Pinch of kosher salt
- 1 large egg
- 1½ cups finely chopped halvah (6½ oz.)
- Sesame seeds and turbinado sugar, for sprinkling

1. Make the dough Whisk the water with the yeast and 1 teaspoon sugar in a small bowl. Let stand 10 minutes, until foamy.

2. Whisk eggs with oil and vanilla in a medium bowl. In the bowl of a stand mixer fitted with the dough hook, combine flour, salt, cinnamon, cardamom, and the remaining ½ cup sugar. Mix to blend. Add the egg and yeast mixtures, and knead until the dough comes together, scraping down the sides and bottom of the bowl, about 3 minutes. Scrape the dough out onto a work surface, and knead until smooth and slightly sticky, 8 to 10 minutes. Transfer dough to an oiled large bowl and cover with plastic wrap. Let stand at room temperature until doubled in bulk, about 2 hours.

3. Meanwhile, make the filling and topping Stir tahini with ⅓ cup of the honey, the vanilla, cinnamon, salt, and 2 tablespoons of water until smooth in a medium

bowl. In a small bowl, beat the egg with the remaining 1 tablespoon honey and 1 tablespoon water.

4. Preheat oven to 375°F and line 2 baking sheets with parchment paper. Divide the dough into 2 equal pieces. Transfer 1 piece to a lightly floured work surface, and keep the other piece covered with a damp kitchen towel. Divide dough on work surface into 3 equal pieces. Using a rolling pin, roll out 1 piece into a 14- × 6-inch rectangle. Spread ¼ cup of the tahini mixture on top, leaving a ½-inch border. Sprinkle ¼ cup of the halvah over tahini in an even layer. With a long side facing you, tightly roll up dough into a log, pressing seam and ends together to seal in filling. Repeat with the other 2 pieces of dough, ½ cup of tahini mixture, and ½ cup of the halvah. Arrange the 3 logs on one of the prepared sheets and braid them together. Brush with egg wash and sprinkle with sesame seeds and turbinado sugar. Repeat with the second piece of dough and the remaining filling, egg wash, and toppings.

5. Bake challahs on the middle and bottom racks of the preheated oven, shifting and rotating halfway through, until deep golden, 30 minutes. Transfer to racks to cool. —MOLLY YEH

MAKE AHEAD The stuffed challahs can be stored at room temperature overnight.

◆ ◆ ◆

Pull-Apart Milk Bread Wreath

ACTIVE 30 MIN; TOTAL 4 HR; SERVES 10

Inspired by Hollywood bakery Bub and Grandma's milk bread, which uses three types of dairy in the loaves they supply to Konbi, the F&W Test Kitchen created this pull-apart version fit for a Thanksgiving spread. Slather it with cranberry sauce, dip it in gravy, and save any leftovers for French toast the morning after.

- 4¾ cups bread flour (about 20¼ oz.), plus more for dusting
- ⅓ cup granulated sugar
- 2¼ tsp. fine sea salt
- 2 (¼-oz.) envelopes quick-rising yeast
- 1 cup whole milk
- ⅔ cup heavy cream
- 7 Tbsp. powdered milk
- 1 large egg
- Cooking spray

- ¼ cup unsalted butter, melted, divided, plus more for brushing
- Flaky sea salt, for garnish

1. Combine flour, sugar, salt, and yeast in the bowl of a stand mixer fitted with the paddle attachment. Whisk together milk, cream, and powdered milk in a medium bowl. Whisk in egg.

2. Add milk mixture to flour mixture. Beat on medium-low speed until combined, about 2 minutes.

3. Fit mixer with the dough hook attachment. Beat on medium speed until dough is smooth, about 10 minutes. (Pull up a section of dough, and stretch as thin as possible. If dough is see-through but does not rip, your dough is complete. If it rips, continue beating until dough can be stretched.)

4. Lightly grease a large bowl with cooking spray, and place dough in greased bowl, turning to coat. Cover with plastic wrap, and let rise until almost doubled in size, about 1 hour and 30 minutes.

5. Transfer dough to a work surface; cut into thirds. Flatten each piece, and tightly roll into tubes. Place tubes, seam sides down, on work surface; cover with lightly greased plastic wrap. Let rest 15 minutes.

6. Working with 1 dough piece at a time, roll into a 20- × 12-inch rectangle on a lightly floured surface. Brush with a scant 1½ tablespoons melted butter; cut lengthwise into 4 strips, and cut strips crosswise into 6 strips each, making 24 rectangles. Stack all 24 dough rectangles. Repeat with remaining 2 dough pieces and remaining melted butter. Arrange stacks in a lightly greased tube pan, standing up like little books, allowing gaps between dough pieces.

7. Cover pan with lightly greased plastic wrap, and let stand in a warm place (80°F), free from drafts, until dough just reaches top edges of pan, about 1 hour. Preheat oven to 325°F.

8. Remove plastic wrap, and bake in preheated oven until bread is golden brown and puffed, 35 to 40 minutes. Transfer to a wire rack, and let stand in pan 5 minutes. Remove from pan, and place on a platter. Brush with melted butter, and sprinkle with flaky sea salt. —MADDY SWEITZER-LAMM

Pull-Apart Milk Bread Wreath

German-Style Pretzels

German-Style Pretzels

ACTIVE 45 MIN; TOTAL 4 HR;
MAKES 8 PRETZELS

*These chewy pretzels from Chef
Hans Röckenwagner develop a shiny,
professional-looking crust as they bake.*

- 3¾ cups bread flour (20 oz.), plus more
  for dusting
- 1½ cups warm water
- 1¼ tsp. active dry yeast
- 2 tsp. kosher salt
- 2 Tbsp. unsalted butter, softened
- 10 cups lukewarm water
- ½ cup food-grade lye micro beads
  (see Note)
- Coarse salt or pretzel salt, for
  sprinkling (see Note)

1. In the bowl of a stand mixer fitted with
the dough hook, combine the 3¾ cups
bread flour with the warm water, yeast,
kosher salt and butter, and knead at
medium speed until the flour is evenly
moistened, 2 minutes. Increase the speed
to high, and knead until a smooth, elastic
dough forms around the hook, 8 minutes.

2. Transfer dough to a lightly floured
surface. Cover loosely with a dry kitchen
towel, and let rest 5 minutes. Cut the dough
into 8 equal pieces, and form each one into
a ball. Cover dough balls with the towel, and
let rest another 5 minutes.

3. On an unfloured surface, roll each dough
ball into an 18-inch-long rope, tapering
slightly at both ends. To shape each
pretzel, form the rope into a U shape. Cross
the ends over each other twice to form the
twist, then bring the ends to the bottom of
the U and press the tips onto it. Arrange
the pretzels on 2 large baking sheets lined
with parchment paper, and let stand,
uncovered, in a warm place until slightly
risen, about 45 minutes. Refrigerate the
pretzels, uncovered, at least 2 hours or
overnight.

4. Preheat oven to 400°F. While wearing
latex gloves, long sleeves, and safety
goggles, fill a large, deep ceramic, plastic,
or glass bowl with the lukewarm water.
Carefully add the lye (be sure to add lye
to water, never the other way around)
and, taking care not to splash, stir the
solution occasionally until all the beads
have fully dissolved, about 5 minutes.
Using a slotted spatula, gently lower a
pretzel into the solution for 15 seconds.
Carefully turn the pretzel over and soak it

for another 15 seconds. With the spatula,
remove the pretzel from the lye solution
and return to baking sheets. Repeat with
remaining pretzels.

5. Sprinkle pretzels with coarse salt, and
bake on the top and middle racks of the
preheated oven until shiny-brown and
risen, about 17 minutes; shift the pans
halfway through baking. Let cool slightly
before serving. — HANS RÖCKENWAGNER

NOTE Food-grade lye can be ordered from
essentialdepot.com.

◆　◆　◆

Buttermilk Biscuits

ACTIVE 15 MIN; TOTAL 30 MIN; SERVES 10

*The butter-to-shortening ratio in these
biscuits from Top Chef champ Kristen Kish
makes them super tender.*

- 7 cups all-purpose flour (about
  30 oz.), plus more for work surface
- 4 tsp. granulated sugar
- 4 tsp. baking powder
- 1 Tbsp. kosher salt
- 1 Tbsp. baking soda
- 1 cup cold unsalted butter, cubed
- ¼ cup vegetable shortening
- 2 cups cold buttermilk
- 2 Tbsp. heavy cream
- 1 tsp. flaky sea salt
- ¼ tsp. black pepper

1. Preheat oven to 425°F. Line a large
rimmed baking sheet with parchment paper.

2. Combine flour, sugar, baking powder,
kosher salt, and baking soda in bowl
of a stand mixer fitted with a paddle
attachment. Beat on low speed until
combined. Add butter and shortening, and
beat on low speed until mixture resembles
coarse crumbs and some pea-size pieces
of butter remain, about 3 minutes. Beat in
buttermilk just until incorporated.

3. Turn dough out onto a lightly floured
surface. Knead and fold dough into thirds,
repeating until it comes together, about
5 times. Dust dough and rolling pin with
flour; roll dough into a ¾-inch-thick (about
12- × 10-inch) rectangle; cut rectangle into
10 (3½-inch) squares. Transfer to prepared
baking sheet, arranging dough squares so
the edges touch. Brush with cream, and
sprinkle with sea salt and black pepper.

4. Bake in preheated oven until golden
brown, about 15 minutes. — KRISTEN KISH

Caraway Rolls with
Garlic-Parsley Butter

PHOTO P. 62

ACTIVE 45 MIN; TOTAL 3 HR 30 MIN;
MAKES 30 ROLLS

*These pull-apart rolls from F&W's Kay Chun
are addictively buttery and garlicky.*

ROLLS

- 1½ cups lukewarm whole milk (100°F to
  105°F)
- 2 tsp. active dry yeast
- ½ tsp. granulated sugar
- 4 cups bread flour
- 1 Tbsp. caraway seeds
- 2 Tbsp. unsalted butter, at room
  temperature, plus more for
  greasing
- 2 tsp. kosher salt

GARLIC-PARSLEY BUTTER

- 2 sticks unsalted butter
- ¼ cup minced garlic
- 1 cup chopped fresh parsley
- Flaky sea salt, for sprinkling

1. Make the rolls In the bowl of a stand
mixer fitted with the dough hook, whisk
milk, yeast, and sugar, and let stand until
foamy. With the mixer running on medium-
low speed, beat in flour, caraway seeds,
2 tablespoons butter, and salt. Knead
dough until smooth but a little tacky,
5 minutes. Transfer to a lightly oiled bowl,
cover with plastic wrap, and let stand in a
warm place until doubled in size, 1 hour.

2. Make the butter Melt butter with garlic
in a small saucepan. Scrape into a medium
bowl and let cool; stir in parsley.

3. Butter a 12-inch cast-iron or nonstick
skillet. Divide dough in half; keep 1 piece
covered with a kitchen towel. Cut other
into 8 pieces; form each into a ball, then
roll in garlic-parsley butter. Arrange in
concentric circles in prepared skillet,
about ¼ inch apart. Repeat with second
piece of dough. Cover loosely with plastic
and let stand in a warm place until doubled
in size, 1 hour.

4. Preheat oven to 350°F. Brush rolls
with butter and bake until golden, about
30 minutes. Brush with remaining butter,
sprinkle with sea salt, and serve. —KAY CHUN

Sweet Potato Yeast Rolls

ACTIVE 40 MIN; TOTAL 2 HR 20 MIN;
MAKES 30 ROLLS

*When shaping the rolls, use tension in
your cupped hand rather than too much
excess flour to coax the dough into a ball.
A generous brushing of melted butter
on the baked rolls adds shine and flavor,
while ajowan seeds offer an herbal bite
reminiscent of thyme and cumin.*

- 2 **medium sweet potatoes (about
  1½ lb.)**
- ½ **cup whole milk**
- 3 **Tbsp. plus 1 tsp. granulated sugar,
  divided**
- 5 **Tbsp. unsalted butter (2½ oz.),
  melted, divided**
- ¼ **cup lukewarm water (100°F to
  110°F)**
- 1 **(¼-oz.) envelope active dry yeast**
- 2 **large eggs, divided**
- 4 **cups all-purpose flour (about
  17 oz.), plus more for work surface**
- 1 **Tbsp. kosher salt**
  Nonstick cooking spray
- 2 **tsp. ajowan, cumin, or caraway
  seeds**

1. Prick sweet potatoes all over using
a fork; place on a microwavable plate.
Microwave on HIGH, turning every
4 minutes, until softened, 8 to 12 minutes
total. Let cool 10 minutes. Peel and discard
skins. Using a fork, mash sweet potatoes in
a medium bowl until mostly smooth.

2. Cook milk, 3 tablespoons sugar, and
3 tablespoons butter in a small saucepan
over medium-low, stirring often, until
sugar just dissolves, about 5 minutes. Let
cool slightly, about 5 minutes. Meanwhile,
stir together ¼ cup lukewarm water, yeast,
and remaining 1 teaspoon sugar in a small
bowl. Let stand at room temperature until
foamy, about 5 minutes.

3. Place milk mixture, yeast mixture,
1 cup (8 ounces) mashed sweet potatoes
(reserve remaining sweet potatoes for
another use), and 1 egg in the bowl of
a stand mixer fitted with a dough hook
attachment. Beat on low speed until
combined, about 30 seconds. Increase
mixer speed to medium-low; gradually
add flour and salt, beating until combined,

about 1 minute. Increase mixer speed
to medium; beat until dough is smooth,
elastic, and slightly sticky, 6 to 8 minutes.
(Dough should stick to bottom of bowl but
pull away from sides.) Transfer dough to
a large bowl lightly greased with cooking
spray. Cover with plastic wrap. Let stand at
room temperature until almost doubled in
size, 45 minutes to 1 hour.

4. Turn out dough onto a lightly floured
work surface, and divide into 30 (about
1-ounce) pieces. Shape into balls. Arrange
dough balls in 6 rows of 5 balls each on a
rimmed 13- × 9-inch baking sheet lightly
greased with cooking spray, spacing about
½ inch apart. Cover loosely with plastic
wrap. Let stand at room temperature until
dough balls have almost doubled in size,
30 minutes to 1 hour.

5. Preheat oven to 375°F. Whisk remaining
egg in a small bowl until lightly beaten.
Uncover rolls; brush lightly with beaten
egg. Sprinkle rolls evenly with ajowan
seeds. Bake in preheated oven until golden
brown and puffy, 14 to 18 minutes. Brush
hot rolls with remaining 2 tablespoons
butter. Serve rolls warm, or transfer to a
wire rack and let cool completely, about
1 hour. — LISA DONOVAN

NOTE Find ajowan seeds at your local
Asian or Indian market, or order from
kalustyans.com.

Two-Bite Parmesan Biscuits

ACTIVE 20 MIN; TOTAL 45 MIN;
SERVES 8 TO 10

*These addictive biscuits are baked on a
bed of grated Parmesan cheese, resulting
in a crispy, cheesy crust around the
bottom of each biscuit. Perfect on their
own, try them drizzled with a bit of honey,
or improvise by tossing a few handfuls of
fresh thyme or chives into the dough to
take them over the top.*

- 1 **(6¼-oz.) Parmesan cheese wedge**
- 3 **cups self-rising flour (about
  12¾ oz.), sifted, plus more for work
  surface**
- 1 **Tbsp. granulated sugar**
- 1 **tsp. black pepper, plus more for
  sprinkling**
- ¾ **cup cold unsalted butter (6 oz.), cut
  into ½-inch pieces**
- 1 **cup cold buttermilk**
- 1 **large egg, beaten**

1. Preheat oven to 425°F. Line a large
rimmed baking sheet with parchment
paper. Break cheese into large chunks;
transfer to a food processor, and pulse
until coarsely ground, 16 to 20 times. (You
should have a little over 1⅔ cups ground
cheese.) Reserve 2 tablespoons cheese.

2. Stir together flour, sugar, pepper,
and 1 cup ground cheese in a large bowl.
Cut butter into flour mixture using a
pastry blender or your fingers until
mixture resembles coarse crumbs. Stir in
buttermilk until a shaggy dough forms.

3. Transfer dough to a floured work
surface. Pat into a 1-inch-thick rectangle,
and cut into quarters; stack quarters on
top of each other. (Dough will be crumbly
at first but will come together as you work.)
Pat stacked dough back into a rectangle.
Repeat cutting and stacking 2 more
times. Roll or pat dough into a ¾-inch-
thick rectangle (about 8½×10 inches).
Cut rounds out of dough using a 1½-inch
round cutter, pressing straight down,
without twisting cutter. (You'll have about
35 biscuits; discard dough scraps.)

4. Sprinkle ⅔ cup ground cheese in a
12- × 8-inch rectangle on prepared baking
sheet. Arrange biscuits ½ inch apart on
cheese. Freeze 10 minutes. Remove from
freezer; brush biscuit tops evenly with egg.
Sprinkle lightly with pepper and reserved
2 tablespoons ground cheese.

5. Bake in preheated oven until biscuits
are golden brown, 12 to 14 minutes. Serve
warm, or let cool to room temperature,
about 30 minutes. — ANNA THEOKTISTO

MAKE AHEAD Biscuits can be prepared
through Step 3 and frozen up to 3 months.
Let thaw 30 minutes; proceed with Step 4,
skipping the 10-minute freezing time.

Two-Bite Parmesan Biscuits

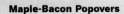

Maple-Bacon Popovers

Cheddar-Scallion Biscuits

ACTIVE 10 MIN; TOTAL 25 MIN;
MAKES 8 BISCUITS

Buttermilk dough bakes atop a pile of grated cheddar, creating a clever textural element in the form of crisp, lacy "feet" around the bottom of each biscuit.

- 2 cups all-purpose flour (about 8½ oz.), plus more for dusting
- 2 tsp. baking powder
- ¾ tsp. baking soda
- ¾ tsp. black pepper
- ½ tsp. kosher salt
- ½ cup cold unsalted butter (4 oz.), cubed
- ½ cup thinly sliced scallions
- 4 oz. sharp cheddar cheese, grated (about 1 cup), divided
- 1 cup buttermilk, divided
- 1 Tbsp. unsalted butter, melted

1. Preheat oven to 425°F. Line a baking sheet with parchment paper. Whisk together flour, baking powder, baking soda, black pepper, and salt in a large bowl until combined. Using a pastry blender or your fingers, work cold butter into flour mixture until butter is in small, flattened pieces and mixture is crumbly. Stir in scallions and ½ cup cheese. Add ¾ cup buttermilk, and stir just until dough comes together, adding up to ¼ cup additional buttermilk, 1 tablespoon at a time, if necessary. (Dough should be neither sticky nor crumbly.)

2. Transfer dough to a lightly floured surface, and knead 3 to 4 times just to bring dough together. Pat dough into an 8- × 6-inch rectangle; fold 1 short side a third of the way over toward center. Fold opposite short side over folded end (business letter fold). Rotate dough clockwise 90 degrees; pat out dough into an 8- × 6-inch rectangle, and repeat folding procedure. Pat dough out into an 8- × 6-inch rectangle (¾ to 1 inch thick); cut dough into 8 rectangular biscuits.

3. Sprinkle remaining ½ cup cheese into 8 mounds about 3 inches apart on prepared baking sheet, scattering cheese just a bit so some cheese will stick out from under biscuits. Place each biscuit rectangle on a mound of cheese on baking sheet. Brush tops with melted butter. Bake biscuits in preheated oven until golden brown, about 15 minutes. — MEGAN SCOTT

Maple-Bacon Popovers

ACTIVE 20 MIN; TOTAL 40 MIN; SERVES 12

Popovers are America's answer to British Yorkshire pudding. Festive and comforting, they're made by adding hot fat (butter, beef drippings, bacon grease) to the bottom of individual popover or muffin tins before pouring in a rich, eggy batter, which causes them to puff up and "pop" over the sides of the pan.

- 1 cup finely chopped thick-cut bacon slices
- ¼ cup unsalted butter, melted, divided
- 1 cup all-purpose flour (about 4¼ oz.)
- 1 tsp. kosher salt
- ¾ cup whole milk, at room temperature
- ¼ cup Grade A Dark pure maple syrup, plus more for brushing
- 4 large eggs, at room temperature

1. Preheat oven to 425°F with oven rack in lower third of oven. Cook chopped bacon in a medium nonstick skillet over medium-high, stirring occasionally, until crisp and golden, 5 to 7 minutes. Using a slotted spoon, transfer to a plate lined with paper towels. Allow drippings to cool slightly in skillet, about 5 minutes; pour into a small heatproof bowl.

2. Add 2 tablespoons melted butter to drippings; stir to combine. Spoon 1 teaspoon drippings mixture into each cup of a 12-cup popover pan or large muffin pan. (Discard any remaining drippings mixture.) Place pan in oven to heat.

3. Stir together flour and salt in a medium bowl. Whisk together milk, maple syrup, eggs, and remaining 2 tablespoons butter in a large bowl. Gradually whisk flour mixture into egg mixture until almost smooth; fold in cooked bacon. Transfer batter to a 4-cup spouted measuring cup.

4. Carefully remove hot pan from oven. Pour batter into popover cups, filling each two-thirds full. Bake in preheated oven until popovers are puffed and golden brown, 18 to 20 minutes. Lightly brush tops with additional maple syrup. Remove from pan, and serve immediately.
— GAIL SIMMONS

Smashed Banana Bread

ACTIVE 30 MIN; TOTAL 2 HR 10 MIN;
MAKES 1 (9-INCH) LOAF

At Dovecote Café in Baltimore, this banana bread is one of many awesome baked goods served on a daily basis. The recipe comes from owner Aisha Pew's mother, Gilda Bain-Pew, and includes super-ripe bananas and a hit of banana liqueur.

- Nonstick cooking spray
- ½ cup pecans, chopped
- 1½ cups all-purpose flour
- ¾ tsp. baking powder
- ¾ tsp. baking soda
- ¾ tsp. fine sea salt
- 2 large eggs
- 1½ cups smashed very ripe banana
- ¼ cup plus 2 Tbsp. sour cream
- 1 tsp. pure vanilla extract
- ¾ tsp. banana liqueur or dark rum
- 5 Tbsp. unsalted butter, softened, plus more for serving
- 1 cup granulated sugar
- Confectioners' sugar, for dusting

1. Preheat oven to 350°F. Grease a 9- × 5-inch metal loaf pan with nonstick cooking spray and line the bottom with parchment paper, allowing 2 inches of overhang on the 2 long sides. Spread pecans on a baking sheet and toast until lightly browned and fragrant, about 7 minutes. Let cool.

2. Whisk flour, baking powder, baking soda, and salt in a medium bowl. Beat eggs, banana, sour cream, vanilla, and banana liqueur until combined in another bowl.

3. Beat 5 tablespoons butter and granulated sugar with a stand mixer fitted with a paddle or using an electric mixer on medium speed until fluffy, about 2 minutes. Reduce speed to low and gradually beat in wet ingredients until just combined; fold in toasted pecans.

4. Scrape batter into prepared pan and bake until a wooden pick inserted into the center of the loaf comes out clean, about 1 hour and 30 minutes. Transfer pan to a rack and let cool 45 minutes, then turn bread out onto rack and let cool completely. Dust top with confectioners' sugar, cut into slices, and serve with softened butter. — GILDA BAIN-PEW

Beef, Pork & Lamb

Sea Salt Rib Roast,
RECIPE P. 77

Parmesan and Herb-Crusted Beef Tenderloin

ACTIVE 40 MIN; TOTAL 1 HR 45 MIN;
SERVES 12 TO 14

This pepper-rubbed roasted beef tenderloin is coated with herbed bread crumbs that have been mixed with anchovies, which add a nice pungent accent to the rich meat.

- 2 (3-lb.) center-cut beef tenderloin roasts, at room temperature
- 2 Tbsp. extra-virgin olive oil, plus more for rubbing
  Salt
- 2 tsp. coarsely cracked black peppercorns
- 2 cups fresh bread crumbs
- ½ cup freshly grated Parmesan cheese
- 3 anchovy fillets, finely chopped
- 1 garlic clove, finely chopped
- 1 Tbsp. finely chopped fresh thyme
- 1 Tbsp. coarsely chopped fresh flat-leaf parsley
  Freshly ground black pepper
- 2 cups dry red wine
- 2 cups veal demiglace (see Note)
- 4 Tbsp. cold unsalted butter, cut into tablespoons

1. Preheat oven to 425°F. Rub the tenderloins all over with olive oil and season with salt and cracked peppercorns. Set tenderloins on a large, heavy-gauge rimmed baking sheet, allowing space between them, and roast in the upper third of oven 20 minutes.

2. In a medium bowl, mix bread crumbs with Parmesan, anchovies, garlic, thyme, and parsley. Blend in the 2 tablespoons olive oil and season with salt and pepper.

3. Carefully pack the bread crumbs on top of each tenderloin. Lower oven temperature to 400°F, and roast the meat about 20 minutes, or until an instant-read thermometer inserted in the center registers 130°F for medium-rare. Using 2 long spatulas, transfer the tenderloins to a carving board and let rest 15 minutes.

4. Meanwhile, set the baking sheet over 2 burners. Add wine and bring to a simmer over medium-high heat, scraping up any browned bits from the bottom. Strain the wine into a medium saucepan and simmer over high heat until reduced to ½ cup.

Whisk in veal demiglace and bring to a boil; simmer 3 minutes. Remove from the heat and let the sauce stand 5 minutes. Whisk in butter, 1 tablespoon at a time, and season with salt and pepper.

5. Using a gentle sawing motion, carve the beef tenderloins into ½-inch-thick slices and serve, passing the remaining sauce at the table. —MARIA HELM SINSKEY

MAKE AHEAD The herbed bread crumbs can be refrigerated overnight. Let the bread crumbs return to room temperature before proceeding.

NOTE Veal demiglace is available at specialty food stores.

WINE There aren't many reds powerful enough to match this super-rich beef, but look for a supple Cabernet Sauvignon or blend of Cabernet Franc and Merlot.

◆———◆———◆

Roasted Dry-Aged Rib of Beef with Creamed Greens

ACTIVE 1 HR; TOTAL 3 HR 30 MIN;
SERVES 10 TO 12

American chef Christina Lecki makes a quick and easy compound butter with parsley, marjoram, and peppercorns to melt over tender beef rib roast.

RIB ROAST

- 1 (10-lb.) beef rib roast, chine bone removed
- 2 Tbsp. extra-virgin olive oil
  Kosher salt and black pepper
- 2 cups chicken stock or low-sodium broth
- 2 fresh rosemary sprigs
- 5 fresh thyme sprigs

MARJORAM BUTTER

- 6 Tbsp. unsalted butter, at room temperature
- ¼ cup chopped fresh parsley
- 2 Tbsp. chopped brined green peppercorns
- 2 Tbsp. chopped fresh marjoram
- 1 Tbsp. chopped fresh thyme
- ½ tsp. finely grated garlic
- ½ tsp. kosher salt
- ½ tsp. black pepper

CREAMED ESCAROLE AND SPINACH

- ¼ cup extra-virgin olive oil
- 2 shallots, minced

- 4 anchovy fillets in oil, drained and chopped
- 3 garlic cloves, finally chopped
- 4 bunches of escarole (2 lb.), trimmed and chopped (24 cups)
- 3 cups heavy cream
- 4 bunches of curly spinach (2 lb.), stemmed (20 cups)
- 1 tsp. finely grated lemon zest plus 2 Tbsp. fresh lemon juice
- ¼ tsp. crushed red pepper
  Kosher salt and black pepper

1. Make the rib roast Preheat oven to 450°F. Set the roast fat-side up on a rack set in a roasting pan. Rub all over with the olive oil and season with salt and pepper. Add the stock and the rosemary and thyme sprigs to the pan. Roast until well browned, about 30 minutes. Reduce oven temperature to 350°F and roast until an instant-read thermometer inserted in the center of the roast registers 125°F for medium-rare, about 2 hours and 30 minutes longer. Transfer to a cutting board and let rest for 30 minutes.

2. Make the marjoram butter Combine 6 tablespoons butter, parsley, green peppercorns, marjoram, thyme, garlic, salt, and pepper in a small bowl. Let the butter stand at room temperature.

3. Make the creamed escarole and spinach Heat the oil in a pot over medium. Add shallots, anchovies, and garlic, and cook, stirring, until anchovies dissolve, about 2 minutes. In batches, stir in escarole until wilted, about 5 minutes. Add heavy cream and bring to a boil. Simmer briskly until cream is slightly reduced, about 10 minutes. Add spinach in batches, stirring, until wilted. Cook, stirring occasionally, until greens are very tender and the cream is reduced and very thick, about 30 minutes longer. Stir in lemon zest, lemon juice, and red pepper, and season with salt and black pepper.

4. Spread marjoram butter all over warm roast. Trim roast off the bone, then thinly slice. Serve with creamed escarole and spinach. — CHRISTINA LECKI

MAKE AHEAD The marjoram butter can be refrigerated for 2 days; bring to room temperature before using. The creamed escarole and spinach can be refrigerated overnight and reheated before serving.

WINE Pair with a spicy, assertive rye whiskey.

Roasted Dry-Aged Rib of
Beef with Creamed Greens

Dry-Aged Rib Eyes with
Burgundy-Truffle Sauce

Sea Salt Rib Roast

PHOTO P. 73

ACTIVE 20 MIN; TOTAL 4 HR 20 MIN;
SERVES 12

Remove the roast from the oven when the internal temperature reaches 120°F; it will continue cooking during the rest time.

- 1 (9-lb.) boneless beef rib roast
- 3 Tbsp. flaky sea salt (such as Maldon)
- 1½ tsp. sel gris
- Morel Cream Gravy (recipe follows)

1. Preheat oven to 425°F with oven rack in lower third of oven. Rub roast all over with sea salt, and place roast, fat cap up, on a wire rack set inside a roasting pan. Let roast stand at room temperature while oven is preheating, about 30 minutes. (Roast may be seasoned and refrigerated, uncovered, up to overnight. Let stand 30 minutes at room temperature before proceeding.) Insert a probe thermometer in thickest part of roast.

2. Roast in preheated oven until meat is lightly browned, 20 to 25 minutes. Without opening oven, reduce oven temperature to 225°F. Continue roasting until internal temperature of meat registers 120°F, about 2 hours and 30 minutes for medium-rare. Transfer roast to a cutting board, and let rest 40 minutes before slicing. Sprinkle slices with sel gris, and serve with Morel Cream Gravy and carving board juices.

WINE Substantial, old-school Bordeaux red: 2015 Château de Pez Saint-Estèphe

Morel Cream Gravy

ACTIVE 45 MIN; TOTAL 55 MIN;
MAKES 3 CUPS

- ¼ cup grapeseed oil, divided
- 1 lb. fresh morel or button mushrooms, sliced (about 7 cups), divided
- ⅓ cup sherry vinegar
- 1½ tsp. fleur de sel
- 4¼ cups heavy cream, divided
- 1½ tsp. chopped fresh tarragon

1. Heat 2 tablespoons oil in a large skillet over high. Add 3½ cups mushrooms, and cook, stirring occasionally, until mushrooms are deeply caramelized, 6 to 8 minutes. Transfer mushrooms to a medium bowl. Repeat browning process with remaining 2 tablespoons oil and remaining mushrooms.

2. Return all mushrooms to skillet over medium. Stir in sherry vinegar and fleur de sel, scraping browned bits off bottom of skillet. Cook until liquid is reduced by half, about 1 minute. Add 4 cups cream, and bring to a simmer, whisking occasionally. Cook, whisking occasionally, until gravy is thickened and reduced to about 3 cups, about 30 minutes. If gravy gets too thick or separates, whisk in up to ¼ cup more cream, 1 tablespoon at a time, until desired consistency is reached. Whisk in tarragon and serve. —SHAUN SEARLEY & JAMES KNAPPETT

Dry-Aged Rib Eyes with Burgundy-Truffle Sauce

ACTIVE 1 HR 10 MIN; TOTAL 2 HR 50 MIN;
SERVES 6

The cold-smoking technique in this recipe captures the flavor of slow-roasting over a wood fire in a fraction of the time.

- 1 (750-ml.) bottle dry red wine (preferably from Burgundy)
- 1 medium yellow onion, halved
- 2 bay leaves
- ½ bunch fresh thyme
- 1 whole star anise
- 2 (32-oz.) 30- or 60-day dry-aged bone-in rib eye steaks (about 1¾ inches thick), patted dry
- 3 Tbsp. plus ¾ tsp. kosher salt, divided
- 1 Tbsp. olive oil
- 4 tsp. beef demi-glace (such as Williams Sonoma)
- 6 oz. high-quality canned escargot, drained, rinsed, and, if desired, roughly chopped (optional)
- ½ cup black truffle butter (such as D'Artagnan), chilled and cut into 8 pieces, divided
- 3 Tbsp. chopped fresh parsley
- ¼ tsp. black pepper
- 1 tsp. flaky sea salt

1. Bring red wine to a boil in a saucepan over medium-high. Reduce heat to medium-low, and simmer, uncovered, until reduced to about 1½ cups, about 45 minutes. Add onion, bay leaves, thyme, and star anise. Simmer until reduced to about 1 cup, about 15 minutes. Pour mixture through a fine wire-mesh strainer into a bowl; discard solids. Set aside.

2. Place 15 charcoal briquettes in an even layer in a chimney starter; light briquettes. When briquettes are covered with a layer of gray ash, use tongs to transfer 5 briquettes to one side of bottom grate of grill. Place about ¼ cup applewood chips and about ¼ cup oak chips on top of charcoal, and insert top grill grate. Cover and adjust vents to bring internal temperature to 85°F to 95°F, adding more briquettes if needed to reach desired temperature.

3. Fill a rimmed baking sheet with a single layer of ice cubes. Place steaks on a wire rack, and set rack over ice. Place baking sheet with steaks on top grill grate over unlit side of grill. Cover and smoke beef, maintaining temperature of 85°F to 95°F and allowing steaks to become infused with smoke flavor, about 15 minutes. Remove steaks from grill, and sprinkle all sides with 3 tablespoons kosher salt. Let stand at room temperature 30 minutes.

4. Preheat oven to 375°F. Heat a large cast-iron skillet over high. Add oil, tilting skillet to evenly coat bottom. Add steaks, and cook, undisturbed, 2 minutes. Flip and cook, undisturbed, 2 minutes. Use tongs to turn steaks upright to sear fat cap and bone. Continue to cook steaks, flipping and turning every minute, until a golden-brown crust develops on both sides and on edges of fat cap, 6 to 8 minutes. Transfer skillet with steaks to preheated oven, and cook until a thermometer inserted in thickest portion of steak registers 110°F, about 10 minutes. Remove steaks from skillet, and let rest on a wire rack 12 minutes.

5. Meanwhile, pour off drippings from skillet. Heat skillet over medium-high. Add wine reduction, and bring to a simmer, stirring and scraping up any browned bits from bottom of skillet. Add demi-glace and, if using, escargot, and cook, stirring constantly, until demi-glace is incorporated and escargot is heated through, about 1 minute. Remove from heat, and gradually stir in 6 tablespoons truffle butter, 2 pieces at a time, allowing butter to emulsify after each addition. Stir in parsley, pepper, and remaining ¾ teaspoon kosher salt.

6. Slice steaks, and arrange on a serving platter. Sprinkle steaks evenly with sea salt, top with remaining 2 tablespoons truffle butter, and serve with Burgundy-truffle sauce. — ANGIE MAR

WINE Pair with a powerful, firmly tannic Burgundy.

Rib Eye Roast with Black Garlic-Red Wine Gravy

ACTIVE 1 HR 45 MIN; TOTAL 6 HR; SERVES 8

Grant Achatz, chef and owner of Alinea in Chicago, gives his elegant roast unexpected flavor with an ultrasavory shallot-and-prune marinade. Pro tip: Using a spoonful of soy sauce in the gravy adds incredible umami.

ROAST

- 1 cup canola oil
- ½ cup pitted prunes
- 4 shallots, chopped
- ⅓ cup fresh rosemary leaves
- 3 Tbsp. juniper berries
- 3 garlic cloves, crushed
- 1½ Tbsp. kosher salt
- 1 tsp. black pepper
- 1 (5- to 6-lb.) cap-on boneless rib eye roast

GRAVY

- 1 stick unsalted butter
- ½ cup finely chopped shallots
- 2 heads of black garlic, peeled (⅓ cup)
- 1 garlic clove, crushed
- ½ cup plus 2 Tbsp. all-purpose flour
- 1½ Tbsp. packed light brown sugar
- 1 cup plus 1 Tbsp. dry red wine
- 1 Tbsp. soy sauce
- 1 qt. beef broth
- 3 fresh thyme sprigs
- 1 fresh rosemary sprig
- 1 tsp. red wine vinegar
  Kosher salt and black pepper

1. Make the roast Combine canola oil, prunes, shallots, rosemary, juniper berries, garlic, salt, and pepper in a blender. Puree until smooth. Set a rack in a roasting pan. Set roast on the rack and rub marinade all over. Let stand at room temperature 2 hours.

2. Preheat oven to 350°F. Roast beef until an instant-read thermometer inserted in the center registers 120°F, about 2 hours Transfer roast to a rack and let stand 30 minutes.

3. Make the gravy Melt butter in a medium saucepan over medium. Add shallots and cook, stirring occasionally, until golden, about 5 minutes. Stir in black garlic, crushed garlic, flour, and sugar, and cook, stirring often, until a golden-brown paste forms, about 5 minutes. Stir in 1 cup wine and soy sauce, and simmer 2 minutes, then add broth, thyme, and rosemary. Bring to a simmer and cook, stirring occasionally, until thickened and reduced to 4 cups, about 30 minutes.

4. Stir remaining 1 tablespoon wine and vinegar into gravy and season with salt and pepper. Strain into a gravy boat. Thinly slice roast across grain and serve gravy alongside. — GRANT ACHATZ

MAKE AHEAD The gravy can be refrigerated for 3 days and reheated before serving.

WINE Pair with a rich Rhône red, such as Côtes du Rhône.

Cranberry-Onion Hanukkah Brisket

ACTIVE 40 MIN; TOTAL 5 HR 50 MIN, PLUS 8 HR REFRIGERATION; SERVES 8 TO 10

This nearly effortless brisket gets a festive red glaze from cranberries; their tart sweetness cuts through the savory onion soup mix and hearty brisket with ease. Rewarming the brisket yields incredibly tender meat that soaks up the concentrated sauce.

- 1½ lb. fresh or thawed frozen cranberries (about 8 cups)
- 1½ cups granulated sugar
- 1 (½-inch) lemon peel strip plus 3 Tbsp. fresh lemon juice
- 2 Tbsp. kosher salt, divided, plus more to taste
- 1 tsp. ground black pepper, divided, plus more to taste
- 2 (2-oz.) envelopes onion soup and dip mix
- 1 (7-lb.) beef brisket, trimmed

1. Preheat oven to 325°F. Combine cranberries, sugar, lemon peel strip, lemon juice, a pinch of salt, and a pinch of pepper in a medium saucepan. Cook over medium-high, stirring and crushing cranberries with a wooden spoon, until cranberries have broken down and mixture has thickened, 10 to 14 minutes. Remove from heat, and stir in onion soup mix; let cool slightly, about 15 minutes.

2. Season brisket with remaining 2 tablespoons salt and remaining 1 teaspoon pepper. Layer 2 large sheets of heavy-duty aluminum foil in a large roasting pan, overlapping slightly to cover bottom of pan and letting foil extend 8 inches past both ends. Repeat with 2 additional sheets of foil placed crosswise (to form an X). Top with a sheet of parchment paper. Spread about a quarter of the cranberry sauce on center of parchment, and place brisket, fat side up, on top. Spread remaining cranberry sauce over top of brisket, top with another sheet of parchment, and wrap foil tightly around beef. Crimp to seal. Place roasting pan on a baking sheet, and braise brisket in preheated oven until fork-tender, 3 hours to 3 hours and 30 minutes. Uncover and let cool completely, about 1 hour and 30 minutes. Cover and refrigerate at least 8 hours or up to 2 days.

3. Preheat oven to 325°F. Uncover brisket, and discard any fat that has solidified on surface of brisket and pan drippings. Scrape off cranberry sauce, place in a bowl, and set aside. Transfer brisket to a carving board, and slice against the grain. Arrange brisket slices in an ovenproof serving dish, and spoon reserved cranberry sauce over top. Cover and bake in preheated oven until heated through, 45 minutes to 1 hour. — JUSTIN CHAPPLE

MAKE AHEAD The unsliced braised brisket can be refrigerated up to 2 days. Slice and heat before serving.

WINE Pair with a rich, full-bodied Zinfandel.

Cranberry-Onion
Hanukkah Brisket

Yemenite Short Ribs

Yemenite Short Ribs

ACTIVE 20 MIN; TOTAL 15 HR 20 MIN;
SERVES 6

Israeli chef Michael Solomonov combines turmeric, black pepper, and cumin to make hawaij, a simple but robust blend that's an essential ingredient in Yemenite cooking. Hawaij is a spice blend often used to flavor soups, stews, and even coffee. Here, it complements rich and tender beef short ribs.

- ½ **cup kosher salt**
- 2 **Tbsp. ground turmeric**
- 1 **Tbsp. black pepper**
- 1 **Tbsp. ground cumin**
- 2 **(5-lb.) beef short rib plates (3 ribs per plate)**
- **Fermented Serrano Schug (recipe follows), for serving**

1. Whisk together salt, turmeric, black pepper, and cumin in a medium bowl until blended. Rub mixture evenly over short rib plates. Place rib plates, bone-sides down, on a wire rack set inside a large rimmed baking sheet. Chill, uncovered, 8 hours or up to overnight. Remove short ribs, and let stand until ribs come to room temperature, about 1 hour and 30 minutes.

2. Preheat oven to 250°F. Transfer short ribs on rack in baking sheet to preheated oven, and cook, uncovered, until meat is tender but not falling apart and a thermometer inserted in the thickest portion registers 190°F, 5 hours and 30 minutes to 6 hours and 30 minutes. (Alternatively, to test for doneness, use a paring knife to pierce the meat between the bones. There should be no resistance.) Remove ribs from oven, tent with aluminum foil, and let rest 30 minutes. Carve each rib plate into individual ribs, and serve with schug.

FERMENTED SERRANO SCHUG Place 1 lb. stemmed serrano chiles and 3 tablespoons kosher salt in a food processor; process until mixture is slightly coarse and loose, about 2 minutes, stopping to scrape down sides as needed. Transfer to an airtight container. Let stand at room temperature 3 days. (If desired, transfer to refrigerator and chill up to 1 week.) Just before serving, add 3 tablespoons fresh lemon juice (from 1 large lemon), 2 tablespoons extra-virgin olive oil, and 2 teaspoons ground coriander to schug, and stir until blended. — MICHAEL SOLOMONOV

MAKE AHEAD To reheat cooked ribs, preheat oven to 300°F. Place ribs in a 13- × 9-inch baking dish. Add ½ cup water, and cover tightly with foil. Bake in preheated oven until warmed through, 45 minutes to 1 hour.

WINE Pair with an earthy, dark-fruited Rhône red.

Boeuf Bourguignon

ACTIVE 1 HR; TOTAL 11 HR; SERVES 4

In this homey version of the classic long-simmered stew, the beef needs to marinate overnight, so plan accordingly.

- 2 **lb. trimmed beef chuck, cut into 1½-inch pieces**
- 1 **bottle (750 ml) Pinot Noir**
- 2 **large onions, thinly sliced**
- 2 **carrots, finely chopped**
- 4 **fresh thyme sprigs**
- 2 **bay leaves**
- 1½ **tsp. herbes de Provence (see Note)**
- 2 **Tbsp. vegetable oil**
- 2 **strips bacon, cut into ¼-inch pieces**
- 2 **Tbsp. all-purpose flour**
- **Salt and freshly ground pepper**
- 2 **Tbsp. unsalted butter**
- ½ **pound white mushrooms, quartered**

1. Cover the beef with the wine in a large bowl, Add onions, carrots, thyme, bay leaves, and herbes de Provence. Cover and refrigerate overnight.

2. The next day, drain meat, vegetables, and herbs, reserving the marinade. Pat meat dry with paper towels. In a medium enameled cast-iron casserole, heat oil. Add bacon and cook over low heat until the bacon is browned and has rendered some fat, about 5 minutes; transfer to a plate.

3. Add meat to the casserole in 3 batches, and brown it well over medium heat, about 5 minutes per batch. Transfer meat to a platter.

4. Add onions and carrots to casserole and cook, stirring occasionally, until browned, about 8 minutes. Stir in flour, then gradually stir in reserved marinade. Add thyme sprigs and bay leaves, and a pinch of salt and pepper. Return the bacon and meat to casserole along with any accumulated juices, and bring to a boil. Reduce heat to low and simmer, stirring occasionally, until the meat is very tender, about 2 hours and 30 minutes.

5. Heat butter in a large skillet. Add mushrooms and season with salt and pepper. Cover and cook over medium-low heat until the liquid from the mushrooms has evaporated and mushrooms have started to brown, about 5 minutes. Uncover and cook over medium heat until nicely browned, about 5 minutes. Stir mushrooms into the stew, season with salt and pepper, and serve. —CHANTAL LEROUX

MAKE AHEAD The stew can be refrigerated for up to 3 days. Reheat gently.

NOTE Herbes de Provence is a blend of dried thyme, rosemary, summer savory, and bay leaves used in stews and on grilled foods. If you can't find it at the store, substitute dried thyme.

WINE A deep, lush red Burgundy with fruity and earthy notes will mirror the Pinot Noir in the marinade. Choose a full-flavored example with some tannin.

Braised Beef Pot Pie

ACTIVE 1 HR 30 MIN; TOTAL 5 HR; SERVES 6

Beef stew enriched with red wine and plenty of winter vegetables gets topped with flaky puff pastry at Bellecour, Gavin Kaysen's Minneapolis restaurant.

- 2½ lb. flat iron steak
-   Kosher salt and black pepper
- 2 Tbsp. canola oil
- ¼ cup unsalted butter
- 2 carrots, peeled and cut into 1-inch pieces
- 1 red onion, cut into 1-inch wedges
- 1 parsnip, peeled and cut into 1-inch pieces
- 1 celery stalk, cut into 1-inch pieces
- 8 oz. rutabaga, peeled and cut into 1-inch pieces
- 8 small cremini mushrooms, halved
- 8 garlic cloves
- 1 (6-inch) fresh rosemary sprig
- 2 dried bay leaves
- 3 Tbsp. tomato paste
- 1½ cups dry red wine
- 1 qt. beef stock or low-sodium beef broth
- 2 (14- to 16-oz.) puff pastry sheets, thawed if frozen
- 1 large egg beaten with 1 tsp. water

1. Preheat oven to 340°F. Season beef generously with salt and pepper. In a large Dutch oven or heavy pot, heat oil over medium-high. Add beef and cook, turning occasionally, until browned all over, about 12 minutes. Transfer beef to a plate; drain oil from pot and discard oil.

2. Return pot to medium-high and add butter, carrots, onion, parsnip, celery, rutabaga, mushrooms, garlic, rosemary, and bay leaves. Cook, stirring occasionally, until just tender, about 10 minutes. Add tomato paste and cook, stirring, 4 minutes. Add wine and boil until liquid is reduced by half, about 8 minutes.

3. Return the beef and any accumulated juices to pot. Add stock; bring to a boil. Cover and transfer to preheated oven. Braise until beef is very tender, about 2 hours and 45 minutes. Carefully remove beef from the braising liquid to a cutting board and let cool slightly. Cut beef into bite-size pieces and return to pot; season with salt and pepper.

4. Increase oven temperature to 400°F. Using top of a 5-inch bowl as a guide, cut 6 rounds from pastry. Transfer rounds to a parchment paper-lined baking sheet. Freeze until firm, about 15 minutes. Brush pastry with egg wash. Bake until pastry is golden, 10 to 12 minutes; cool.

5. Remove and discard the bay leaves. Ladle the hot stew into bowls, and top each with a pastry round. Serve immediately.
— GAVIN KAYSEN

WINE Pair with a spicy California Rhône-style blend.

Apple and Pumpkin Seed Stuffed Pork Loin

ACTIVE 1 HR; TOTAL 3 HR; SERVES 8 TO 10

Food stylist and recipe developer Laura Rege stuffs her pork loin with a tasty combination of toasted rye bread, apples, and pumpkin seeds. To serve the juicy roast, she drizzles it with luscious unrefined pumpkin seed oil.

- ¼ cup extra-virgin olive oil, divided
- 1 cup finely chopped onion
- 6 garlic cloves, finely chopped
- 2 Fuji apples, peeled, cored, and cut into ¼-inch dice
- ¼ cup plus 2 Tbsp. apple cider vinegar
- 4 oz. rye bread, cut into ¼-inch cubes and toasted
- ¼ cup pumpkin seeds, lightly toasted
- 2 Tbsp. chopped fresh parsley
-   Kosher salt and black pepper
- 1 (3½-lb.) pork loin, skin removed and reserved, meat butterflied ½ inch thick (have your butcher do this)
- 8 Lady apples, halved crosswise and seeded
-   Unrefined pumpkin seed oil, for drizzling

1. Heat 2 tablespoons oil in a large skillet over medium-high. Add the onion and garlic and cook, stirring, until soft and light golden, about 3 minutes. Stir in Fuji apples and ¼ cup apple cider vinegar, and boil over medium-high until the liquid is reduced by half, about 2 minutes. Transfer to a large bowl and stir in toasted bread cubes, pumpkin seeds, and parsley. Season stuffing with salt and pepper.

2. Using a sharp knife, score pork skin at ¼-inch intervals. Lay pork loin butterflied-side up on a work surface, and season with salt and pepper. Spread stuffing over pork loin, then roll up meat, leaving seam on top. Drape pork skin over seam. Using kitchen twine, tightly tie loin at 1-inch intervals. Season with salt and pepper, wrap in plastic, and refrigerate for at least 1 hour or up to 24 hours.

3. Preheat oven to 475°F. Toss Lady apples with remaining 2 tablespoons each vinegar and oil.

4. Unwrap pork and transfer skin-side up to a rimmed baking sheet. Roast until skin is browned and bubbly, 20 minutes. Reduce oven temperature to 325°F and roast 25 minutes more. Scatter apples around pork and scrape any liquid from the bowl over them. Continue to roast until an instant-read thermometer inserted in the center of the meat registers 140°F, about 20 minutes longer.

5. Transfer pork to a cutting board and set apples on a platter. Scrape pan drippings into a small bowl. Let pork rest 15 minutes, then discard strings. Thickly slice pork and transfer to platter. Drizzle with pan drippings and pumpkin seed oil, and serve.
— LAURA REGE

WINE Pair with a dry, full-bodied Riesling from Alsace.

Braised Beef Pot Pie

Pork-and-Brisket Chili, RECIPE P. 86

Celery Root, Apple, and Fennel Slaw, RECIPE P. 86

CASUAL SUNDAY SUPPER

Making a festive Sunday dinner for family and friends is a tradition that seems to have faded across the country. But that's not the case at the home of Megan and Colby Garrelts, the couple behind the acclaimed Kansas City restaurants Bluestem and Rye. Both chefs grew up in the Midwest, an experience that not only shapes their food but also their family life.

Scallion-Corn Muffins,
RECIPE P. 87

MoKan Nut Pie,
RECIPE P. 87

CASUAL SUNDAY SUPPER MENU

Pork-and-Brisket Chili

ACTIVE 1 HR 45 MIN; TOTAL 4 HR, PLUS
OVERNIGHT SOAKING; SERVES 10 TO 12

Colby Garrelts makes a giant pot of chili for his family's Sunday supper, often using venison that he has hunted himself. Here, he uses a mix of pork shoulder and brisket for a super-decadent and satisfying bowl of chili.

BEANS

- 1 lb. small dried pink beans, soaked overnight and drained
- 5 garlic cloves
- 1 small yellow onion, quartered through the core
- 1 medium carrot, halved crosswise
- 1 celery rib, halved crosswise
- 1½ Tbsp. kosher salt, plus more to taste, divided

CHILI

- 3½ lb. boneless pork shoulder, cut into 1½-inch pieces
- 2 lb. brisket, cut into 1½-inch pieces
  Kosher salt and black pepper
- 3 Tbsp. vegetable oil
- 3 medium yellow onions, chopped
- 1 green bell pepper, stemmed, seeded, and chopped
- 10 garlic cloves, chopped
- ¼ cup tomato paste
- ¼ cup chili powder
- 2 Tbsp. packed light brown sugar
- 1 Tbsp. mustard powder
- 1 Tbsp. ground cumin
- 1 (16-oz.) jar roasted green Hatch chiles (medium heat)
- 1 (16-oz.) can crushed tomatoes
- 5 qt. chicken stock or low-sodium broth
- ¼ cup fresh oregano leaves
  Sour cream, shredded cheese, and thinly sliced scallions, for serving

1. Make the beans Combine beans, garlic, onion, carrot, celery rib, salt, and 4 quarts water in a large saucepan; bring to a boil. Simmer over medium-low heat until the beans are just tender, about 1 hour. Drain well and discard the vegetables.

2. Make the chili Season pork and brisket generously with salt and pepper. Heat oil in a large pot over medium-high until shimmering. In batches, cook pork and brisket, turning occasionally, until browned all over, about 10 minutes per batch. Using a slotted spoon, transfer meat to a baking sheet.

3. Add onions, bell pepper, garlic, and a generous pinch of salt. Cook over medium-high, stirring frequently, until just starting to soften and brown, about 5 minutes. Add tomato paste, chili powder, brown sugar, mustard powder, and cumin, and cook, stirring, until fragrant and vegetables are coated, about 3 minutes. Add Hatch chiles and tomatoes, and cook, stirring, until bubbling, about 5 minutes. Add stock and bring to a boil. Add meat and oregano, and simmer over medium, stirring occasionally, until meat is barely tender, about 1 hour.

4. Stir beans into chili and simmer over medium, stirring occasionally, until meat and beans are tender, about 1 hour and 15 minutes longer. Serve hot with sour cream, shredded cheese, and thinly sliced scallions. — MEGAN & COLBY GARRELTS

MAKE AHEAD The chili can be refrigerated for up to 5 days. Reheat gently before serving.

Celery Root, Apple, and Fennel Slaw

TOTAL 45 MIN; SERVES 8

The Garreltses serve this sweet and crunchy slaw as an accompaniment to their rich and meaty Pork-and-Brisket Chili, but it also would also be excellent alongside barbecued meat and chicken.

- 1 lb. celery root, peeled, and julienned on a mandoline
- ½ cup sugar
- 1 tsp. kosher salt, plus more for seasoning
- ¼ cup extra-virgin olive oil
- 2 Tbsp. apple cider vinegar
- 1 Tbsp. Dijon mustard
- 1 Tbsp. drained capers, chopped
- 1 Tbsp. drained prepared horseradish
- 2 Braeburn or Lady apples, cored, and julienned on a mandoline
- 5 celery ribs, thinly sliced, plus ½ cup lightly packed celery leaves
- 1 small fennel bulb, halved, cored, and julienned on a mandoline
- ½ cup lightly packed fresh parsley leaves
- 2 Tbsp. finely chopped fresh oregano
  Black pepper

1. Toss celery root, sugar, and 1 teaspoon salt in a large bowl; let stand 15 minutes. Drain celery root well in a colander, and squeeze out some of the excess liquid. Wipe out bowl.

2. Whisk oil, vinegar, Dijon, capers, and horseradish in same bowl. Add celery root, apples, celery ribs and leaves, fennel, parsley, and oregano; toss well. Season with salt and pepper, and toss again. Serve right away. — MEGAN & COLBY GARRELTS

Scallion-Corn Muffins

ACTIVE 20 MIN; TOTAL 45 MIN; MAKES 24

These deliciously moist muffins get fantastic flavor from corn kernels and scallions.

Nonstick cooking spray

1¾ cups fine cornmeal

1¼ cups all-purpose flour

¾ cup sugar

1½ Tbsp. baking powder

2 tsp. kosher salt

2 large eggs

1½ cups whole milk

1 stick unsalted butter, melted

1 cup fresh or thawed frozen corn kernels

¼ cup finely chopped scallions

1. Preheat oven to 350°F. Grease the cups of two 12-cup muffin pans with nonstick cooking spray.

2. In a large bowl, whisk cornmeal with flour, sugar, baking powder, and salt. In a medium bowl, beat eggs with milk and butter until smooth. Stir the wet ingredients into the dry until combined, then fold in corn kernels and scallions.

3. Spoon the batter into the prepared muffin cups. Bake about 15 minutes, until a wooden pick inserted in the center of a muffin comes out clean. Let the muffins cool in the pan 10 minutes before serving. — MEGAN & COLBY GARRELTS

MAKE AHEAD The corn muffins can be stored in an airtight container overnight. Warm in a low oven before serving.

MoKan Nut Pie

ACTIVE 1 HR; TOTAL 9 HR 30 MIN; MAKES 1 (9-INCH) PIE

This riff on pecan pie from Megan Garrelts is called MoKan because it refers to Missouri and Kansas; when Megan makes it, she uses Missouri pecans and Kansas black walnuts. It has a great flaky crust and plenty of fragrant nuts, with a classic sticky pecan pie filling.

CRUST

1¼ cups all-purpose flour, plus more for dusting

1½ tsp. sugar

½ tsp. kosher salt

4 Tbsp. unsalted butter, cubed and frozen

4 Tbsp. rendered pork lard, cubed and frozen

⅓ cup ice water

FILLING

1½ cups pecans, chopped

1½ cups walnuts, chopped

1 stick plus 2 Tbsp. unsalted butter, cubed

6 large eggs, at room temperature

1 cup sugar

1 cup cane syrup or dark corn syrup

2½ Tbsp. bourbon

2 tsp. kosher salt

1 tsp. pure vanilla extract

Unsweetened whipped cream, for serving

1. Make the crust Combine 1¼ cups flour, sugar, and salt in a food processor; pulse until combined. Add butter and lard, and pulse until mixture resembles coarse meal. Drizzle ice water on top and pulse until dough just comes together. Turn dough out onto a work surface, gather any crumbs, and pat into a disk. Wrap in plastic and refrigerate until well chilled, about 4 hours or overnight.

2. On a lightly floured work surface, roll out dough to a 13-inch round. Ease dough into a 9-inch deep-dish pie plate. Fold overhang under itself and crimp decoratively. Freeze crust until well chilled, at least 1 hour.

3. Preheat oven to 375°F. Place crust on a large rimmed baking sheet. Line crust with parchment paper and fill with pie weights or dried beans. Bake until crust is just set, about 20 minutes. Remove parchment and weights. Bake until just starting to brown, about 15 minutes longer. Let cool completely.

4. Make the filling Preheat oven to 350°F. Spread pecans and walnuts on a large rimmed baking sheet. Toast in the oven, until fragrant and lightly browned, 8 to 10 minutes. Let cool.

5. Cook butter in a medium skillet over medium-low, stirring occasionally, until foamy, about 5 minutes. Continue to cook, stirring frequently, until milk solids turn brown and butter smells nutty, about 4 minutes longer. Pour brown butter through a fine wire-mesh strainer into a heatproof bowl. Let cool to room temperature.

6. Beat eggs, cooled brown butter, sugar, cane syrup, bourbon, salt, and vanilla in a large bowl until smooth. Stir in the pecans and walnuts.

7. Pour filling into cooled crust. Bake until the filling is nearly set, about 45 minutes. Transfer pie to a rack and let cool completely, about 4 hours. Cut into wedges and serve with unsweetened whipped cream. — MEGAN & COLBY GARRELTS

MAKE AHEAD The pie can be covered and kept at room temperature for 3 days.

WINE Pair this menu with a robust California Syrah.

Standing Pork Rib Roast with Cracklings

Spiced Pork Crown Roast with Roasted Vegetables

ACTIVE 45 MIN; TOTAL 4 HR 15 MIN; SERVES 16

American chef Christina Lecki makes a toasty, fragrant spice rub for a celebratory cut of pork; as the meat cooks, the delicious juices flavor the vegetables in the pan.

- 1½ Tbsp. whole cloves
- 1½ Tbsp. whole allspice berries
- 6 whole star anise
- 1 (1½-inch) cinnamon stick
- 3 bay leaves
- 1 dried Thai chile, stemmed
- 1 tsp. ground mace
- 1 (16-rib) crown roast of pork (about 10 lb.), tied, bones frenched
- Kosher salt and black pepper
- 16 torpedo onions or large shallots, peeled
- 1½ lb. medium fingerling potatoes
- 1½ lb. parsnips, peeled and cut into 2½-inch pieces
- 1½ lb. medium turnips, peeled and cut into 2½-inch pieces
- 1 lb. rutabaga, peeled and cut into 2½-inch pieces
- 1 cup sage leaves
- 12 garlic cloves, peeled
- 2 Tbsp. canola oil
- Nonstick cooking spray

1. Combine cloves, allspice, star anise, cinnamon stick, bay leaves, and chile in a small skillet over medium-high. Toast, stirring, until spices just start to smoke, 2 to 3 minutes. Transfer to a spice grinder and let cool, then add mace and grind to a powder.

2. Season pork roast with salt and pepper, and rub spice mixture all over it. Let stand at room temperature 1 hour.

3. Meanwhile, preheat oven to 325°F. Toss onions, potatoes, parsnips, turnips, rutabaga, sage, garlic, and canola oil in a very large roasting pan. Season with salt and pepper.

4. Set pork roast on top of vegetables. Lightly coat 16 small squares of foil with nonstick spray and wrap each rib bone to prevent burning. Roast pork until beginning to brown, 2 hours. Increase oven temperature to 450°F and roast until vegetables are tender and an instant-read thermometer inserted in the thickest part of the pork registers 140°F, about 40 minutes longer. Transfer roast to a platter and let rest 15 minutes. Carve pork roast between ribs and serve with roasted vegetables. — CHRISTINA LECKI

MAKE AHEAD The spice mix can be made up to 3 days ahead.

◆ ◆ ◆

Standing Pork Rib Roast with Cracklings

ACTIVE 20 MIN; TOTAL 7 HR, PLUS OVERNIGHT SALTING; SERVES 8

Allowing the salted roast to stand overnight draws the moisture out of the skin, which creates the crispy, delicious cracklings.

- 1 (8-rib) pork loin roast with skin (about 5½ lb.), ribs frenched, skin scored at ½-inch intervals, and tied
- ½ cup kosher salt, divided

1. Place pork loin on a rimmed baking sheet. Season generously all over with ¼ cup salt, then sprinkle skin with remaining ¼ cup salt; be sure to push salt into crevices in skin at each score. Refrigerate uncovered overnight.

2. Let pork stand at room temperature for 3 hours. Preheat oven to 275°F. Set a rack in a large roasting pan. Using a damp towel, brush excess salt off roast, then transfer to pan skin-side up. Bake until an instant-read thermometer inserted in the thickest part registers 115°F, about 1 hour and 30 minutes.

3. Increase heat to 450°F and continue to roast, until the skin is crisp and an instant-read thermometer inserted in the thickest part registers 135°F, about 50 minutes longer. Transfer roast to a carving board and let rest for 30 minutes. Remove and discard ties. Using a sharp serrated knife, slice meat and serve. — ERIKA NAKAMURA

WINE Pair with a smoky, spicy Merlot from California.

Sausage-and-Potato Pan Roast

ACTIVE 20 MIN; TOTAL 50 MIN; SERVES 4 TO 6

For the perfect cold-weather weeknight dinner, F&W's Justin Chapple makes this one-pan dish, roasting sweet sausages with potatoes and shallots, and tossing them with brightly flavored arugula and lemon before serving.

- 2 large red potatoes, cut into 1½-inch pieces
- 2 Yukon Gold potatoes, cut into 1-inch wedges
- 1 large baking potato, cut into 1½-inch pieces
- 10 medium unpeeled shallots, halved
- ⅓ cup extra-virgin olive oil, plus more for brushing
- Kosher salt and black pepper
- 1½ lb. sweet Italian sausage, cut into 3-inch lengths
- 1 8-oz. bunch arugula, stemmed and chopped
- 1 Tbsp. fresh lemon juice

1. Preheat oven to 425°F. Toss red potatoes, Yukon Golds, baking potatoes, shallots, and ⅓ cup oil on a large rimmed baking sheet. Season generously with salt and pepper. Roast until potatoes are lightly browned, about 15 minutes. Brush sausage with oil and add to baking sheet. Roast until the potatoes are tender and the sausage is cooked through, 20 to 25 minutes longer.

2. Transfer everything on baking sheet to a platter. Fold in arugula and lemon juice, season with salt and pepper, and serve. — JUSTIN CHAPPLE & KAY CHUN

WINE Pair with a fruity, spicy Spanish Rioja.

BEST OF BOTH WORLDS

Roasting pork at a relatively low temperature allows the fat to render better under the skin, resulting in extra-juicy, tender meat. Though our standing pork rib roast recipe calls for finishing the pork under high heat to puff the skin and get those crispy cracklings, if skin isn't your thing, you can skip that step and simply continue cooking the roast at 275°F until the internal temperature hits 140°F.

Clove-and-Cider Glazed Ham

ACTIVE 30 MIN; TOTAL 2 HR; SERVES 12

For entertaining, chef Carla Hall glazes a spiral-cut ham with apple cider, brown sugar, mustard, bourbon, and sweet spices.

- 1 (7- to 8-lb.) spiral-cut ham
- 1 cup fresh apple cider
- ½ cup packed light brown sugar
- 3 Tbsp. unsalted butter
- 2 Tbsp. Dijon mustard
- 2 Tbsp. bourbon
- 1 Tbsp. apple cider vinegar
- 1 (3-inch) cinnamon stick
- 6 whole cloves
- ½ tsp. black peppercorns
- ½ tsp. grated nutmeg

1. Preheat oven to 375°F. Place ham in a 13- × 9-inch baking dish.

2. Combine apple cider, brown sugar, butter, mustard, bourbon, vinegar, cinnamon stick, cloves, peppercorns, and nutmeg in a small sauce-pan over medium-low. Simmer, whisking occasionally. Cook until reduced to ¾ cup, about 25 minutes. Pour glaze over ham, leaving spices on meat. Cover tightly with foil. Bake, basting every 15 minutes, until heated through, about 1 hour and 15 minutes. Transfer to a platter.

3. Strain pan juices into a small saucepan. Bring to a boil and cook until reduced to a glaze, 8 to 10 minutes. Spoon glaze over ham, and serve. — CARLA HALL

WINE Pair with a spiced, red-berried medium-bodied red, such as Garnacha.

◆━━◆━━◆

Spiced Brown Sugar Ham with Apple Jus

ACTIVE 20 MIN; TOTAL 5 HR 30 MIN; SERVES 8 TO 10

Keep the ham wrapped in foil while resting (2 hours is ideal) so the meat can reabsorb any moisture released during cooking. "If you can't pick up the foil-wrapped ham without burning yourself, then it's not done resting!" says Atlanta restaurateur Kevin Gillespie.

- 1 (1-lb.) box light brown sugar
- 2 Tbsp. freshly ground black pepper
- 1½ tsp. ground cloves
- 1½ tsp. ground cinnamon
- 1 (8- to 10-lb.) bone-in smoked ham, skin removed
- 3 medium Fuji apples, peeled, cored, and thinly sliced
- 2 Tbsp. apple cider vinegar
  Kosher salt

1. Preheat oven to 350°F. Mix sugar, pepper, cloves, and cinnamon in a medium bowl.

2. Place ham fat-side up on two large pieces of aluminum foil and, using your hands, rub sugar mixture all over the top and sides; it should form a thick layer. Wrap ham tightly in foil and transfer to a large roasting pan. Bake until glossy on the outside and a thermometer inserted in the thickest part of the meat registers 125°F, about 3 hours. Transfer ham to a work surface, and let rest in foil at room temperature until cool enough to handle, about 2 hours.

3. Unwrap ham and slice; transfer to a large platter and tent with foil to keep warm. Pour accumulated juices into a large measuring cup and spoon off any fat. You should have about 3¼ cups.

4. Combine Fuji apples and 2 tablespoons water in a medium saucepan over medium. Cover and cook, stirring occasionally, until tender, about 10 minutes. Using a slotted spoon, transfer apples to a blender and puree with ham juices and vinegar until smooth. Pour apple jus through a fine-mesh strainer into a gravy boat and season with salt. Serve ham, passing apple jus at the table. — KEVIN GILLESPIE

WINE Pair with a fruit-forward Zinfandel.

◆━━◆━━◆

Ruby Port Ham Glaze

TOTAL 5 MIN; MAKES ½ CUP

This glaze works especially well with city ham (as opposed to saltier, drier country ham), but you can use it on either style.

- 3 Tbsp. packed light brown sugar
- 2 Tbsp. ruby port
- 2 tsp. Dijon mustard

Whisk together brown sugar, port, and mustard until smooth. Refrigerate until ready to use, up to 1 week. — MARY-FRANCES HECK

Herb-Crusted Rack of Lamb

TOTAL 1 HR; SERVES 10 TO 12

The Thanksgiving spread at the home of Food Network star and cookbook author Ayesha Curry features this classic rack of lamb as well as traditional turkey and sides inspired by her Jamaican heritage.

- ¼ cup extra-virgin olive oil, divided
- 2 racks of lamb, frenched (2 lb. each)
  Kosher salt and black pepper
- 2 Tbsp. whole-grain mustard
- 1 tsp. honey
- ¾ cup plain dry bread crumbs
- 2 Tbsp. finely chopped fresh parsley
- 1 Tbsp. finely chopped fresh mint leaves
- 1 Tbsp. finely chopped fresh rosemary
- 1 tsp. finely grated lemon zest
- 1 lb. cherry tomatoes, preferably on the vine

1. Preheat oven to 400°F. Preheat a large cast-iron skillet, then heat 1 tablespoon oil over medium-high. Season the lamb all over with salt and pepper. In batches if necessary, add lamb racks to skillet, fat-side down, and cook until browned, about 3 minutes. Turn lamb fat-side up and cook 2 minutes longer. Transfer lamb, fat-side up, to a large rimmed baking sheet.

2. Mix mustard and honey in a small bowl. Mix bread crumbs, parsley, mint, rosemary, lemon zest, remaining 3 tablespoons oil, and a generous pinch each salt and pepper in another small bowl. Brush lamb with honey mustard and coat with bread crumb mixture, pressing to help it adhere.

3. Roast lamb for 15 minutes. Scatter tomatoes around it, and roast until an instant-read thermometer inserted in the center of the meat registers 130°F for medium-rare, 20 to 25 minutes longer. Transfer lamb to a carving board and let rest for 10 minutes. Cut racks into chops and serve with tomatoes. — AYESHA CURRY

WINE Pair with a full-bodied Napa Valley Cabernet.

Spiced Brown Sugar
Ham with Apple Jus

**Roast Leg of Lamb with
Minty Salsa Verde**

Spiced Leg of Lamb

ACTIVE 25 MIN; TOTAL 11 HR; SERVES 8

Palestinian cookbook author Reem Kassis says her mother, Nisreen, would serve leg of lamb to guests because it was "a sign of utmost respect." Large cuts of meat were reserved for special occasions and celebratory gatherings. Kassis roasts it low and slow until the meat is nearly falling apart, then finishes it at a higher temperature to crisp the outside.

- 8 large garlic cloves, 4 cloves minced, 4 cloves smashed
- 3 Tbsp. pomegranate molasses
- 2 Tbsp. extra-virgin olive oil
- 1 Tbsp. kosher salt
- 1 Tbsp. ground coriander
- 1 Tbsp. ground cumin
- 2 tsp. ground dill seeds
- 2 tsp. sumac
- 1 tsp. Nine-Spice Mix (recipe follows)
- ½ tsp. cayenne pepper
- 1 (4½- to 5½-lb.) bone-in leg of lamb (shank end)
- 3 fresh bay leaves
- ½ cup water, plus more as needed

1. Whisk minced garlic, pomegranate molasses, oil, salt, coriander, cumin, dill, sumac, Nine-Spice Mix, and cayenne in a small bowl until a smooth paste forms.

2. Using a paring knife, cut slits all over lamb. Rub spice mixture over lamb, pressing into slits. Tuck bay leaves and smashed garlic into 4 of the slits. Transfer lamb to a wire rack set in a large roasting pan. Refrigerate, uncovered, at least 6 hours or up to overnight. Let lamb stand at room temperature 1 hour before roasting.

3. Preheat oven to 425°F. Roast lamb, uncovered, in preheated oven until spice mixture just begins to brown, about 15 minutes. Remove lamb from the oven, and reduce oven temperature to 325°F. Add ½ cup water to roasting pan, and cover tightly with aluminum foil. Return lamb to oven and roast at until tender and almost falling apart, about 3 hours, adding more water if necessary. (Water in pan may evaporate too quickly.)

4. Increase oven temperature to 425°F. (Do not remove pan from oven.) Uncover roasting pan, and continue to roast until top is browned, 5 to 10 minutes. Transfer lamb to a cutting board; tent with foil, and let rest 15 minutes. Pull meat into large chunks and serve. — REEM KASSIS

WINE Pair with a spicy, cool-climate Syrah.

◆ ◆ ◆

Nine-Spice Mix

ACTIVE 20 MIN; TOTAL 1 HR 20 MIN
MAKES ABOUT ¾ CUP

As a child, Reem Kassis would walk through Jerusalem's old city with her mother, where they'd buy whole spices to make this fragrant, all-purpose blend. Toasting the spices before grinding brings out their fruity notes, resulting in an intensely aromatic mixture.

- 6 Tbsp. whole allspice
- 6 cassia bark sticks or cinnamon sticks
- 3 Tbsp. coriander seeds
- 1 Tbsp. black peppercorns
- 1 tsp. cardamom seeds
- ½ tsp. cumin seeds
- 10 whole cloves
- 2 blades mace
- ½ whole nutmeg, crushed

1. Combine allspice, cassia bark, coriander seeds, black peppercorns, cardamom seeds, cumin seeds, cloves, mace, and nutmeg in a large skillet over medium-low. Cook until very fragrant but not burned, about 10 minutes, stirring often for the first 4 minutes and stirring constantly during the last 6 minutes. Remove from heat, and let cool completely, at least 1 hour.

2. Working in 3 batches, transfer spice mixture to a spice grinder, and grind until mixture becomes a fine powder, about 30 seconds. Transfer to an airtight container. — REEM KASSIS

MAKE AHEAD The spice mixture may be stored in an airtight container for up to 3 months.

Roast Leg of Lamb

ACTIVE 20 MIN; TOTAL 2 HR 30 MIN;
SERVES 6 TO 8

The modern match for this leg of lamb from British chef April Bloomfield is a refreshing, piquant mint salsa.

- 1 (4½-lb.) leg of lamb, tied
- 3 garlic cloves
- ½ cup rosemary needles, chopped
- 3 Tbsp. extra-virgin olive oil
  Kosher salt and black pepper
  Minty Salsa Verde (recipe follows)

1. Let the lamb stand at room temperature for 1 hour. Preheat oven to 400°F. Using the back of a knife, smash garlic to a paste. Scrape into a small bowl, and whisk in rosemary and oil. Season generously with salt and pepper, and rub paste all over lamb. Transfer to a shallow roasting pan.

2. Roast lamb until an instant-read thermometer inserted in the thickest part registers 130°F, about 1 hour and 15 minutes. Transfer lamb to a carving board and let rest for 15 minutes. Carve lamb and serve with Minty Salsa Verde. — APRIL BLOOMFIELD

WINE Pair with a gamey, intense Rhône red.

◆ ◆ ◆

Minty Salsa Verde

TOTAL 15 MIN; SERVES 6 TO 8

- 3 salt-packed anchovies, rinsed, soaked, and filleted
- 1 Tbsp. drained capers
- ½ small garlic clove
- ¼ cup plus 2 Tbsp. extra-virgin olive oil
- 3 Tbsp. red wine vinegar
- 1 Tbsp. Dijon mustard
- 2 cups packed fresh mint leaves
- 1½ cups packed fresh parsley leaves
  Flaky sea salt and black pepper

Combine anchovies, capers, and garlic in a food processor; pulse until a paste forms. Add oil, vinegar, and mustard, and pulse until incorporated. Add herbs and pulse until finely chopped. Scrape mixture into a small bowl. Season with salt and pepper, and serve. — APRIL BLOOMFIELD

MAKE AHEAD The salsa verde can be refrigerated overnight.

Buttermilk-Brined Roast Chicken, RECIPE P. 108

Poultry

Clementine-and-
Garlic Roast Turkey

Clementine-and-Garlic Roast Turkey

ACTIVE 1 HR; TOTAL 4 HR 30 MIN; SERVES 10

To make the tastiest, quickest, easiest jus for turkey, F&W's Justin Chapple includes juicy clementines and garlic in the roasting pan, adding excellent flavor.

- 1½ sticks unsalted butter, softened
- 6 clementines, zested (1½ Tbsp.) and halved crosswise, divided
- 4 large garlic cloves, finely grated, plus 6 whole garlic heads, halved crosswise
- 2 tsp. finely chopped fresh thyme, plus 10 sprigs
- 1 (12- to 14-lb.) turkey, rinsed and patted dry
- Kosher salt and black pepper
- 2 cups chicken stock or low-sodium broth

1. Mix butter, clementine zest, grated garlic, and chopped thyme in a medium bowl. Loosen breast and thigh skin of turkey, and spread butter mixture under and over skin. Season turkey inside and out with salt and pepper. Transfer to a rack set in a roasting pan, and let come to room temperature, about 1 hour.

2. Preheat oven to 400°F. Roast until lightly browned, about 30 minutes. Add stock to pan and roast for 30 minutes. Scatter clementine halves, garlic heads, and thyme sprigs in pan. Roast, rotating the pan a few times, until an instant-read thermometer inserted in the inner thigh registers 165°F, about 1 hour longer. Transfer turkey to a cutting board; let rest for 30 minutes. Transfer clementines, garlic heads, and thyme to a plate, tent with foil and keep warm.

3. Meanwhile, skim fat off pan juices and transfer juices to a medium saucepan. Squeeze roasted garlic from 1 head and whisk into pan juices. Bring to a boil over medium-high and cook, whisking frequently, until slightly reduced, about 5 minutes. Season roasted garlic jus with salt and pepper. Carve turkey and transfer to a platter. Arrange roasted clementines, garlic heads, and thyme around turkey and serve with jus. — JUSTIN CHAPPLE & LAURA REGE

MAKE AHEAD The seasoned, uncooked turkey can be refrigerated overnight. Bring to room temperature before roasting.

WINE Pair with a citrusy, full-bodied Chenin Blanc.

Vinegar-Brined Roast Turkey

ACTIVE 25 MIN; TOTAL 15 HR; SERVES 12

Top Chef champ Kristen Kish deemed it her brother's job to make the turkey for Thanksgiving. She taught him how to brine the bird in cider vinegar, which helps tenderize it and yields flavorful drippings that are perfect for pan jus.

BRINE

- 2 gal. warm water
- 2 cups apple cider vinegar
- 2 cups kosher salt
- 1 cup packed light brown sugar
- 3 Tbsp. whole black peppercorns
- 6 bay leaves
- Large handful of fresh flat-leaf parsley stems (leaves reserved for turkey)

TURKEY

- 1 (12- to 14-lb.) fresh turkey, neck and giblets removed
- ¾ cup unsalted butter (6 oz.), at room temperature
- 2 Tbsp. chopped fresh flat-leaf parsley
- 1 Tbsp. chopped fresh thyme
- 1 lemon, zested and halved, divided
- 2 tsp. kosher salt, divided
- 1½ tsp. black pepper, divided
- 6 Tbsp. extra-virgin olive oil, divided
- 3 medium carrots, cut into 1-inch pieces
- 3 celery stalks, large diced
- 1 large yellow onion, quartered and petals separated
- ½ cup dried cremini mushrooms (about ⅜ oz.)
- 2 shallots, halved
- 1 garlic head, halved crosswise
- 5 fresh rosemary sprigs
- 4 fresh sage sprigs
- 3 fresh marjoram sprigs

1. Make the brine Stir together 2 gallons warm water, vinegar, salt, brown sugar, peppercorns, bay leaves, and parsley stems in a 14-quart stockpot until sugar and salt dissolve, about 1 minute and 30 seconds. Let brine cool to room temperature, about 30 minutes.

2. Make the turkey Place turkey in brine, cover, and refrigerate 12 to 24 hours. Remove turkey from brine; discard brine. Pat turkey dry with paper towels. Preheat oven to 350°F. Stir together butter, parsley, thyme, lemon zest, 1½ teaspoons salt, and 1 teaspoon pepper in a medium bowl until combined. Using your fingers, gently loosen skin from turkey breast and thighs. Spread some butter mixture under skin; carefully replace skin. Spread remaining butter mixture over skin of breast and thighs. Drizzle turkey with 2 tablespoons oil, and sprinkle with remaining ½ teaspoon salt and remaining ½ teaspoon pepper. Place turkey, breast-side up, on a wire rack in a roasting pan. Toss together carrots, celery, onion, and remaining ¼ cup oil in a large bowl; scatter vegetable mixture around turkey in roasting pan. Stuff turkey cavity with lemon halves, dried mushrooms, shallots, garlic, rosemary, sage, and marjoram. Tie legs together with kitchen twine; tuck wing tips under.

3. Roast turkey in preheated oven until golden brown and an instant-read thermometer inserted in thickest part of thigh registers 155°F, about 2 hours. Transfer turkey to a carving board; remove rack from roasting pan. Let turkey rest until thermometer registers 165°F, about 30 minutes. Scoop out herb-and-mushroom mixture from inside of turkey, and add to roasting pan with vegetables. Set roasting pan on stovetop over medium-high; stir in 2 cups water, and simmer, scraping up browned bits from bottom of pan, 10 minutes. Remove from heat. Pour mixture through a fine wire-mesh strainer over a bowl; discard solids. Carve turkey, and serve with gravy. — KRISTEN KISH

WINE Pair with a light-bodied, berry-rich Beaujolais.

Turkey Leg Roulade

ACTIVE 1 HR; TOTAL 2 HR 30 MIN; SERVES 6

For lovers of dark meat—the most flavorful part of the bird—a turkey leg roulade offers an elegant alternative to the whole bird for the holiday. Deboned turkey legs are wrapped around a leek-and-currant stuffing, tied, poached in white wine, and then roasted—a method that yields perfectly cooked, juicy meat and crackling bronze skin in a fraction of the time. The best part? The process can be started several days in advance, needing only a quick blast in a hot oven on T-day to crisp the skin before serving.

- 2 (2-lb.) turkey leg quarters, patted dry
- 4 tsp. kosher salt, divided, plus more for seasoning
- 2 tsp. freshly ground black pepper, divided
- 3 cups Melted Leeks with Currants and Sage (recipe follows)
- 2 qt. chicken stock
- 1 cup dry white wine

1. Place one turkey leg, skin-side down, on a cutting board. (a) Using a sharp, thin knife, cut along white membrane that runs lengthwise down thigh and leg until blade hits bone. (b) Continue cutting along and around thigh and drumstick bones until bones are fully exposed. (c) Slip knife under thigh bone and separate from meat. Repeat with drumstick bone. Taking care not to pierce meat and skin around joint, use tip of knife to trace around joint until it is free. Remove bone; reserve for another use. Repeat procedure with remaining leg.

2. Place one leg, skin-side down, with a short end closest to you. Season with 2 teaspoons salt and 1 teaspoon pepper. Spread half of leeks in an even layer over meat, leaving a ½-inch border. Repeat procedure with remaining leg, salt, pepper, and leeks.

3. Working with one leg at a time, roll turkey leg by tucking the skin side into stuffing to form a long cylinder. Arrange, seam-side down, on work surface. Repeat procedure with remaining leg.

4. Secure legs with butcher's twine at 1-inch intervals, tying tightly to secure. Stuffed turkey legs may be wrapped in plastic wrap and chilled in the refrigerator for up to 2 days.

5. Bring stock and wine to a simmer in a large Dutch oven, and season lightly with salt. Carefully place legs in broth. Add more broth if necessary to cover.

Reduce heat to low to maintain a very gentle simmer. Cover and cook until a thermometer inserted in legs registers 165°F, about 1 hour. Carefully transfer legs to a large rack set over a rimmed baking sheet. Let meat rest for 15 minutes. Strain cooking liquid; discard solids. Reserve strained cooking liquid for gravy, if desired. If serving turkey later, let cool to room temperature, wrap tightly in plastic wrap, and refrigerate up to 2 days.

6. Preheat oven to 400°F. Roast turkey until skin is crisp, about 20 minutes. Let stand 5 minutes. Slice into ½-inch rounds.
— MARY-FRANCES HECK

WINE Pair with a full-bodied California Chardonnay.

Melted Leeks with Currants and Sage

TOTAL 30 MIN; MAKES 3 CUPS

This sweet-and-savory stuffing is studded with wine-soaked currants and fresh herbs, which lend their flavors to the poached and roasted turkey legs.

- ½ cup currants
- ½ cup dry white wine
- ½ cup unsalted butter (4 oz.)
- 4 cups thinly sliced leeks, white and light green parts only

STEP-BY-STEP

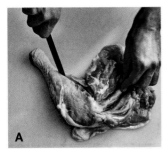

BUTTERFLY THE LEG Place one turkey leg, skin-side down, on a cutting board. (A) Using a sharp, thin knife, cut along the white membrane that runs lengthwise down the thigh and leg until the blade hits bone. (B) Continue

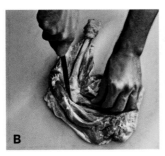

cutting along and around the thigh and drumstick bones until the bones are fully exposed. (C) Slip knife under thigh bone and separate from meat. Repeat with drumstick bone. Taking care not to pierce the meat and skin

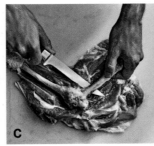

around the joint, use the tip of knife to trace around joint until it is free. Remove bone; reserve for another use. Repeat procedure with remaining leg.

SPREAD THE STUFFING Place one leg, skin-side down, with a short end closest to you. Season with 2 teaspoons salt and 1 teaspoon pepper. Spread half of leeks in an even layer over meat, leaving a ½-inch border. Repeat procedure with remaining leg, salt, pepper, and leeks.

- 2 cups thinly sliced kale or collard greens
- ½ cup finely chopped celery
- 2 tsp. kosher salt
- 1 Tbsp. chopped fresh thyme
- 1 Tbsp. chopped fresh rosemary
- 1 Tbsp. chopped fresh sage
- 1 tsp. finely grated lemon zest

1. Place currants and wine in a small bowl, and set aside.

2. Melt butter in a large skillet over medium. Using a silicone spatula, fold in leeks until coated. Cook, stirring often, until leeks are wilted to half their original volume, about 5 minutes. Fold in kale and celery, and season with salt. Continue cooking until vegetables are tender, about 10 minutes. Stir in thyme, rosemary, sage, currants, and wine. Increase heat to high, and cook until all liquid is evaporated, about 4 minutes. Remove from heat, stir in zest, and let cool before using.

— MARY-FRANCES HECK

ROLL IT UP Working with one leg at a time, roll turkey leg by tucking the skin side into the stuffing to form a long cylinder. Arrange, seam-side down, on work surface. Repeat procedure with remaining leg.

TIE WITH TWINE Secure legs with butcher's twine at 1-inch intervals, tying tightly to secure. Stuffed turkey legs may be wrapped in plastic wrap and chilled in the refrigerator for up to 2 days.

POACH AND REST Bring stock and wine to a simmer in a large Dutch oven, and season with salt. Add legs and more stock, if necessary, to cover. Reduce heat to low to maintain a very gentle simmer. Cover and cook until a thermometer inserted in legs registers 165°F, about 1 hour.

ROAST AND CARVE Preheat oven to 400°F. Roast turkey until skin is crisp, about 20 minutes. Let stand 5 minutes. Slice into ¹/₂-inch rounds.

Simple Smoked Turkey

ACTIVE 1 HR; TOTAL 5 HR 15 MIN, PLUS 12 HR
BRINING; SERVES 8 TO 12

*Smoking a turkey yields juicy and tender
meat. The keys to success are seasoning
the bird with a dead-simple saltwater brine,
then controlling the temperature of the
smoker for even cooking. The added bonus
of smoking the Thanksgiving turkey? It
frees up the oven for sides and pies.*

- 2 gal. filtered water, divided
- 1½ cups plus 1 tsp. fine sea salt, divided
- 1 (12- to 16-lb.) fresh or thawed
  frozen whole natural turkey, giblets
  removed
- 1 large yellow onion, quartered
- 2 garlic heads, halved
- 2 small lemons, halved
- 3 fresh sage sprigs
- 1 Tbsp. olive oil
- ½ cup apple cider vinegar

1. Combine ½ gallon water and 1½ cups
salt in a large saucepan. Cook over
medium, whisking constantly, until salt
dissolves, about 3 minutes. Pour mixture
into a very large stockpot or other large
container; add remaining 1½ gallons
water. Place turkey in brine. Place a plate
upside down on top of turkey to submerge
completely. Cover; refrigerate 12 hours.

2. Remove turkey from brine; discard
brine. Pat turkey dry with paper towels,
including cavity. Let stand 1 hour at
room temperature. Stuff cavity with
onion, garlic, lemons, and sage. Rub oil
over turkey breasts and legs. Sprinkle
with remaining 1 teaspoon salt. Tie legs
together with kitchen twine; tuck wing
tips under.

3. Open vent of smoker completely.
Prepare a charcoal fire in smoker
according to manufacturer's instructions,
and push coals to one side. Bring internal
temperature to 300°F to 325°F; maintain
temperature 15 to 20 minutes. Place
4 cups soaked applewood chips on coals.
Position grate in smoker, and place turkey,
breast-side up, over side without coals.
(Legs should be pointing toward coals.)
Smoke turkey, covered with smoker lid,
maintaining temperature inside smoker
between 300°F and 325°F and brushing
with vinegar every 45 minutes, until a

thermometer inserted into thickest part
of breast registers 155°F, 12 to 15 minutes
per pound, approximately 2 hours and
30 minutes to 4 hours. Transfer turkey to
a cutting board; let rest 30 minutes. Carve
turkey and serve. — ALECIA MOORE & ROBBY
GRANTHAM-WISE

WINE Pair with an elegant, structured
Cabernet Franc.

Bulgur-Stuffed Poussin with Preserved Lemon-Honey Glaze

ACTIVE 35 MIN; TOTAL 3 HR 10 MIN;
SERVES 4

*Poussin turns tender, juicy, and fragrant
thanks to a Persian-inspired, sweet spice
marinade and preserved lemon-honey
glaze. The dried fruit-studded bulgur
filling gives you a built-in side dish. One
poussin makes a perfect single serving; if
using plumper Cornish hens, split each in
half to serve two.*

- ¼ cup olive oil
- ¼ cup fresh lemon juice (from
  2 lemons)
- 3½ tsp. kosher salt, divided
- 1 tsp. ground coriander
- 1 tsp. ground cumin
- 1 tsp. ground ginger
- ½ tsp. ground cinnamon
- ½ tsp. black pepper
- 4 (1-lb.) poussins or 2 (1½-lb.)
  Cornish game hens
- ½ cup uncooked coarse or medium
  bulgur, rinsed in cool water and
  drained
- ¼ cup dried apricots, chopped
- ¼ cup unsweetened dried cranberries
- 1¼ cups lower-sodium chicken broth,
  divided
- ¼ cup salted roasted pistachios,
  chopped
- ¼ cup toasted walnuts, chopped
- ¼ cup chopped fresh flat-leaf parsley
- ¼ cup honey
- ¼ tsp. saffron threads
- 1½ Tbsp. thinly sliced preserved lemon
  peel
- 2 Tbsp. fresh mint leaves, torn
- 2 Tbsp. fresh basil leaves, torn

1. Whisk together oil, lemon juice,
1½ teaspoons salt, coriander, cumin,
ginger, cinnamon, and pepper in a large
bowl. Sprinkle poussins evenly with
1½ teaspoons salt. Add poussins to
marinade, turning to coat and rubbing
marinade all over birds, inside and out.
Cover and chill 2 hours.

2. About 1 hour before roasting the birds,
make the stuffing. Stir together bulgur,
apricots, cranberries, and remaining
½ teaspoon salt in a medium heatproof
bowl. Bring ¾ cup broth to a simmer in a
small saucepan over medium-high. Pour
hot broth over bulgur mixture. Let stand
until liquid is absorbed, about 1 hour. Fluff
with a fork. (The bulgur should still have a
little tooth to it. It will finish cooking inside
the poussins.) Add pistachios, walnuts,
and parsley; stir to combine.

3. Preheat oven to 500°F. Remove
poussins from marinade, and pat dry
with paper towels. Discard marinade.
Stuff poussins evenly with bulgur mixture
(about ½ cup each). Loosely tie legs
together with kitchen twine and tuck
wing tips under. Place poussins on a wire
rack set inside a shallow roasting pan or
rimmed baking sheet.

4. Roast in preheated oven until lightly
browned, about 15 minutes. Decrease
oven temperature to 350°F without
opening oven door, and roast until
poussins are golden brown, juices run
clear when poussin is pierced with a knife,
and stuffing temperature registers 160°F,
25 to 30 minutes.

5. Transfer poussins to a platter or tray;
cover to keep warm. Remove wire rack
from pan. Pour remaining ½ cup broth into
pan with poussin drippings; stir and scrape
bottom with a wooden spoon to loosen
browned bits. Pour broth mixture into a
small saucepan. Add honey and saffron,
and bring to a simmer over medium-low,
stirring often. Add preserved lemon peel,
and simmer until syrupy, 5 to 8 minutes.

6. To serve, divide poussins among
4 plates. If serving Cornish hens, spoon
about ½ cup stuffing onto each of 4 plates.
Cut Cornish hens in half; divide among
plates. Spoon lemon-honey glaze over
birds, and garnish with mint and basil.
— CARA CHIGAZOLA-TOBIN

WINE Pair with an herby, peppery
Lebanese red.

Simple Smoked Turkey

Dry-Brined Spatchcocked Turkey

ACTIVE 45 MIN; TOTAL 3 HR 15 MIN, PLUS
2 DAYS REFRIGERATION; SERVES 10

A dry brine is not only an easier technique, but it also results in crispier skin and more flavorful meat than a classic wet brine.

- 1 (12- to 14-lb.) fresh or thawed frozen natural whole turkey, patted dry (see Note)
- 3½ Tbsp. kosher salt (preferably Diamond Crystal) or 3 Tbsp. Morton kosher salt, divided
- 2 (3-oz.) limes, quartered
- 1 (2-inch) piece fresh ginger, cut into ¼-inch coins
- 1 garlic head, halved crosswise
- ½ cup unsalted butter (4 oz.), cut into 8 pieces, divided
- 2 cups unsalted chicken stock
  Coconut-Lemongrass Gravy (recipe follows)

1. Place turkey, breast-side down, on a work surface. Using poultry shears and beginning at tail end, cut along each side of backbone, separating it from turkey. Turn turkey breast-side up. Using the heels of your hands, press firmly against breast bone until it cracks and breast flattens. Trim excess fat around neck.

2. Starting at neck end, using your fingers, gently loosen and lift skin from breast and legs. Rub 1 tablespoon salt under skin; carefully replace skin. Rub remaining 2½ tablespoons salt all over skin and in turkey cavity, rubbing more salt where meat is thickest. Place turkey on a wire rack set snugly inside an 18- × 13-inch rimmed baking sheet. Tuck wing tips under turkey. Turn turkey breast-side down. Cover with plastic wrap; refrigerate 36 hours.

3. Spread limes and ginger in a single layer on a clean rimmed baking sheet; add garlic head halves. Place a wire rack on lime mixture in baking sheet. Remove turkey from refrigerator. Uncover and place, breast-side up, on rack; pat dry with paper towels. Refrigerate, uncovered, at least 6 hours or up to 12 hours.

4. Remove turkey from refrigerator. Let stand at room temperature 1 hour. Meanwhile, preheat oven to 450°F with oven rack in lower third of oven. Place 2 butter pieces under loosened skin of each breast and 2 butter pieces under loosened skin of each leg. Pour stock into baking sheet.

5. Roast turkey in preheated oven until an instant-read thermometer inserted in thickest part of breast registers 150°F, 1 hour to 1 hour and 10 minutes, rotating baking sheet halfway through roasting time. Transfer turkey to a cutting board, and let rest 30 minutes. (Reserve aromatics and pan drippings for Coconut-Lemongrass Gravy.) Carve turkey, and transfer to a platter. Serve with Coconut-Lemongrass Gravy. — KELSEY YOUNGMAN

NOTE For dry brining, select a natural, heritage, or organic turkey that is not processed with water or salt.

WINE Pair with a citrus-scented, dry Riesling.

Coconut-Lemongrass Gravy

TOTAL 15 MIN; MAKES 1¼ CUPS

- 1 cup pan drippings
  Chicken stock
- ¼ cup well-shaken and stirred unsweetened coconut milk
- 2 Tbsp. unsalted butter
- 2 tsp. finely chopped fresh lemongrass
- 2 tsp. packed light brown sugar
- 1 tsp. cornstarch

1. Pour aromatics and pan drippings through a fine wire-mesh strainer into a medium bowl, pressing on solids; discard solids. Skim off and discard fat from drippings (there should be about 1 cup drippings remaining; top up with chicken stock, if needed.

2. Transfer drippings to a blender. Add coconut milk, butter, lemongrass and light brown sugar. Process until smooth, about 30 seconds. Set aside 2 tablespoons coconut milk mixture. Pour remaining coconut milk mixture into a small saucepan. Stir together cornstarch and reserved 2 tablespoons coconut milk mixture. Bring coconut milk mixture in saucepan to a simmer over medium; stir in cornstarch mixture. Simmer, stirring often, until slightly thickened, about 2 minutes. — KELSEY YOUNGMAN

STEP-BY-STEP

SPATCHCOCK Place turkey, breast-side down, on a work surface. Using poultry shears and beginning at tail end, cut along each side of backbone, separating backbone from turkey. Remove backbone; save for stock or discard.

FLATTEN TURKEY Turn turkey breast-side up on work surface. Using the heels of your hands, press firmly against breastbone until it cracks and turkey breast flattens.

PRESEASON Loosen skin from breast and legs by gently pushing your fingers between skin and meat. Rub kosher salt under skin, on skin, and in turkey cavity.

AIR CHILL Place turkey on a wire rack set snugly inside an 18- × 13-inch rimmed baking sheet. Tuck wing tips under turkey (so they don't burn when roasted). Turn turkey breast-side down. Cover with plastic wrap, and refrigerate 36 hours.

PREPARE AROMATICS Spread ginger, limes, and garlic in an even layer on a clean rimmed baking sheet. Top with a wire rack. Add turkey, breast-side up; pat skin dry with paper towels. Refrigerate, uncovered, 6 to 12 hours.

BUTTER AND ROAST Remove turkey from refrigerator. Let turkey stand at room temperature 1 hour. Place butter under loosened skin of breast and legs. Pour stock into baking sheet. Bake in preheated oven as directed.

Whole-Grain Stuffing with Mustard Greens, Mushrooms, and Fontina, RECIPE P. 106

Porchetta-Spiced Turkey with Pan Gravy, RECIPE P. 106

THE PLENTY PROJECT

Food & Wine's *Justin Chapple and Kay Chun created an astonishing holiday menu, then turned the ingredient scraps—beet peels, bread crusts, radish greens, and more—into an ingenious array of delicious recipes for a Thanksgiving without food waste.*

Caramelized Vegetables with Dijon Butter,
RECIPE P. 107

Sweet and Savory Cranberry Conserva,
RECIPE P. 107

Sautéed Collard Greens with Pepperoni,
RECIPE P. 107

THE PLENTY PROJECT MENU

Porchetta-Spiced Turkey with Pan Gravy

ACTIVE 1 HR; TOTAL 3 HR 15 MIN, PLUS
OVERNIGHT MARINATING; SERVES 12

Porchetta, the fennel-scented, crackly-skinned Roman pork roast, is the inspiration for this succulent turkey.

- 3 Tbsp. fennel seeds
- 7 garlic cloves, minced
- 2 Tbsp. chopped fresh oregano plus 3 oregano sprigs
- 1 Tbsp. chopped fresh sage
- 1 Tbsp. chopped fresh rosemary
- 1 Tbsp. chopped fresh thyme
- 1 tsp. coarsely ground black pepper
- 2 tsp. finely grated lemon zest plus 1 Tbsp. fresh lemon juice
- ½ tsp. crushed red pepper
- 1 stick plus 3 Tbsp. unsalted butter, at room temperature
- 1 (12-lb.) turkey
- 2 Tbsp. extra-virgin olive oil
- Kosher salt and black pepper
- ¼ cup all-purpose flour
- 4 cups low-sodium chicken broth
- 2 Tbsp. chopped fresh parsley
- Caramelized lemon halves, for garnish (see Note)

1. Blend fennel seeds, garlic, chopped oregano, sage, rosemary, thyme, coarsely ground black pepper, lemon zest, red pepper, and 1 stick butter in a bowl.

2. Put the turkey on a rack set over a flameproof roasting pan. Using your fingers and starting at neck end, gently loosen skin from breast. Spread all but 2 tablespoons spiced butter under skin in an even layer. Spread remaining 2 tablespoons spiced butter all over skin. Refrigerate turkey uncovered overnight.

3. Preheat oven to 425°F. Rub oil all over turkey, and season with salt and pepper. Roast until the turkey is golden and an instant-read thermometer inserted in the inner thigh registers 160°F, about 1 hour and 45 minutes.

4. Transfer turkey to a cutting board. Carefully tilt turkey and pour cavity juices into a medium bowl. Let turkey rest for 30 minutes.

5. Meanwhile, pour off all but ¼ cup of fat from roasting pan. Add flour and set roasting pan over low heat. Cook, stirring, until flour is golden, 1 to 2 minutes. Stir in broth, turkey cavity juices, and oregano sprigs, and bring to a simmer, scraping up any browned bits. Cook until thickened, 4 to 5 minutes. Whisk in remaining 3 tablespoons butter and lemon juice, and season with salt and pepper. Pour gravy through a fine wire-mesh strainer into a gravy boat, and stir in parsley.

6. Carve turkey, and serve with pan gravy and caramelized lemon halves. —KAY CHUN

NOTE To caramelize lemon halves, sear them cut-side down in a hot cast-iron skillet until browned, about 3 minutes.

Whole-Grain Stuffing with Mustard Greens, Mushrooms, and Fontina

ACTIVE 1 HR; TOTAL 2 HR 30 MIN; SERVES 12

This stuffing is substantial enough to double as a vegetarian main dish (just substitute mushroom broth or water for the chicken stock).

- 4 Tbsp. unsalted butter, plus more for greasing
- 1 cup farro
- 1 lb. whole-wheat bread, crusts removed, bread cut into 1-inch dice (8 cups)
- ¼ cup extra-virgin olive oil
- 3 leeks, light green and white parts only, thinly sliced
- 6 garlic cloves, finely chopped
- 1 lb. mustard greens, stemmed and coarsely chopped (12 packed cups)
- Kosher salt and black pepper
- 1 lb. cremini mushrooms, quartered
- 1½ cups chicken stock or low-sodium broth
- 1 Tbsp. fresh lemon juice
- 3 large eggs, beaten
- 3 scallions, thinly sliced
- 2 cups shredded Italian Fontina cheese (6 oz.), divided

1. Preheat oven to 400°F. Butter a 4-quart baking dish.

2. In a medium saucepan of salted boiling water, cook farro until al dente, about 20 minutes. Drain well; transfer to a very large bowl.

3. Meanwhile, spread bread on a large baking sheet and toast until golden and crisp, about 15 minutes. Transfer to the bowl.

4. In a large nonstick skillet, melt 2 tablespoons butter in 2 tablespoons oil. Add leeks and garlic, and cook over medium, stirring occasionally, until softened, about 8 minutes. Stir in mustard greens in batches, and cook until wilted. Season with salt and pepper. Add vegetables to bowl.

5. In the same skillet, melt 1 tablespoon butter in 1 tablespoon oil. Add half the mushrooms and season with salt and pepper. Cook over medium-high, stirring, until golden, about 3 minutes. Transfer to the bowl. Repeat with remaining 1 tablespoon butter, 1 tablespoon oil, and mushrooms.

6. Add stock, lemon juice, eggs, scallions, and 1 cup Fontina cheese to the bowl and mix well. Transfer stuffing to prepared baking dish and cover with foil. Bake for 40 minutes. Scatter remaining 1 cup Fontina cheese on top and bake, uncovered, until golden, 25 to 30 minutes longer. —KAY CHUN

MAKE AHEAD The assembled stuffing can be covered and refrigerated overnight.

Sweet and Savory Cranberry Conserva

TOTAL 30 MIN; MAKES 3 CUPS

- 2 Tbsp. canola oil
- 1 large shallot, minced
- 1 garlic clove, minced
- 1 tsp. ground fennel
- 1 lb. fresh cranberries
- 1 cup packed light brown sugar
- ¼ cup unseasoned rice vinegar
- 2 Tbsp. whole-grain mustard
- 2 tsp. Dijon mustard
- Kosher salt and black pepper

Heat canola oil in a medium saucepan over medium. Add shallot, garlic, and fennel, stirring, until softened, 3 minutes. Add ⅓ cup water, cranberries, sugar, vinegar, whole-grain mustard, and Dijon, and bring to a boil. Simmer over medium-high, stirring occasionally, until the cranberries are coated in a thick sauce, about 7 minutes. Season with salt and pepper. Scrape into a bowl and let cool; serve. —JUSTIN CHAPPLE

MAKE AHEAD The conserva can be refrigerated for up to 2 weeks.

Mashed Potatoes with Parmesan Cream

ACTIVE 30 MIN; TOTAL 1 HR; SERVES 12

For the fluffiest mashed potatoes, be sure to put them through a ricer while still warm.

- 6 lb. large Yukon Gold potatoes, scrubbed, peeled, and cut into large chunks
- Kosher salt and pepper
- 1½ sticks unsalted butter
- 1½ cups heavy cream
- 1½ cups whole milk
- 1¼ cups freshly grated Parmigiano-Reggiano cheese

1. In a pot, cover potatoes with water; bring to a boil. Add a generous pinch of salt and simmer over medium until tender, 20 minutes. Drain.

2. Meanwhile, in a saucepan, combine butter, cream, and milk; bring to a simmer. Add cheese and let stand 1 minute; whisk until smooth.

3. Pass the warm potatoes through a ricer into the pot. Fold in Parmesan cream. Season generously with salt and pepper, and serve. —JUSTIN CHAPPLE

MAKE AHEAD The potatoes can be refrigerated for up to 3 days. Reheat gently, adding milk if too thick.

Sautéed Collard Greens with Pepperoni

TOTAL 45 MIN; SERVES 12

Collards are often paired with bacon, but spicy pepperoni is a fun, tasty twist.

- ⅓ cup extra-virgin olive oil
- 6 oz. pepperoni, julienned
- 2 large shallots, thinly sliced
- 6 garlic cloves, thinly sliced
- 4 lb. collard greens, stemmed and coarsely chopped
- Kosher salt and black pepper
- 3 Tbsp. fresh lemon juice

1. Heat oil in a pot over medium-high. Add pepperoni, shallots, and garlic, and cook, stirring, until the shallots are softened, 3 to 5 minutes. Add collard greens in large handfuls, stirring and letting each handful wilt slightly before adding more.

2. When all of the collards have wilted, add ¼ cup water and a generous pinch of salt. Cook over medium-high, stirring occasionally, until greens are crisp-tender and most of the liquid has evaporated, about 10 minutes. Stir in lemon juice and season with salt and pepper. Transfer to a bowl and serve. —JUSTIN CHAPPLE

MAKE AHEAD The cooked collard greens can be refrigerated overnight.

Caramelized Vegetables with Dijon Butter

ACTIVE 40 MIN; TOTAL 1 HR 20 MIN; SERVES 12

Carrots, fennel, and beets get a double dose of mustard butter: first to bake in the flavor before roasting, and again at the very end for a rich, pungent finish.

- 1 stick unsalted butter, at room temperature, divided
- 3 Tbsp. Dijon mustard, divided
- 1 Tbsp. coriander seeds, crushed in a mortar
- Kosher salt and black pepper
- 1½ lb. carrots, scrubbed and halved lengthwise
- 3 fennel bulbs (1½ lb.), cut into 1-inch-thick wedges
- 1½ lb. beets, peeled and cut into 1-inch-thick wedges
- Kosher salt and black pepper
- 2 Tbsp. chopped fresh dill

1. Preheat oven to 425°F. Mix 6 tablespoons butter, 2 tablespoons Dijon, and coriander in a bowl. Season with salt and pepper.

2. Scatter carrots and fennel on a large rimmed baking sheet. Arrange beets on another large rimmed baking sheet. Dollop spiced butter over each baking sheet, and season with salt and pepper. Toss and rub to evenly coat. Roast, stirring occasionally and rotating the sheets halfway through, until the vegetables are tender and caramelized, about 40 minutes.

3. Meanwhile, mix remaining 2 tablespoons butter and 1 tablespoon mustard in a small bowl. Dollop butter over warm vegetables and toss to evenly coat. Transfer vegetables to a serving platter and garnish with dill. —KAY CHUN

Buttermilk-Brined Roast Chicken

PHOTO P. 94

ACTIVE 30 MIN; TOTAL 1 HR 30 MIN, PLUS
6 HR BRINING; SERVES 4

Douglas fir is a signature ingredient at Sarah and Evan Rich's flagship San Francisco restaurant, Rich Table. Here, sprigs are incorporated into the brine for the flavorful chicken, but rosemary serves as a nice substitute.

- ¼ cup kosher salt, plus more to taste
- 11 garlic cloves, 9 smashed, 2 thinly sliced
- 2 Tbsp. sugar
- 2 Tbsp. chopped fresh rosemary or 5 Douglas fir sprigs
- 1 bay leaf
- 2 cups water plus 2 cups cold water
- ½ cup dried porcini mushrooms
- 1 qt. buttermilk
- 1 (3½-lb.) whole chicken
- 1 tsp. unsalted butter, softened
- 2 Tbsp. extra-virgin olive oil

1. Combine ¼ cup salt, smashed garlic, sugar, rosemary, bay leaf, and 2 cups water in a medium saucepan. Bring to a simmer, stirring to dissolve salt and sugar. Transfer mixture to a very large bowl and stir in 2 cups cold water.

2. Place mushrooms in a spice grinder; grind to a powder. (You should have about 3 tablespoons.) Whisk mushroom powder and buttermilk into salt mixture. Place chicken in buttermilk brine, cover with plastic wrap, and refrigerate at least 6 hours or up to 12 hours.

3. Preheat oven to 425°F. Remove chicken from brine and pat dry; discard brine. Tuck wing tips behind breasts, tie legs with kitchen twine, and set chicken, breast-side up, in a rack over a roasting pan. Season all over with salt.

4. Roast chicken 15 minutes. Brush butter all over chicken, and roast until an instant-read thermometer inserted in the thickest part of the thigh registers 165°F, about 45 minutes longer. Transfer to a cutting board and let rest 15 minutes.

5. Heat oil and sliced garlic in a small skillet over medium-high. Simmer, stirring occasionally, until the garlic just starts to brown and oil is hot and fragrant, about 3 minutes. Remove from heat and let cool.

6. Carve chicken and arrange on a platter. Brush with some garlic oil and serve right away, passing around remaining oil at the table. — SARAH & EVAN RICH

WINE Pair with a fruity, rich Pinot Noir.

◆ ◆ ◆

Pan-Roasted Chicken with Warm Farro Salad

ACTIVE 30 MIN; TOTAL 1 HR 15 MIN; SERVES 4

F&W's Kay Chun makes a super fall-friendly dish of simple roast chicken with a side of nutty farro with roasted carrots and mushrooms, which she flavors with lemon juice and hazelnuts.

- 1 (4-lb.) whole chicken, backbone removed and chicken cut in half
- 5 Tbsp. extra-virgin olive oil, divided
  Kosher salt and black pepper
- 2 Tbsp. unsalted butter
- 3 fresh sage sprigs
- ½ lb. small (not baby) carrots
- 1 lb. mixed mushrooms, chopped, any tough stems discarded
- 1½ cups farro
- 1 Tbsp. fresh lemon juice, plus wedges for serving
- ½ cup chopped toasted hazelnuts
  Chopped fresh parsley, for garnish

1. Preheat oven to 450°F. Set racks in the middle and lower thirds of the oven. Rub chicken all over with 2 tablespoons oil and season with salt and pepper. Melt butter in a large cast-iron skillet. Add sage sprigs, then chicken, skin-side down, and cook over medium-high until golden, about 5 minutes. Turn chicken over and roast in middle of oven, basting occasionally, until cooked through, about 40 minutes. Transfer chicken to a cutting board and let rest for 10 minutes. Reserve pan juices but discard sage.

2. Meanwhile, toss carrots, mushrooms, and remaining 3 tablespoons oil on a rimmed baking sheet; season with salt and pepper. Roast vegetables on lower rack of oven until golden and tender, about 20 minutes. Let cool slightly, then slice carrots. Transfer carrots and mushrooms to a large bowl.

3. Meanwhile, in a medium saucepan of salted boiling water, cook farro until al dente, 15 to 20 minutes; drain well. Add farro, lemon juice, half the hazelnuts,

and ½ cup reserved chicken pan juices to the vegetables; mix well. Transfer to plates, top with remaining hazelnuts, and garnish with parsley. Carve chicken and serve it with farro, lemon wedges, and the remaining pan juices. — JUSTIN CHAPPLE & KAY CHUN

MAKE AHEAD The farro can be refrigerated for 2 days and rewarmed before using.

WINE Pair with an earthy Pinot Noir.

CARVE LIKE A PRO

No matter what type of bird you've roasted, carving follows the same progression.

TOOLS NEEDED: sharp, thin-bladed boning knife, and a sturdy carving board with a trough to catch the juices

1. REMOVE THE LEGS: Take hold of a drumstick with one hand; with the other hand, use the knife to cut through the skin that connects the leg to the breast. Apply pressure to the leg to push it back and expose the ball-and-socket joint where the thigh connects to the body. Keep bending the leg away until you can clearly see the joint. (A duck or goose requires a lot of force to pry the legs away from the body; don't be timid.) Once you expose the joint, use the tip of the knife to slice through the cartilage to free the leg piece. If you hit bone, wiggle the knife around until it slices easily through the joint. Repeat with the second leg.

2. IF DESIRED, separate each leg into two pieces (thigh and drumstick): Locate the joint, and cut through the cartilage, trying not to chop the bone.

3. REMOVE THE BREAST: Stabilize the bird with a meat fork or tongs, and position the knife to one side of breastbone. Slice down, doing your best to guide the knife tip along the breastbone and down along the rib cage, to remove one side of the breast in one piece. Repeat with second breast half.

4. CARVE THE BREAST: Set the breast on the cutting board, and slice crosswise into thick or thin pieces, as desired.

Pan-Roasted Chicken
with Warm Farro Salad

Roast Chicken with
Sauce Chasseur

Roast Chicken with Sauce Chasseur

ACTIVE 40 MIN; TOTAL 1 HR: SERVES 4

Sauce Chasseur is classically thickened with a rich demiglace, but this version uses cream which allows the flavors of the herbs, tomatoes, and acidic wine to come through.

- 1 Tbsp. grapeseed or other neutral oil
- 4 (8-oz.) skin-on airline chicken breasts or boneless skinless chicken breasts
- 1½ tsp. kosher salt, plus more to taste
- ½ tsp. black pepper
- 4 large shallots, halved lengthwise, root ends trimmed
- 8 thyme sprigs
- ½ cup dry white wine (such as Aligoté or lightly oaked Chardonnay)
- 2 cups lower-sodium chicken broth
- 2 Tbsp. unsalted butter
- 8 oz. fresh wild mushrooms, cleaned and cut into bite-size pieces (about 3 cups)
- ½ cup heavy cream
- 1 large plum tomato, chopped
- 1 Tbsp. finely chopped fresh chives
- 1 Tbsp. finely chopped fresh tarragon

1. Preheat oven to 350°F. Heat oil in a 12-inch stainless-steel ovenproof skillet over medium-high. Season chicken with salt and pepper. Sear chicken in skillet, skin-side down, until skin is crisp and golden brown, about 4 minutes. Flip chicken; add shallots, cut-sides down, and press into skillet. Cook chicken and shallots until shallots are browned, about 4 minutes. Add thyme and wine to skillet. Bring to a simmer over medium-high; add broth, and return to a simmer. Carefully transfer skillet (so skin of chicken stays dry) to preheated oven, and roast until thermometer inserted into thickest part of breast registers 155°F, about 20 minutes.

2. Remove skillet from oven. Using tongs, place chicken breasts and shallots on a plate; tent with aluminum foil to keep warm while making sauce. Pour broth mixture through a fine wire-mesh strainer into a heatproof bowl or measuring cup, and set aside. Wipe skillet clean, and return to high heat.

3. Melt butter in skillet, and add mushrooms in a single layer. Cook, without stirring, until browned on one side, about 2 minutes. Shake skillet to loosen mushrooms; cook, without stirring, until mushrooms just begin to release their juices, about 2 minutes. Add strained broth mixture and cream to skillet, and bring to a boil over high. Reduce heat to medium-low, and simmer, stirring occasionally, until mushrooms are tender and sauce is thick enough to coat the back of a spoon, 10 to 15 minutes. Remove from heat, and stir in tomato, chives, and tarragon; season with salt to taste.

4. Slice chicken breasts crosswise into 1-inch-thick pieces. Divide chicken among plates, and serve with sauce chasseur.
— MARY-FRANCES HECK

NOTE Sauce chasseur, or hunter's sauce, balances earthy wild mushrooms with bright tomatoes, wine, and fine herbs.

WINE Pair with an herb-scented Burgundy.

◆————◆————◆

Goose Stuffed with Apples and Armagnac-Soaked Prunes

ACTIVE 1 HR; TOTAL 4 HR 50 MIN; SERVES 8

Nadine Levy Redzepi, cookbook author and wife of Noma chef René Redzepi, soaks prunes in Armagnac until they're superboozy and plump, then combines them with apples and garlic to create an elegant stuffing for roast goose. If boozy flavors aren't your thing, you can soak the prunes for as little as 2 hours.

- ½ lb. pitted prunes, halved
- 1 cup Armagnac
- 1 (9-lb.) goose, neck reserved, giblets finely chopped, goose at room temperature
- 3 Granny Smith apples, cored and cut into ¾-inch pieces
- 6 garlic cloves, peeled
  Canola oil
  Kosher salt and black pepper
- 2 cups chicken stock or low-sodium broth
- 1 cup heavy cream
- 2 Tbsp. sherry vinegar
- 2 Tbsp. currant jelly

1. Combine prunes and Armagnac in a small bowl. Cover and refrigerate at least 2 hours or up to 1 week. Drain the prunes well and reserve the liquid for another use.

2. Preheat oven to 325°F. Using paper towels, pat goose completely dry. Toss prunes, apples, and garlic in a large bowl. Stuff goose with prune mixture, and tie legs together with twine. Rub goose all over with canola oil and season with salt. Transfer goose, breast-side up, to a rack set in a roasting pan. Place neck in the bottom of the roasting pan. Roast for 40 minutes, then remove pan from the oven. Carefully tilt pan and spoon fat into a small heatproof bowl.

3. Return goose to oven and increase temperature to 350°F. Roast for 50 minutes; remove pan. Carefully tilt pan and spoon the fat into bowl. Remove goose neck and reserve for snacking, if desired.

4. Return goose to oven and increase temperature to 400°F. Roast until the skin is golden brown and an instant-read thermometer inserted in the inner thigh registers 160°F, about 40 minutes longer. Transfer goose to a work surface, and tent with foil to keep warm. Pour ½ cup boiling water into pan and scrape up any browned bits from bottom. Pour pan juices into a heatproof bowl.

5. Heat 2 tablespoons reserved goose fat in a medium saucepan over high. Add giblets and cook until browned, about 1 minute. Add stock and reserved pan juices, and bring to a boil. Reduce heat to low and simmer for 5 minutes. Add cream and simmer for 3 minutes. Stir in vinegar and jelly, and season with salt and pepper. Pour gravy through a fine wire-mesh strainer into a gravy bowl or small pitcher. Carve goose and transfer to a platter. Spoon prunes and apples into a serving bowl, and serve with gravy.
— NADINE LEVY REDZEPI

WINE Pair with a savory white Burgundy.

Juniper-Rubbed Roast Duck with Cherry Jus

ACTIVE 1 HR 10 MIN; TOTAL 21 HR 45 MIN; SERVES 4

New York City chef Angie Mar models her roast duck on the one her father made every Christmas. Mar rubs her version with crushed juniper berries, which can be found in the spice aisle and impart a fresh, woodsy flavor. She serves the duck with a rich sauce of reduced duck broth and tart cherries—a nod to the cherry trees in the Pacific Northwest where she grew up—and a kirsch flambé for a showstopping holiday centerpiece.

- 1 (5- to 5½-lb.) Pekin duck (aka Long Island duck), with giblets and neck
- 2 Tbsp. plus 1 tsp. dark brown sugar, divided
- 2 Tbsp. plus ½ tsp. kosher salt, divided
- 1 Tbsp. juniper berries, finely crushed
- 1 medium yellow onion, quartered
- 1 small carrot, peeled and cut crosswise into 2-inch pieces
- 1 celery stalk, cut crosswise into 2-inch pieces
- 2 tsp. vegetable oil
- 4 cups cold water, divided
- 4 bunches fresh thyme, divided
- 2 Tbsp. kirsch (cherry brandy)
- ¾ cup frozen pitted tart cherries
- 3 Tbsp. cold unsalted butter, cut into ½-inch pieces

1. Using a sharp knife or poultry shears, cut off last 2 joints of duck wings; set aside for broth. Trim and discard excess skin around neck cavity. Remove neck and giblets from cavity; reserve for broth. Reach into cavity; pull away any fat deposits and discard. Using a metal or wooden skewer, prick skin of duck all over at a 45-degree angle, taking care not to pierce the meat.

2. Stir together 2 tablespoons brown sugar, 2 tablespoons salt, and juniper berries in a small bowl. Sprinkle 1 tablespoon brown sugar mixture inside cavity of duck, and rub remaining mixture over skin. Place duck on a nonreactive wire rack set inside a rimmed baking sheet, and chill, uncovered, 18 to 24 hours.

3. While duck chills, preheat oven to 375°F. Chop reserved wing tips and neck into 2-inch pieces. Place on a rimmed baking sheet with onion, carrot, and celery; add oil and ¼ teaspoon salt, and toss to coat. Spread in

a single layer, and roast in preheated oven, stirring occasionally, until well browned, about 55 minutes. Add 1 cup cold water to baking sheet, stirring and scraping up browned bits from bottom of pan. Transfer mixture to a large saucepan; add reserved heart and gizzards. (Save liver for another use.) Stir in remaining 3 cups cold water and 2 thyme sprigs from 1 bunch. Bring mixture just to a simmer over medium-low. Partially cover, and simmer very gently (do not boil) until reduced to 1½ cups, 1 hour and 30 minutes to 2 hours, skimming and discarding any foam that accumulates on surface. Pour mixture through a fine wire-mesh strainer over a bowl; discard solids. Chill broth until ready to use.

4. Preheat oven to 250°F with oven racks in lowest and middle positions. Let duck stand at room temperature 30 minutes. Pour water to a depth of ¾ inch in a large baking pan, and place on lowest oven rack. Transfer duck, breast-side up, to a roasting rack set inside a deep, aluminum foil-lined roasting pan; insert 2 bunches of thyme into main cavity. Prick skin all over once again with a skewer to ensure rendering. Place roasting pan on middle oven rack, and roast at 250°F until a thermometer inserted in thigh and thickest part of breast registers 145°F, about 1 hour and 30 minutes. (Breast may take longer to register 145°F.) Remove roasting pan; drain and discard cavity juices and drippings in pan. Remove water pan from oven, and increase oven temperature to 450°F.

5. Once oven has preheated to 450°F, return duck in drained roasting pan to middle oven rack. Roast until skin is dark and crisp, about 20 minutes. Meanwhile, skim fat off surface of chilled duck broth and discard. Transfer skimmed broth to a small saucepan, and bring to a simmer over medium. Stir in remaining 1 teaspoon brown sugar. Cook until reduced to ⅓ cup, about 20 minutes. Stir in remaining ¼ teaspoon salt; set aside and keep warm.

6. Remove roasting rack with duck from roasting pan. Drain and discard foil and drippings from pan; wipe pan clean. Return roasting rack with duck to roasting pan; set on a heatproof surface, and let rest 15 minutes. Remove and discard thyme in cavity. Run remaining 2 bunches thyme under water to dampen; stuff into cavity.

7. Place kirsch in a heatproof measuring cup with a spout. Heat a small saucepan over medium until warm, about

30 seconds. Remove saucepan from heat, turn off burner, and pour in kirsch. Using a utility lighter, carefully ignite fumes just above surface of kirsch. Slowly and carefully pour flaming liquid over duck. Once flames extinguish, transfer duck to a cutting board. Pour residual kirsch from roasting pan into reduced broth. Add frozen cherries, and cook over medium, stirring occasionally, until cherries are heated through, about 3 minutes. Remove from heat. Swirl in butter until emulsified. Carve duck, and serve with sauce.
— ANGIE MAR

WINE Pair with a savory, cherry-inflected Pinot Noir.

HOW TO FLAMBÉ

Angie Mar flambés roasted duck tableside. Here's how to do it safely at home. You'll need a small saucepan, handled glass or heatproof measuring cup with a spout, and a utility lighter.

1. Wipe the roasting pan clean of drippings and grease. Set on a heatproof surface in a well-ventilated area, far from flammable elements. Ensure nothing is hanging above pan. Secure loose garments and hair. Keep a lid nearby to smother flames if needed.

2. Measure 80- or 100-proof alcohol (120 proof and higher can be dangerous) into a handled Pyrex or heatproof cup with a spout. Never pour from the bottle. Dampen any herbs stuffed into the bird's cavity with water.

3. Heat a dry, small, high sided, long-handled saucepan over medium just until warm, about 30 seconds. Remove pan from heat, turn off the burner, and set pan on heatproof surface. (Do not hold pan while lighting.)

4. Carefully pour alcohol into warm pan.

5. Immediately ignite a utility lighter a few inches above hot alcohol (igniting the fumes, not the liquid).

6. Slowly pour flaming alcohol over bird. Do not carry the flaming dish from kitchen totable—allow flames to extinguish on their own before transporting.

Juniper-Rubbed Roast
Duck with Cherry Jus

Smoked Duck
Breasts with Apple-
Brandy Caramel

Smoked Duck Breasts with Apple-Brandy Caramel

ACTIVE 2 HR 10 MIN; TOTAL 2 HR 35 MIN, PLUS 8 HR REFRIGERATION; SERVES 4 TO 6

Seek out small, 2-inch-wide apples for this recipe; they will be perfectly tender by the time the caramel thickens and turns deep amber in color. Cold-smoking the duck breast adds an extra layer of flavor; for a quicker preparation, skip smoking the ducks, and score and sear as directed.

- 2 (15-oz.) skin-on duck breasts
- 1½ Tbsp. kosher salt, divided
  - Ice cubes
- 2 Tbsp. duck fat or unsalted butter
- 1½ lb. small Gala apples
- ¼ cup unsalted butter
- 1 cup granulated sugar
- 3 cups duck or chicken stock
- 2 Tbsp. (1 oz.) brandy
- 8 fresh winter savory or thyme sprigs

1. Using a sharp knife, score duck skin in a crosshatch pattern at ¾-inch intervals, about ⅛ inch deep (being careful to avoid cutting into meat). Sprinkle duck breasts with 1 tablespoon salt, and chill, skin-sides up, uncovered, 8 hours or overnight.

2. Place 15 charcoal briquettes in an even layer in a chimney starter; light briquettes. Once briquettes are covered with gray ash, use tongs to transfer 5 briquettes to one side of bottom grate of grill. Place 1 oak chunk on top of charcoal, and insert top grill grate. Cover and adjust vents to bring internal temperature to 85°F to 95°F.

3. Fill a rimmed baking sheet with a single layer of ice cubes. Place duck breasts, skin-sides up, on a wire rack, and set rack over ice. Place baking sheet with duck on top grill grate over unlit side of grill. Cover and smoke duck, maintaining temperature of 85°F to 95°F and allowing duck breasts to become infused with smoke flavor, about 20 minutes. Remove duck breasts from grill, and set aside.

4. Heat duck fat in a large, high-sided skillet over medium-high. Add apples, and cook, stirring occasionally, until browned on all sides, about 6 minutes. Add butter, and swirl skillet to melt. Stir in sugar and remaining ½ tablespoon salt. Cook, stirring occasionally, until sugar melts and forms a golden caramel, 5 to 6 minutes. Reduce heat to medium, and carefully add duck stock. (Caramel will initially seize up and splatter.) Cook, stirring occasionally, until caramel is thick, syrupy, deep amber in color, and reduced to about ¾ cup, and apples are fork-tender, about 1 hour. Remove caramel from heat.

5. Place brandy in a heatproof measuring cup with a spout. Pour brandy over caramel. Using a long match or lighter, carefully ignite fumes just above surface of caramel. Allow flames to extinguish. Stir to combine. Keep caramel warm over low while preparing duck breasts.

6. Heat a large skillet over medium. Place duck breasts, skin-sides down, in skillet, and reduce heat to medium-low. Cook, undisturbed, until fat is rendered and skin is golden brown, about 15 minutes, occasionally spooning off drippings from skillet. Increase heat to medium-high, and flip duck breasts. Cook until a meat thermometer inserted into thickest portion of breast registers 130°F for medium-rare, 6 to 9 minutes. Transfer duck breasts to a cutting board; let rest 10 minutes. Carefully add winter savory to skillet. Cook until crisp, 10 to 20 seconds. Transfer to a paper towel-lined plate.

7. Cut duck breasts into ½-inch-thick slices, and arrange on a serving platter with apples. Drizzle with caramel sauce, and garnish with crispy winter savory. — ANGIE MAR

BOURBON Pair with a subtly oaky bourbon.

◆ ◆ ◆

Roast Hen with Yassa Marinade

ACTIVE 15 MIN; TOTAL 2 HR 10 MIN; SERVES 4

Chef and author Joseph "JJ" Johnson seasons Cornish hens with a West African yassa-style marinade, which includes onion and lemon as well as tamari, herbs, and Dijon mustard.

- 1½ cups tamari
- 1½ cups grapeseed or canola oil
- ¼ cup fresh mint leaves with stems
- 1 medium onion, chopped
- 1 fresh Thai bird chile with stem
- 1 Tbsp. finely grated lemon zest
- 1 Tbsp. Dijon mustard
- 1 tsp. fresh thyme leaves with stems
- ½ tsp. kosher salt, plus more for seasoning
- 4 (1¼- to 1½-lb.) Cornish game hens

1. Combine tamari, grapeseed oil, mint, onion, chile, lemon zest, Dijon, and thyme in a food processor; pulse.

2. In a large bowl, season hens with salt. Add marinade and rub it all over hens and in the cavities. Cover and refrigerate for 1 to 3 hours.

3. Preheat oven to 375°F. Set a rack over a large rimmed baking sheet. Arrange hens on rack, leaving some of marinade in the cavities. Roast until an instant-read thermometer inserted in the inner thighs registers 165°F and the juices run clear, about 1 hour. Transfer hens to a cutting board, and let rest 10 minutes before serving. — JOSEPH "JJ" JOHNSON

WINE Pair with a savory Sicilian red.

GAME BIRDS AT A GLANCE

GUINEA HEN
AVERAGE WEIGHT: About 3 lb.
SERVES: 2 to 4
FYI The dark leg and thigh meat of a guinea hen remain juicy when slow-cooked, but the delicate breast meat can dry out if not basted with fat.

QUAIL
AVERAGE WEIGHT: About 4 oz.
SERVES: 1 (1 to 2 quail per person)
FYI Quail are often sold semi-boneless for ease of cooking and eating. Use a knife and fork to tackle the boneless breast, and nibble the legs and thighs.

POUSSIN
AVERAGE WEIGHT: 1 to 1¼ lb.
SERVES: 1
FYI These tender little birds (also called spring chickens) are best cooked with high heat until just cooked through, leaving a hint of pink in the juices.

DUCK
AVERAGE WEIGHT: About 5 lb.
SERVES: 2 to 4 (lower-than-average yield because of high ratio of fat and bone to meat)
FYI Breast meat is best when not cooked past medium.

West African-Spiced Fried Guinea Hen

ACTIVE 40 MIN; TOTAL 4 HR 40 MIN;
SERVES 2 TO 4

Grains of paradise, also known as melegueta or Guinea pepper, is a West African spice with a slightly citrusy, floral burn that gives this peanut butter and lime-based marinade lingering heat. The marinade's heavy use of spice (plus an extra dose in the coating) turns the crust aromatic and dark when frying.

- 1 (2½- to 3-lb.) guinea hen or chicken
- ½ cup vegetable oil, plus more for frying
- ¼ cup creamy peanut butter
- 2 tsp. lime zest plus 2 Tbsp. fresh lime juice (from 2 limes), divided
- 2 Tbsp. garlic powder
- 2 Tbsp. onion powder
- 2 Tbsp. smoked paprika
- 2 red Thai chiles, stemmed and finely chopped
- 2 Tbsp. plus 1 tsp. kosher salt, divided
- 1 Tbsp. ground cinnamon, divided
- 1 Tbsp. finely ground grains of paradise, divided
- 2 cups white rice flour (about 10½ oz.)

1. To cut guinea hen into 8 pieces, first remove the leg quarters: Tug one leg away from body, and insert a knife tip into joint that connects thigh to backbone. Separate leg quarter from backbone, and repeat on opposite side. Turn each quarter skin-side down, and locate the white membrane line that runs between leg and thigh. Use line as a guide to cut through the joint separating leg and thigh. Next, using sharp scissors or poultry shears, cut through rib bones along both sides of backbone, and remove backbone. (Save backbone to make stock.) Turn breast portion bone-side up, and use tip of knife to uncover and remove the thin, rigid breastbone. Cut down middle (where breastbone was) to create 2 breast halves. Cut each breast half crosswise on an angle, resulting in one piece with wing attached and one without.

2. Whisk together oil, peanut butter, and lime juice in a medium bowl until smooth. Stir in garlic powder, onion powder, paprika, chiles, 1 tablespoon salt, 2 teaspoons cinnamon, 1 teaspoon grains of paradise, and lime zest. Transfer to a large zip-top plastic bag; add guinea hen

pieces. Seal bag, pressing out air, and turn until hen pieces are well coated. Chill 4 to 8 hours.

3. Pour oil to a depth of 1 inch into a deep, heavy skillet, and heat over medium to 350°F. Set a wire rack inside a rimmed baking sheet. Whisk together rice flour, 1 tablespoon salt, remaining 2 teaspoons grains of paradise, and remaining 1 teaspoon cinnamon in a pie plate or 8-inch square baking dish. Remove guinea hen pieces from marinade (do not scrape off excess), and add to seasoned flour; discard marinade. Turn to coat guinea hen pieces; shake off excess seasoned flour.

4. Using tongs, carefully lower 4 coated guinea hen pieces into hot oil. Fry, turning every 3 minutes, until pieces are very dark and crisp, and a thermometer inserted in thickest portion registers 165°F, 8 to 12 minutes. Transfer to prepared rack to drain, and sprinkle with ½ teaspoon salt. Repeat with remaining 4 guinea hen pieces and remaining ½ teaspoon salt. Serve hot.
—JOSEPH "JJ" JOHNSON

WINE Pair with an earthy, robust Monastrell.

◆ ◆ ◆

Buttermilk-Marinated Quail with Herbed Raita and Blood Oranges

ACTIVE 35 MIN; TOTAL 8 HR 35 MIN;
SERVES 4 TO 8

Sizzling broiled quail, spiced with toasty garam masala, are served with creamy herbed raita and cooling, jeweled blood orange supremes for a stunning dinner-party appetizer or main course.

- 1 bunch fresh cilantro (about 2 cups packed)
- 1 bunch fresh mint (about ¾ cup packed)
- 1 cup buttermilk
- 8 garlic cloves, peeled
- 2 medium Indian green chiles or serrano chiles, stems removed
- 1 (1-inch) piece fresh ginger, peeled and sliced into ¼-inch rounds
- 1 Tbsp. ground toasted cumin
- 1 Tbsp. ground coriander
- 2 tsp. garam masala
- 4½ tsp. kosher salt, divided
- 8 (4-oz.) semiboneless quail
- 1 cup plain whole-milk yogurt
- 2 Tbsp. finely chopped scallion

- 2 Tbsp. chopped fresh cilantro
- 1½ Tbsp. chopped fresh mint
- 4 tsp. fresh lime juice
- ¾ tsp. black pepper
- 4 blood oranges
- ¼ cup unsalted butter, melted
- ½ tsp. chaat or garam masala

1. Combine bunch cilantro, bunch mint, buttermilk, garlic, chiles, ginger, cumin, coriander, garam masala, and 2 teaspoons salt in a blender. Process until smooth, about 40 seconds. Transfer marinade to a large zip-top plastic bag, and add quail. Seal bag, pressing out air, and turn until quail are well coated. Place in a dish (to protect against leaks), and chill 8 to 24 hours.

2. Stir together yogurt, scallion, chopped cilantro, chopped mint, lime juice, black pepper, and 1½ teaspoons salt in a medium bowl until combined. Cover raita, and chill until ready to serve.

3. Using a small sharp knife, cut off tops and bottoms of oranges, exposing red flesh and making the fruit sit flat on the cutting surface. Arc knife along natural contours of the fruit to remove peel, including bitter white pith. Once peel is removed, hold orange over a strainer set over a large bowl, and carefully cut on either side of each section to free it from membrane. Drop the segments (supremes) into strainer as you work. Remove or cut around any seeds you encounter. Cover and chill supremes until ready to serve.

4. Remove quail from marinade, scraping off excess. Discard marinade. Pat quail dry with paper towels, and sprinkle with remaining 1 teaspoon salt.

5. Preheat broiler to high with oven rack 6 inches from heat. Brush quail with melted butter, and arrange, breast-sides down, on a wire rack set inside a rimmed baking sheet. Broil in preheated oven until lightly browned and crispy, about 2 minutes. Flip quail, and broil until lightly browned and crispy but still rosy and juicy inside, 4 to 5 minutes.

6. If desired, cut each quail into halves or quarters. Divide quail among 4 dinner plates or 8 appetizer plates. Sprinkle with chaat masala, and serve with blood orange supremes and herbed raita for dipping.
— MANEET CHAUHAN

WINE Pair with a substantial California rosé.

West African-Spiced
Fried Guinea Hen

LOVE YOUR LEFTOVERS

Kentucky Hot Brown

ACTIVE 30 MIN; TOTAL 1 HR 10 MIN;
MAKES 8 SANDWICHES

*Restaurateur and celebrity host Bobby
Flay describes this dish as a smart way to
repurpose holiday leftovers: roast turkey,
odds and ends from cheese plates, and
breads that didn't make it into the stuffing.*

SAUCE

- 2¼ cups whole milk
- 2 Tbsp. unsalted butter
- 2 Tbsp. all-purpose flour
- 2 cups shredded sharp white cheddar cheese (6 oz.)
- ¼ cup freshly grated Parmigiano-Reggiano cheese
- Pinch of freshly grated nutmeg
- Few dashes of hot sauce
- Kosher salt and black pepper

SANDWICHES

- 16 slices of thick-cut bacon
- 2 tomatoes, cut into eight ¼-inch-thick slices
- 1 Tbsp. canola oil
- Kosher salt and black pepper
- 8 (½-inch-thick) slices of day-old white sandwich bread
- 4 Tbsp. unsalted butter, cut into pieces

- 2 lb. roast turkey breast, sliced ¼ inch thick
- 1½ cups shredded sharp white cheddar cheese (6 oz.)
- ½ cup freshly grated Parmigiano-Reggiano cheese
- Chopped fresh chives and parsley, for garnish

1. Make the sauce Bring milk to a simmer
in a small saucepan. Melt butter in a
medium saucepan. Add flour and whisk
over medium, 1 minute. Gradually whisk
in hot milk and bring to a boil. Cook,
whisking, until thickened, about 5 minutes.
Remove pan from heat, and whisk in white
cheddar cheese and Parmigiano cheese
until melted. Stir in nutmeg and hot sauce,
and season with salt and pepper.

2. Make the sandwiches Preheat oven to
425°F. Arrange bacon on a rack set over a
baking sheet. Cook until golden and crisp,
about 30 minutes.

3. Preheat broiler. Arrange tomato slices
on a baking sheet, drizzle with oil, and
season with salt and pepper. Broil 6 inches
from heat until lightly charred, 1 to
2 minutes per side; keep warm.

4. Arrange bread on a foil-lined baking
sheet, and spread each slice with
½ tablespoon butter; season with salt
and pepper. Broil until lightly toasted,
about 2 minutes. Flip bread and toast for
1 minute. Top each toast with some turkey
and a slice of tomato. Spoon sauce on top,
and sprinkle with white cheddar cheese
and Parmigiano-Reggiano cheese. Broil
until cheese is melted and golden brown,
2 to 3 minutes. Transfer sandwiches
to plates and top with bacon. Garnish
with chives and parsley, and serve hot.
— BOBBY FLAY

WINE Pair with a vibrant Barbera d'Alba.

Farmhouse Turkey Hot Dish

ACTIVE 1 HR; TOTAL 3 HR 40 MIN;
SERVES 6 TO 8

*Hot dish is Minnesotan for baked layers
of starch, meat, vegetable, and, typically,
canned soup. Chef and Twin Cities native
Andrew Zimmern's version, crisp brown
Tater Tots provide the starch. He uses
freshly braised turkey legs and a velouté
sauce made from the braising liquid
instead of the soup. This simplified version
takes advantage of leftover turkey meat.*

- 7 Tbsp. unsalted butter, divided
- 2 small carrots, chopped
- 1 celery rib, thinly sliced
- ½ small onion, chopped
- ¼ fennel bulb, chopped
- 1 tsp. dried thyme
- Pinch of freshly grated nutmeg
- ¼ cup all-purpose flour
- 4 cups chicken stock
- 4 cups shredded leftover turkey meat
- ½ cup heavy cream
- ½ cup thawed frozen peas
- ¼ cup minced parsley
- Kosher salt and black pepper
- ½ lb. mixed mushrooms, such as shiitake caps, cremini, white button, chanterelle, and oyster,

1 (32-oz.) bag frozen Tater Tots
Flaky sea salt
Hot sauce (optional)

1. Preheat oven to 425°F. Melt 4 tablespoons butter in a large pot. Add carrots, celery, onion, fennel, thyme, and nutmeg, and cook over medium-high, stirring occasionally, until lightly browned, about 5 minutes. Add flour and cook, stirring, 1 minute. Add stock, bring to a boil, and cook, stirring occasionally, until sauce is thickened, about 5 minutes. Add turkey, cream, peas, and parsley; season with kosher salt and pepper, and cook over medium, stirring occasionally, 5 minutes. Spread in a 13- × 9-inch baking dish.

2. Melt the remaining 3 tablespoons butter in a large skillet. Add mushrooms, and cook over medium- high, stirring occasionally, until browned, about 5 minutes. Add leeks and cook, stirring occasionally, until softened, about 5 minutes. Stir in tarragon. Spread mushroom mixture over turkey in baking dish.

3. Spread Tots over the mushroom mixture. Bake until bubbling and golden, 45 minutes. Sprinkle with sea salt and serve with hot sauce, if desired.
— ANDREW ZIMMERN

WINE Pair with a robust, berry-rich Zinfandel.

Turkey Mole Rojo

ACTIVE 2 HR 50 MIN: TOTAL 8 HR 40 MIN; SERVES 8

Chef T.J. Steele, of the Oaxacan-influenced restaurant Claro in Brooklyn, has a suggestion for easy, foolproof mole: Simmer it in a slow cooker, which will prevent scorching.

7 oz. dried ancho chiles, stemmed and seeded
2 oz. dried guajillo chiles, stemmed and seeded
3¼ qt. warm water
8 black peppercorns
5 whole cloves

1 (1-inch) canela cinnamon stick
1 garlic head, cloves separated
1 medium yellow onion, halved
3 Tbsp. coconut oil, divided
⅓ cup raisins
¼ tsp. fresh oregano leaves
2 fresh thyme sprigs
½ cup toasted whole pecans
⅓ cup toasted whole almonds
1 (15-oz.) can whole peeled tomatoes
¾ cup plus 2 Tbsp. toasted sesame seeds, plus more for garnish
1½ tsp. packed light brown sugar, plus more to taste
1 tsp. kosher salt, plus more to taste
4 cups turkey or chicken broth
3 lb. leftover roasted turkey, warmed

1. Heat a large cast-iron skillet over medium-low. Working in batches, arrange ancho and guajillo chiles in a single layer in skillet; cook, turning once, until lightly toasted, about 30 seconds per batch. Transfer to a large bowl; add 3¼ quarts warm water, and let stand until chiles are soft and pliable, about 30 minutes. Drain chiles, reserving 5 cups soaking water.

2. Add peppercorns, cloves, and cinnamon to skillet; toast over medium-low, stirring constantly, until aromatic, about 30 seconds. Transfer mixture to a plate.

3. Add garlic and onion halves to skillet. Increase heat to medium-high; cook, turning garlic often, until cloves are tender and charred, 12 to 15 minutes. Transfer garlic to plate with spice mixture. Continue cooking onion, turning once, until tender and charred, about 5 minutes more. Transfer to plate with spice mixture and garlic. Peel garlic cloves; discard skins.

4. Melt 1 tablespoon coconut oil in skillet. Add raisins and cook, stirring constantly, until raisins puff up, about 40 seconds. Stir in oregano and thyme; remove from heat.

5. Working in batches, process soaked chiles, spice mixture, garlic, onion, raisin mixture, pecans, almonds, tomatoes with juices, sesame seeds, and 4 cups reserved soaking water in a high-speed blender, scraping down sides of blender as necessary to loosen mixture, until mixture is the texture of a thick and coarse tomato sauce, about 1 minute and 15 seconds per batch. Add splashes of reserved soaking liquid as needed to reach desired texture. Pour mixture through a wire-mesh strainer into a large bowl; discard solids.

6. Melt remaining 2 tablespoons coconut oil in a 12-inch high-sided skillet over medium. Carefully pour in strained mole mixture. (It will splatter.) Cook, stirring often, until warmed through, 7 to 10 minutes. Transfer mole mixture to a large slow cooker. Cook, uncovered, on high, stirring every 30 minutes, until mixture resembles consistency of wet sand, 6 hours and 30 minutes to 7 hours. Remove from heat; stir in brown sugar and salt.

7. Place turkey broth in a saucepan. Bring to a boil over high; whisk in 2 cups of the mole mixture. Reduce heat to low; simmer, stirring occasionally, until slightly thickened, 20 to 25 minutes. Season to taste with brown sugar and salt. Serve mole sauce over warmed leftover turkey, and garnish with sesame seeds. — T.J. STEELE

MAKE AHEAD Prepare mole mixture through Step 6; store prepared mole mixture, covered, in refrigerator up to 1 week or in freezer up to 3 months.

WINE Pair with a fruity Primitivo blend from Italy.

Red Wine Gravy

ACTIVE 30 MIN; TOTAL 4 HR; MAKES ABOUT
5 CUPS

*Roasted turkey necks and a store-bought
smoked turkey drumstick add body and
depth to this rich gravy. Choose a good-
quality Cabernet Sauvignon; the flavor will
concentrate as the wine reduces.*

- 4 lb. fresh turkey necks, rinsed and
  patted dry
- 1 large yellow onion, coarsely
  chopped
- 2 celery stalks, coarsely chopped
- 2 medium carrots, coarsely chopped
- 2 Tbsp. olive oil
- 2 cups Cabernet Sauvignon wine
- 1 (12-oz.) smoked turkey drumstick
- 1 large garlic head, halved
- 2 fresh bay leaves
- 1 Tbsp. black peppercorns
- 4 fresh thyme sprigs
- 5 fresh parsley sprigs
- 3 qt. turkey or chicken broth
- 1/3 cup unsalted butter (2²/₃ oz.)
- 1/3 cup plus 2 Tbsp. all-purpose flour
  (about 1⁵/₈ oz.)
- 1/2 tsp. kosher salt
- 1/2 tsp. coarsely ground black pepper
- 1 fresh rosemary sprig

1. Preheat oven to 425°F. Toss together
turkey necks, onion, celery, carrots,
and oil in a large bowl. Spread in a single
layer on 2 rimmed baking sheets. Roast
in preheated oven until browned, 1 hour
to 1 hour and 15 minutes, turning once
halfway through roasting.

2. Place roasted turkey necks and
vegetables in a stockpot. Divide wine
evenly between hot baking sheets, stirring
and scraping up browned bits from bottom
of pot; add wine mixture to stockpot. Add
drumstick, garlic, bay leaves, peppercorns,
thyme sprigs, parsley sprigs, and broth.
Bring to a boil over high. Reduce heat
to medium-low, and simmer, skimming
and discarding foam from top as needed,
until reduced to about 6 cups, 1 hour
and 45 minutes to 2 hours. Pour mixture
through a fine wire-mesh strainer into a
large heatproof bowl; discard solids. Let
stand 10 minutes; skim off and discard fat.

3. Melt butter in a large saucepan over
medium. Add flour and cook, whisking
often, until golden brown, about 5 minutes.

Gradually pour in hot stock mixture,
whisking constantly until smooth. Bring to
a simmer over medium. Simmer, whisking
often, until mixture thickens, about
15 minutes. Stir in salt and pepper. Hold
rosemary sprig at one end, and swirl in
gravy until it imparts a subtle herb flavor.
— ALECIA MOORE & ROBBY GRANTHAM-WISE

MAKE AHEAD Gravy can be made through
Step 2 and refrigerated up to 2 days
in advance.

NOTE Look for smoked turkey drumsticks
refrigerated at the grocery store near the
bacon or at your butcher.

Best-Ever Turkey Gravy

TOTAL 25 MIN; SERVES 16

*This simple, silky-smooth gravy stays
lump-free with a trick of loosening the
roux with a splash of broth before whisking
it into the pot.*

- 1/4 cup rendered turkey fat from Rich
  Turkey Broth (recipe right) or
  unsalted butter
- 7 Tbsp. all-purpose flour (about 2 oz.)
- 4 cups Rich Turkey Broth (recipe left),
  divided
- 1 Tbsp. chopped fresh thyme or sage
- 1¼ tsp. kosher salt
- 1/2 tsp. black pepper

Melt turkey fat in a small skillet over
medium. Add flour and cook, whisking
constantly, until mixture turns golden
brown, 5 to 6 minutes. Gradually add
3/4 cup Rich Turkey Broth, whisking
constantly until smooth. Remove roux from
heat; cover to keep warm. Bring remaining
3¼ cups Rich Turkey Broth to a boil in a
large stockpot over high. Whisk roux into
boiling stock until smooth. Reduce heat
to medium-low; simmer, whisking often,
until mixture thickens and no floury taste
remains, 5 to 6 minutes. Stir in thyme, salt,
and pepper. —KELSEY YOUNGMAN

PORCINI GRAVY Simmer 1/2 oz. (1/2 cup)
dried porcini mushrooms and 4 cups
Rich Turkey Broth in a stockpot over low
20 minutes. Strain stock; finely chop and
reserve mushrooms. Use porcini-infused
broth in place of Rich Turkey Broth; stir
finely chopped mushrooms into gravy.

PIMENTÓN GRAVY For a smoky bite,
stir 1 teaspoon smoked paprika into
2 cups gravy.

Rich Turkey Broth

ACTIVE 50 MIN; TOTAL 4 HR 10 MIN;
MAKES 4 CUPS

*Simmering roasted giblets, bones, and
aromatics in a simple chicken stock with
lean ground turkey yields an ultra-rich
broth that's the key to our Best-Ever Turkey
Gravy (recipe at left).*

- 4 medium carrots, peeled and cut
  into 3-inch pieces
- 4 celery stalks, cut into 3-inch pieces
- 2 small yellow onions, peeled and
  quartered
- 1 garlic head, halved crosswise
- 1 turkey neck
- 1 turkey liver
- 1 turkey heart
- 1 turkey gizzard
- 3 Tbsp. vegetable oil
- 3/4 tsp. kosher salt
- 1/2 tsp. black pepper
- 3 cups unsalted chicken stock,
  divided
- 2 lb. lean ground turkey

1. Preheat oven to 400°F. Toss together
carrots, celery, onions, garlic, neck,
liver, heart, gizzard, oil, salt, and pepper
on a large rimmed baking sheet. Roast
in preheated oven until well browned,
about 1 hour, stirring once halfway
through cooking. Transfer mixture to a
large stockpot. Add 1/2 cup stock to hot
baking sheet, scraping up any browned
bits with a wooden spoon; pour mixture
into stockpot.

2. Add ground turkey, 3 cups water, and
remaining 2½ cups stock to stockpot.
Bring mixture to a simmer over high;
reduce heat to medium, and cook,
uncovered, skimming foam occasionally,
45 minutes. Using a slotted spoon, remove
and discard as many large pieces as
possible. Pour mixture through a fine wire-
mesh strainer into a large heatproof bowl;
discard solids.

3. Return strained broth to stockpot. Bring
to a boil over high; cook, undisturbed,
until reduced to 4 cups, about 20 minutes.
Remove from heat; let cool completely,
about 2 hours. Cover and refrigerate until
ready to use. Skim off rendered turkey fat
from chilled broth before using; reserve
for Best-Ever Turkey Gravy (recipe at left).
—KELSEY YOUNGMAN

Best-Ever Turkey Gravy

Buttermilk-Poblano Gravy

Buttermilk-Poblano Gravy

ACTIVE 35 MIN; TOTAL 45 MIN; SERVES 6

This vibrant buttermilk-poblano gravy comes from Los Angeles food writer Javier Cabral, who grew up in a Mexican-American family. Fire-roasted poblanos add smokiness and flavor without the heat (unlike a jalapeño or serrano, which would be an automatic turnoff to the heat-averse). The buttermilk adds a refreshing tang that will keep you ladling more and more over turkey, chicken, or potatoes. It would even be a great base for the most memorable pot pie you'll ever have. And since it's roux-based, it maintains the rib-sticking properties that a good gravy should always have. "Go ahead and dip some tortilla chips into it while you're at it," Javier says. "No judgement here."

- 2 large (3-oz.) poblano chiles
- 3 Tbsp. unsalted butter, divided
- ½ cup diced yellow onion
- 1½ cups vegetable stock or turkey stock, warmed, divided
- 1 Tbsp. all-purpose flour
- 2 Tbsp. whole buttermilk
- 1½ tsp. kosher salt
  Ground white pepper, to taste

1. Using kitchen tongs, hold 1 chile directly over a medium flame of a gas stovetop. Cook until skin is blackened, 4 to 6 minutes per side. Repeat with remaining chile. Place chiles in a bowl, cover with plastic wrap, and let steam 10 minutes.

2. Using same piece of plastic wrap, partially cover your hands, and rub off skin from chiles, removing as much of the blackened skin as you can. (Don't worry if all the skin doesn't come off.) Remove and discard stems and seeds. Finely dice 1 chile; cut remaining chile into strips, and set aside separately.

3. Melt 1 tablespoon butter in a medium skillet over medium-high. Add onion and chile strips. Cook until onion is soft, about 4 minutes. Combine onion mixture and ½ cup warm stock in a blender, and process until smooth, about 30 seconds.

4. Melt remaining 2 tablespoons butter in same skillet over medium. Whisk in flour, and reduce heat to low. Cook, whisking constantly, until mixture is golden brown, about 3 minutes. Increase heat to medium. Add onion-chile puree and remaining 1 cup warm stock, and cook, whisking constantly, until thick enough to coat the back of a spoon, about 2 minutes. Reduce heat to low; add buttermilk and diced chile. Simmer gently to allow flavors to meld, about 2 minutes. Season with salt and white pepper. — JAVIER CABRAL

MAKE AHEAD Poblano peppers can be roasted, peeled, and cut 2 days ahead.

NOTE You can roast poblanos under broiler, turning often, until charred.

Cranberry Kosho

TOTAL 15 MIN, PLUS 3 DAYS FERMENTATION; MAKES ABOUT 3 CUPS

Kosho—a Japanese condiment—is traditionally prepared with yuzu and red or green chiles. This version uses sweet-tart cranberries and gets its heat from jalapeños and their seeds. The resulting puree is sour, spicy, and salty, the perfect pairing for juicy turkey at the holiday table.

- 4 cups fresh or frozen cranberries
- 2 cups jalapeños, stemmed (do not remove seeds)
- ¼ cup granulated sugar
- 1½ tsp. kosher salt

1. Working in 2 batches, place cranberries and jalapeños in a food processor; pulse until cranberries and jalapeños are broken up, about 10 times. Transfer mixture to a large bowl. Stir in sugar and salt until dissolved. Transfer mixture to 1 or more jars with tight-fitting lids; loosely attach lids, and let stand 2 days at room temperature. Transfer jars to refrigerator, and continue to age at least 1 day or up to 12 days.

2. Before serving, return cranberry mixture to food processor, and pulse until mixture forms a chunky paste. — OSET BABUR

MAKE AHEAD Cranberry kosho may be made up to 2 weeks ahead. Cover and chill until ready to serve.

Cranberry Relish

TOTAL 15 MIN; MAKES 4 CUPS

"This is delicious and truly one of the easiest recipes in the world as long as you use a food processor," said the late chef and author Anthony Bourdain about his simple relish recipe. "It contains a shocking amount of sugar, which you should not balk at. It's a holiday."

- 1 large navel orange, scrubbed and cut into 1-inch pieces
- 12 oz. fresh cranberries (3¼ cups)
- 1 cup sugar

Place orange and cranberries in a food processor, and pulse until very finely chopped. Scrape mixture into a medium bowl, and stir in sugar. Cover and refrigerate. Serve chilled or at room temperature. — ANTHONY BOURDAIN

MAKE AHEAD The relish can be refrigerated for 1 week.

Roasted Cranberry
Grape Sauce

Lemon-Pomegranate Cranberry Sauce

ACTIVE 10 MIN; TOTAL 40 MIN; SERVES 10

A quick whirl in a food processor is all it takes to make this fresh-tasting sauce—no cooking required. For a savory upgrade, stir in finely ground toasted coriander (see Note).

- 1 lb. fresh or thawed frozen cranberries (4 cups)
- 1 lemon, seeded and cut into 1-inch pieces
- ¾ cup granulated sugar
- 1 Tbsp. minced peeled fresh ginger (from 1 [1-inch] piece)
- 1 tsp. kosher salt
- ½ cup pomegranate arils

Place cranberries, lemon, sugar, ginger, and salt in a food processor, and process until cranberries and lemon are very finely chopped, 1 to 2 minutes. Scrape into a bowl, and stir in pomegranate arils. Cover and refrigerate at least 30 minutes or up to 24 hours before serving. — JUSTIN CHAPPLE

NOTE Place 2 teaspoons coriander seeds in a small skillet over medium, and cook, shaking pan, until very fragrant, about 3 minutes. Transfer to a spice grinder, and let cool about 5 minutes. Grind seeds into a powder, then fold into cranberry sauce before chilling.

Molded Cranberry Sauce

ACTIVE 30 MIN; TOTAL 4 HR; SERVES 10 TO 12

Chef Tyler Florence makes his not-too-sweet molded cranberry sauce with chunks of pineapple.

- 2 lb. fresh or frozen cranberries, divided
- 3 cups sugar
- 2 cups finely chopped fresh pineapple (8 oz.)
- 1 Tbsp. finely grated orange zest
- 1 Tbsp. fresh lemon juice
- Kosher salt and black pepper
- Shaved celery, snipped fresh chives, and chopped toasted walnuts, for garnish

1. Line a 1½-quart glass bowl or mold with plastic wrap, allowing 4 inches of overhang all around.

2. Reserve ¼ cup cranberries for garnish. Combine remaining cranberries, sugar, pineapple, orange zest, lemon juice, and ½ cup water in a large saucepan; bring to a boil. Cook over medium-low, stirring frequently, until cranberries are broken down and mixture is thick, 30 to 35 minutes. Season with salt and pepper.

3. Scrape sauce into prepared bowl and let cool for 30 minutes. Cover with overhanging plastic. Refrigerate until chilled and set, at least 3 hours or overnight.

4. Peel back plastic and carefully invert cranberry mold onto a plate; remove plastic wrap. Garnish with reserved cranberries, shaved celery, snipped chives, and chopped walnuts, and serve cold. — TYLER FLORENCE

MAKE AHEAD The molded cranberry sauce can be refrigerated for up to 3 days.

Roasted Cranberry-Grape Sauce

ACTIVE 5 MIN; TOTAL 1 HR; SERVES 10

In this clever and tasty riff on traditional cranberry sauce, F&W's Laura Rege tosses cranberries with juicy red grapes before roasting in the oven.

- 1 lb. seedless red grapes, stemmed
- 2 (10-oz.) bags fresh or thawed frozen cranberries (5 cups)
- ⅔ cup sugar
- 6 fresh thyme sprigs
- 2 tsp. finely grated lemon zest plus 1 Tbsp. fresh lemon juice
- Pinch of kosher salt

Preheat oven to 425°F. Toss grapes, cranberries, sugar, thyme, lemon zest, lemon juice, and salt on a parchment paper-lined baking sheet. Roast until cranberries and grapes just start to burst, 20 minutes, stirring halfway through. Let cool before serving. — LAURA REGE

MAKE AHEAD The sauce can be refrigerated for up to 3 days.

Seafood

The Snappiest Shrimp,
RECIPE P. 139

Roasted Side of Salmon

ACTIVE 30 MIN; TOTAL 1 HR 30 MIN;
SERVES 6

Fish only needs to brine for an hour—its shorter muscle fibers take a fraction of the time to denature and absorb seasoning compared to red meat. A saltwater soak also improves the look of the finished dish, minimizing the white protein called albumin that appears on the surface of cooked fish. The added water content helps to keep the fish from overcooking, even if it roasts for a minute too long. Use fine sea salt to evoke the natural brininess of ocean water. This method can be used on any 1-inch-thick fillet of flaky fish.

8 cups cold water
¼ cup fine sea salt
¼ cup granulated sugar
1 (2-lb.) skin-on wild salmon side
2 Tbsp. Dijon mustard
2 Tbsp. packed light brown sugar

1. Combine 8 cups water, salt, and granulated sugar in a deep roasting pan large enough to fit fish; stir to dissolve salt and sugar. Add fish, and let stand at room temperature 1 hour. Remove fish from brine; rinse under cold running water, and pat dry. Place salmon, skin-side down, on a parchment-paper-lined baking sheet, and chill, uncovered, at least 1 hour and up to 3 hours.

2. Preheat oven to 450°F with oven rack in top third of oven. Stir together mustard and brown sugar in a small bowl. Brush glaze over flesh side of fish. Roast in preheated oven on top rack until fish is opaque around edges, about 8 minutes. Turn broiler to high, and broil until fish is cooked through and glaze is bubbly and browned, about 8 minutes. Let stand 5 minutes. — ROBIN BASHINSKY

WINE Pair this with a complex, fragrant white Burgundy.

Herb-Roasted King Salmon with Pinot Noir Sauce

ACTIVE 50 MIN; TOTAL 1 HR; SERVES 10

Originally served at Seattle's Hotel Sorrento by chef David Pisegna (and included in The Best of F&W *collection from 1988), this throwback salmon dish stands the test of time. We simplified the original recipe but didn't change a thing about the velvety, wine-blushed beurre blanc; keep it warm and serve it immediately for the best results.*

2 Tbsp. plus 4 tsp. vegetable oil, divided
⅔ cup coarsely chopped fresh wild mushrooms (about 2¼ oz.)
2 large shallots, chopped
1 cup Pinot Noir wine
10 fresh tarragon sprigs, divided, plus tarragon leaves, for garnish
10 fresh thyme sprigs, divided
10 fennel frond sprigs, divided, plus chopped fennel fronds, for garnish
1 cup fish stock or bottled clam juice
½ cup heavy cream
1 cup unsalted butter (8 oz.), cut into ½-inch pieces, divided
2 tsp. fresh lemon juice
1¾ tsp. kosher salt, divided
¾ tsp. black pepper, divided
1 (3½-lb.) skin-on salmon side (preferably king salmon), cut into 10 (5½-oz.) portions and patted dry

1. Preheat oven to 400°F. Heat 4 teaspoons oil in a medium saucepan over medium-high. Add mushrooms and shallots, and cook, stirring often, until shallots are softened, about 3 minutes. Stir in wine, 2 tarragon sprigs, 2 thyme sprigs, and 2 fennel sprigs. Return mixture to a simmer over medium-high, and cook until wine is reduced by half, 4 to 5 minutes. Stir in stock and cream, and return to a simmer. Cook, stirring occasionally, until reduced to about ⅔ cup, 18 to 22 minutes.

2. Remove sauce from heat, and gradually whisk in ½ cup butter. (You may need to return saucepan to heat briefly to melt butter; do not let mixture come to a simmer or sauce will break.) Pour sauce through a fine wire-mesh strainer into a small heatproof bowl; discard solids. Stir in lemon juice, ½ teaspoon salt, and ¼ teaspoon pepper; cover to keep warm.

3. Season tops of salmon fillets with remaining 1¼ teaspoons salt and remaining ½ teaspoon pepper. Heat 1 tablespoon oil in a large nonstick or cast-iron skillet over medium-high. Add 5 salmon fillets, flesh-sides down, and sear until lightly browned, about 1 minute. Flip fillets, and sear until skin is lightly browned, about 1 minute. Transfer cooked fillets, skin-sides down, to an aluminum foil-lined rimmed baking sheet, spacing fillets ½ inch apart. Wipe skillet clean, and repeat process with remaining 1 tablespoon oil and remaining 5 salmon fillets.

4. Top fillets with remaining ½ cup cubed butter, remaining 8 tarragon sprigs, remaining 8 thyme sprigs, and remaining 8 fennel sprigs. Bake in preheated oven to desired degree of doneness, 6 to 8 minutes for medium.

5. Spoon about 2 tablespoons warm wine sauce onto each of 10 dinner plates. Using a spatula, carefully slide salmon fillets off their skins, leaving skins and herb sprigs on baking sheet. Pat bottoms of cooked fish with paper towels. Place fillets on sauce, skinned-sides down. Garnish with tarragon leaves and fennel fronds, and serve immediately. — DAVID MCCANN & DAVID PISEGNA

WINE Pair with a complex, raspberry-scented Oregon Pinot Noir.

Herb-Roasted King
Salmon with Pinot
Noir Sauce

Trout Saltimbocca

Tomato-Braised Baccalà with Olives and Polenta

TOTAL 1 HR 45 MIN. PLUS 2 DAYS SOAKING; SERVES 6

Simmering soaked salt cod in a tomato sauce laced with peppers, onions, and olives infuses the fish with flavor and leaves it flaky and tender. Sweet and creamy polenta, enriched with lightly tangy mascarpone, sops up the sauce and balances the brightly flavored fish.

- 1 lb. baccalà (dried salted cod)
- 6 cups water
- 1 Tbsp. kosher salt, divided
- 1½ cups uncooked polenta
- ½ cup mascarpone cheese
- ¼ cup plus 2 Tbsp. extra-virgin olive oil, divided
- 2 cups thinly sliced yellow onion
- 2 Tbsp. sliced garlic
- ½ tsp. crushed red pepper
- 1 cup dry white wine
- 1 (28-oz.) can San Marzano tomatoes, crushed by hand
- ⅔ cup pitted whole Gaeta or Kalamata olives
- ¼ tsp. dried oregano
- ¼ tsp. black pepper
- 2 fresh bay leaves
- 2 Tbsp. chopped fresh flat-leaf parsley
  Lemon wedges, for serving

1. Place baccalà in a large bowl; add cold water to cover, and let soak in refrigerator 48 hours, changing cold water twice a day. Drain baccalà, and cut into 6 pieces (about 3 ounces each). Set aside.

2. Bring 6 cups water and 2½ teaspoons salt to a boil in a medium saucepan over medium-high. Gradually add polenta, whisking constantly. Return mixture to a boil, whisking constantly. Reduce heat to medium-low, and cook, uncovered, whisking occasionally, until polenta is tender and creamy, 45 minutes to 1 hour. Remove from heat, and whisk in mascarpone until smooth. Cover to keep warm until ready to serve.

3. Heat 2 tablespoons oil in a large skillet over medium. Add onion, garlic, and red pepper, and cook, stirring occasionally, until softened and onion is translucent, about 6 minutes. Add wine and cook, stirring occasionally, until mostly evaporated, 8 to 10 minutes. Add crushed tomatoes and their juices, olives, oregano, black pepper, bay leaves, and remaining ¼ cup oil. Cook, stirring often, until sauce is slightly thickened, about 8 minutes.

4. Add cod to tomato sauce, and simmer, stirring occasionally, until cod flakes easily when pressed with a fork, 16 to 20 minutes, flipping cod pieces after 10 minutes. Stir in remaining ½ teaspoon salt or more to taste. Remove and discard bay leaves. Serve cod and sauce over polenta. Sprinkle with parsley, and serve with lemon wedges. — REBECCA WILCOMB

WINE Pair with a crisp, earthy Pinot Nero.

Trout Saltimbocca

TOTAL 45 MIN; SERVES 4

Chef, television host, and Minnesota native Andrew Zimmern landed a lake trout in the North Country one day and came up with this bright and savory dish, inspired by the state's first Italian immigrants. The pancetta wrapping helps keep the whole grilled fish from falling apart.

- 1¾ lb. trout, cleaned
  Kosher salt and black pepper
- 20 sage sprigs
- 12 thin lemon slices
- 1 lb. very thinly sliced pancetta
  Canola oil, for brushing
- 4 Tbsp. unsalted butter
- 1 small shallot, minced
- 1 Tbsp. minced fresh parsley
- 1 Tbsp. minced fresh tarragon
- 1 Tbsp. minced scallion
- 1 Tbsp. minced fresh mint
- 1 tsp. tomato paste
- 2 Tbsp. dry white wine
- ¼ cup heavy cream
- ½ tsp. fresh lemon juice
- 3 Tbsp. Dijon mustard
- 2 Tbsp. apple cider vinegar
- 2 Tbsp. unrefined hazelnut oil
- 2 Tbsp. unrefined peanut oil
- 8 oz. baby watercress
- 2 Tbsp. chopped fresh chives

1. Season fish with salt and pepper. Fill each cavity with 1 sprig sage and 1 slice lemon. Place 2 sprigs sage and 1 slice lemon on both sides of each fish.

2. Place a sheet of wax paper on a work surface. Arrange 6 to 8 slices pancetta in 2 overlapping rows to form a 6- × 8-inch rectangle. Set 1 fish at bottom edge of pancetta. Using wax paper as a guide, tightly roll up fish in pancetta. Carefully peel off wax paper. Brush fish with canola oil and transfer to a rimmed baking sheet. Repeat with remaining fish and pancetta and more oil.

3. Preheat a grill or a broiler with a rack in the top third of the oven. Grill or broil fish, flipping halfway through, until cooked through, about 6 minutes per side. Season with pepper.

4. Meanwhile, melt butter in a small skillet. Cook over medium-high, stirring occasionally, until browned, 2 to 3 minutes. Stir in shallot, parsley, tarragon, scallion, mint, and tomato paste. Cook, stirring, for 20 seconds. Add wine, bring sauce to a boil, and cook for 1 minute. Add 2 tablespoons cream and cook until sauce thickens, about 1 minute. Scrape sauce into a small heatproof bowl and stir in lemon juice. Season with salt.

5. Combine mustard and vinegar in a large bowl. Slowly drizzle in hazelnut oil and peanut oil, whisking constantly, until incorporated. Whisk in remaining 2 tablespoons cream. Season with salt and pepper. Add watercress and chives, and toss to coat. Serve fish with butter sauce. — ANDREW ZIMMERN

WINE Pair with a vibrant Washington state dry Riesling.

Irish Fish Pie

ACTIVE 45 MIN; TOTAL 1 HR 30 MIN;
SERVES 4 TO 6

A staple in Irish and Irish-American households, fish pie is usually topped with a puree of white potatoes. But swap white potatoes for sweet potatoes, and it turns out that the mild brininess of the fish is fantastic with the slightly sweet topping. Piping the sweet potato puree onto the casserole is the easiest way to seal in the filling.

- 1½ lb. orange-flesh sweet potatoes
- ½ lb. fresh cod
- ½ lb. large shrimp, shelled and deveined
- ½ lb. bay scallops
- 6 Tbsp. unsalted butter, at room temperature
- 1 small onion, finely chopped
- 2 cups whole milk
- 2 bay leaves
- 2 fresh thyme sprigs
- Kosher or fine sea salt
- Freshly ground black pepper
- 2 Tbsp. all-purpose flour
- ¼ cup chopped fresh chives

1. Peel the sweet potatoes and cut them into 1-inch cubes. Place sweet potatoes in a large saucepan and add cool water to cover by 1 inch. Bring to a boil over medium-high. Reduce the heat to low to maintain a gentle simmer, and cook until sweet potatoes are fully tender, about 15 minutes. Drain sweet potatoes, reserving the cooking liquid.

2. Pass the sweet potatoes through a food mill or press them through a potato ricer, discarding any pulpy, stringy flesh. Give the milled sweet potatoes a good stir with a spoon, and add 1 to 2 tablespoons of the reserved cooking liquid if the puree seems dry or tacky. For a coarser puree, simply mash sweet potatoes with the back of a fork or a potato masher. They will collapse into a relatively smooth mass that should not require additional liquid to remain moist. Set aside 2 cups puree for the fish pie; reserve the rest for another use.

3. Preheat oven to 375°F. Cut cod into 1-inch pieces. Peel and devein shrimp. Pick over scallops for bits of shell, and remove tough band of muscle adhered to one side of each scallop. Refrigerate the seafood until ready to use.

4. Melt 2 tablespoons butter in a medium saucepan over medium. Add onion and cook, stirring, until translucent and soft, about 5 minutes. Pour milk into the pan and add bay leaves and thyme sprigs. Bring to a gentle simmer, stirring often. Stir in ½ teaspoon salt.

5. Poach each type of seafood individually: Place the cod in the simmering milk and cook until the fish is nearly cooked through, 1 to 2 minutes. Lift cod from milk with a slotted spoon, and place in a 2- to 3-quart casserole dish. Add the scallops to milk and poach until opaque, about 30 seconds. Lift from milk with a slotted spoon, and add to the dish with the fish. Add shrimp and poach until they just begin to curl, about 1 minute. Lift them from milk with a slotted spoon, and add to the dish. Use your hands or a fork to flake cod into bite-size pieces. Season fish with ½ teaspoon salt and ¼ teaspoon pepper.

6. In a small bowl, mash 2 tablespoons butter with flour. Remove bay leaves and thyme sprigs from milk. Bring milk to a simmer once again, and whisk the butter mixture into the milk until no lumps remain. Reduce heat to low and simmer, stirring, until the mixture thickens, about 5 minutes.

7. Pour béchamel over seafood in casserole dish. Add chives and fold gently to combine everything. Taste the filling and adjust seasoning with salt or black pepper, if needed.

8. Reheat the 2 cups sweet potato puree in the microwave, stirring every 30 seconds, or in a pot, stirring constantly, until warm. Stir remaining 2 tablespoons butter into sweet potatoes until it melts, and season lightly with salt. If desired, transfer warm sweet potato puree to a piping bag fitted with a star tip. Pipe or spread puree over filling, sealing edges.

9. Bake until filling is bubbly and topping is browned, about 20 minutes. Let stand for a few minutes before serving.
—MARY-FRANCES HECK

MAKE AHEAD Let the puree cool, and then refrigerate it in an airtight container for up to 3 days. To freeze, place cupfuls of puree in sandwich-size plastic zip-top bags, flatten the bags as you seal them, and stack them in the freezer.

Salmon with Lentil-Beet Salad

TOTAL 50 MIN; SERVES 4

The crisp, buttery skin-on salmon fillet in this healthy dish is perfect with the tangy lentil salad, but the salad itself is so good, it could easily stand on its own. If you can't find frisée, use escarole and chicory instead.

- 1 cup French green lentils
- Kosher salt and black pepper
- 6 baby golden beets, scrubbed and cut into ½-inch wedges
- 2 Tbsp. sherry vinegar
- 2 Tbsp. minced shallot
- 2 tsp. Dijon mustard
- ¼ cup plus 1 Tbsp. extra-virgin olive oil
- 3 cups torn frisée, white and light green parts only
- 2 red endives, halved lengthwise, cored, and sliced crosswise on the diagonal
- 4 (5- to 6-oz.) skin-on salmon fillets

1. Place lentils in a large saucepan, and add water to cover by 2 inches; bring to a boil. Simmer over medium until just tender, about 20 minutes. Remove from heat, add a generous pinch of salt, and let stand 5 minutes. Drain well and spread lentils on a baking sheet to cool.

2. Rinse out saucepan and put a steamer basket in it. Add 1 inch of water and bring to a boil. Scatter beets in the basket; cover and steam until tender, about 10 minutes. Let cool.

3. Whisk vinegar, shallot, mustard, and ¼ cup oil in a large bowl. Season with salt and pepper. Add lentils, beets, frisée, and endives, and toss to coat. Season with salt and pepper, and toss again.

4. Season salmon with salt and pepper. Heat remaining 1 tablespoon oil in a large nonstick skillet over medium-high until shimmering. Add salmon, skin-side down, and press gently with a spatula to flatten. Cook until the skin is browned and crisp, about 3 minutes. Flip salmon and cook until it is medium within, about 3 minutes longer. Transfer salmon to plates, and serve with lentil salad. — JUSTIN CHAPPLE & KAY CHUN

MAKE AHEAD The lentil salad can be refrigerated overnight. Fold in the frisée and endives before serving.

WINE Pair with a Sonoma County Pinot Noir.

Salmon with Lentil-Beet Salad

New England-Style Crab Dip with Brown-Butter Crumbs, RECIPE P. 136

Raw Oysters with Cava Mignonette, RECIPE P. 136

HORS D'OEUVRES OF THE SEVEN FISHES

Chefs across the country have long reinterpreted the classic plateau de fruits de mer, *or seafood tower. Boston chef Matt Jennings offers this array of hors d'oeuvres that's like a modern take on the traditional Italian Christmas Eve Feast of the Seven Fishes.*

Pink Peppercorn and Fennel Gravlax, RECIPE P. 137

Roasted Shrimp-and-Fennel Skewers with Mustard Chimichurri, RECIPE P. 137

White Anchovy Toasts with Parsnip Butter, RECIPE P. 136

Sea Scallop Lollipops, RECIPE P. 137

Smoky Mussel Stew, RECIPE P. 136

HORS D'OEUVRES OF THE SEVEN FISHES MENU

Raw Oysters with Cava Mignonette

TOTAL 5 MIN; MAKES ABOUT ¾ CUP

- ½ cup chilled cava
- ¼ cup minced shallot
- 1 Tbsp. white wine vinegar
- ¼ tsp. freshly ground black pepper
- Raw oysters on the half shell, for serving

Stir together cava, shallot, vinegar, and pepper in a small bowl. Serve mignonette with oysters. — MATT JENNINGS

New England-Style Crab Dip with Brown-Butter Crumbs

ACTIVE 30 MIN; TOTAL 1 HR 15 MIN; SERVES 12

- 1 cup mayonnaise
- ¼ cup minced celery
- ¼ cup minced green bell pepper
- 2 Tbsp. finely grated sweet onion
- 2 Tbsp. finely chopped fresh parsley
- 1 tsp. finely grated lemon zest plus 1 Tbsp. fresh lemon juice
- ½ tsp. hot sauce
- ⅛ tsp. cayenne pepper
- 1 lb. jumbo lump crabmeat, picked over
- Kosher salt and black pepper
- 4 oz. day-old rustic white bread, torn into 1-inch pieces (4 cups)
- 4 Tbsp. unsalted butter
- Crostini, chips, or radicchio leaves, for serving

1. Stir together mayonnaise, celery, bell pepper, onion, parsley, lemon zest, lemon juice, hot sauce, and cayenne in a large bowl. Fold in crab and season with salt and pepper. Refrigerate for 1 hour.

2. Meanwhile, preheat oven to 400°F. Place bread in a food processor, and pulse until fine crumbs form. Spread bread crumbs on a rimmed baking sheet and toast about 8 minutes, until crisp.

3. Cook butter over medium until milk solids turn dark golden, about 4 minutes.

Stir in toasted bread crumbs and season with salt.

4. Scrape crab mixture into a 10-inch round baking dish or skillet. Sprinkle brown-butter crumbs evenly on top. Bake until golden on top and bubbling at the edge, 20 to 25 minutes. Let cool for 5 minutes before serving with crostini, chips or radicchio leaves. — MATT JENNINGS

MAKE AHEAD Dip can be prepared through Step 3 and refrigerated overnight.

White Anchovy Toasts with Parsnip Butter

ACTIVE 1 HR; TOTAL 1 HR 30 MIN; MAKES 24

PARSNIP BUTTER
- 1¼ lb. parsnips, peeled and cut into 1-inch chunks
- 2 Tbsp. unsalted butter
- ⅓ cup half-and-half
- Kosher salt and black pepper

BASIL OIL
- ½ cup lightly packed fresh basil
- ¼ cup lightly packed fresh parsley
- 1 small garlic clove
- ¼ cup plus 2 Tbsp. extra-virgin olive oil
- Kosher salt and black pepper

TOASTS
- 24 baguette slices, cut on the diagonal ⅓ inch thick (from 1 baguette)
- Extra-virgin olive oil, for brushing
- 24 white anchovy fillets (alici or boquerones)

1. Make the parsnip butter Cook parsnips in a large saucepan of boiling salted water until tender, 8 to 10 minutes. Drain well and transfer to a food processor. Add butter and half-and-half, and puree until smooth. Scrape puree into a medium saucepan and cook over medium-low, stirring frequently, until thick, 15 minutes. Season with salt and pepper. Transfer to a medium bowl and press a sheet of plastic wrap directly on butter. Let cool completely, then refrigerate until chilled, 30 minutes.

2. Make the basil oil Combine basil, parsley, and garlic in a food processor, and

pulse until finely chopped. With machine on, stream in oil until smooth. Season basil oil with salt and pepper.

3. Make the toasts Preheat oven to 400°F. Arrange baguette slices on a baking sheet and brush both sides with oil. Toast until golden, 8 to 10 minutes; let cool.

4. Spread toasts with parsnip butter and arrange on a platter. Top with anchovies, drizzle with basil oil, and serve. — MATT JENNINGS

MAKE AHEAD The parsnip butter can be covered and refrigerated for up to 2 days.

Smoky Mussel Stew

ACTIVE 40 MIN; TOTAL 1 HR; SERVES 12 AS AN HORS D'OEUVRE

- ¾ lb. Yukon Gold potatoes, peeled and cut into ½-inch pieces
- 3 Tbsp. extra-virgin olive oil
- Kosher salt and black pepper
- ½ lb. Brussels sprouts, quartered
- 1 lb. fresh mussels, scrubbed and debearded
- 1 cup dry white wine
- 1 medium white onion, quartered through the core and peeled
- 2 medium shallots, chopped
- 2 Tbsp. unsalted butter
- 2 fresh parsley sprigs, plus chopped parsley for garnish
- 2 fresh thyme sprigs
- 1 bay leaf
- Pinch of cayenne pepper
- 2 cups heavy cream
- 1 large egg yolk
- ½ lb. smoked mussels
- 2 Tbsp. fresh lemon juice

1. Preheat oven to 375°F. On one side of a large rimmed baking sheet, toss potatoes with 2 tablespoons oil and season with salt and pepper. On other side of baking sheet, toss Brussels sprouts with remaining 1 tablespoon oil and season with salt and pepper. Roast until the vegetables are tender and charred in spots, about 25 minutes.

2. Meanwhile, combine mussels, wine, onion, shallots, butter, parsley sprigs, thyme, bay leaf, and cayenne in a large saucepan over high; bring to a boil. Cover and cook over medium-high until mussels open, 6 to 8 minutes. Using a slotted spoon, transfer mussels to a bowl. Remove mussels from their shells; discard shells and any mussels that do not open. Strain broth through a fine wire-mesh strainer.

3. Wipe out saucepan. Add strained broth along with accumulated mussel broth and bring to a boil. Add cream and bring just to a boil. Beat egg yolk and 2 tablespoons hot cream in a small bowl, then gradually whisk mixture into saucepan. Simmer soup over medium, whisking, until thickened slightly, 3 to 5 minutes. Stir in Brussels sprouts, potatoes, cooked mussels, and smoked mussels, and simmer until hot, about 3 minutes. Stir in lemon juice and season with salt and pepper. Serve stew in small ramekins, garnished with parsley. — MATT JENNINGS

Roasted Shrimp-and-Fennel Skewers with Mustard Chimichurri

TOTAL 45 MIN; MAKES 24 SMALL SKEWERS

- 2 cups lightly packed fresh parsley
- 1 cup snipped fresh chives
- 2½ Tbsp. sherry vinegar
- 1½ Tbsp. fresh lemon juice
- 1 Tbsp. finely grated peeled fresh horseradish
- 2 garlic cloves, finely chopped
- 1 tsp. crushed red pepper
- 1 tsp. honey
- ¼ cup plus 3 Tbsp. extra-virgin olive oil, plus more for brushing
- 1½ Tbsp. whole-grain mustard
  Kosher salt and black pepper
- 2 medium fennel bulbs, halved lengthwise, cored, and cut into thin wedges
- 24 large medium, shelled and deveined

1. Preheat oven to 375°F. Combine parsley, chives, vinegar, lemon juice, horseradish, garlic, red pepper, honey, ¼ cup plus

2 tablespoons oil, and ¼ cup water in a food processor; pulse until finely chopped. Scrape into a bowl, stir in mustard, and season with salt and black pepper.

2. Arrange fennel on half of a large rimmed baking sheet, keeping wedges intact. Brush with oil and season with salt and pepper. Roast until tender, 25 to 30 minutes.

3. Toss shrimp and remaining 1 tablespoon oil in a medium bowl; season with salt and black pepper. Spread shrimp on other half of baking sheet and roast until just cooked through, about 5 minutes.

4. Thread shrimp onto twenty-four 6-inch skewers and arrange on a platter with fennel wedges. Serve with mustard chimichurri. — MATT JENNINGS

MAKE AHEAD The chimichurri can be made early in the day and refrigerated. Bring to room temperature before serving.

Pink Peppercorn and Fennel Gravlax

ACTIVE 30 MIN; TOTAL 3 DAYS; SERVES 10 TO 12

- ½ cup plus 2 Tbsp. kosher salt
- 1 (2-lb.) skin-on center-cut salmon fillet, pinbones removed
- 2 Tbsp. pink peppercorns
- 2 Tbsp. caraway seeds
- 2 Tbsp. coriander seeds
- 2 Tbsp. fennel pollen
- 1 tsp. freshly ground white pepper
- ¼ cup sugar
- 1 large bunch fresh dill
  Rye crackers, sour cream, sliced onions, and drained capers, for serving

1. Fill a large bowl with water, add 2 tablespoons salt, and stir until dissolved. Submerge salmon in water and let stand for 10 minutes. Drain fish and pat dry.

2. Meanwhile, toast pink peppercorns, caraway seeds, and coriander seeds in a small skillet over medium, stirring, until very fragrant, about 2 minutes. Cool slightly, then coarsely grind in a mortar or spice grinder. Transfer to a small bowl and

stir in fennel pollen, white pepper, sugar, and remaining ½ cup salt.

3. Line a rimmed baking sheet with plastic wrap. Arrange half of dill down the center of the baking sheet. Sprinkle half the spice mixture evenly over dill, then top with salmon, skin-side down. Sprinkle remaining spice mixture over top and sides of salmon in an even layer. Top with remaining dill. Wrap salmon tightly in plastic wrap, and place skin-side down on baking sheet. Top with a second baking sheet and heavy canned goods to weigh it down. Refrigerate for 1 day.

4. Unwrap fish and pat dry. Rewrap fish and seasonings in a clean sheet of plastic, leaving behind any liquid and squeezing out excess liquid from dill. Place skin-side up on baking sheet. Top with baking sheet and weights and refrigerate for 2 days, until flesh feels firm in the center.

5. Rinse fish, pat it dry, and thinly slice. Serve with rye crackers, sour cream, sliced onions, and capers. — MATT JENNINGS

MAKE AHEAD The gravlax can be rinsed, wrapped in a fresh sheet of plastic, and refrigerated for 3 days.

Sea Scallop Lollipops

TOTAL 20 MIN; MAKES 12

- ½ cup mayonnaise
- 2 Tbsp. gochujang
- 2 Tbsp. minced dill pickle
  Kosher salt and black pepper
- 2 Tbsp. canola oil
- 12 large sea scallops (1 lb.)
  Lollipop sticks or small skewers, for serving

1. Stir mayonnaise, gochujang, and pickle in a small bowl; season with salt.

2. Heat oil in a large cast-iron skillet over medium-high. Season scallops with salt and pepper, and cook, turning once, until golden and just cooked through, about 3 minutes. Skewer scallops on lollipop sticks and arrange on a platter. Serve with gochujang mayo. — MATT JENNINGS

MAKE AHEAD The gochujang mayo can be

Provençal Fish Stew

Provençal Fish Stew

ACTIVE 35 MIN; TOTAL 55 MIN; SERVES 4

How could a classic like bouillabaisse simultaneously be simplified and made more elegant? Enter Clare de Boer and Jess Shadbolt of King in Soho, who distill the essence of the dish by serving sweet seafood in a fresh tomato sauce made with concentrated aromatics, like fennel seeds and chile flakes, and a generous glug of wine. The result is bright and fresh, with simmered-all-day flavor achieved in under an hour.

AÏOLI

- 1 Tbsp. fresh lemon juice
- 1 small garlic clove, peeled
- Pinch of saffron threads
- ¾ tsp. flaky sea salt, divided
- 1 large pasteurized egg yolk
- ⅔ cup mild-tasting extra-virgin olive oil

STEW

- 3 garlic cloves, thinly sliced
- 2 tsp. crushed fennel seeds
- ⅛ tsp. crushed red pepper
- 5 Tbsp. olive oil, divided
- 3¼ tsp. flaky sea salt, divided
- ¾ tsp. black pepper, divided
- 2 lb. ripe tomatoes, roughly chopped (about 5 cups)
- 1 cup dry white wine
- Pinch of saffron threads
- 2 (1¼-lb.) live lobsters
- 1 (1-lb.) skin-on red snapper fillet or any skin-on flaky whitefish fillet, cut into 8 pieces
- 1 lb. littleneck clams (about 12 clams), scrubbed and thoroughly rinsed
- 1 lb. mussels (about 32 mussels), scrubbed and debearded

ADDITIONAL INGREDIENTS

Crusty bread, toasted

Leafy green salad (optional)

1. Make the aïoli Using a mortar and pestle, mash together lemon juice, garlic, saffron, and ¼ teaspoon salt until smooth and combined. Scrape mixture into a medium bowl; whisk in egg yolk. (Alternatively, using flat side of a knife, mash garlic and ¼ teaspoon salt on a cutting board to form a paste. Transfer to a medium bowl; whisk in lemon juice, saffron, and egg yolk.) Slowly drizzle in oil, whisking constantly, until emulsified. Whisk in remaining ½ teaspoon salt; cover and refrigerate up to 1 day.

2. Make the stew Stir together garlic, fennel seeds, red pepper, 2 tablespoons oil, ¾ teaspoon salt, and ⅛ teaspoon black pepper in a large Dutch oven. Cook over medium, stirring occasionally, until garlic begins to sizzle, about 3 minutes. Stir in tomatoes, wine, and saffron, and bring to a simmer. Reduce heat to medium-low, and cook, stirring occasionally, until sauce is slightly reduced, 12 to 15 minutes. Stir in 1 teaspoon salt and ⅛ teaspoon black pepper. Transfer tomato mixture to a bowl. Wipe Dutch oven clean.

3. Place a damp paper towel on a work surface. Top with a rimmed baking sheet; line with another damp paper towel. Fit a cutting board inside baking sheet. Place 1 lobster on cutting board, and straighten tail. With blade of a chef's knife over the head, pierce lobster straight down through the midline of the carapace (where the head connects to the body) until knife tip reaches cutting board. Using a lever motion, cut lobster's head in half. Rotate lobster 180 degrees, and cut lengthwise through the midline, through the body and tail, to separate lobster into 2 halves. Remove and discard stomach sac from head, intestinal tract, and tomalley. If desired, using back of knife, crack claws on inner side, and loosen shells. Remove and discard rubber bands, if necessary. Repeat procedure with remaining lobster.

4. Sprinkle cut sides of lobsters with ½ teaspoon salt and ¼ teaspoon black pepper. Sprinkle snapper pieces with remaining 1 teaspoon salt and remaining ¼ teaspoon black pepper. Heat 1 tablespoon oil in Dutch oven over medium. Add 2 lobster halves, cut sides down, making sure claws are in contact with bottom of Dutch oven. Cook until meat is lightly browned, about 2 minutes. Flip and cook until claws are bright red, 1 to 3 minutes. Remove from Dutch oven. Add 1 tablespoon oil to Dutch oven, and repeat with remaining 2 lobster halves. Remove from Dutch oven. Add remaining 1 tablespoon oil to Dutch oven. Place snapper pieces in Dutch oven, skin-sides down. Top with lobster halves, shell-sides down. Add clams and mussels. Pour tomato mixture over seafood. Bring to a simmer over medium. Reduce heat to medium-low, cover, and cook until clams and mussels open and lobster claws are cooked through, 10 to 12 minutes. Discard any clams and mussels that do not open.

5. Serve stew immediately on warm plates or a platter with toasted bread spread with aïoli and, if desired, salad. — CLARE DE BOER & JESS SHADBOLT

The Snappiest Shrimp

PHOTO P. 127

ACTIVE 20 MIN; TOTAL 1 HR 20 MIN; SERVES 6

Head-on jumbo wild shrimp make a festive holiday main course. But while they are quick to prepare, they are easy to overcook and a pain to peel at the table. Before asking your guests to roll up their sleeves, brine the raw shrimp in a slushy solution of sea salt and baking soda. Alkaline baking soda slightly alters the pH of the shrimp, making for extra-plump meat that is as succulent as lobster and resists overcooking. Added bonus: The meat pulls away from the shells while cooking, so you get all the flavor of shell-on shrimp with none of the struggle of peeling them.

- ½ cup fine sea salt
- 2 Tbsp. baking soda
- 3 lb. raw head-on jumbo pink or brown wild Gulf shrimp
- 3 cups cracked ice
- ¼ cup olive oil
- 1 tsp. black pepper

1. Combine 8 cups water, salt, and baking soda in a large bowl, and stir until salt and baking soda dissolve and water is clear, about 1 minute and 30 seconds. Add shrimp and ice. Chill 1 hour. Remove shrimp from brine, and pat dry. Discard brine. Chill shrimp until ready to cook, up to 1 hour.

2. Preheat oven to 400°F. Toss shrimp with oil and black pepper, and spread in an even layer on a large rimmed baking sheet. Roast in preheated oven until heads are just opaque, about 12 minutes. Transfer to a platter, and serve immediately. — ROBIN BASHINSKY

WINE Pair with a crisp, lemon-zesty Albariño.

Pan-Roasted Lobster with Chive Beurre Blanc

TOTAL 1 HR 30 MIN; SERVES 4

Fresh Maine lobster bathed in white wine butter sauce makes for an elegant holiday meal, inspired by chef and restaurateur Jasper White's classic New England preparation. Butchering live lobsters might seem intimidating; once you get the hang of handling them, the rest of the dish is easy. If live lobsters are unavailable, substitute eight thawed frozen Maine lobster tails, 3 pounds large head-on shrimp, or 2 pounds diver scallops simply seared and served with the sauce.

- 2 Tbsp. unsalted butter, melted
- 4 (1½-lb.) live Maine lobsters
- 2 cups cold unsalted butter (16 oz.), cubed, divided
- 1 cup finely chopped shallots (about 6 shallots)
- 1 (750-ml.) bottle unoaked dry white wine
- 1 tsp. fresh lemon juice
- 1 tsp. kosher salt, plus more to taste
- 2 Tbsp. (1 oz.) high-proof bourbon (optional)
- ½ lb. linguine or fettuccine, cooked according to package directions
- ¼ cup minced fresh chives
- 2 to 4 Tbsp. water

1. Place a damp paper towel on a work surface. Top with a large rimmed baking sheet; line with another damp paper towel. Fit a cutting board inside baking sheet. Place 1 lobster on cutting board, belly side up. Using your left hand, curl tail into body, and hold. Arrange claws facing right. Carefully plunge tip of knife through mouth of lobster, killing lobster instantly. (Although it may still move, the lobster is dead.) Continue cutting in a downward motion until edge of knife makes contact with cutting board, cutting head in half. Remove knife, turn lobster over, belly-side down, rotate lobster 180 degrees, and flatten tail. Insert knife at point of first cut, and cut downward through carapace and tail, cutting lobster in half. If lobster is female, it will have dark green roe where the body meets the tail. Remove 1 tablespoon roe, and place in a small bowl; discard remaining roe. Set bowl aside. Discard light green tomalley, vein running through tail, and head sac. Cut crosswise between tail and carapace to separate.

2. Remove claws and knuckles by twisting from body. Grip claw with a kitchen towel, and crack claws between spikes with back of knife, twisting knife left and right to crack shell. Arrange lobster tail halves, cut-sides down, and claws on buttered baking sheet. Repeat procedure with remaining lobsters. Chill lobsters in refrigerator until ready to cook, up to 2 hours. (If desired, use poultry shears to cut off legs, and place in a steamer basket over simmering water. Steam 4 minutes, and serve as an appetizer.)

3. Preheat oven to 450°F. Melt 2 tablespoons cubed butter in a large saucepan over medium. Add shallots, and cook, stirring often, until shallots are translucent, 4 to 6 minutes. Stir in wine, and bring to a rapid boil over high. Reduce heat to medium-high, adjusting heat as necessary to maintain a vigorous simmer; cook until wine is reduced to just below top of shallots, 30 to 35 minutes. Reduce heat to low, and cook, whisking in remaining cubed butter, a few cubes at a time, until sauce is creamy and thickened. Remove from heat; stir in lemon juice and salt, and cover. Set beurre blanc in a warm spot until ready to use, up to 30 minutes.

4. Transfer lobsters to preheated oven, and roast 5 minutes. Carefully remove from oven, and use tongs to flip lobster tails cut-sides up. Return to oven, and roast until lobster shells are bright red and meat is opaque and plump, 3 to 5 minutes. Working quickly, transfer baking sheet to stovetop. If desired, drizzle lobsters with bourbon, and carefully ignite the vapor with a long match or long multipurpose lighter. Let stand until flames disappear. Line a warmed platter with hot cooked linguine; using tongs, place lobsters on pasta. Tent platter with aluminum foil.

5. Pour liquid drippings from baking sheet into a large skillet over medium; discard white albumen on baking sheet. Add reserved roe to skillet, and cook, whisking constantly, until roe begins to turn bright red and is the texture of soft scrambled eggs, about 30 seconds. Remove skillet from heat, and whisk in beurre blanc and chives. If sauce is very thick, whisk in water, 1 tablespoon at a time, to reach desired consistency. Season with salt to taste. Remove and discard foil from lobsters, and pour beurre blanc over lobsters and pasta. Serve immediately.
— MARY-FRANCES HECK

MAKE AHEAD Lobster may be butchered up to 2 hours before cooking. Keep chilled in refrigerator.

NOTE Frozen raw Maine lobster tails are available from Luke's Lobster in the freezer section of Whole Foods.

WINE Pair with a racy, citrusy Albariño.

Pan-Roasted Lobster
with Chive Beurre Blanc

Vegetarian Mains

Savory Leek and Greens
Hand Pies, RECIPE P. 147

Wild Mushroom Shepherd's Pie with Potato-Chestnut Topping

ACTIVE 1 HR 30 MIN; TOTAL 4 HR 45 MIN;
SERVES 8 TO 10

Chicago chef Grant Achatz swaps out mushrooms for the usual meat and adds woodsy chestnuts to the potato topping in his vegetarian take on shepherd's pie.

SAUCE

- 3 lb. white mushrooms, coarsely chopped
- 1 lb. leeks, white and light green parts only, chopped
- 1 carrot, chopped
- 3 garlic cloves, crushed
- 2 bay leaves
- 1½ Tbsp. kosher salt
- 1 Tbsp. fresh thyme leaves
- 1 Tbsp. black peppercorns
- ½ tsp. hot curry powder
- 2 cups heavy cream
- 6 Tbsp. unsalted butter
- ¼ cup plus 2 Tbsp. all-purpose flour

FILLING

- 6 Tbsp. unsalted butter
- 1 large shallot, finely chopped
- 2 garlic cloves, minced
- 8 oz. rutabaga, peeled and cut into ⅓-inch dice
- 8 oz. turnips, peeled and cut into ⅓-inch dice
- ¼ lb. sunchokes, peeled and cut into ⅓-inch dice
- 1 small carrot, cut into ⅓-inch dice
- 1 small parsnip, peeled and cut into ⅓-inch dice
- Kosher salt and black pepper
- 1 lb. shiitake mushrooms, stemmed and caps quartered
- 2 lb. mixed cremini, oyster, maitake, and portobello mushrooms, cut into bite-size pieces
- ½ cup finely chopped fresh parsley
- ½ cup chopped fresh chives
- 2 Tbsp. chopped fresh thyme

TOPPING

- 2 lb. Yukon Gold potatoes, peeled and cut into large chunks
- 1 (5-oz.) pkg. roasted chestnuts
- 1 small parsnip, peeled and cut into 1-inch pieces
- 1 qt. heavy cream
- ½ tsp. freshly grated nutmeg
- 1 Tbsp. kosher salt
- 4 large egg yolks
- ¼ cup mixed chopped fresh parsley, chives, and thyme

1. Make the sauce Working in 4 batches, place mushrooms in a food processor, and pulse until finely chopped; transfer to a 12-quart pot. Add leeks, carrot, garlic, bay leaves, salt, thyme, peppercorns, and curry powder to food processor, and pulse until very finely chopped; transfer to pot. Add cream and 1 quart water, and bring to a boil over high, then simmer over medium, stirring occasionally, for 1 hour.

2. Pour stock mixture through a fine wire-mesh strainer into a large heatproof bowl, pressing on solids to extract as much liquid as possible; discard solids. Return stock to pot and boil over medium-high, until reduced to 3 cups, about 10 minutes. Pour stock into the bowl.

3. Wipe out pot and melt butter in it. Whisk in flour and cook over medium, whisking often, until well browned, about 7 minutes. Gradually whisk in stock until smooth, and bring to a boil. Simmer over medium-low, whisking often, until thickened and no floury taste remains, about 15 minutes. Scrape sauce into bowl.

4. Make the filling Wipe out pot and melt butter in it. Add shallot and garlic, and cook over medium-high, stirring, until softened, about 2 minutes. Add rutabaga, turnips, sunchokes, carrot, parsnip, and a generous pinch of salt. Cook, stirring occasionally, until just softened, about 7 minutes. Add all mushrooms and cook, stirring occasionally, until tender and their liquid evaporates, 10 to 12 minutes. Add sauce and cook over medium-low, stirring often, until vegetables are coated in a creamy sauce, 10 to 15 minutes. Remove pot from heat and stir in herbs. Season with salt and pepper. Spread filling in a 13- × 9-inch gratin dish.

5. Make the topping Combine potatoes, chestnuts, and parsnip in a large saucepan. Cover with cream and 1 quart water, and bring to a boil over medium-high. Stir in nutmeg and 1 tablespoon salt, and simmer over medium, stirring occasionally, until vegetables are tender, about 30 minutes.

6. Drain vegetables in a colander set over a heatproof bowl. Transfer half the vegetables to a food processor, add ¾ cup cooking liquid, and puree until smooth. Scrape into a large bowl. Repeat with remaining vegetables and another ¾ cup cooking liquid. Let puree cool slightly, then stir in egg yolks and chopped herbs and season with salt. Spread topping over filling and swirl decoratively.

7. Preheat oven to 375°F. Bake pie until the filling bubbles, about 40 minutes. Turn on broiler and broil 8 to 10 inches from heat, until the top is lightly browned, 2 to 3 minutes. Let stand for 20 minutes. Sprinkle with salt and serve. — GRANT ACHATZ

MAKE AHEAD The shepherd's pie can be prepared through Step 6 and refrigerated overnight. Let stand at room temperature for at least 45 minutes before baking.

WINE Pair with an earthy, lush, full-bodied Champagne.

Wild Mushroom
Shepherd's Pie with
Potato-Chestnut Topping

Curried Squash Galette

Savory Leek and Greens Hand Pies

PHOTO P. 143

ACTIVE 20 MIN; TOTAL 1 HR; SERVES 6

Using a blend of greens creates a slightly bitter filling with sweet notes from the sautéed leeks and onions. Lean on store-bought pizza dough from your grocer's deli to crank out these savory pies quickly; be sure to let the dough come to room temperature for easy rolling.

- 1 lb. mixed fresh greens (such as cabbage, Swiss chard, collard greens, and dandelion greens), chopped (about 8 cups)
- 1 medium white onion, chopped
- ½ cup celery leaves
- 3 Tbsp. olive oil
- 2 medium leeks, white parts only, thinly sliced
- 1 Tbsp. kosher salt
- ½ tsp. black pepper
- 2 Tbsp. finely chopped fresh mint leaves
- 2 Tbsp. finely chopped fresh flat-leaf parsley leaves
- 1½ lb. fresh prepared pizza dough
- All-purpose flour, for work surface

1. Preheat oven to 500°F. Place a pizza stone on bottom oven rack. Working in batches, pulse greens, onion, and celery leaves in a food processor until finely chopped, about 5 times per batch.

2. Heat oil in a large skillet over medium-high. Add chopped greens mixture, leeks, salt, and pepper, and cook, stirring often, until greens are very tender and liquid has evaporated, about 10 minutes. Remove from heat; let cool 20 minutes. Stir in mint and parsley.

3. Roll and stretch pizza dough into a 25- × 16-inch rectangle on a floured work surface. Cut out 8 (6-inch) rounds from dough; place 3 dough rounds on each of 2 baking sheets lined with parchment paper; set remaining 2 dough rounds aside. Roll the dough rectangle scraps into a 14-inch square. Cut out 4 (6-inch) rounds. Discard remaining dough scraps.

4. Divide cooled greens mixture evenly among the 6 dough rounds on baking sheets (about ½ cup per round). Lightly brush edges of filled rounds with water. Place remaining 6 dough rounds on top of each filled round; pinch edges to seal. Using your hands, flatten and spread filling to edges of each sealed pie. Make a ½-inch hole in center of each pie using a knife to allow steam to escape.

5. Transfer pies onto hot pizza stone in preheated oven; bake until golden brown, about 10 minutes. Let cool 5 minutes; serve warm. — NAOMI POMEROY

Curried Squash Galette

ACTIVE 40 MIN; TOTAL 2 HR; SERVES 6 TO 8

With a super-flaky crust (the secret: frozen grated butter) and a lightly spiced sweet-savory winter squash filling, this rustic galette from F&W's Justin Chapple makes a perfect vegetarian meal; serve it with a green salad.

- 1¼ cups all-purpose flour
- ¾ tsp. kosher salt
- ¾ tsp. black pepper
- 1 stick unsalted butter, frozen
- ⅓ cup ice water

FILLING

- 1 lb. butternut squash, peeled, seeded, and cut into ¼-inch-thick slices
- 1 lb. kabocha squash, peeled, seeded, and cut into ¼-inch-thick slices
- 1 red onion, cut through the core into ½-inch wedges
- ¼ cup extra-virgin olive oil
- 2 tsp. Madras curry powder
- Kosher salt and black pepper
- ½ cup sour cream
- ½ cup shredded Manchego cheese, divided, plus more for serving

1. Make the dough Whisk flour, ¾ teaspoon salt, and ¾ teaspoon pepper in a large bowl. Working over bowl, grate butter on large holes of a box grater. Gently toss grated butter in flour. Stir in ⅓ cup ice water until dough is evenly moistened. Scrape out dough onto a work surface, gather up any crumbs, and knead gently just until dough comes together. Pat into a disk, wrap in plastic, and refrigerate until chilled, about 1 hour.

2. Make the filling Preheat oven to 425°F. Toss together butternut squash, kabocha squash, onion, oil, and curry powder on a large rimmed baking sheet. Season generously with salt and pepper. Roast until squash is tender but not falling apart, 15 to 20 minutes. Let cool.

3. Increase oven temperature to 450°F. On a lightly floured work surface, roll out dough to a 14-inch round. Carefully transfer to a parchment paper-lined baking sheet. Spread sour cream over dough, leaving a 1½-inch border. Sprinkle ¼ cup cheese on top. Arrange squash and onion over sour cream, and sprinkle remaining ¼ cup cheese on top. Fold pastry edge up and over vegetables to create a 1½-inch border.

4. Bake squash galette until crust is browned, 30 to 35 minutes; let cool slightly. Sprinkle with shredded cheese, cut into wedges, and serve warm.
— JUSTIN CHAPPLE

WINE Pair with a rich, spicy Pinot Gris.

Roasted Butternut Squash Parmesan

ACTIVE 30 MIN; TOTAL 1 HR 55 MIN;
SERVES 4

Food writer and recipe developer Raquel Pelzel made version after version of this dish before she perfected it—but she finally did. She describes it as "a double-decker of squash-marinara-oozy cheese with main-dish gravitas. It was hearty, way less fussy than making a traditional parm, and my stovetop didn't need to be degreased post-cooking."

BREAD CRUMBS

- 2 country-style white bread slices, roughly torn
- 6 Tbsp. finely grated Parmigiano-Reggiano cheese, divided
- 2 medium garlic cloves, roughly chopped
- 2 Tbsp. nutritional yeast
- ½ tsp. kosher salt
- 2 Tbsp. extra-virgin olive oil

SQUASH PARMESAN

- 1 (2½-lb.) butternut squash
- 2 Tbsp. finely minced fresh sage
- 1 Tbsp. extra-virgin olive oil
- 1 tsp. finely minced fresh thyme
- 1 tsp. honey
- ½ tsp. kosher salt
- 2 cups marinara sauce
- 1½ Tbsp. soy sauce
- 4 oz. mozzarella cheese (not fresh mozzarella), grated (about 2 cups)
- 4 oz. Fontina cheese, grated (about 2 cups)
- 2 Tbsp. finely grated Parmigiano-Reggiano cheese

1. Make the bread crumbs Preheat oven to 375°F with oven rack in middle position. Combine torn bread, ¼ cup Parmigiano-Reggiano, garlic, nutritional yeast, and salt in a food processor. Pulse until fine bread crumbs form, 3 to 4 times. While pulsing, drizzle in oil, and process until crumbs are coated in oil (you should end up with about 1 cup bread crumbs). Transfer crumbs to a rimmed baking sheet, and bake in preheated oven until golden brown, crisp, and toasted, about 7 minutes, stirring once halfway through. Remove from oven, transfer to a large plate, and set aside.

2. Make the squash Increase oven temperature to 400°F. Keep one oven rack in middle position, and place another rack in upper-middle position. Use a vegetable peeler to peel squash. Separate neck from round base. Cut neck in half crosswise, then cut lengthwise into ½-inch-thick planks. Cut round base in half, and use a spoon to scoop out and discard seeds. Turn squash halves cut-sides down, and cut into ½-inch-thick half moons. Toss squash slices, sage, oil, thyme, honey, and salt in a large bowl. Transfer squash mixture to a rimmed baking sheet, and arrange in a single layer. Roast squash at 400°F until slightly tender, about 15 minutes. Let cool 5 minutes.

3. Meanwhile, stir together marinara and soy sauce in small bowl; layer half of squash in an 11- × 7-inch baking dish. Spread 1 cup marinara mixture evenly over squash; sprinkle evenly with 1 cup mozzarella and 1 cup Fontina. Repeat layering with remaining squash, marinara mixture, mozzarella, and Fontina. Sprinkle evenly with Parmigiano-Reggiano. Cover with heavy-duty aluminum foil, and bake at 400°F, for 1 hour. Uncover and bake until squash is tender and cheese is golden brown, 20 to 25 minutes. Sprinkle with bread crumbs, and serve. —RAQUEL PELZEL

Spinach-and-Grape-Leaf Pie

ACTIVE 1 HR; TOTAL 4 HR 30 MIN; SERVES 8

Chef and New York restaurateur Alex Raij makes this big, impressive pie—which she calls pastel de parra *or "grape pie" in Spanish—as a snack, but a big slice is also satisfying as a vegetarian meal.*

DOUGH

- 2 cups all-purpose flour, plus more for dusting
- 1 tsp. kosher salt
- 2 sticks cold unsalted butter, cut into small pieces
- 1 cup heavy cream

FILLING

- 4 large whole eggs plus 1 large egg, lightly beaten
- ¼ cup extra-virgin olive oil
- 1 medium onion, minced
  Kosher alt

- 4 garlic cloves, minced
- 1 (10-oz.) jar of grape leaves, stems removed and leaves thinly sliced (about 3 cups)
- 2 bunches scallions, thinly sliced
- 6 (10-oz.) pkg. frozen leaf spinach, thawed and squeezed dry, or 3 lb. fresh spinach, stemmed and blanched
- 2 cups frozen peas, thawed
- 8 oz. fresh ricotta (1 cup)
- 1 oz. Parmigiano-Reggiano cheese, freshly grated (¼ cup)
  Juice of 1 lemon
- ½ tsp. freshly grated nutmeg
- ½ cup finely chopped fresh mint
  Freshly ground black pepper
- 1 large egg yolk beaten with 1 Tbsp. milk, for glazing

1. Make the dough Combine 2 cups flour and salt in a food processor, and pulse a few times to blend. Add half of the butter, and pulse until mixture resembles large peas. Add remaining butter, and pulse until mixture resembles baby peas. Make holes in flour mixture and drizzle in cream. Pulse until dough starts to come together.

2. Scrape dough onto a lightly floured work surface. Gently knead it a few times and form dough into a ball. Cut off one-third of the dough and gently form into a disk. Gently flatten larger piece of dough into a disk. Wrap both disks tightly in plastic and refrigerate until firm, at least 2 hours or up to 24 hours.

3. Make the filling Place 4 whole eggs in a medium saucepan, and add water to cover; bring to a boil. Boil for 2 minutes, then drain eggs and cover with cold water. Lightly crack shells, and let cool; peel.

4. Heat oil in a large, deep skillet over medium. Add onion and a large pinch of salt, and cook until translucent, about 7 minutes. Add garlic and cook until fragrant, about 3 minutes. Add grape leaves. Cover and cook over low, stirring occasionally, until tender, about 10 minutes. Add scallions and cook over medium until softened, about 3 minutes. Stir in spinach. Cover and cook, stirring occasionally, until spinach is heated through and thoroughly incorporated, about 5 minutes.

5. Scrape greens from skillet into a large bowl and let cool to room temperature. Stir in peas, ricotta, Parmigiano-Reggiano, beaten egg, lemon juice, nutmeg, and mint. Season filling with salt and pepper.

6. Preheat oven to 425°F. Heat a large rimmed baking sheet in the oven. On a lightly floured work surface, roll out large piece of dough to a 16-inch round slightly less than ¼ inch thick. Fold dough in half and transfer to a 10-inch springform pan. Unfold dough and gently press into pan and up sides. Trim overhang to ½ inch. Refrigerate dough in pan. Roll out smaller piece of dough to a 10-inch round, slightly less than ¼ inch thick. Slide round onto a cookie sheet and chill until firm, 5 minutes. Trim round to 9 inches.

7. Arrange whole cooked eggs in dough-lined pan and cover with filling, smoothing the top. Place 9-inch dough round on top and brush edge with some egg-milk glaze. Fold overhanging dough over center round and pinch edges together to seal. Brush top and edge of pie with glaze.

8. Transfer pie to preheated baking sheet, and bake for 10 minutes. Reduce oven temperature to 375°F, and bake until crust is richly browned and the filling is hot, about 50 minutes. Transfer pie to a rack, and let cool to warm.

9. Remove side of pan. Cut pie into wedges, and serve warm or at room temperature. — ALEX RAIJ

MAKE AHEAD The dough, filling, and cooked eggs can be refrigerated separately overnight. Bring the filling to room temperature before proceeding. The baked pie can be kept at room temperature up to 4 hours or covered and refrigerated up to 2 days; reheat gently in a 375°F oven.

WINE Pair with a citrusy, full-bodied white Rioja.

Winter Galette

ACTIVE 1 HR; TOTAL 2 HR 30 MIN, PLUS COOLING; SERVES 6 TO 8

Food writer and cookbook author Gail Simmons' former boss—chef Daniel Boulud—created seven vegetable dishes for her wedding feast. The fabulous array was the stimulus for this seasonal rustic tart. In colder months, she tops it with paper-thin slices of vegetables she has on hand, from winter squash to celery root. The dough is easy to prepare and shape into a freeform crust, while fresh ricotta, infused with herbs and lemon zest, forms a creamy base.

DOUGH

- ¾ cup all-purpose flour, plus more for dusting
- ¾ cup whole-wheat flour
- ½ tsp. kosher salt
- 1 stick unsalted butter, cubed and chilled
- ¼ cup sour cream
- 2 Tbsp. ice water
- 1 Tbsp. fresh lemon juice

FILLING

- 2 Tbsp. extra-virgin olive oil, divided
- 1 large shallot, thinly sliced
   Kosher salt and black pepper
- 1 cup whole-milk ricotta
- 1½ tsp. finely grated lemon zest plus 1 tsp. fresh lemon juice
- 1 large garlic clove, finely grated
- 1 tsp. fresh thyme leaves, plus more for sprinkling
- 1 tsp. minced fresh oregano, plus leaves for sprinkling
- ½ tsp. minced fresh rosemary, plus leaves for sprinkling
- ½ lb. acorn squash, seeded, peeled, and shaved into ribbons
- ½ lb. celery root, peeled and shaved into ribbons
- 1 small baking potato, peeled and shaved into ribbons
- 1 large egg beaten with 1 Tbsp. water
- ¼ cup freshly grated Parmigiano-Reggiano
- 2 tsp. honey, warmed

1. Make the dough Combine all-purpose flour, whole-wheat flour, and salt in a food processor; pulse to mix. Add butter, and pulse until mixture resembles peas. Add sour cream, ice water, and lemon juice, and pulse until dough just begins to hold together. Transfer to a lightly floured work surface and pat into a disk. Wrap in plastic and refrigerate until chilled, about 1 hour.

2. Make the filling Preheat oven to 400°F. Line a baking sheet with parchment paper. Heat 1 tablespoon oil in a small skillet over medium-low. Add shallot and season with salt, and cook, stirring, until softened, about 5 minutes. Let cool.

3. Mix ricotta, lemon zest, garlic, 1 teaspoon thyme, 1 teaspoon oregano, and ½ teaspoon rosemary in a small bowl. Season with salt and pepper. Toss squash, celery root, potato, and remaining 1 teaspoon oil in a large bowl. Season with salt and pepper.

4. On a lightly floured work surface, roll out dough to a 13-inch round. Transfer to prepared baking sheet. Spread ricotta on dough, leaving a 1-inch border. Pile squash mixture on ricotta and fold 1½ inches of dough edge over vegetables. Sprinkle with thyme, oregano, and rosemary leaves. Brush dough edge with beaten egg.

5. Bake galette until starting to brown, 15 minutes. Sprinkle Parmigiano-Reggiano over filling, and bake until vegetables are tender and crust is golden, 15 to 20 minutes.

6. Mix honey and lemon juice in a small bowl. Drizzle lemon honey over galette. Serve warm or at room temperature. — GAIL SIMMONS

MAKE AHEAD The galette can be baked up to 3 hours ahead and rewarmed before serving.

WINE Pair with a full-bodied California Chardonnay.

Spicy Eggplant Gratin

Spicy Eggplant Gratin

ACTIVE 30 MIN; TOTAL 2 HR; SERVES 6

Chef and author Chris Behr roasts his eggplant instead of breading and frying it for this fresh, lighter take on eggplant Parm. In place of regular mozzarella, he opts for gooey smoked Scamorza cheese, which pairs perfectly with the creamy eggplant.

- 3 lb. eggplant, cut into 1-inch pieces
- ½ cup plus 3 Tbsp. extra-virgin olive oil, divided
- Kosher salt and black pepper
- 1 medium yellow onion, finely chopped
- 3 garlic cloves, chopped
- 1 tsp. crushed red pepper
- 30 fresh basil leaves, divided
- 2 (28-oz.) cans whole peeled tomatoes, crushed
- 6 oz. smoked Scamorza or mozzarella cheese, cubed (1½ cups), divided
- 3 oz. Parmigiano-Reggiano, finely grated (1 cup), divided
- Crusty bread, for serving

1. Preheat oven to 375°F. Position racks in the upper and lower thirds of the oven. Line 2 large rimmed baking sheets with foil. Divide eggplant between prepared baking sheets, and drizzle with 2 tablespoons oil; toss to coat. Season with salt and pepper, and spread out in a single layer. Bake until golden brown, 45 minutes, rotate the baking sheets halfway through. Keep the oven on.

2. Meanwhile, heat ¼ cup oil in a large enameled cast-iron casserole over medium-low. Add onion and season with salt, and cook, stirring occasionally, until softened, 8 minutes. Add garlic, red pepper, and 5 basil leaves, and cook, stirring, until garlic is softened and fragrant, 1 minute. Add tomatoes, and simmer, stirring occasionally, until sauce is thickened, about 45 minutes. Let cool slightly, then transfer to a food processor and pulse until almost smooth; season with salt. You should have about 6 cups of tomato sauce.

3. Spread 1 cup sauce in the bottom of a 2½-quart shallow baking dish. Top with half the eggplant and remaining basil leaves. Drizzle with 1 tablespoon oil. Spread 2 cups sauce on top, and sprinkle with 3 ounces Scamorza and 1½ ounces Parmigiano-Reggiano. Drizzle with 1 tablespoon oil. Top with remaining eggplant, sauce, 3 ounces Scamorza, and 1 tablespoon oil.

4. Bake gratin in upper third of the oven until bubbling, about 30 minutes. Remove from oven and preheat broiler to high. Sprinkle remaining 1½ ounces Parmigiano-Reggiano over top, and broil until golden brown, about 3 minutes. Let cool for 10 minutes before serving.
— CHRIS BEHR

MAKE AHEAD The gratin can be assembled through Step 3 and refrigerated overnight. Bring to room temperature before baking.

◆ ◆ ◆

Cacio e Pepe Broccolini with Crispy White Beans and Burrata

TOTAL 40 MIN; SERVES 4

Cookbook author Hetty McKinnon's riff on cacio e pepe *is as comforting and uncomplicated as the original. This warm salad captures the rich, elegant flavors of the classic Italian pasta dish and rounds them out with bitter charred Broccolini and crispy, creamy, flash-fried white beans. It makes a winning dinner party salad— perfect for sharing.*

- 2 bunches fresh Broccolini (about 1 lb.), trimmed and stems halved lengthwise
- 7 Tbsp. extra-virgin olive oil, divided, plus more for drizzling
- 1 tsp. fine sea salt, divided
- 2 (15.5-oz.) cans cannellini or navy beans, drained, rinsed, and patted dry
- 1 red Fresno chile, thinly sliced
- 1 garlic clove, finely chopped
- ¼ cup chopped fresh flat-leaf parsley
- 8 oz. Burrata cheese
- 1½ oz. pecorino Romano cheese, grated (about ⅓ cup)
- ½ to 1 tsp. black pepper
- ½ lemon, cut into 4 wedges

1. Heat a large skillet over medium-high until very hot, 4 to 5 minutes. Toss together Broccolini and 3 tablespoons oil in a large bowl until coated. Add half of Broccolini to skillet, and spread in an even layer. Cook until slightly charred and crisp-tender, 2 to 3 minutes per side. Transfer to a large bowl, and repeat with remaining Broccolini. Toss Broccolini with ¾ teaspoon salt.

2. Carefully wipe skillet clean, and return to heat over medium-high. Add 2 tablespoons oil; swirl to coat. Add half the beans; spread in an even layer. Cook, undisturbed, until outer skins of beans begin to peel back, crisp, and brown slightly, about 1 minute and 30 seconds. Add chile and garlic, stir, and cook, undisturbed, until fragrant, 15 to 30 seconds. Transfer mixture to bowl with Broccolini. Repeat procedure with remaining 2 tablespoons oil and remaining beans.

3. Gently toss Broccolini and beans with parsley and remaining ¼ teaspoon salt. Arrange Burrata in center of serving bowl, and surround with Broccolini and beans mixture. Sprinkle with pecorino Romano and black pepper. Drizzle with oil, and serve with lemon wedges. — HETTY MCKINNON

WINE Pair with a lemony, zesty Italian white.

Charred Vegetable Ragù

Pickled Pepper Macaroni and Cheese

ACTIVE 30 MIN; TOTAL 1 HR; SERVES 8

A mix of sweet and hot pickled peppers adds piquancy to and balances the richness of this mac and cheese. Crispy panko bread crumbs add crunch.

- 3 Tbsp. unsalted butter, melted, plus more for brushing
- 4 cups half-and-half
- 2 Tbsp. all-purpose flour
- 2 tsp. kosher salt
- 1 tsp. black pepper
- 1 cup water
- 1 lb. uncooked extra-wide egg noodles
- 2 cups shredded Fontina cheese
- 2 cups shredded sharp white cheddar cheese
- 1 cup chopped mixed hot and sweet pickled peppers, plus more for garnish
- 1 cup panko

1. Preheat oven to 425°F. Brush a 13- × 9-inch baking dish with butter.

2. Whisk half-and-half, flour, salt, pepper, and 1 cup water in a medium bowl. Stir in noodles, Fontina, white cheddar cheese, and mixed peppers. Scrape noodle mixture into prepared baking dish, and bake until bubbling and noodles are tender, about 30 minutes.

3. Preheat broiler and position a rack 8 inches from heat. Toss panko with 3 tablespoons butter in a small bowl until evenly moistened. Sprinkle panko mixture over macaroni and cheese, and broil until browned, 1 to 2 minutes. Garnish with peppers and serve. — JUSTIN CHAPPLE

WINE Pair with a full-bodied, creamy Chardonnay.

Charred Vegetable Ragù

ACTIVE 40 MIN; TOTAL 1 HR; SERVES 4

Comfort food takes the form of a slow-simmered Sunday sauce for F&W Associate Food Editor Kelsey Youngman. But when time is short, a quick but intense cooking method does the trick. In this case, broiling infuses this hearty vegetarian ragù with smoky richness. Ladled over a pile of tagliatelle and topped with cheese, this nourishing sauce tastes slow-cooked and comforting, especially on a wintry weeknight.

- 4 large portobello mushrooms, stemmed and quartered
- 1 garlic head
- 1 yellow onion, peeled and quartered
- 2 celery stalks, cut into thirds
- 2 carrots, peeled and cut into thirds
- 6 Tbsp. extra-virgin olive oil, divided
- 8 oz. fresh cremini mushrooms, stemmed and quartered
- ½ cup tomato paste
- 2 tsp. dried oregano
- ½ cup dry red wine
- 1 tsp. kosher salt, plus more to taste
- ½ tsp. black pepper
- 12 oz. uncooked bronze-cut durum wheat tagliatelle pasta
- 2 oz. Parmigiano-Reggiano cheese, grated (about ½ cup), plus more for serving

1. Preheat broiler to low with oven rack in middle of oven. Toss together portobellos, garlic, onion, celery, carrots, and 1 tablespoon oil on a large rimmed baking sheet lined with parchment paper. Spread in a single layer. Broil in preheated oven until vegetables are charred in spots, about 20 minutes, rotating pan and flipping vegetables halfway through. Let cool 5 minutes. Squeeze roasted garlic out of skins; discard skins. Transfer garlic and vegetable mixture to a food processor. Pulse until finely chopped, about 4 times; set aside.

2. Heat 3 tablespoons oil in a large, deep skillet over medium-high. Add mushrooms, and cook until bottoms are browned, about 3 minutes. Stir and cook until browned on all sides, 5 to 8 minutes. Stir in tomato paste and oregano, and cook, stirring constantly, about 1 minute. Add wine, and cook, stirring constantly, until slightly thickened, about 1 minute. Stir in roasted vegetable mixture and season with salt and pepper. Remove from heat.

3. Bring a large pot of salted water to a boil over high. Cook pasta according to package directions for al dente. Drain, reserving 1½ cups cooking liquid. Transfer cooked pasta to skillet with sauce, and return to heat over medium. Add Parmigiano-Reggiano and remaining 2 tablespoons oil. Stir in reserved cooking liquid, ½ cup at a time, until sauce is creamy, about 3 minutes. Season with salt to taste. Divide pasta among 4 warm bowls; top with additional Parmigiano-Reggiano. — KELSEY YOUNGMAN

MAKE AHEAD Ragù can be prepared, cooled completely, and stored in an airtight container in refrigerator up to 3 days.

NOTE To make this dish vegan, omit the cheese, or use vegan cheese.

WINE Pair with a smoky Italian red.

Baharat-Spiced Eggplant with Hazelnuts, Cherries, and Tarragon

TOTAL 1 HR; SERVES 4

F&W Best New Chefs 2017 Sara Kramer and Sarah Hymanson, of L.A.'s Kismet, brine eggplant before coating it in a fragrant spice mix and pan-frying. They create a magical plate of that eggplant along with pickled onions, sweet cherries, toasted hazelnuts, creamy labneh, and herbs.

EGGPLANT

- 8 cups warm water
- 1½ cups kosher salt
- 1 cup sugar
- 4 Chinese eggplants, cut crosswise into 3-inch pieces

ONIONS

- 3 cipollini onions, peeled and thinly sliced crosswise
- ½ cup warm water
- ½ cup distilled white vinegar
- 1 Tbsp. kosher salt
- 2 tsp. sugar

BAHARAT SPICE MIXTURE

- 1 Tbsp. whole allspice berries
- 2 tsp. coriander seeds
- 1 tsp. cumin seeds
- ¾ tsp. whole cloves
- 1 (½-inch) piece of cinnamon stick
- ¼ tsp. black peppercorns
- 11 cardamom pods, smashed and seeded (¼ tsp. seeds), pods discarded

ASSEMBLY

- 2 Tbsp. extra-virgin olive oil
- ½ garlic clove
- 2 cups Rainier cherries, halved and pitted
- 1 Tbsp. sugar
- 1 Tbsp. fresh lemon juice
  Kosher salt
  Canola oil, for frying
- ¼ cup hazelnuts, toasted, plus grated hazelnuts for serving
- ¼ cup fresh parsley leaves
- 2 Tbsp. fresh tarragon leaves
- 1 cup labneh
  Finely grated lemon zest, for serving

1. **Brine the eggplant** Mix 8 cups warm water, salt, and sugar in a large bowl; stir until dissolved. Cut a ⅛-inch-deep slit lengthwise down one side of each eggplant piece; do not cut in half. Add eggplant to brine and cover with a plate to submerge. Cover with plastic wrap and refrigerate for at least 3 hours or preferably overnight. Drain well and discard the brine.

2. **Make the onions** Place onions in a small bowl, and add ice water to cover; soak for 15 minutes. Drain. Mix ½ cup warm water, vinegar, salt, and sugar in the same bowl. Add soaked onions. Cover and refrigerate for at least 3 hours or overnight.

3. **Make the spice mixture** Combine allspice, coriander, cumin, cloves, cinnamon, black peppercorns, and cardamom pods in a dry skillet over medium-high. Toast until fragrant, about 2 minutes. Transfer to a spice grinder and let cool, then grind to a powder.

4. **Assemble the dish** Heat oil in a small skillet over medium-high. Add garlic and cook, stirring occasionally, until fragrant, about 3 minutes. Remove from heat and let garlic oil cool. Meanwhile, toss cherries, sugar, lemon juice, and a pinch of salt in a medium bowl.

5. In a large cast-iron skillet, heat 2 inches of canola oil to 325°F. Add drained eggplant and fry in batches, turning occasionally, until eggplant is completely tender, about 5 minutes per batch. Using a slotted spoon, transfer eggplant to a paper towel-lined baking sheet to drain. When cool enough to handle, open up eggplant pieces along cut side so they are flattened but still intact. Sprinkle eggplant all over with spice mixture and season all over with salt.

6. Carefully pour off all but 1 tablespoon hot canola oil from skillet. Heat skillet over medium-high and cook half the eggplant, turning once, until golden brown, about 4 minutes. Transfer to a plate and brush with garlic oil. Repeat with remaining eggplant.

7. Just before serving, drain onions. Transfer to a bowl and toss with toasted hazelnuts, parsley, and tarragon. Spread labneh on 4 plates and top with eggplant, cherries, and onion-herb mixture. Top with grated lemon zest and grated hazelnuts and serve. —SARA KRAMER & SARAH HYMANSON

MAKE AHEAD The spice mixture can be stored in an airtight container for up to 2 weeks.

Coconut Chickpeas with Winter Squash

ACTIVE 35 MIN; TOTAL 1 HR 10 MIN; SERVES 6 TO 8

Sweet plantain and lime peel round out this comforting vegan braise. If you have leftovers, rejoice—the flavors meld overnight in the refrigerator, making for an even tastier dish the day after.

- 3 Tbsp. olive oil
- 1 red onion, chopped
- 5 garlic cloves, finely chopped
- 1½ lb. butternut squash, peeled, seeded, and cut into 1-inch pieces
- 1 lb. delicata squash, halved, seeded, quartered, and cut into ½-inch-thick slices
- 1 large carrot, cut into ½-inch-thick slices
- 1 celery stalk, cut into ½-inch-thick slices
- 1 firm-ripe plantain, cut into ½-inch-thick slices
- 2 Tbsp. chopped fresh cilantro, plus ½ cup whole fresh cilantro leaves for garnish
- 1 bird chile, stemmed and thinly sliced
- 1 tsp. ground cumin
- 1 tsp. kosher salt, plus more
- 1 (13.5-oz.) can well-stirred unsweetened coconut milk
- 2 long lime zest strips
- 2 (15.5-oz.) cans chickpeas, rinsed and drained
- 2 Tbsp. fresh lime juice

1. Heal oil in a large enameled cast-iron Dutch oven or heavy pot over medium. Add onion and cook, stirring occasionally, until softened, about 5 minutes. Add garlic and cook, stirring, until fragrant, about 1 minute. Add butternut squash, delicata squash, carrot, celery, plantain, chopped cilantro, chile, cumin, and 1 teaspoon salt. Cook, covered, until vegetables start to soften, about 10 minutes. Add coconut milk, lime zest strips, and 2 cups water, and bring to a boil. Reduce heat to medium-low, and simmer, covered, until vegetables are tender, 20 to 25 minutes.

2. Add chickpeas and simmer until heated through, about 5 minutes. Season with salt. Stir in lime juice. Discard lime zest strips, and garnish with cilantro leaves before serving. — JOSEPH "JJ" JOHNSON

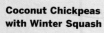

**Coconut Chickpeas
with Winter Squash**

Pasta & Grains

Caviar Carbonara,
RECIPE P. 163

15-Yolk Tagliolini

Preserved-Tomato Paccheri

ACTIVE 1 HR; TOTAL 6 HR; SERVES 6

For her unconventional tomato sauce, chef Missy Robbins marinates canned tomatoes in a mix of garlic, spices, citrus, and warm olive oil. The result is a supple, chunky, rich coating for paccheri (PAH-kur-ee), the wide tube-shape pasta.

- 4 (28-oz.) cans whole San Marzano tomatoes, drained, halved lengthwise, and seeded
- 4½ tsp. sugar
- 4½ tsp. kosher salt
- 1 Tbsp. fennel seeds
- 1 Tbsp. coriander seeds
- 2 cups plus 3 Tbsp. extra-virgin olive oil
- 7 garlic cloves, 2 crushed and 5 thinly sliced
- Wide strips of zest from 2 small lemons plus 1 tsp. finely grated zest
- Wide strips of zest from 1 small orange
- 2 fresh basil sprigs
- 2 fresh marjoram sprigs, plus 2 tsp. marjoram leaves
- 1½ tsp. crushed red pepper
- 1 lb. paccheri or other wide, tubular pasta
- ¼ cup freshly grated pecorino Romano cheese

1. Place tomato halves in a colander set over a bowl. Sprinkle with sugar and salt, and toss gently. Let stand at room temperature for 2 hours.

2. Meanwhile, in a small skillet over medium-low, toast the fennel and coriander seeds, shaking pan, until very fragrant, about 2 minutes. Transfer seeds to a spice grinder or mortar and let cool slightly, then coarsely grind.

3. Combine 2 cups oil, crushed seeds, crushed garlic, lemon and orange zest, and basil and marjoram sprigs in a small saucepan. Warm over low until oil begins to bubble, 7 minutes. Transfer drained tomatoes to a deep ceramic baking dish and pour warm oil over them. Let stand at room temperature for 3 hours.

4. Using a slotted spoon, transfer preserved tomatoes to a bowl. Using your hands or a metal spoon, coarsely crush them; you should have 3 cups.

5. Heat remaining 3 tablespoons oil in a large skillet over medium. Add sliced garlic, and cook, stirring, until fragrant but not browned, about 2 minutes. Add crushed tomatoes and red pepper, and cook until tomatoes are warmed through, about 2 minutes; keep warm over low.

6. In a pot of salted boiling water, cook paccheri until al dente; drain. Add to skillet and stir to coat. Stir in grated lemon zest and marjoram leaves. Transfer paccheri to a bowl, garnish with pecorino, and serve.

— MISSY ROBBINS

MAKE AHEAD The tomatoes can be refrigerated in the oil for up to 4 days. The strained oil can be reserved for another use.

WINE Pair with an aromatic Piedmontese red, such as a Barbera d'Asti.

◆ ◆ ◆

15-Yolk Tagliolini

ACTIVE 1 HR 30 MIN; TOTAL 2 HR; MAKES 1 LB. PASTA

White truffles call for fresh, homemade pasta, and this ultra-rich version, made with 15 egg yolks, creates a tender, silky base for freshly shaved truffles.

- 2¼ cups 00 flour (about 9 oz.), plus more for dusting (see Note)
- Kosher salt
- 15 large egg yolks

1. Combine flour and a pinch of salt in a food processor. With machine on, slowly pour in egg yolks. Process until ingredients come together, about 1 minute.

2. Remove dough from food processor. Transfer to a well-floured work surface, and knead until dough is smooth and springs back when pressed with thumb, about 15 minutes. Wrap dough tightly in plastic wrap, and refrigerate at least 30 minutes or up to overnight.

3. Let dough return to room temperature. Cut into 6 pieces. Working with one piece at a time, keeping others covered, pass pasta through a pasta machine set to widest setting. Reduce width to second-widest setting, and run through again. Fold dough in thirds (like a letter), and repeat passing procedure through widest and second-widest settings. Set dough sheet on a floured surface, and dust with more flour. Repeat with remaining pieces.

4. Let pasta sheets dry until leathery, about 10 minutes. Run one sheet through the spaghetti-cutting attachments of pasta machine. (Alternatively, loosely roll sheets from short end to short end, and cut with a knife into ⅛-inch strips.) Shake out excess flour, and place portion on a floured baking sheet; sprinkle with flour. Repeat with remaining sheets.

— MARY-FRANCES HECK

NOTE Doppio zero ("double zero," or 00) is a fine Italian flour available at specialty food shops and from amazon.com.

MAKE AHEAD Uncooked pasta will keep overnight, tented loosely with plastic wrap. To freeze, place baking sheet with individual coils in freezer until solid, about 6 hours, then transfer to a freezer bag. Pasta will keep up to a month in freezer; cook directly from frozen, adding 1 to 2 minutes to cooking time.

Baked Orecchiette with Pork Sugo

ACTIVE 1 HR; TOTAL 4 HR; SERVES 8

In Italian cuisine, a sugo is a gravy or sauce. The dish is an excellent alternative to the usual baked pasta, because it's not as heavy and cheesy but still delicious and satisfying.

- 3¼ lb. boneless pork shoulder, cut into 1-inch pieces
- Kosher salt
- Freshly ground black pepper
- 3 Tbsp. extra-virgin olive oil
- 4 carrots, cut into ¼-inch dice
- 4 celery ribs, cut into ¼-inch dice
- 1 large sweet onion, cut into ¼-inch dice
- 4 garlic cloves, very finely chopped
- 1 (14-oz.) can diced tomatoes
- 1½ cups dry red wine
- 4 fresh thyme sprigs
- 5 cups chicken stock or low-sodium broth
- 2 Tbsp. chopped fresh flat-leaf parsley
- 1 Tbsp. chopped fresh oregano
- ½ tsp. crushed red pepper
- 1½ lb. orecchiette
- 2 cups freshly grated Parmigiano-Reggiano cheese (7 oz.)

1. Season pork with salt and black pepper. In a large enameled cast-iron casserole, heat olive oil until shimmering. Add pork in a single layer and cook over medium high until the pieces are golden brown all over, about 12 minutes. Add carrots, celery, onion, and garlic, and cook until softened and browned in spots, about 8 minutes. Add tomatoes and their juices, and bring to a simmer. Add red wine and thyme sprigs, and cook over high until the wine is reduced by half, about 5 minutes. Add stock and bring to a boil. Cover and simmer over low until pork is very tender, about 2 hours.

2. Using a slotted spoon, transfer the pork and vegetables to a food processor; discard thyme sprigs. Pulse just until pork is shredded. Scrape shredded pork and vegetables back into the casserole. Stir in chopped parsley, oregano, and red pepper, and season with salt and black pepper.

3. Preheat oven to 375°F. Cook orecchiette in a large pot of boiling salted water until it is still firm to the bite, about 5 minutes; drain well. Add orecchiette to the casserole

and toss with pork sauce. Scrape pasta into an extra-large baking dish and sprinkle with Parmigiano-Reggiano. Bake casserole in the upper third of preheated oven until golden brown on top and bubbling, about 35 minutes. Let stand 10 minutes before serving. —ETHAN STOWELL

♦   ♦   ♦

Cavatelli with Sparerib Ragù

ACTIVE 1 HR; TOTAL 3 HR; SERVES 10 TO 12

This hearty ragù from New York City chef Josh Laurano features both little riblets and tender chunks of sparerib meat in a decadent tomato sauce.

- 1 (4-lb.) rack of pork spareribs, rack cut crosswise through the rib bones into 3 strips (have your butcher do this)
- ¼ cup plus 1 Tbsp. extra-virgin olive oil, divided
- Kosher salt and black pepper
- 1 large yellow onion, finely chopped
- 5 carrots, finely chopped
- 4 celery ribs, finely chopped
- 4 garlic cloves, crushed
- 2 Tbsp. chopped fresh thyme
- ½ lb. pork skin, cut into small dice (optional)
- 2 cups dry red wine
- 1 (28-oz.) can crushed tomatoes
- 2 lb. cavatelli
- 1 cup freshly grated Parmigiano-Reggiano cheese (3 oz.), plus more for serving

1. Preheat oven to 450°F. Cut center strip of spareribs into individual riblets and set on a baking sheet. Cut each outer strip into 3 equal pieces and add to baking sheet. Drizzle ribs with 2 tablespoons oil, season with salt and pepper, and turn to coat. Roast until golden, 20 minutes. Let cool slightly, then tie individual ribs in a cheesecloth bundle.

2. Heat 2 tablespoons oil in a large enameled cast-iron casserole over medium. Add onion, carrots, celery, garlic, thyme, and pork skin, if using. Cook, stirring, until vegetables are softened, 15 minutes. Add wine, and cook until reduced by half, 5 minutes. Stir in tomatoes, 2 cups water, and roasted rib strips, and bring to a simmer. Cook over low, stirring occasionally, 45 minutes. Add cheesecloth rib bundle. Cook, stirring, until sauce is thick and all ribs are tender, about 1 hour longer. Remove cheesecloth bundle and reserve riblets.

3. Transfer rib strips to a work surface and remove meat from bones. Add meat to ragù; discard bones.

4. In a large pot of salted boiling water, cook pasta until al dente. Drain, reserving 1 cup pasta water. Return pasta to pot and add reserved water, ragù, remaining 1 tablespoon oil, and 1 cup Parmigiano-Reggiano. Season with salt and pepper, and toss until well coated. Mound pasta in bowls, garnish with riblets, and serve, passing additional cheese at the table. — JOSH LAURANO

WINE Pair with a bright, firm Italian red, such as L'Aspetto Toscana.

♦   ♦   ♦

White Truffle Tagliolini

TOTAL 20 MIN; SERVES 4

Generous portions of this pasta dish perfectly showcase the white truffle's heady aroma. Use the tagliolini recipe on the previous page, or purchase fresh spaghetti.

- 1 lb. fresh tagliolini (recipe, p. 159) or spaghetti
- Kosher salt
- ½ cup best-quality butter (4 oz.), divided
- 2 oz. Parmesan cheese, grated (about ½ cup)
- 1 oz. fresh Alba truffle, shaved

1. Bring a large pot of lightly salted water to a boil. Add pasta, and stir gently with tongs. Boil until pasta is cooked but still slightly chewy, about 2 minutes.

2. While pasta cooks, melt ¼ cup butter in a large skillet over high. Using tongs, transfer cooked pasta to skillet, and stir to evenly coat with butter. Use a ladle to add about 1 cup pasta cooking liquid to skillet, and continue stirring rapidly. Add remaining ¼ cup butter, and shake and stir pan until the simmering water reduces slightly and forms a creamy sauce that clings to the pasta. Remove from heat, sprinkle pasta with Parmesan, and continue stirring until pasta partially absorbs cooking liquid and forms a creamy sauce. If pasta looks dry, add a splash more cooking liquid. Divide pasta among 4 bowls, and top with shaved truffle. Serve immediately. — MARY-FRANCES HECK

WINE Pair with an aromatic Piedmontese red, such as a Barbera d'Asti.

White Truffle Tagliolini

**Toasted Capellini with
Clams and Dashi**

Caviar Carbonara

PHOTO P. 157

ACTIVE 1 HR; TOTAL 2 HR 30 MIN; SERVES 4

There's no better night than New Year's Eve to enjoy silky ribbons of fresh pasta topped with copious amounts of caviar.

PASTA

- 1¾ cups 00 flour, plus more for dusting (see Note, p. 159)
- 2 tsp. kosher salt
- 4 large egg yolks
- 1 large egg
- 1½ Tbsp. extra-virgin olive oil

CARBONARA

- 3 large egg yolks
- 1 large egg
- ½ cup finely grated Parmigiano-Reggiano
- 1 Tbsp. finely grated lemon zest
- ½ tsp. kosher salt
- 1 tsp. black pepper
- 60 grams caviar
- Snipped fresh dill, for garnish

1. Make the pasta Place 1¾ cups flour and salt in a food processor; pulse to mix. Beat egg yolks, whole egg, and oil in a medium bowl. Add to flour in food processor, and pulse until dough just comes together. Transfer to a lightly floured work surface and knead until very smooth but stiff, 5 to 10 minutes. Cover with plastic wrap and let stand at room temperature for 1 hour.

2. Divide dough into 4 pieces and work with 1 piece at a time, keeping the rest covered. Press dough to flatten it. Using a pasta machine set at widest setting, run dough through successively narrower settings until you reach sixth one. Cut pasta sheet into a 10-inch length, lay it on a lightly floured work surface, and generously dust with flour. Repeat with remaining dough.

3. Loosely roll up pasta sheets and then, using a very sharp knife, cut into scant ¾-inch-wide ribbons. Transfer pappardelle to a large baking sheet and gently toss with more flour. Let stand at room temperature for 30 minutes.

4. In a large pot of salted boiling water, cook pasta until al dente, 2 to 3 minutes. Drain, reserving 1 cup cooking water.

5. Make the carbonara Beat egg yolks, whole egg, cheese, lemon zest, ½ teaspoon salt, and 1 teaspoon pepper in a large bowl. Very gradually whisk in ½ cup reserved hot pasta water to temper eggs. Add pasta and half the caviar, and vigorously toss until hot and creamy, 1 to 2 minutes. Transfer to bowls and top with dill and dollops of remaining caviar. — JUSTIN CHAPPLE

MAKE AHEAD The uncooked pappardelle can be covered with plastic wrap and refrigerated overnight.

WINE Pair with an elegant, brioche-scented Champagne.

◆ ◆ ◆

Toasted Capellini with Clams and Dashi

TOTAL 1 HR 15 MIN; SERVES 2

Chef Joshua Pinsky created this Asian-accented version of the classic Portuguese dish fideos by infusing noodles with a flavorful broth made with, among other ingredients, dashi and soy sauce.

- 1 tsp. dashi powder (see *Note)
- 2 dozen littleneck clams, scrubbed
- ¾ cup fresh apple cider
- 2 Tbsp. Asian fish sauce
- 1 Tbsp. plus 1 tsp. white soy sauce (see **Note)
- 1 Tbsp. tobanjan (see **Note)
- 1 Tbsp. unsalted butter
- 4 oz. capellini, broken in half
- 1 cup coarsely chopped green cabbage
- 1 garlic clove, thinly sliced
- 1 (2-inch) piece fresh ginger, peeled and cut into matchsticks
- 1 small leek, white and light green parts only, thinly sliced
- 1 serrano chile, halved lengthwise, seeded, and thinly sliced on the diagonal
- 1 cup coarsely chopped escarole
- 1 Tbsp. small fresh oregano leaves

1. Preheat oven to 450°F. Bring ¾ cup water to a boil in a small saucepan. Stir in dashi powder until dissolved.

2. Bring 2½ cups water to a boil in a large pot. Add clams, cover, and cook over medium-high 5 to 7 minutes; transfer to a baking sheet as they open, and discard any that don't. Strain ¾ cup clam cooking liquid into a large saucepan. Add dashi, apple cider, fish sauce, white soy sauce, and tobanjan to make a clam broth.

3. Melt butter in a medium skillet. Add capellini, and toast over medium-high, stirring, until golden, 3 to 4 minutes. Add half the clam broth and layer cabbage, garlic, ginger, leek, and serrano chile on top; do not stir. Bake until all the broth is absorbed and pasta is al dente, about 15 minutes.

4. Add steamed clams to remaining broth in saucepan. Stir in escarole, and simmer until heated through. Stir in oregano. Transfer pasta and vegetables to bowls, top with steamed clams and escarole, and serve. — DAVID CHANG

*NOTE Dashi powder is available at many health food stores and at Asian markets.

**NOTE White soy sauce, also known as shoyu, and tobanjan, a spicy, fermented bean paste also known as doubanjiang, are available at Asian markets, too.

MAKE AHEAD The dashi can be refrigerated for 3 days.

WINE Pair with a green and flinty Italian white, such a Vigneto Reiné Mataòssu.

Ricotta-Filled
Handkerchief Pasta with
Pesto and Marinara

Ricotta-Filled Handkerchief Pasta with Pesto and Marinara

TOTAL 2 HR 15 MIN; SERVES 8

Known as mandilli, *this dish from Boston chef Tim Cushman has something for everyone who loves Italian classics. First he coats delicate sheets of pasta with pesto, then stuffs them with ricotta and sets them atop a pool of tomato sauce.*

PASTA

- 1½ cups (8 oz.) 00 flour (see Note, p. 159)
- ½ cup durum semolina flour, plus more for dusting
- 1 tsp. kosher salt
- 10 large egg yolks
- 1 Tbsp. extra-virgin olive oil

PESTO

- 1¼ cups blanched almonds
- 4 garlic cloves
- 2¼ cups extra-virgin olive oil
- ¼ cup water
- 4 cups fresh basil leaves
- 2 cups freshly grated Parmigiano-Reggiano cheese (6 oz.)
- 1¼ cups freshly grated pecorino Romano cheese (4 oz.), plus more for garnish
- ⅓ cup mascarpone cheese
- Kosher salt

MARINARA

- 2 (28-oz.) cans whole peeled San Marzano tomatoes
- 2 Tbsp. extra-virgin olive oil
- 1 garlic clove, minced
- Pinch of sugar
- Kosher salt
- 2 cups fresh ricotta cheese (1 lb.), divided

1. Make the pasta Whisk 00 flour, ½ cup semolina flour, and salt in a medium bowl. Whisk egg yolks, oil, and ¼ cup water in another bowl. Mound flour mixture on a work surface and make a well in center. Pour beaten yolks into well and gradually incorporate flour with a fork, starting with inner rim of well and working your way out until all flour is incorporated and a soft dough forms. Knead dough until smooth and elastic, about 10 minutes. Wrap in plastic and refrigerate for 1 hour.

2. Cut dough into 8 equal pieces and cover with a kitchen towel. Lightly dust 1 piece of dough with semolina flour and flatten slightly. Run dough twice through a pasta machine at widest setting. Run dough twice through successively narrower settings until it is ⅛- to 1/16-inch thick and 14 to 16 inches long. Lay pasta sheet on a semolina-dusted baking sheet and generously dust with more semolina. Repeat with remaining 7 pieces of dough. Keep pasta sheets covered with a damp kitchen towel.

3. Make the pesto Combine almonds, garlic, and oil in a food processor; pulse until smooth. Add basil, and pulse until finely chopped. Add Parmesan, 1¼ cups pecorino, and mascarpone, and pulse until smooth. Season pesto with salt and scrape into a large bowl.

4. Make the marinara Place tomatoes with their juices in a food processor, and pulse until almost smooth. Heat oil in a large saucepan over medium. Add garlic, and cook, stirring, until fragrant, 1 minute. Add pureed tomatoes and sugar. Season with salt and bring to a simmer. Cook over medium-low, stirring occasionally, until thickened, about 30 minutes; keep warm.

5. Meanwhile, preheat oven to 450°F. Line 2 rimmed baking sheets with parchment paper. In a very large pot of salted boiling water, cook 2 pasta sheets until al dente, about 3 minutes. Using a slotted spoon, lift out pasta sheets and drain slightly, then turn gently in pesto to coat. Lay one pasta sheet on a prepared baking sheet, and dollop ¼ cup ricotta near one end. Fold one-third of pasta sheet over ricotta, then fold rest of sheet over onto itself. Repeat to fill second pesto-coated sheet, then repeat entire process with remaining pasta sheets, pesto, and ricotta. Cover folded handkerchief pasta with foil and bake until hot throughout, 10 minutes.

6. Spoon marinara sauce into shallow bowls. Top with stuffed pasta handkerchiefs, garnish with pecorino, and serve. — TIM CUSHMAN

MAKE AHEAD The pesto and marinara sauce can each be refrigerated for 3 days.

WINE Pair with a fruit-forward Italian red, such as Barbara d'Asti.

Busiate with Brussels Sprouts, Mint, and Two Cheeses

TOTAL 40 MIN; SERVES 6

Michelin-starred chef Ignacio Mattos' first rule of pasta: "Make sure your cooking water is well salted, so it tastes like the sea." His second rule is to use just a few well-chosen ingredients—like Brussels sprouts, lemon, mint, and pecorino—to make a wonderfully satisfying dish.

- 1 lb. busiate or other corkscrew pasta
- ½ cup extra-virgin olive oil, divided
- 12 oz. Brussels sprouts, thinly sliced on a mandoline (6 cups)
- 2 shallots, thinly sliced
- 1 garlic clove, thinly sliced
- ¼ cup fresh ricotta cheese
- 1 tsp. finely grated lemon zest
- Pinch of crushed red pepper
- Kosher salt and black pepper
- ¼ cup chopped fresh mint, plus more for garnish
- Freshly grated pecorino Romano cheese, for garnish

1. In a pot of salted boiling water, cook busiate until al dente; drain, reserving 2 cups pasta water. Wipe out pot.

2. Heat 3 tablespoons oil in a large skillet over medium. Add Brussels sprouts and cook, stirring, until softened, about 3 minutes. Add shallots, garlic, and 1 tablespoon oil, and cook until Brussels sprouts are lightly golden, about 3 minutes. Stir in ricotta, lemon zest, and red pepper, and season with salt and black pepper.

3. Return pasta and pasta water to pot. Add Brussels sprout mixture, remaining ¼ cup oil, and ¼ cup mint, and toss until a sauce forms, 2 minutes. Garnish with black pepper, pecorino, and mint, and serve. — IGNACIO MATTO

WINE Pair with a flinty, minerally Sicilian white, such as Pietramarina Etna Bianco Superiore.

Baked Rigatoni with Milk-Braised Pork, Ricotta, and Lemon

ACTIVE 45 MIN; TOTAL 4 HR 30 MIN; SERVES 8

Chef Ryan Hardy of Pasquale Jones in New York's Little Italy creates dishes like this sumptuous baked pasta with tender braised pork. The pureed garlic-infused milk that the pork cooks in makes an incredibly flavorful sauce.

- ¼ cup extra-virgin olive oil, divided
- 1 (4-lb.) boneless pork shoulder roast
  Kosher salt and black pepper
- 12 garlic cloves, minced
- ½ cup dry white wine
- 3 qt. whole milk
- 6 fresh rosemary sprigs, plus chopped rosemary for garnish
- 1 bay leaf
- 5 (3-inch) strips of lemon zest
- 1 lb. rigatoni
- 2 cups fresh ricotta cheese (1 lb.)
  Freshly grated pecorino Romano cheese

1. Preheat oven to 375°F. Heat 2 tablespoons oil in a large enameled cast-iron casserole over medium-high. Rub pork all over with remaining 2 tablespoons oil and season with salt and pepper. Add to casserole and cook until browned all over, about 8 minutes; transfer to a plate. Add garlic to casserole, and cook, stirring, until golden, 1 to 2 minutes. Add wine, and cook until almost evaporated, about 2 minutes.

2. Add milk, rosemary sprigs, bay leaf, and lemon zest to casserole, and bring to a simmer. Add pork, and braise in oven until meat is very tender, about 3 hours. Let pork cool in casserole to room temperature.

3. Transfer pork to a work surface and cut in half. Coarsely chop 1 piece; reserve remaining pork for another use. Working in 2 batches, puree cooking liquid in a blender until smooth. Strain through a fine wire-mesh strainer, pressing down on solids; discard solids.

4. Preheat oven to 425°F. Lightly grease a 3½- or 4-quart baking dish. In a pot of salted boiling water, cook pasta until al dente. Drain and transfer to a large bowl. Add chopped pork and 3 cups cooking liquid, season with salt and pepper, and toss to coat. Transfer pasta to prepared baking dish and dollop ricotta on top. Cover with foil and bake until pasta is tender, about 20 minutes. Uncover and bake until golden on top, about 15 minutes longer. Garnish with pepper and chopped rosemary. Serve with grated pecorino.
— RYAN HARDY & TIM CASPARE

MAKE AHEAD The braised pork can be refrigerated in its cooking liquid for 3 days.

WINE Pair with a fruity, lightly floral red, such as St.-Joseph (French Syrah).

◆━━━━◆━━━━◆

Soft Polenta with Mixed Mushrooms and Gremolata

TOTAL 1 HR; SERVES 6 TO 8

Los Angeles chef Suzanne Goin adores the straightforward flavors in this vegetarian dish: the sautéed mushrooms and greens, and the tangy mascarpone that melts into the creamy polenta.

- 1½ cups medium-grain polenta
  Kosher salt
- 6 Tbsp. unsalted butter
  Freshly ground black pepper
- ½ cup chopped flat-leaf parsley
- 1 tsp. chopped garlic
- 1 Tbsp. finely grated lemon zest
- ¼ cup extra-virgin olive oil
- 1½ lb. mixed mushrooms, such as cremini, oyster, and stemmed shiitake, thickly sliced or quartered
- 4 oz. young greens, such as spinach, Russian kale, or pea shoots, coarsely chopped (4 cups packed)
- ½ cup mascarpone cheese

1. In a large saucepan, bring 8 cups water to a boil. Whisk in polenta in a slow, steady stream. Add 1 tablespoon salt and cook over medium-low, whisking frequently, until polenta is thickened and tender, about 30 minutes. Whisk in 4 tablespoons butter and season with salt and pepper. Press plastic wrap directly on surface of polenta to prevent a film from forming; cover and keep warm.

2. Meanwhile, on a work surface, mince parsley, garlic, and lemon zest. Transfer gremolata to a small bowl.

3. In a large skillet, melt 1 tablespoon butter in 2 tablespoons olive oil. Add half the mushrooms and season with salt and pepper. Cook over medium-high, stirring occasionally, until the mushrooms are golden and tender, about 5 minutes. Stir in half the chopped greens and cook for 1 minute; transfer the mixture to a large bowl. Repeat with the remaining butter, oil, mushrooms, and chopped greens.

4. Pour the polenta onto a large platter; if the polenta is very thick, reheat with ½ cup water before serving. Spoon the mushrooms and greens on top and garnish with the mascarpone. Sprinkle the gremolata over the polenta and serve warm. — SUZANNE GOIN

MAKE AHEAD The cooked polenta can be refrigerated overnight. Rewarm with a little water before serving.

WINE Earthy Rhône reds, like the 2011 Le Pigoulet en Provence Vin de Pays de Vaucluse, and rich Rhône whites, like the 2010 Gilles Robin Les Marelles Crozes Hermitage Blanc.

Baked Rigatoni with
Milk-Braised Pork,
Ricotta, and Lemon

Black Rice with Ginger
and Cardamom,
RECIPE P. 170

Red Lentil Dal with
Mustard Seeds,
RECIPE P. 171

BLACK RICE FEAST

While prime rib may have been the centerpiece of your holiday feast for years, consider reinventing your celebration this season with something completely different. Chef Akasha Richmond of Los Angeles's Akasha created this menu for a fantastic Indian meal centered on bowls of aromatic black rice and nutty brown basmati.

Masala Prawns,
RECIPE P. 170

Ginger Turkey Meatballs,
RECIPE P. 171

BLACK RICE FEAST MENU

Black Rice with Ginger and Cardamom

ACTIVE 15 MIN; TOTAL 1 HR; SERVES 8 TO 10

This rich-tasting black rice is fragrant with cardamom.

- 2 Tbsp. ghee (see Note)
- 1 large shallot, thinly sliced
- 2 Tbsp. minced peeled fresh ginger
- 2 cups black rice (14 oz.), rinsed and drained
- 1 Tbsp. green cardamom pods, cracked
- Sea salt
- Thinly sliced scallions, for garnish

Heat ghee in a medium saucepan over medium. Add shallot and ginger, and cook, stirring occasionally, until softened and lightly browned, about 5 minutes. Stir in rice and cardamom, and cook, stirring, for 2 minutes. Add 3 cups water and a generous pinch of sea salt, and bring to a boil. Cover and cook over low until rice is tender and water is absorbed, about 30 minutes. Remove from heat and let steam for 15 minutes. Fluff rice with a fork and season with salt. Transfer to a serving bowl, garnish with scallions, and serve. — AKASHA RICHMOND

NOTE Ghee is a clarified butter that's available at Indian markets, Whole Foods, and amazon.com.

Brown Basmati Rice with Coconut and Turmeric

TOTAL 1 HR 10 MIN; SERVES 8 TO 10

The nutty flavor of brown basmati rice is amped up here with coconut milk, turmeric, and fresh mint.

- 2 cups brown basmati rice (12 oz.), rinsed and drained
- 1 cup unsweetened coconut milk
- 1 (2-inch) piece of fresh turmeric, peeled and finely grated (1 Tbsp.)
- Kosher salt
- Fresh mint leaves, for garnish

Combine rice, 2 cups water, coconut milk, turmeric, and a generous pinch of salt in a medium saucepan. Bring to a boil, cover, and cook over low until rice is tender and liquid has been absorbed, 35 to 40 minutes. Remove from heat and let steam for 15 minutes. Fluff rice with a fork and season with salt. Transfer to a serving bowl, garnish with mint leaves, and serve. — AKASHA RICHMOND

Masala Prawns

TOTAL 1 HR; MAKES 24 SHRIMP

A soak in a mix of spices, shallots, ginger, and lime before grilling punches up the flavor of these meaty shrimp.

- ⅓ cup fresh lime juice
- 2 small shallots, minced
- 3 Tbsp. minced peeled fresh ginger
- 2 Tbsp. canola oil, plus more for brushing
- 1 Tbsp. chaat masala (see Note*)
- 2 garlic cloves, minced
- 1½ tsp. ground fenugreek
- 1½ tsp. dried mango powder (see Note**)
- 1½ tsp. fine sea salt
- ¾ tsp. ground coriander
- ¾ tsp. crushed red pepper
- 24 large shrimp, shelled and deveined
- Lime wedges and fresh cilantro leaves, for serving

1. Combine lime juice, shallots, ginger, canola oil, chaat masala, cloves, fenugreek, mango powder, sea salt, coriander, and red pepper in a medium bowl. Add shrimp; toss well. Cover and refrigerate at least 30 minutes or up to 2 hours.

2. Preheat a grill pan and brush with canola oil. Remove shrimp from marinade and scrape off some of excess marinade. Grill over medium-high, turning once, until just cooked through, 4 minutes. Transfer shrimp to a platter, and serve with lime wedges and cilantro. — AKASHA RICHMOND

NOTE* Chaat masala is an Indian spice blend made with black sea salt.

NOTE** Dried mango powder (amchoor) is a citrusy seasoning made from unripe green mangoes. Look for these products at Indian markets and on amazon.com.

WINE Pair with a rich, tropical-fruit-inflected Riesling.

Red Lentil Dal with Mustard Seeds

ACTIVE 35 MIN; TOTAL 1 HR; SERVES 8 TO 10

Cumin, ginger, and bay leaf flavor these fragrant Indian-style stewed lentils.

- 4 cups red lentils (1½ lb.), picked over
- 2 bay leaves
- 1 tsp. ground turmeric
- ¼ cup ghee (see Note in recipe at far left)
- 1½ Tbsp. brown mustard seeds
- 2 tsp. cumin seeds
- 1 large onion, minced
- ¼ cup minced peeled fresh ginger
- 1 (28-oz.) can whole peeled tomatoes, drained and chopped
- 1 serrano chile, minced
- 2 tsp. ground coriander
- Kosher salt and black pepper
- Yogurt and chopped fresh cilantro, cucumber, and tomato, for serving

1. Combine red lentils, bay leaves, turmeric, and 12 cups water in a large cast-iron casserole; bring to a boil. Simmer over medium, stirring frequently, until lentils break down to a thick puree, about 40 minutes. Discard bay leaves.

2. Meanwhile, heat ghee in a large skillet over medium-high. Add mustard and cumin seeds, and cook, stirring, until seeds start to pop, about 1 minute. Add onion and ginger, and cook, stirring occasionally, until onion is softened and lightly browned, about 8 minutes. Stir in tomatoes, chile, and coriander, and cook until tomatoes just start to break down, about 5 minutes. Season tomato mixture with salt and black pepper.

3. Stir tomato mixture into dal, and cook over medium, stirring occasionally, about 10 minutes. Season with salt and black pepper. Serve with yogurt, cilantro, cucumber, and tomato. — AKASHA RICHMOND

MAKE AHEAD The dal can be refrigerated for 3 days. Reheat gently before serving.

Ginger Turkey Meatballs

TOTAL 45 MIN; MAKES 40

- 2 lb. 85% lean ground turkey
- ½ cup minced red onion
- 3 Tbsp. finely grated peeled fresh ginger
- 3 Tbsp. sambar masala (see Note)
- 1 tsp. finely grated peeled fresh turmeric
- 1½ tsp. fine sea salt
- 2 Tbsp. canola oil, divided
- Fresh cilantro leaves, for garnish

1. Preheat oven to 400°F. Mix ground turkey, onion, ginger, masala, turmeric, and salt in a large bowl. Using a 2-tablespoon scoop, scoop and roll meatballs and place on a large baking sheet.

2. Heat 1 tablespoon canola oil in a very large skillet over medium. Add half the meatballs and cook, turning, until browned all over, 5 to 7 minutes. Using a slotted spoon, transfer meatballs to baking sheet. Repeat with remaining 1 tablespoon canola oil and meatballs.

3. Bake meatballs until cooked through, about 8 minutes. Arrange meatballs on a platter, garnish with cilantro, and serve. — AKASHA RICHMOND

NOTE Sambar masala is a spice blend made with myriad spices, including coriander, fenugreek, and cumin. Look for it at Indian markets and on amazon.com.

MAKE AHEAD The meatballs can be made up to 6 hours ahead; serve at room temperature or reheat gently.

WINE Pair with a berry-forward, lightly floral Beaujolais.

Soups,
Salads
& Sides

**Escarole and Golden
Beet Salad with Toasted
Hazelnuts,** RECIPE P. 182

Caramelized Onion
and Bread Soup
with Bruléed
Bleu Cheese

Caramelized Onion and Bread Soup with Bruléed Bleu Cheese

ACTIVE 1 HR 20 MIN; TOTAL 1 HR 40 MIN; SERVES 6

4½ lb. mixed onions (such as 2 large yellow onions, 2 large red onions, and 2 large sweet onions), halved and thinly sliced lengthwise (about 16 cups)

2 Tbsp. extra-virgin olive oil

2 Tbsp. unsalted butter

¼ cup oloroso sherry

6 cups low-sodium vegetable broth

8 fresh thyme sprigs

1 Tbsp. kosher salt, plus more

¾ tsp. freshly ground black pepper, plus more

2 tsp. sherry vinegar

6 day-old whole-grain rustic bread slices, halved

4 oz. Stilton cheese, chilled and thinly sliced or crumbled

1. In a stockpot over medium-high, toss together onions, oil, and butter. Cook, stirring occasionally, until onions start to caramelize, about 20 minutes. Reduce heat to medium, and continue to cook, stirring and scraping any browned bits from bottom of pot, until onions are tender and caramelized, about 25 minutes.

2. Add sherry and cook, scraping up browned bits from bottom of pot. Simmer over medium, stirring constantly, until sherry is almost evaporated, 2 to 3 minutes. Stir in broth, thyme, salt, and pepper. Increase heat to high, and bring to a boil. Reduce heat to medium-low, and simmer, partially covered, until flavors marry, 20 to 25 minutes. Stir in vinegar and cook 1 minute; add salt and pepper to taste.

3. Preheat oven to broil with oven rack 6 inches from heat. Remove and discard thyme sprigs. Divide hot soup evenly among 6 ovenproof crocks or bowls, and place on a rimmed baking sheet. Place 2 bread pieces on each bowl, and gently push them down until half-submerged but still at top of soup. Add cheese slices (or a handful of crumbles) to each bowl. Broil until cheese is melted, bubbly, and browned in spots, 2 to 3 minutes. —DANA FRANK & ANDREA SLONECKER

WINE Pair with an oloroso sherry. For a red wine, try Listán Negro.

Truffle-Infused French Onion Soup

ACTIVE 1 HR 30 MIN; TOTAL 3 HR 30 MIN; SERVES 10

4 Tbsp. unsalted butter

3 lb. sweet onions, sliced ¼ inch thick

2 bay leaves

½ cup water

¼ cup all-purpose flour

1 cup dry red wine

3 qt. beef stock, preferably homemade

10 fresh thyme sprigs, tied with cotton string

Kosher salt and freshly ground black pepper

1 baguette, sliced ⅓ inch

¼ cup extra-virgin olive oil

10 oz. truffled pecorino cheese, coarsely shredded (3 cups)

1. Melt the butter in a large heavy casserole. Add the onions and bay leaves, cover and cook over medium-high heat, stirring occasionally, until the onions are very soft, about 15 minutes. Uncover and cook over medium heat, stirring occasionally, until the onions are deeply browned, about 1½ hours. Add water, one tablespoon at a time, if the onions dry out.

2. Add the flour to the onions and cook, stirring constantly, for 2 minutes. Add the wine and cook, stirring constantly, until nearly evaporated, about 2 minutes. Add the beef stock and thyme, and simmer over medium-low until reduced to 10 cups, about 35 minutes. Discard the thyme bundle and bay leaves, and season the soup with salt and pepper.

3. Preheat the oven to 350°F. Brush the baguette slices with the olive oil, arrange on a baking sheet and toast until golden and crisp, about 12 minutes.

4. Preheat the broiler. Ladle the hot soup into 10 heatproof bowls. Float 3 baguette toasts in each bowl and scatter the cheese on top. Set the bowls on a sturdy baking sheet and broil about 4 inches from the heat source until the cheese has melted, about 2 minutes. —MICHAEL MINA

WINE Cru Beaujolais, made from the Gamay grape, go well with this rich, truffle-infused soup.

Barley Soup with Scotch

ACTIVE 40 MIN; TOTAL 40 MIN; SERVES 4

The idea for this hearty, risotto-style soup came to Frédéric Morin while he was sitting on a combine in his uncle's barley field. He could smell the peat from the neighboring farm, which reminded him of Scotch whisky.

6 cups vegetable broth

1 cup barley grits (see Note)

2 Tbsp. plus 1 tsp. vegetable oil

1 large onion, finely diced

1 Tbsp. Scotch whisky

2 Tbsp. unsalted butter

Salt and freshly ground black pepper

¼ cup celery leaves

1 oz. dry salami, sliced paper-thin (about 20 slices)

Crème fraîche, for serving

1. In a medium saucepan, bring the broth to a boil. Cover and keep hot over low heat. In a large skillet, cook the barley over medium-high, stirring constantly, until lightly browned, about 2 minutes. Transfer to a plate to cool.

2. Add the 2 tablespoons of vegetable oil to the skillet and add the onion. Cook over medium heat, stirring occasionally, until softened, about 10 minutes. Add the barley and stir. Add 1 cup of the hot broth and cook over medium heat, stirring frequently, until most of the broth has been absorbed. Continue adding more broth, 1 cup at a time, and stirring between additions. The soup is finished when all of the broth has been added and the barley is just tender, about 25 minutes. Add the Scotch whisky, then stir in the butter. Season the soup with salt and pepper.

3. In a small skillet, heat the remaining 1 teaspoon of vegetable oil. Add the celery leaves and cook over medium-high, tossing, just until wilted, about 10 seconds. Ladle the soup into shallow bowls. Top with the salami, crème fraîche, and celery leaves. —FRÉDÉRIC MORIN

MAKE AHEAD The soup can be refrigerated overnight. Add more stock as necessary.

NOTE Barley grits are either pearled barley or whole-grain barley that has been cut into small pieces. They're available at health food stores or specialty markets.

Creamy Parsnip Soup with Pear and Walnuts

ACTIVE 45 MIN; TOTAL 1 HR; SERVES 8 TO 10

"I add pear and walnuts for sophistication and crunch," says chef Marcus Samuelsson about this earthy, Indian-spiced soup. If you can't find sunchokes (also called Jerusalem artichokes), use all parsnips instead.

SOUP

- 2 Tbsp. extra-virgin olive oil
- 1¾ lb. parsnips, peeled and chopped (6 cups)
- ¾ lb. sunchokes, peeled and chopped (2 cups)
- 4 garlic cloves, chopped
- 4 tsp. garam masala
- 2 tsp. ground cumin
- 1 tsp. ground turmeric
- 1 tsp. kosher salt, plus more
- 4 cups water
- 3 cups chicken stock or low-sodium chicken broth
- 1½ cups heavy cream
- 1 Tbsp. fresh lemon juice
  Black pepper

TOPPING

- 1 tsp. extra-virgin olive oil
- ½ cup walnuts, chopped
- 1 garlic clove, minced
- 1 Tbsp. fresh lemon juice
- ½ Tbsp. walnut oil
- 1 small Bosc or d'Anjou pear, finely chopped
- 1 Tbsp. chopped fresh parsley
- 1 Tbsp. chopped fresh tarragon
  Kosher salt and black pepper

1. Make the soup Heat oil in a large saucepan over medium. Add parsnips, sunchokes, and garlic and cook, stirring, until lightly golden, 5 minutes. Stir in garam masala, cumin, turmeric, and salt. Cook, stirring, until fragrant, 2 minutes. Add 4 cups water, stock, and cream. Bring to a simmer; cook until vegetables are soft, 25 minutes.

2. Working in batches, puree soup in a blender until very smooth. Pour soup into a clean saucepan and stir in lemon juice. Season with salt and pepper.

3. Make the topping Heat oil in a medium skillet over medium-low. Add walnuts and cook, stirring, until golden, 3 minutes. Remove from heat and stir in garlic and lemon juice. Scrape mixture into a small

bowl and toss with walnut oil. Cool to room temperature, then stir in the pear, parsley, and tarragon; season with salt and pepper. Serve soup sprinkled with the topping.

— MARCUS SAMUELSSON

MAKE AHEAD The soup can be refrigerated for 3 days and reheated gently before serving.

WINE Pair with a lively, pear-scented Oregon Pinot Gris.

◆   ◆   ◆

Roasted Carrot Soup with Fresh Cheese and Black Bread

ACTIVE 50 MIN; TOTAL 1 HR 10 MIN; SERVES 4

Baltic black bread, traditionally made with rye flour and sourdough starter, is dense and sour, with a tight crumb. Its rye flavor gives this vegetarian soup earthy depth.

- 2 lb. carrots, peeled and cut into 2-inch pieces
- 2 Tbsp. canola oil, divided
- 1¼ tsp. kosher salt, divided
- ¼ tsp. cumin seeds
- ¼ tsp. caraway seeds
- 3 Tbsp. unsalted butter, divided
- 1 large yellow onion, finely chopped
- 1 qt. best-quality vegetable broth
- 3 Tbsp. sour cream
- 5 oz. Baltic black bread, heavy dark rye bread, or pumpernickel bread, torn into bite-size pieces (about 2½ cups)
- ½ cup crumbled farmer's cheese
- ½ cup roughly torn fresh dill
- 2 Tbsp. finely chopped fresh chives

1. Preheat oven to 400°F. Toss together carrots, 1 tablespoon canola oil, 1 teaspoon salt, cumin seeds, and caraway seeds in a large bowl until evenly coated. Spread carrots in an even layer on a rimmed baking sheet lined with aluminum foil; roast in preheated oven until very tender and browned in spots, about 1 hour, stirring halfway through roasting.

2. Melt 1 tablespoon butter in a large saucepan over medium. Add onion and cook, stirring often, until softened, about 6 minutes. Stir in roasted carrots and broth, and bring to a simmer over medium-high. Reduce heat to medium-low, and gently simmer until flavors meld, about 15 minutes. Transfer to a blender; add sour cream and remaining ¼ teaspoon

salt. Secure lid on blender, and remove center piece to allow steam to escape. Place a over opening. Process until soup has a smooth and silky consistency, about 1 minute and 30 seconds. Keep warm.

3. Melt remaining 2 tablespoons butter and 1 tablespoon canola oil in a large skillet over low. Add bread pieces and cook, stirring occasionally, until bread is crisp outside and slightly chewy in center, 10 to 12 minutes. Transfer to a bowl, and sprinkle with salt.

4. Divide soup among 4 warm shallow bowls. Top each bowl with 2 tablespoons bread and 2 tablespoons crumbled cheese. Sprinkle servings evenly with dill and chives. — SIMON BAJADA

WINE Pair with a skin-contact Sicilian white wine.

◆   ◆   ◆

Creamy Pumpkin Soup

ACTIVE 20 MIN; TOTAL 45 MIN; SERVES 6

This creamy pumpkin soup is even better if it's made a day ahead of time.

- 3 Tbsp. unsalted butter
- 1 small white onion, chopped
- 1 garlic clove, minced
- 1 Tbsp. firmly packed light brown sugar
- ½ tsp. freshly ground cinnamon
- ¼ tsp. white pepper
- ¼ tsp. freshly ground nutmeg
- ⅛ tsp. cayenne pepper
- 1 (15-oz.) can pure pumpkin puree
- 3 cups low-sodium vegetable broth
- ½ cup heavy whipping cream
  Kosher salt
  Crème fraîche, for garnish (optional)

1. Melt butter in a large pot over medium. Once the butter is just beginning to brown, add onion and sauté 5 minutes. Add garlic, sugar, cinnamon, white pepper, nutmeg, and cayenne, and cook 3 minutes. Add the pumpkin puree and broth, stir to incorporate, season with salt, and bring to a boil. Reduce heat to low and simmer 20 minutes. Stir in cream and let cool for 10 minutes.

2. Transfer soup to a blender (or use an immersion blender in the pot) and puree until smooth. If needed, add additional water or broth to reach desired consistency. Return mixture to the pot or a large saucepan. Serve warm and drizzle with crème fraîche, if desired. — EMILY FARRIS

Beet and Red Cabbage Borscht

ACTIVE 40 MIN; TOTAL 6 HR; SERVES 20

Food stylist Alison Attenborough and chef husband Jamie Kimm make borscht around the holidays. One year, they had roasted fennel left over after a day of food styling and added it to the soup pot; they've been making borscht with fennel ever since.

2 lb. medium beets

2 lb. trimmed beef chuck, cut into ½-inch pieces

Salt and freshly ground black pepper

All-purpose flour, for dusting

¼ cup plus 2 Tbsp. extra-virgin olive oil

1 2½-lb. head red cabbage, cored and cut into 1-inch pieces

2 medium onions, coarsely chopped

2 medium fennel bulbs, halved, cored and cut into ½-inch dice

2 garlic cloves, minced

¼ cup sweet paprika

¼ cup balsamic vinegar, plus more for seasoning

2 Tbsp. honey

3½ qt. low-sodium chicken broth

4 fresh thyme sprigs

2 cups sour cream

1 (12 oz.) jar prepared horseradish, drained

¾ cup minced fresh chives

1. Preheat the oven to 400°F. In a shallow baking dish, cover the beets with foil and bake until tender, about 1 hour. When cool enough to handle, peel the beets and cut into ½-inch dice.

2. Meanwhile, season the meat with salt and pepper and toss with flour just until lightly coated. In a large enameled cast-iron casserole, heat 1 tablespoon of the oil. Add half of the meat and cook over medium-high until browned all over; transfer to a bowl with a slotted spoon. Repeat with 1 tablespoon of oil and the remaining meat.

3. Add the remaining ¼ cup of oil to the casserole. Stir in the red cabbage, onions, fennel, garlic and paprika. Cook over medium, stirring occasionally, until the vegetables begin to soften, about 10 minutes. Add the vinegar and honey, and cook over medium-high t until the vegetables start sticking to the casserole and browning lightly, about 3 minutes. Add

the beets, browned meat, chicken broth, and thyme sprigs and bring to a boil. Cover and simmer over low heat until the meat is very tender, about 1 hour and 15 minutes.

4. In a medium bowl, mix the sour cream with the horseradish and chives and season with salt and pepper.

5. Discard the thyme sprigs and season the borscht to taste with salt, pepper, vinegar and honey. Serve in cups or bowls with the horseradish cream.
—ALISON ATTENBOROUGH & JAMIE KIMM

MAKE AHEAD The borscht and horseradish cream can be refrigerated separately overnight. Bring the horseradish cream to room temperature and reheat the borscht before serving.

Judith's Dungeness Crab Cioppino

ACTIVE 1 HR; TOTAL 1 HR 30 MIN; SERVES 10

For Christmas Eve dinner, Judith Tirado, Michael Mina's late mother-in-law, always prepared cioppino—the San Francisco seafood stew that owes its origins to fishermen from Italy's Ligurian coast.

¼ cup extra-virgin olive oil

8 large garlic cloves, 6 finely chopped, 2 whole

3 jalapeños, seeded and minced

2 red bell peppers, finely chopped

1 large onion, finely chopped

1 large bay leaf

2 Tbsp. tomato paste ½ cup dry red wine

1 (28-oz.) can peeled tomatoes, finely chopped, juices reserved

4 (8-oz.) bottles clam broth

1½ cups water

Salt and freshly ground black pepper

½ cup packed basil leaves

½ tsp. crushed red pepper

4 steamed Dungeness crabs, about 2 lb. each (see Note)

24 littleneck clams, scrubbed

2 lb. firm, white-fleshed fish fillets such as halibut, skinned and cut into 1½-inch chunks

2 lb. large shrimp, peeled and deveined

2 lb. mussels, scrubbed

1 lb. sea scallops, halved vertically if large

Crusty bread, for serving

1. In a very large soup pot, heat ¼ cup of the olive oil until shimmering. Add the chopped garlic, jalapeños, bell peppers, onion, and bay leaf and cook, stirring occasionally, over medium-high until softened and beginning to brown, about 10 minutes. Add the tomato paste and cook, stirring, for 1 minute. Add the wine and cook until nearly evaporated, about 1 minute longer. Add the chopped tomatoes and their juices and cook over medium-high until slightly thickened, about 5 minutes. Add the clam broth and water, season lightly with salt and generously with pepper, and bring to a boil. Simmer over medium heat until the broth is reduced to about 8 cups, about 20 minutes.

2. Meanwhile, in a mini food processor, combine the basil leaves with the whole garlic and process until the garlic is finely chopped. Add the remaining ½ cup of olive oil and the crushed red pepper, and process the basil puree until smooth. Season with salt and pepper.

3. Working over the sink, pull off the flap on the undersides of the crabs. Remove the top shells and discard. Pry out the brownish insides and pull off the feathery lungs and discard. Rinse the crab bodies in cold water and quarter them so that each piece has body and leg.

4. Add the crabs and clams to the pot. Cover and cook over high, stirring occasionally, until the clams begin to open, about 5 minutes. Using tongs, transfer the crabs to a large platter. Add the fish, shrimp, mussels and scallops to the pot, pushing them into the broth. Return crabs to the pot, cover and cook, stirring occasionally, until clams and mussels are fully open and fish, shrimp and scallops are cooked through, about 8 minutes longer.

5. Ladle cioppino into deep bowls and drizzle each serving with some of the basil puree. Serve with crusty bread and pass the remaining basil puree. —MICHAEL MINA

MAKE AHEAD The Dungeness crab cioppino can be prepared through Step 1 and refrigerated for up to 3 days.

NOTE Have the fishmonger steam the crabs for you.

WINE Choose a dry Barbera from Italy's Piedmont.

Pumpkin and Shellfish Bisque with Pumpkin Seed Pistou

ACTIVE 30 MIN; TOTAL 1 HR; SERVES 4

Sweet pumpkin lends a creamy, silky texture to this autumnal soup, while fresh pistou brightens it up. Serve extra pistou with grilled meats, roasted vegetables, and buttered pasta.

PISTOU

- 1 Tbsp. vegetable oil
- ½ cup raw pepitas
- 1 cup chopped fresh flat-leaf parsley
- ½ cup olive oil, divided,
- 1½ Tbsp. fresh lemon juice
- 1 Tbsp. fresh oregano leaves
- 1½ tsp. kosher salt
- 1 medium garlic clove
  Pinch of crushed red pepper

BISQUE

- 2 Tbsp. vegetable oil
- 1 small yellow onion, chopped
- 1 large pumpkin or other winter squash, peeled and cut into large cubes (about 4 cups)
- 4 cups seafood stock
- 3 fresh thyme sprigs, tied into a bundle
- ½ cup heavy cream
- 2 Tbsp. unsalted butter, cubed
- 1 Tbsp. kosher salt

1. Make the pistou Heat vegetable oil in a small saucepan over medium. Add pepitas; cook, stirring and tossing often, until slightly puffed and toasted, about 3 minutes. Let cool slightly, about 5 minutes.

2. Combine parsley, ¼ cup olive oil, lemon juice, oregano, salt, garlic, red pepper, and cooled pepitas in a blender. Process on medium speed, slowly drizzling in remaining ¼ cup olive oil, until mixture is slightly smooth yet still textured, 20 to 30 seconds.

3. Transfer mixture to a container with a tight-fitting lid. Set aside at room temperature until ready to use, up to 3 hours.

4. Make the bisque Heat oil in a medium stockpot over high. Add onion; cook, stirring often, until softened, about 5 minutes. Add pumpkin and stock; bring to a boil over medium-high. Reduce heat to medium-low, and add thyme. Simmer, uncovered, until pumpkin is fall-apart tender, about 30 minutes. Remove

stockpot from heat. Remove and discard thyme; stir in cream.

5. Working in batches if needed, pour soup into a blender. Secure lid on blender, and remove center piece to allow steam to escape. Place a clean towel over opening. Process on high speed until smooth, about 30 seconds. With blender running on medium speed, gradually add butter; process until silky-smooth, 1 minute and 30 seconds to 2 minutes. Transfer soup to a clean large pot; stir in salt.

6. Ladle soup evenly into 4 bowls. Top each bowl with about 2 tablespoons pistou. — JUSTIN DEVILLIER & JAMIE FELDMAR

MAKE AHEAD Pistou can be stored in an airtight container in refrigerator up to 2 days; bring to room temperature and stir before using. Soup may be stored, without pistou garnish, covered, in refrigerator up to 3 days.

WINE Pair with a crisp, lemony Chenin Blanc.

◆━━━━◆━━━━◆

Red Wine Venison Stew

ACTIVE 1 HR 50 MIN; TOTAL 4 HR; SERVES 8

Made with venison, this stew is intensely flavored and has a silky, thick sauce that clings to the vegetables and meat as they slowly cook together. Beef chuck roast works well here, too, but may add more fat, so be sure to skim the final stew before serving.

- ¼ cup all-purpose flour
- 1 Tbsp. kosher salt, plus more to taste
- ½ tsp. black pepper, plus more to taste
- 1 (4-lb.) boneless venison or chuck roast, trimmed and cut into 2-inch cubes
- 7 to 8 Tbsp. bacon drippings (from about 1 lb. thick-cut bacon, cooked) or vegetable oil, divided
- 8 fresh thyme sprigs
- 4 whole cloves, crushed
- 8 juniper berries, crushed
- 3 bay leaves
- 3 (2-inch) lemon peel strips plus 3 Tbsp. fresh lemon juice (from 2 lemons), divided
- 3 medium yellow onions, large diced
- 4 medium carrots, peeled and large diced

- 10 oz. sliced fresh cremini mushrooms (about 3½ cups)
- 4 large garlic cloves, chopped
- 1 (28-oz.) can whole peeled plum tomatoes, crushed
- 4 cups beef bone broth
- 1½ cups full-bodied, robust red wine (such as Cabernet Sauvignon)
  Cooked egg noodles
  Chopped fresh flat-leaf parsley and sour cream, for serving

1. Preheat oven to 350°F. Toss together flour, salt, and pepper in a large bowl; add venison, and toss to coat.

2. Heat 2 tablespoons bacon drippings in a large Dutch oven over medium. Working in 4 batches, add venison, and cook, turning occasionally, until well browned, about 15 minutes per batch. Transfer venison to a plate. Add more bacon drippings, 1 tablespoon at a time, between batches as needed. (If necessary, deglaze the Dutch oven with water [save this water and return to pan when adding broth], and wipe clean. Then start next batch with 2 tablespoons bacon drippings.)

3. Place thyme, cloves, juniper berries, bay leaves, and lemon peel strips in a double layer of cheesecloth. Gather edges of cheesecloth; tie securely with kitchen twine, and set aside.

4. Add onions, carrots, mushrooms, garlic, and remaining 2 tablespoons bacon drippings to Dutch oven. Cook, stirring occasionally, until onions are softened, about 15 minutes. Add tomatoes, broth, cheesecloth bundle, lemon juice, and browned venison along with any drippings accumulated on plate. Return to a simmer over medium-high; transfer to preheated oven. Braise, uncovered, until venison is fork-tender, about 2 hours, stirring in wine after 1 hour.

5. Return Dutch oven to stovetop, and bring to a simmer over medium. Reduce heat to low, and gently simmer until sauce has thickened slightly, 10 to 15 minutes. Remove from heat, and skim and discard fat from surface of stew. Remove and discard cheesecloth bundle. Season with salt and pepper to taste. Serve over egg noodles with parsley and sour cream. — RAY ISLE

WINE Pair with a powerful, spicy Petite Sirah.

Pumpkin and Shellfish Bisque with Pumpkin Seed Pistou

Posole Rojo

Posole Rojo

ACTIVE 2 HR 10 MIN; TOTAL 5 HR 25 MIN;
SERVES 10

Posole began as a ceremonial dish for the ancient Aztecs because corn was considered a sacred crop. Today it can be found all across Mexico, typically made by families on weekends or for special occasions.

- 1 (3-lb.) boneless pork shoulder (Boston butt), trimmed and cut into 2-inch pieces
- 1 (3-lb.) rack pork spareribs, cut in half crosswise
- 6 qt. water, plus more
- 2 Tbsp. plus 2 tsp. kosher salt, divided
- 1 large white onion, quartered
- 3 large garlic cloves
- 1 (2-inch) piece fresh ginger, peeled
- 3 bay leaves
- 1 Tbsp. dried oregano, plus more for serving
- 3 (25-oz.) cans white hominy, drained and rinsed (about 8 cups)
- 5 large dried ancho chiles (see Note)
- 5 large dried guajillo chiles (see Note)
- 2 Tbsp. grapeseed oil
- 10 (5-inch) corn tostada shells
- 4 cups thinly sliced iceberg lettuce (from ½ head lettuce)
- 3 cups chicharrones (optional)
- 1 cup crumbled Cotija cheese (optional)
- 8 red radishes, thinly sliced
- 2 ripe avocados, thinly sliced
- 5 limes, halved

1. Combine pork shoulder, spareribs, 6 quarts water, and 1 tablespoon salt in a large stockpot. Bring to a boil over high, skimming off and discarding foam from surface during first 10 minutes of cooking. Place onion, garlic, ginger, bay leaves, and oregano in center of a large piece of cheesecloth; gather edges of cheesecloth together, and secure with twine. Add to pot; reduce heat to medium-low, and gently simmer, uncovered, 1½ hours.

2. Remove cheesecloth bundle from pot. Remove onion, garlic, and ginger; set aside. Discard bay leaves and oregano. Add hominy to pot; simmer over medium-low, uncovered, until rib bones can be easily removed from spareribs, about 1½ hours.

3. While pork mixture simmers, split ancho and guajillo chiles; remove and discard stems and seeds. Place half of the chiles in a large, deep skillet over medium. Cook, turning occasionally, until toasted evenly on both sides, about 1 minute. Remove to a plate; repeat with remaining chiles. Return all toasted chiles to skillet; add water just to cover chiles. Bring to a gentle simmer over medium; cook until chiles are soft and rehydrated, about 15 minutes. Remove from heat; cool slightly, about 15 minutes. Drain chiles, reserving cooking liquid. Taste cooking liquid; if it tastes bitter, discard. If it tastes faintly of raisins, reserve ½ cup.

4. Transfer rehydrated chiles and either the reserved ½ cup chile cooking liquid or ½ cup water to a blender. Add onion, garlic, ginger, and 1 tablespoon salt. Process until smooth, adding stock from pork mixture in stockpot as needed to reach consistency of applesauce, about 1 minute. Pour through a fine wire-mesh strainer into a bowl; discard solids.

5. Heat oil in a 10-inch skillet over medium-high. Carefully pour strained chile mixture into skillet. (Mixture will splatter.) Cook, stirring often, until reduced by half and darkened in color, about 30 minutes. (Partially cover skillet to reduce splatters, if desired.) Remove from heat, and set aside.

6. When pork mixture has finished simmering, remove spareribs from stockpot, and set aside until cool enough to handle, about 5 minutes. Remove and discard rib bones and tendons from spareribs. Chop meat into bite-size pieces, and return to stockpot. Stir in reserved chile sauce. Bring to a simmer over medium-low; cook until flavors meld, about 1 hour, skimming fat from surface, if desired. Stir in remaining 2 teaspoons salt.

7. Place tostada shells, lettuce, chicharrones, Cotija (if using), radishes, avocados, and limes in separate bowls for topping soup. Ladle soup among 10 large bowls, add a pinch of oregano. Serve soup alongside bowls of toppings. — PRIYA KRISHNA

MAKE AHEAD Prepare soup through Step 6; cool soup, cover, and chill up to 3 days. Prepare garnishes for Step 7 just before serving. Rewarm soup gently.

NOTE Soaking dried chiles draws out their flavor, including bitterness, if prevalent. If the resulting liquid is sweet, incorporate it into the dish. Discard it if it tastes bitter.

Okra Gumbo with Blue Crabs and Shrimp

ACTIVE 35 MIN; TOTAL 1 HR 15 MIN;
SERVES 8

In this recipe from The Dooky Chase Cookbook, *chef Leah Chase uses okra (and lots of it) to thicken the dish.*

- ¼ cup vegetable oil
- 3 lb. okra, thinly sliced crosswise
- 4 live blue crabs
- 1½ cups finely chopped onion
- ½ cup finely chopped green bell pepper
- ½ cup finely chopped celery
- 2 Tbsp. tomato paste
- 1½ qt. water
- 1 tsp. minced garlic
- 1 tsp. crushed red pepper
- 1 tsp. paprika
- ½ tsp. cayenne pepper
- ½ tsp. dried thyme
- 2 bay leaves
- Kosher salt
- 1 lb. medium shrimp, shelled and deveined
- Steamed white rice, for serving

1. Heat the oil in a large pot. Add the okra and cook over low, stirring, until softened, 20 minutes. Add the crabs, onion, bell pepper and celery, cover and cook, stirring to prevent the okra from sticking to the bottom of the pot, until the vegetables are tender and the crabs are partially cooked, 15 minutes.

2. Stir in the tomato paste, water, garlic, red pepper, paprika, cayenne, thyme and bay leaves; season with salt. Bring to a boil. Reduce the heat to medium, and simmer until crabs are bright red, 10 minutes. Stir in the shrimp and cook until pink, 10 minutes.

3. Transfer the crabs to a work surface and pull off the triangular shells on the underside of each one. Using a sharp knife, cut each crab in half and transfer to bowls. Ladle the gumbo into the bowls and serve with rice. — LEAH CHASE

SUGGESTED PAIRING Clean, mellow pale ale.

Escarole and Golden Beet Salad with Toasted Hazelnuts

PHOTO P. 173

TOTAL 45 MIN; SERVES 12

This superfresh, crunchy salad stars very thinly sliced golden beets, which have a sweet, earthy flavor.

- 1 cup hazelnuts
- 1 medium shallot, minced
- ¼ cup Champagne vinegar
- 2 tsp. honey
- 2 tsp. Dijon mustard
- ⅓ cup extra-virgin olive oil
- Kosher salt and black pepper
- 2 (1¼-lb.) heads of escarole, white and light green leaves only, torn
- ½ lb. small golden beets, peeled and very thinly sliced or julienned
- ¾ cup snipped fresh chives

1. Preheat oven to 375°F. Spread hazelnuts in a pie plate, and bake until fragrant and lightly browned, 10 to 12 minutes. Transfer hazelnuts to a kitchen towel and rub them together in towel to release skins. Let hazelnuts cool, then coarsely chop.

2. Whisk shallot, vinegar, honey, and mustard in a serving bowl. Gradually whisk in oil and season with salt and pepper. Add escarole, beets, chives, and toasted hazelnuts, and toss well. Season with salt and pepper, toss again, and serve.

— JUSTIN CHAPPLE

Winter Chicory Salad with Kumquats and Date Dressing

TOTAL 20 MIN; SERVES 6

A mix of young chicories, like endive, frisée, and radicchio, creates pops of welcome color. Use paper-thin slices of unpeeled clementines if kumquats are not available.

- ½ cup extra-virgin olive oil
- 3 Tbsp. sherry vinegar
- 3 Tbsp. fresh orange juice
- 1 Tbsp. finely chopped shallot
- 2 cups kumquats, sliced into ⅛-inch rounds, seeds removed, divided
- ½ cup dried pitted dates, thinly sliced, divided
- 1 tsp. kosher salt, divided
- ½ tsp. black pepper, divided
- 4 Belgian endive leaves, sliced (about 1 cup)
- 2 cups bright yellow frisée leaves (from 1 large head, use yellow leaves only)
- 2 cups packed fresh arugula
- 1 cup packed fresh mizuna
- 1 cup sliced Treviso or Chioggia radicchio
- ½ cup loosely packed fresh flat-leaf parsley leaves
- 1 Tbsp. fresh mint leaves, cut into thin strips
- ½ cup toasted salted pistachios
- 4 oz. aged pecorino Romano cheese, shaved with a Y-shape vegetable peeler (about 2 cups)

1. Whisk together oil, sherry vinegar, orange juice, and shallot in a small bowl. Stir in 1 tablespoon kumquats and 1 tablespoon dates until blended. Season with ½ teaspoon salt and ¼ teaspoon pepper.

2. Place remaining kumquats and dates in a large bowl. Reserve and set aside 6 tablespoons vinaigrette. Drizzle remaining vinaigrette over kumquat mixture, and, using your hands, pull dates apart into individual slices. Add endive, frisée, arugula, mizuna, radicchio, parsley, and mint; gently toss to coat. Season with remaining ½ teaspoon salt and remaining ¼ teaspoon pepper.

3. To serve, divide salad evenly among 6 plates; drizzle 1 tablespoon of the reserved vinaigrette over top and around each salad. Garnish with pistachios and shaved pecorino. — NINA FRIEND

Torn Escarole Salad with Warm Bacon Vinaigrette

TOTAL 30 MIN; SERVES 6 TO 8

Lightly spicy croutons tossed in chile-sesame oil before toasting, smoky bacon, and crumbled blue cheese add rich, savory dimension to this quick, dinner-worthy salad. A dollop of apple butter adds a natural sweetness to the dressing, but honey can be used in its place.

- 6 cups torn crusty Italian bread
- ⅓ cup hot chile-sesame oil or olive oil
- ¾ tsp. kosher salt, divided
- 4 thick-cut applewood-smoked bacon slices, cut into ½-inch pieces
- ¼ cup finely chopped shallot
- 3 Tbsp. olive oil
- 2 Tbsp. apple butter or 2 tsp. honey
- 1½ Tbsp. red wine vinegar
- 1½ tsp. Dijon mustard
- 6 cups torn escarole
- 2 small Honey Crisp apples, cut into matchsticks
- 4 oz. mild blue cheese, crumbled (about 1 cup)

1. Preheat oven to 400°F. Toss together bread, chile-sesame oil, and ½ teaspoon salt on a rimmed baking sheet; spread in an even layer. Bake in preheated oven, stirring occasionally, until golden brown and crisp, about 20 minutes.

2. Meanwhile, cook bacon in a large skillet over medium, stirring occasionally, until crisp, 10 to 12 minutes. Transfer bacon to a paper towel-lined plate, reserving 3 tablespoons drippings in skillet. Add shallot to skillet, and cook over low, scraping any browned bits from bottom of skillet, until shallot is softened, about 2 minutes. Remove from heat; whisk in oil, apple butter, vinegar, Dijon, and remaining ¼ teaspoon salt.

3. Toss together escarole, apples, cheese, and bacon in a large bowl. Add shallot dressing; toss to coat. Transfer to a large platter; sprinkle with croutons.

— LIZ MERVOSH

MAKE AHEAD Croutons can be made a day ahead and stored in an airtight container at room temperature.

Winter Chicory Salad
with Kumquats and
Date Dressing

**Tuscan Kale Salad with
Gorgonzola Croutons**

Butter Lettuce Salad with Fresh Cranberry Vinaigrette

TOTAL 30 MIN; SERVES 12

TV chef Carla Hall tosses dried cranberries, apricots, and nuts with greens and minces fresh cranberries in her vinaigrette.

VINAIGRETTE

- ½ cup fresh cranberries
- 1 Tbsp. sugar
- 1 tsp. grated lemon zest plus 2 Tbsp. fresh lemon juice
- ¼ cup extra-virgin olive oil
  Kosher salt and black pepper

SALAD

- 2 heads of butter lettuce
- 2 oz. goat cheese, crumbled (½ cup)
- ¼ cup sliced dried apricots
- ¼ cup dried cranberries
- ½ cup pecans, toasted and chopped

1. Make the vinaigrette Place cranberries and sugar in a food processor, and pulse until finely chopped. Transfer half of the cranberries to a bowl. Add lemon zest and juice to the processor, and pulse to combine. Slowly drizzle in oil. Add vinaigrette to bowl; season with salt and pepper.

2. Make the salad Arrange lettuce, goat cheese, dried apricots, dried cranberries, and pecans on a platter. Drizzle with vinaigrette, and serve. — CARLA HALL

◆ ◆ ◆

Brussels Sprouts and Arugula Salad with Buttermilk Dressing

TOTAL 15 MIN; SERVES 10

Instead of roasting Brussels sprouts, toss them with arugula, parsley, and a light, satisfying buttermilk dressing. If you have time, quick-pickled shallot rings add color, texture, and tang to the salad (see Note).

- 1 cup sliced almonds
- ½ cup buttermilk
- ¼ cup mayonnaise
- 1 small garlic clove, grated
- 1 tsp. kosher salt
- 1 tsp. black pepper
- 1 lb. Brussels sprouts, very thinly sliced
- 12 oz. arugula, thick stems trimmed
- 2 cups lightly packed fresh flat-leaf parsley leaves

1. Preheat oven to 350°F. Spread almonds on a large rimmed baking sheet. Bake in preheated oven until golden, 6 to 7 minutes. Remove from pan, and let cool 10 minutes.

2. Whisk together buttermilk, mayonnaise, garlic, salt, and pepper in a very large bowl. Add Brussels sprouts, arugula, and parsley; toss well to coat. Sprinkle with toasted almonds, and serve.
— JUSTIN CHAPPLE

NOTE Combine ½ cup red wine vinegar, ¼ cup water, 2 tsp. granulated sugar, and 2 tsp. kosher salt in a jar with a tight-fitting lid. Attach lid and shake well. Remove lid; add ½ cup thinly sliced shallot rings. Attach lid and shake well. Refrigerate 30 minutes. Drain. Scatter on salad.

◆ ◆ ◆

Tuscan Kale Salad with Gorgonzola Croutons

ACTIVE 30 MIN; TOTAL 1 HR 30 MIN; SERVES 8

Cozy Italian flavors come together in this easy make-ahead salad. Lacinato kale (also known as Tuscan kale) is slightly more tender than other varieties, making it ideal for raw preparations. The croutons are the real star of this salad, combining creamy Gorgonzola and rye bread to deliver a cheesy, irresistible crunch.

- 6 small (1½- to 2-oz.) golden beets, trimmed, peeled, and quartered
- 6 small (1½- to 2-oz.) hakurei turnips or baby turnips, trimmed and quartered
- ¾ cup extra-virgin olive oil, divided
- 3 tsp. kosher salt, divided
- 1 tsp. ground black pepper, divided
- 4 oz. Gorgonzola or other creamy blue cheese
- ¼ cup unsalted butter, melted
- 14 oz. rye bread, crusts removed, torn into 1½-inch pieces
- 1 cup white wine vinegar
- 2 Tbsp. granulated sugar
- ⅔ cup thinly sliced red onion
- 1 Tbsp. Dijon mustard
- 2 tsp. honey
- 2 (7-oz.) bunches Tuscan kale, stemmed and torn into bite-size pieces (about 10 loosely packed cups)

1. Preheat oven to 400°F. Arrange racks in upper and lower thirds of oven.

2. Place beets and turnips on a baking sheet lined with parchment paper. Drizzle with 2 tablespoons oil, and sprinkle with ¾ teaspoon salt and ½ teaspoon pepper; toss gently to coat. Arrange in a single layer on baking sheet.

3. Place Gorgonzola in a large bowl; mash with a fork until smooth. Add 6 tablespoons oil; stir well with fork. Stir in melted butter. Add bread pieces; toss gently to coat. Arrange bread in a single layer on a baking sheet lined with parchment paper.

4. Place bread on upper oven rack and beet mixture on lower oven rack. Bake in preheated oven 15 minutes. Stir vegetables and bread, and return both to oven on same racks. Bake until bread is crisp and browned, 8 to 10 minutes. Remove bread from oven, and set aside. Continue to roast vegetables until tender when pierced with a knife, about 10 minutes. Cool to room temperature, about 30 minutes.

5. Meanwhile, stir together vinegar, ½ cup water, sugar, and 1½ teaspoons salt in a small saucepan; bring to a boil. Add onion; boil 1 minute. Remove from heat, and let cool to room temperature, about 30 minutes. Drain onions, reserving 3 tablespoons pickling liquid.

6. Whisk together reserved pickling liquid, mustard, honey, remaining ¾ teaspoon salt, and remaining ½ teaspoon pepper in a large bowl. Gradually add remaining ¼ cup oil, whisking constantly, until emulsified. Add kale, beets, and turnips; toss gently to combine. Transfer to a large, shallow bowl. Top with pickled onions and croutons. — ANN TAYLOR PITTMAN

MAKE AHEAD Onions can be pickled up to 3 days in advance.

Cauliflower Salad with Yogurt Sauce and Pomegranate

ACTIVE 20 MIN; TOTAL 35 MIN; SERVES 8

Inspired by her mother's (much richer) fried eggplant salad, Palestinian cookbook author Reem Kassis tops fried cauliflower with toasted nuts, pomegranate arils, and yogurt laced with lemon and garlic.

Canola oil, for frying

2 medium heads cauliflower (about 1½ lb. each), cored and cut into 1½-inch florets (about 16 cups)

2 tsp. kosher salt, divided

1½ cups plain whole-milk Greek yogurt

½ tsp. fresh lemon juice

1 small garlic clove, crushed

1 cup mixed fresh herbs and greens (such as arugula, dill, and chives)

¾ cup lightly toasted mixed nuts (such as almonds, pistachios, and hazelnuts)

¼ cup pomegranate arils

1. Pour canola oil to a depth of 1 inch into a large skillet. Heat over medium-high to 350°F. Working in batches, fry cauliflower until just golden and tender, about 3 minutes per batch. Using a slotted spoon, transfer cauliflower to paper towels to drain; season with 1½ teaspoons salt.

2. Meanwhile, whisk together yogurt, lemon juice, and garlic in a medium bowl. Season yogurt mixture with remaining ½ teaspoon salt. Chill at least 15 minutes or up to 1 hour; remove and discard crushed garlic before using.

3. To serve, arrange cauliflower on a platter; spoon yogurt mixture over top. Garnish with herbs and greens, mixed nuts, and pomegranate arils. — REEM KASSIS

Endive Salad with Kumquats and Pomegranate Arils

TOTAL 15 MIN; SERVES 6

Any bitter chicory, like escarole or radicchio, works in place of endive in this colorful salad. Leave the cheese crumbles on the larger side; they add creamy balance to the dish.

2 Tbsp. Champagne vinegar

1 Tbsp. finely chopped shallot

1½ tsp. granulated sugar

1 tsp. Dijon mustard

1 tsp. kosher salt

¼ tsp. black pepper

⅓ cup extra-virgin olive oil

6 small heads red and green endive, quartered lengthwise (about 14 oz.)

½ cup kumquats (about 2¾ oz.), seeded and thinly sliced

¼ cup pomegranate arils

2 Tbsp. salted roasted pepitas

1½ oz. ricotta salata cheese or goat cheese, crumbled (about ⅓ cup)

½ cup loosely packed fresh flat-leaf parsley leaves

1. Stir together vinegar and shallot in a small bowl; let stand 5 minutes. Whisk in sugar, mustard, salt, and pepper. Whisk in oil until mixture is smooth.

2. Arrange endive quarters on a large platter. Sprinkle evenly with kumquat slices, pomegranate arils, roasted pepitas, and crumbled cheese. Drizzle dressing evenly over salad; sprinkle with parsley. — ANNA THEOKTISTO

MAKE AHEAD The dressing can be made and stored in an airtight container in refrigerator up to 2 days ahead of time.

Fall Salad with Sherry Vinaigrette

TOTAL 30 MIN; SERVES 10 TO 12

Star chef Tyler Florence tosses three types of lettuce with sweet apple, persimmons, and crisp fennel in this bountiful and beautiful fall salad.

¾ cup pecans

½ cup sherry vinegar

¼ cup Dijon mustard

2 Tbsp. honey

1 tsp. fresh thyme leaves

1½ cups extra-virgin olive oil

Sea salt and black pepper

1 head of red leaf lettuce, leaves torn

2 heads of Treviso or Chioggia radicchio, cored and leaves torn

1 head of frisée (4 oz.), white and light green leaves only

2 Fuyu persimmons, cored and very thinly sliced crosswise on a mandoline

1 Pink Lady apple, cored and very thinly sliced on a mandoline

1 medium fennel bulb, cored and very thinly sliced on a mandoline

Nasturtium leaves, for garnish (optional)

1. Preheat oven to 375°F. Spread pecans in a pie plate, and toast until golden, about 7 minutes. Let cool, then coarsely chop.

2. Whisk vinegar, mustard, honey, and thyme in a medium bowl. Gradually whisk in oil and season with sea salt and pepper.

3. Toss lettuce, Treviso, and frisée in a very large serving bowl. Scatter persimmons, apple, fennel, and pecans on top, and if desired, garnish with nasturtium leaves. Serve salad, passing dressing at the table. — TYLER FLORENCE

MAKE AHEAD The nuts can be stored in an airtight container for up to 2 days. The dressing can be refrigerated overnight.

Endive Salad with
Kumquats and
Pomegranate Arils

**Broccoli and Beer
Cheese Cocottes**

Broccoli and Beer Cheese Cocottes

ACTIVE 35 MIN; TOTAL 1 HR 5 MIN; SERVES 6

An update on the classic broccoli-cheese casserole, these individual servings of bubbly lager-spiked Red Leicester cheese sauce over broccoli with crunchy croutons are crowd-pleasers.

Nonstick cooking spray

4 qt. water

⅓ cup plus 2¼ tsp. kosher salt, divided, plus more to taste

12 cups roughly chopped broccoli (from 3 large broccoli heads, stems discarded)

½ cup plus 2 Tbsp. unsalted butter (5 oz.), divided

1 cup finely chopped yellow onion

⅔ cup all-purpose flour (about 2⅞ oz.)

1 (12-oz.) bottle lager beer

1 cup half-and-half

12 oz. Red Leicester cheese or mild cheddar cheese, grated (about 3 cups)

1 tsp. Worcestershire sauce

1 tsp. dry mustard

¾ tsp. black pepper

2 oz. rye bread (about 2 slices), torn into ½-inch pieces (about 1 cup)

1. Preheat oven to 425°F. Lightly coat 6 (8-ounce) cocottes or ramekins with cooking spray; set aside. Bring 4 quarts water to a boil in a large pot over high. Add ⅓ cup salt; let water return to a boil. Add broccoli; cook, stirring occasionally, until just tender, about 3 minutes; drain. Transfer broccoli to a large bowl filled with ice water; let stand 5 minutes. Drain. Arrange broccoli in a single layer on a baking sheet lined with paper towels; pat dry. Transfer broccoli to a large bowl; set aside.

2. Melt ½ cup butter in a large saucepan over medium. Add onion; cook, stirring occasionally, until softened, about 8 minutes. Gradually whisk in flour; cook, whisking constantly, until flour is completely incorporated and lightly browned, about 2 minutes. Gradually whisk in beer and half-and-half, and cook, whisking constantly, until sauce thickens and begins to bubble, 3 to 4 minutes. Gradually whisk in cheese, Worcestershire, dry mustard, pepper, and 2 teaspoons salt until smooth.

3. Pour cheese sauce over broccoli; stir to combine. Season with salt to taste. Spoon mixture evenly into prepared cocottes, and arrange on a rimmed baking sheet.

4. Microwave remaining 2 tablespoons butter in a medium-size microwavable bowl on HIGH until melted, 30 seconds to 1 minute. Add bread pieces and remaining ¼ teaspoon salt; toss to coat. Sprinkle mixture evenly over broccoli mixture in cocottes. Bake, uncovered, in preheated oven until bread is golden brown and cheese is bubbly, 16 to 20 minutes. — PAIGE GRANDJEAN

MAKE AHEAD Broccoli can be prepared and refrigerated up to 1 day ahead.

NOTE Recipe may be prepared in a 9-inch square baking dish.

Red Cabbage Salad with Baked Cherries, Apples, and Almond Dukkah

ACTIVE 30 MIN; TOTAL 40 MIN; SERVES 8 TO 10

This crisp shredded cabbage salad gets a triple hit of stone fruit flavor from sweet roasted cherries, dried cherries, and cherry vinegar. Toasty dukkah adds a nutty crunch to this refreshing side.

1½ cups frozen pitted dark sweet cherries (about 11 oz.), thawed

2 Tbsp. sherry vinegar

¼ cup olive oil, divided

2½ Tbsp. honey, divided

¾ tsp. kosher salt, divided

¾ tsp. black pepper, divided

¼ cup cherry vinegar (such as Pojer e Sandri) or balsamic vinegar

½ head red cabbage, quartered, cored, and thinly sliced on a mandoline (about 6 cups)

3 apples (such as Honey Crisp, Red Delicious, or Gala), quartered, cored, and thinly sliced on a mandoline (about 5 cups)

Almond Dukkah (recipe follows)

2 Tbsp. dried cherries, for garnish

1. Preheat oven to 330°F. Stir together cherries, sherry vinegar, 2 tablespoons oil, 1 tablespoon honey, ¼ teaspoon salt, and ¼ teaspoon pepper in a small baking dish; spread in a single layer. Bake in preheated oven until cherries are tender and infused with vinegar mixture, 12 to 16 minutes. Set aside.

2. Whisk together cherry vinegar, ¼ teaspoon pepper, remaining 2 tablespoons oil, and remaining 1½ tablespoons honey in a small bowl until well blended.

3. Just before serving, toss together cabbage, apples, roasted cherries and 2 tablespoons roasted cherry juice, cherry vinaigrette, remaining ½ teaspoon salt, and remaining ¼ teaspoon pepper. (Save remaining roasted cherry juice for another use.) Transfer salad to a large serving platter, and sprinkle with almond dukkah. Garnish with dried cherries. Serve immediately. — ALECIA MOORE & ROBBY GRANTHAM-WISE

MAKE AHEAD The cherry vinaigrette can be made up to 3 days in advance. The sweet cherries may be roasted 1 day ahead; let cool, cover, and chill.

NOTE Cherry vinegar is available from markethallfoods.com.

Almond Dukkah

TOTAL 15 MIN; SERVES 8 TO 10

Dukkah is an Egyptian condiment made up of toasted nuts and seeds ground to a powder. Sprinkled over salads, soups, and dips, it adds a warm flavor and delightful crunch.

½ cup blanched almonds

2 tsp. fennel seeds

1 Tbsp. cumin seeds

2 Tbsp. salted roasted sunflower seed kernels

1 Tbsp. toasted sesame seeds

2 tsp. pure maple syrup

½ tsp. paprika

½ tsp. kosher salt

1. Toast almonds and fennel seeds in a small skillet over low, stirring often, until fragrant and slightly darkened, about 5 minutes. Transfer to a small plate, and let cool 5 minutes. Roughly chop almonds.

2. Place cumin seeds in skillet, and toast over low, stirring often, until fragrant, about 45 seconds. Transfer to a work surface, and lightly crush with the flat side of a large knife.

3. Stir together chopped almonds, fennel seeds, crushed cumin seeds, sunflower seed kernels, sesame seeds, maple syrup, paprika, and salt in a small bowl until thoroughly combined. Store in an airtight container at room temperature. — ALECIA MOORE & ROBBY GRANTHAM-WISE

Roots Remoulade with Smoked Trout

ACTIVE 35 MIN; TOTAL 1 HR 5 MIN; SERVES 4

Thinly sliced root vegetables like carrots, kohlrabi, and radishes make this salad bright and crisp. Topped with a luxe crème fraîche dressing and whole-grain mustard, then paired with smoked trout, this salad makes a crunchy and satisfying weeknight meal.

- 1¼ cups crème fraîche
- 3 Tbsp. French whole-grain mustard
- 3 Tbsp. fresh lemon juice
- ¾ tsp. fine sea salt, plus more to taste
  Freshly ground black pepper
- 1½ lb. mixed root vegetables (such as celery root, parsnips, orange and yellow carrots, kohlrabi, golden beets, watermelon radishes, and black radishes), peeled
- 4 oz. smoked trout
- ¼ cup chopped fresh flat-leaf parsley or ½ cup fresh chervil leaves
- 1 cup nasturtium leaves or watercress leaves

1. Whisk together crème fraîche, mustard, lemon juice, salt, and several grinds of pepper in a large bowl. Set aside.

2. Cut vegetables into thin strips either by hand using a chef's knife or in a food processor fitted with the julienne attachment. Toss vegetables in crème fraîche mixture until well coated. Cover and refrigerate 30 minutes or up to 1 day.

3. Flake fish into bite-size chunks; add fish and parsley to vegetable salad, and gently toss. Add salt and pepper to taste. Transfer salad to a large, shallow serving bowl. Scatter nasturtium over top, and serve. — DANA FRANK & ANDREA SLONECKER

WINE Pair with an acidic white wine.

Speck-Wrapped Haricots Verts with Date Molasses

ACTIVE 20 MIN; TOTAL 30 MIN; SERVES 8

A cousin of prosciutto, cold-smoked speck has a sturdier texture, which makes it perfect for wrapping bundles of crisp-tender beans. Date molasses is thinner than regular molasses; if substituting regular molasses, reduce the cook time slightly.

- ⅓ cup plus 1¼ tsp. kosher salt, divided
- 1 lb. haricots verts (French green beans), trimmed
- ⅓ cup date molasses or regular unsulfured molasses
- 3 Tbsp. sherry vinegar
- 3 Tbsp. olive oil
- ¾ tsp. black pepper
- 8 thin speck slices
- ¼ to ½ cup fried shallots

1. Preheat oven to 475°F. Bring 4 quarts water to a boil in a large pot over medium-high. Add ⅓ cup salt, and return to a boil. Add haricots verts, and cook until crisp-tender, about 4 minutes; drain. Transfer to a large bowl filled with ice water; let stand 3 minutes. Drain. Dry beans thoroughly.

2. Stir together molasses and vinegar in a small skillet; bring to a simmer over medium. Cook, stirring occasionally, until mixture coats back of a spoon and reduces to about ⅓ cup, about 4 minutes. Remove from heat; let cool 5 minutes.

3. Meanwhile, toss together beans, oil, pepper, and remaining 1¼ teaspoons salt in a large bowl. Divide haricots verts evenly into 8 bundles. Place 1 bundle at the short end of 1 speck slice; roll up lengthwise. Repeat process with remaining haricots verts and speck.

4. Place 3 tablespoons cooled molasses mixture in a small bowl; reserve for serving. Arrange bundles, seam-sides down, on a rimmed baking sheet lined with aluminum foil. Brush bundles evenly with remaining molasses mixture. Bake in preheated oven until bundles are glazed and ends begin to char, 8 to 10 minutes.

5. Arrange bundles on a serving platter. Drizzle with reserved molasses mixture, and sprinkle with desired amount of fried shallots. — PAIGE GRANDJEAN

MAKE AHEAD Green beans can be blanched and refrigerated 1 day ahead.

Garlicky Haricots Verts with Hazelnuts

TOTAL 20 MIN; SERVES 8

Fresh haricots verts are quickly cooked in beef fat just until they're crisp-tender, giving them deeply savory flavor without overcooking them. The acidic lemon juice and licoricey tarragon add just enough bright, light flavor to this rich side dish.

- ¼ cup rendered beef fat or unsalted butter (see Note)
- 2 lb. haricots verts (French green beans), trimmed
- 1 cup roughly chopped raw hazelnuts
- 3 Tbsp. chopped garlic (about 8 garlic cloves)
- 3 Tbsp. unsalted butter
- 2 Tbsp. fresh lemon juice
- 1 Tbsp. chopped fresh tarragon
- 1 Tbsp. kosher salt
- ¾ tsp. black pepper

Heat beef fat in a large, high-sided skillet over medium-high until shimmering, about 2 minutes. Add haricots verts, and cook, stirring often, until bright green, about 4 minutes. Add hazelnuts, garlic, and butter, and cook, stirring often, until hazelnuts are toasted and haricots verts are crisp-tender, 4 to 6 minutes. Remove from heat; stir in lemon juice, tarragon, salt, and black pepper. Serve immediately. — ANGIE MAR

NOTE To make ½ cup of rendered beef fat, gently heat 8 ounces of beef trimmings in a small saucepan over medium-low for 1 hour. Strain the rendered fat before using.

Roots Remoulade
with Smoked Trout

Roasted Beets and
Charred Green Beans

Roasted Beets and Charred Green Beans

ACTIVE 40 MIN; TOTAL 4 HR 30 MIN;
SERVES 8

An homage to the jarred pickled beets and bean salad she ate as a kid, Top Chef *champ Kristen Kish pairs roasted beets and cast-iron-charred haricots verts with an herby vinegar dressing.*

- 3 lb. small to medium red beets
- 8 fresh thyme sprigs
- 5 Tbsp. extra-virgin olive oil, divided
- 2½ tsp. kosher salt, divided
- 1 tsp. black pepper, divided
- ½ cup plus 2 Tbsp. grapeseed oil, divided
- 1 lb. haricots verts, trimmed, divided
- ¼ cup apple cider vinegar
- 2 Tbsp. granulated sugar
- 1 Tbsp. whole-grain mustard
- 1 Tbsp. finely chopped fresh oregano
- 2 tsp. chopped fresh thyme
- 2 large shallots, thinly sliced on a mandoline
- Roasted hazelnuts, for garnish
- Chopped fresh flat-leaf parsley, for garnish

1. Preheat oven to 350°F. Toss together beets, thyme sprigs, 3 tablespoons olive oil, ½ teaspoon salt, and ¼ teaspoon pepper in a roasting pan or baking dish; cover tightly with aluminum foil. Bake in preheated oven until beets are tender, about 1 hour and 15 minutes. Remove foil, and let stand until cool enough to handle. Peel cooled beets, and cut into wedges. Discard thyme sprigs.

2. Heat 1 tablespoon grapeseed oil in a large cast-iron skillet over high until smoking. Add half of the haricots verts in an even layer. Cook, without stirring, until charred on one side, about 2 minutes. Cook, stirring often, until tender-crisp, about 3 minutes. Transfer to a plate. Repeat process with 1 tablespoon grapeseed oil and remaining haricots verts. Sprinkle beans with ½ teaspoon salt and ¼ teaspoon pepper.

3. Toss together beets, haricots verts, vinegar, sugar, mustard, oregano, thyme, and remaining 2 tablespoons olive oil. Season with remaining 1½ teaspoons salt and remaining ½ teaspoon pepper. Cover and refrigerate at least 2 hours or up to 2 days.

4. Stir together shallots and remaining ½ cup grapeseed oil in a small saucepan. Cook over medium-high, stirring occasionally, until golden brown and crisp, about 15 minutes. Using a slotted spoon, transfer fried shallots to paper towels to drain. Top salad with fried shallots; garnish with hazelnuts and parsley. — KRISTEN KISH

Green Beans with Roasted Almond Crumble

TOTAL 45 MIN; SERVES 12

TV chef Carla Hall brightens up roasted green beans with citrus and fresh herbs, then tops them with a crunchy almond crumb topping.

- 2 cups (3 oz.) crustless white bread cubes (½-inch pieces)
- ¼ cup extra-virgin olive oil
- Kosher salt and black pepper
- ½ cup finely chopped salted roasted almonds
- 2 lb. green beans, trimmed
- ¼ tsp. finely grated orange zest plus 1 Tbsp. fresh orange juice
- 2 Tbsp. chopped fresh tarragon
- 2 Tbsp. chopped fresh basil

1. Preheat oven to 450°F. Toss bread with 1 tablespoon oil on a baking sheet; season with salt and pepper. Bake until golden, 8 minutes. Cool, then finely chop. Transfer to a bowl; stir in almonds.

2. Meanwhile, toss green beans with remaining 3 tablespoons oil on a rimmed baking sheet; season with salt and pepper. Roast, stirring occasionally, until lightly browned, 20 minutes. Add orange zest, orange juice, tarragon, and basil, and toss. Transfer beans to a platter, top with almond crumble, and serve. — CARLA HALL

Roasted Beets with Beet Green Salsa Verde

ACTIVE 30 MIN; TOTAL 1 HR 30 MIN;
SERVES 10 TO 12

Chef Tyler Florence uses beets and their greens to make this fresh and vibrant side dish for Thanksgiving. If you can't find beets with beautiful greens, Swiss chard or curly spinach leaves can be used instead.

- 2¼ lb. small to medium beets, scrubbed
- 1 lb. fresh ricotta cheese
- Sea salt and black pepper
- ½ cup extra-virgin olive oil
- ¼ cup sherry vinegar
- 2 cups beet greens, halved lengthwise and very thinly sliced crosswise into ribbons
- ½ cup minced beet green stems
- ½ red onion, finely chopped
- ½ cup chopped fresh dill, plus sprigs for garnish
- ½ cup pomegranate seeds

1. Preheat oven to 400°F. Wrap beets in foil and transfer to a rimmed baking sheet. Bake until tender when pierced, about 1 hour. Unwrap and let cool.

2. Spread ricotta on a platter. Cut beets into chunks and arrange on cheese. Season lightly with sea salt.

3. Whisk oil and vinegar in a medium bowl. Add beet greens and stems, onion, and chopped dill, and mix well. Season salsa verde with sea salt and pepper, and spoon over the beets. Scatter pomegranate seeds on top, garnish with dill sprigs, and serve. — TYLER FLORENCE

MAKE AHEAD The roasted beets can be refrigerated for 2 days. Return to room temperature before serving.

Chile-Mint Parsnips

TOTAL 25 MIN; SERVES 6 TO 8

The key to tender parsnips is removing the fibrous core. It's simple to do once the parsnips are quartered; just slice away the tough center of each piece. Barberries offer a punchy sourness to these earthy, sweetly spiced parsnips. Substitute unsweetened dried cranberries or cherries if barberries are unavailable.

- 1 Tbsp. thin lemon peel strips (about 1½ inches long) plus 1 Tbsp. fresh lemon juice (from 1 lemon), divided
- ¼ tsp. cornstarch
- 7 Tbsp. unsalted butter (3½ oz.), cut into pieces, divided
- 1½ tsp. cumin seeds
- 1 (4-inch) Ceylon cinnamon stick
- 3 fresh mint sprigs plus ¼ cup loosely packed small tender fresh mint leaves, divided
- 2 lb. parsnips, quartered lengthwise, tough fibrous cores removed
- 1½ cups water
- 1 Tbsp. honey
- 1¾ tsp. kosher salt, divided
- 1½ Tbsp. dried barberries or chopped unsweetened dried cranberries
- 1½ tsp. ground Urfa biber (Urfa pepper) (see Note) or a pinch of crushed red pepper

1. Whisk together lemon juice and cornstarch in a small bowl; set aside.

2. Melt ¼ cup butter in a deep 12- to 14-inch skillet over medium. Cook, stirring often, until milk solids turn nut-brown, 5 to 8 minutes.

3. Working quickly, add lemon peel strips, cumin seeds, cinnamon stick, and mint sprigs to butter. (Mint will cause mixture to splatter.) Cook over medium, stirring constantly, until fragrant, about 30 seconds. Add parsnips, 1½ cups water, honey, and 1 teaspoon salt.

4. Bring parsnip mixture to a boil over high. Boil, stirring occasionally, 5 minutes. Cover and reduce heat to medium; simmer, undisturbed, until parsnips are crisp-tender, 3 to 5 minutes. Uncover;

stir in lemon juice mixture, remaining 3 tablespoons butter, and remaining ¾ teaspoon salt. Cook, stirring constantly, until mixture is creamy and parsnips are glazed, about 1 minute.

5. Transfer parsnips to a large platter. Remove and discard cinnamon stick and mint sprigs. Drizzle glaze over parsnips. Sprinkle with mint leaves, barberries, and Urfa biber. Serve immediately or at room temperature. — LIZ MERVOSH

NOTE Urfa biber is a ground dried Turkish chile pepper with smoky heat and a raisin-like flavor. You can purchase it at burlapandbarrel.com.

Creamed Kale

ACTIVE 40 MIN; TOTAL 1 HR 15 MIN; SERVES 10 TO 12

This rich and delicious creamed kale from chef Tyler Florence is an excellent swap for more traditional creamed spinach.

- 3½ lb. Tuscan kale, 4 leaves left whole, the rest stemmed and chopped
- ¼ cup plus 1 Tbsp. extra-virgin olive oil
- Kosher salt and black pepper
- 2 Tbsp. unsalted butter
- 2 white onions, finely chopped
- 1½ cups heavy cream
- 1 Tbsp. honey

1. Preheat oven to 350°F. Rub whole kale leaves with 1 tablespoon oil on a large baking sheet; season with salt and pepper. Bake until crispy, about 15 minutes. Let cool.

2. Meanwhile, melt the butter in remaining ¼ cup oil in a large pot. Add onions, season with salt, and cook over medium-high, stirring occasionally, until softened and just starting to brown, 8 to 10 minutes. Add chopped kale and cook, stirring occasionally, until wilted, about 5 minutes. Add cream and honey, and bring to a simmer. Cover and cook over medium, stirring occasionally, until the kale is very tender and coated in a thick sauce, 35 to 40 minutes.

3. Transfer half of the creamed kale to a food processor, and puree until nearly smooth. Stir puree into pot and season with salt and pepper. Transfer creamed kale to a serving bowl. Top with crispy kale leaves, and serve. — TYLER FLORENCE

Creamed Spinach

ACTIVE 20 MIN; TOTAL 30 MIN; SERVES 8

New York City butcher Erika Nakamura makes a mean creamed spinach, using a combo of Cognac and Pernod to add complex flavor to the steakhouse staple.

- 2 cups chicken stock or low-sodium broth
- 3 (8-oz.) bags baby spinach
- ½ stick unsalted butter
- 2 large shallots, minced
- 3 large garlic cloves, finely grated
- 2 Tbsp. Cognac
- 1 Tbsp. Pernod
- 1 cup heavy cream
- 2 fresh thyme sprigs
- Freshly grated nutmeg
- Kosher salt and white pepper

1. Bring stock to a boil over medium-high in a large pot. Add spinach, cover, and cook for 1 minute. Toss spinach with tongs, cover, and cook until just wilted, 1 minute longer. Drain spinach and let cool, then squeeze out as much liquid as possible.

2. Cook butter, shallots, and garlic in a large, shallow pot over medium, stirring occasionally, until soft and translucent but not browned, about 5 minutes. Remove pot from heat, and add Cognac and Pernod. Carefully tilt pan over burner to ignite alcohol; cook until flames subside. (Alternatively, remove pan from heat and ignite with a long match, then return to heat.) Stir in drained spinach, cream, and thyme. Bring to a boil and cook, stirring, until thickened, about 2 minutes. Discard thyme sprigs. Season with a pinch of nutmeg, salt, and white pepper, and transfer to a bowl. Serve creamed spinach hot. — ERIKA NAKAMURA

MAKE AHEAD The creamed spinach can be refrigerated overnight.

Creamed Kale

Ginger-and-Molasses-
Glazed Root Vegetables

Sautéed Collards and Cabbage with Gremolata

TOTAL 45 MIN; SERVES 12

These crunchy sautéed greens from TV chef and cookbook author Carla Hall get big flavor from garlic, lemon, and crushed red pepper.

- ¾ cup finely chopped fresh parsley
- 1½ tsp. minced garlic plus 2 thinly sliced garlic cloves
- 1 Tbsp. finely grated lemon zest plus ¼ cup fresh lemon juice, divided
- ½ cup plus 2 Tbsp. extra-virgin olive oil, divided
- Kosher salt and black pepper
- 4 shallots, halved and thinly sliced (¾ cup)
- 1½ lb. green cabbage, cored and sliced ¼ inch thick (9 cups)
- 1½ lb. collard greens, stems discarded, leaves sliced ¼ inch thick (12 cups)
- ¾ tsp. crushed red pepper

1. Combine parsley, minced garlic, lemon zest, 3 tablespoons lemon juice, and 6 tablespoons oil in a small bowl. Season with salt and black pepper and mix well.

2. Heat 2 tablespoons olive oil in a large pot over medium. Add shallots and sliced garlic, and cook, stirring occasionally, until light golden, about 5 minutes. Add green cabbage, collard greens, and remaining 2 tablespoons oil; season with salt and black pepper. Cook over medium-high, stirring, until the collards and cabbage are wilted and crisp-tender, 7 to 8 minutes. Stir in red pepper and remaining 1 tablespoon lemon juice. Transfer greens to a platter, top with gremolata, and serve. — CARLA HALL

MAKE AHEAD The gremolata can be made up to 3 hours ahead and kept covered at room temperature.

Creamed Pearl Onions with Sage and Thyme

ACTIVE 40 MIN; TOTAL 1 HR 15 MIN; SERVES 8

This was a classic dish on the late Anthony Bourdain's Thanksgiving table. Blanching the pearl onions makes them infinitely easier to peel.

- Kosher salt
- 2 lb. pearl onions
- 2 tsp. black peppercorns, plus ground pepper for seasoning
- 2 bay leaves
- 4 Tbsp. unsalted butter, divided
- ¼ cup all-purpose flour
- 2⅔ cups whole milk
- 6 fresh sage leaves, finely chopped
- ½ tsp. finely chopped fresh thyme

1. Preheat oven to 375°F. Set up an ice water bath. Bring a large saucepan of water to a boil; add 1 tablespoon salt. Add pearl onions and blanch just until the skins loosen, 1 to 2 minutes. Using a slotted spoon, transfer onions to ice bath to cool. Drain onions and pat dry. Trim off root ends and pinch off skins.

2. Add peppercorns and bay leaves to saucepan of water, and bring to a boil. Add peeled onions and simmer over medium-high until just tender, 5 to 8 minutes. Drain well and pat dry. Transfer onions to a 13- × 9-inch baking dish.

3. Melt butter over medium-low in a medium saucepan. Add flour and cook, stirring constantly with a wooden spoon, until bubbling and just beginning to turn color, about 3 minutes. Gradually whisk in milk, and simmer, stirring, until sauce is thick enough to coat back of a spoon and no floury taste remains, about 5 minutes. Stir in sage and thyme, and season generously with salt and pepper. Pour sauce over onions and bake, until bubbling and just starting to brown at the edge, 20 minutes. Let stand for 5 minutes before serving. — ANTHONY BOURDAIN

MAKE AHEAD The onions can be refrigerated overnight in their sauce. Bring to room temperature before baking.

Ginger-and-Molasses-Glazed Root Vegetables

TOTAL 50 MIN; SERVES 8

Plucked from the F&W archives, this simple side is a must-have for your Thanksgiving spread. The original matchstick knife cuts were updated for easier rounds and half-moons and added parsnips for earthy sweetness. The hot bite of ginger brings an extra zip that will make your guests demand seconds.

- 1 lb. carrots, peeled and cut diagonally into ⅛-inch-thick coins
- 1 lb. parsnips, peeled and cut diagonally into ⅛-inch-thick coins
- 1 lb. turnips, peeled, halved, and cut into ⅛-inch-thick half-moons
- 6 Tbsp. unsalted butter (3 oz.), cut into pieces, divided
- 2 tsp. grated garlic
- 2 tsp. grated peeled fresh ginger
- 2 Tbsp. unsulfured molasses
- 1 tsp. kosher salt
- ¼ tsp. coarsely ground black pepper
- Chopped fresh flat-leaf parsley, for garnish

1. Bring a large pot of salted water to a boil over high. Meanwhile, fill a large bowl with ice water; set aside. Add carrots and parsnips to boiling water, and cook 3 minutes. Add turnips, and cook until vegetable mixture is crisp-tender, about 2 minutes. Using a slotted spoon, immediately transfer vegetable mixture to ice bath to cool. Drain and transfer to a paper towel-lined baking sheet. Pat dry.

2. Melt ¼ cup butter in a large skillet over medium until sizzling. Add garlic and ginger. Cook, stirring often, until fragrant and no longer raw, about 2 minutes. Add carrot mixture, molasses, 2 tablespoons water, salt, pepper, and remaining 2 tablespoons butter. Cook, stirring constantly, until vegetable mixture is glazed, 2 to 4 minutes. Remove from heat, and transfer to a serving platter. Garnish with parsley, and serve immediately. — DAVID MCCANN

MAKE AHEAD Carrots, parsnips, and turnips may be blanched 1 day ahead.

Roasted Citrus with Crunchy Three-Seed Brittle

ACTIVE 20 MIN; TOTAL 50 MIN; SERVES 6 TO 8

Quickly roasting sliced citrus makes it extra sweet and juicy in this elegant winter salad. A sweet and savory brittle spiked with chile oil and studded with sesame, pumpkin, and sunflower seeds is the perfect counterpoint to the mixed citrus.

- ¼ cup white sesame seeds
- ¼ cup black sesame seeds
- ¼ cup raw pepitas
- ¼ cup salted roasted sunflower seed kernels
- 2 Tbsp. dark brown sugar
- 2 Tbsp. plus ¾ tsp. hot chile-sesame oil, divided
- ½ tsp. orange zest
- ½ tsp. kosher salt, divided
- 1 Tbsp. plus 2 tsp. honey, divided
- 1½ Tbsp. fresh lime juice
- 4 lb. mixed fresh citrus fruits (such as blood oranges, grapefruit, and Meyer lemons), peeled and cut crosswise into ½-inch rounds
  Flaky sea salt

1. Preheat oven to 350°F. Position one oven rack 3 inches from heat; position second rack in middle of oven. Line a rimmed baking sheet with parchment paper.

2. Stir together white sesame seeds, black sesame seeds, pepitas, sunflower seed kernels, brown sugar, ¾ teaspoon chile-sesame oil, orange zest, and ¼ teaspoon kosher salt in a small bowl. Gradually drizzle in 1 tablespoon honey, stirring to combine. Transfer to prepared baking sheet; press mixture into an 8-inch square.

3. Bake on middle rack in preheated oven until sugar melts, 8 to 10 minutes. Let cool on baking sheet 25 minutes (brittle will harden as it cools). Break into bite-size pieces.

4. Stir together lime juice, 1 tablespoon chile-sesame oil, remaining 2 teaspoons honey, and remaining ¼ teaspoon kosher salt in a small bowl; set aside.

5. Increase oven temperature to high broil. Gently toss together citrus and remaining 1 tablespoon chile-sesame oil in a large bowl. Arrange citrus in an even layer on a wire rack set inside a rimmed baking sheet. Broil on top rack in preheated oven until sizzling, 1 minute and 30 seconds to 2 minutes.

6. Transfer roasted citrus to a large platter. Drizzle evenly with lime juice mixture; garnish with sea salt, and top with brittle.
— LIZ MERVOSH

MAKE AHEAD Brittle can be made up to 2 days ahead and stored in an airtight container at room temperature.

◆ ◆ ◆

Roasted Butternut Squash with Curry Leaves

ACTIVE 15 MIN; TOTAL 50 MIN; SERVES 4

The first time food blogger and author Nik Sharma hosted Thanksgiving was during college, when he decided to rely on his dorm's oven to cook a whole turkey. The oven's capricious behavior resulted in a bird that was dry and slightly charred in some spots. The turkey might have been a disaster, but the unexpected tropical notes of coconut and fragrant curry leaves in this simple squash side dish helped save the day.

- 1 (2½-lb.) butternut squash, peeled, seeded, and cut into ¾-inch cubes
- 1 Tbsp. coconut oil, melted
- 1½ tsp. marash chile flakes (see Note)
- 1½ tsp. fine sea salt
- 1 tsp. black mustard seeds
- 24 fresh curry leaves
- 1 Tbsp. fresh lime juice

Preheat oven to 425°F with oven rack in lower third of oven. Toss butternut squash with coconut oil, chile flakes, salt, mustard seeds, and curry leaves in a medium bowl until evenly coated. Transfer to a baking dish, and roast in preheated oven until squash is tender and slightly browned, about 35 minutes, stirring halfway through roasting. Remove from oven; drizzle with lime juice, and serve warm. — NIK SHARMA

MAKE AHEAD Butternut squash can be peeled and cubed 1 day ahead.

NOTE Substitute Aleppo pepper for the marash chile flakes, if desired. Find curry leaves at your local Asian grocery store.

Ombré Potato and Root Vegetable Gratin

ACTIVE 45 MIN; TOTAL 3 HR; SERVES 12

This colorful gratin can be made ahead of time and refrigerated overnight. Reheat gently before serving.

- Unsalted butter, for greasing
- 2 cups heavy cream
- 3 garlic cloves, minced
- 1 small shallot, minced
- ½ tsp. freshly grated nutmeg
- 1½ tsp. kosher salt
- ½ tsp. black pepper
- 1¾ cups freshly grated Parmigiano-Reggiano cheese (5 oz.)
- 1 lb. red beets, peeled and sliced on a mandoline ¹⁄₁₆ inch thick
- 1 lb. sweet potatoes or garnet yams, peeled and sliced on a mandoline ¹⁄₁₆ inch thick
- 1 lb. Yukon Gold potatoes, peeled and sliced on a mandoline ¹⁄₁₆ inch thick
- 1 lb. turnips, peeled and sliced on a mandoline ¹⁄₁₆ inch thick

1. Preheat oven to 375°F. Lightly butter a 13- × 9-inch baking dish. Whisk cream, garlic, shallot, nutmeg, salt, and pepper in a medium bowl. Stir in 1 cup Parmigiano-Reggiano.

2. Gently toss beets with one-fourth of the cream mixture in a large bowl. Arrange beets in baking dish in an even layer, overlapping them slightly. Scrape any remaining cream from bowl over beets. Repeat this process with sweet potatoes, Yukon Golds, and turnips, using one-fourth of the cream mixture for each vegetable. Press a sheet of parchment paper on top of turnips, then cover dish tightly with foil.

3. Bake gratin until the vegetables are tender, about 1 hour and 30 minutes. Uncover and top with remaining ¾ cup Parmigiano-Reggiano. Bake until golden on top, about 15 minutes longer. Transfer gratin to a rack and let cool for at least 15 minutes before serving. — CARLA HALL

MAKE AHEAD The gratin can be refrigerated overnight. Reheat gently before serving.

Roasted Citrus with Crunchy Three-Seed Brittle

Chile-Infused
Mashed Potatoes

Potato Rösti with Pastrami

ACTIVE 25 MIN; TOTAL 50 MIN; SERVES 4

For the laciest, crispiest rösti, use a spiralizer to cut starchy russet potatoes into long, curly shoestrings. The extra steps of rinsing away the excess starch, salting the potatoes to draw out their moisture, then patting them dry helps to crisp the potatoes. Attentively cooking so the potatoes brown evenly, then baking on a rack—makes for a greaseless, light result. Consider the cooked rösti a blank canvas for decadent toppings like melted raclette, runny fried eggs, sour cream, and caviar, or—as Swiss chef Daniel Humm suggests here—New York-style thinly sliced pastrami, grainy mustard, and dill pickles.

- 3 lb. large russet potatoes, peeled and spiralized or julienned (about 7 cups)
- 1½ tsp. kosher salt
- ½ cup plus 1 tsp. canola oil, divided
- ¼ cup crème fraîche
- 3 oz. thinly sliced best-quality pastrami
- 2 Tbsp. finely chopped fresh chives
- 2 Tbsp. fresh dill sprigs
- 1 Tbsp. whole-grain mustard
- 2 long dill pickle slices, halved lengthwise

1. Preheat oven to 400°F. Place potatoes in a large bowl, and rinse under cold water, agitating with your hands until water runs clear. Working in batches, pat potatoes dry with a clean kitchen towel. Place potatoes in a colander, and toss with salt. Let stand 10 minutes. Working in batches, pat dry again with a clean kitchen towel until potatoes no longer glisten with water.

2. Heat 1 teaspoon canola oil in a medium stainless-steel or cast-iron skillet over high until it begins to smoke. Reduce heat to low; pour out oil, and wipe out skillet with a paper towel. (This process will help keep the potatoes from sticking.) Increase heat to medium, and add ¼ cup canola oil.

3. When oil is very hot and begins to shimmer, quickly pull skillet off heat, and carefully add potatoes in an even layer. Return skillet to heat over medium. Using a metal or heat-resistant spatula, loosen potatoes from sides of pan, and press down in center to form a cake.

4. Pour remaining ¼ cup canola oil around and down sides of potato cake. Cook until bottom is slightly crisp and lightly browned, 7 to 8 minutes, giving skillet a quarter turn every 2 minutes to ensure even browning.

5. Slide rösti onto a large plate. Place a second large plate on top, and invert. Slide rösti back into skillet. Cook until bottom is slightly crisp and browned, 7 to 8 minutes, giving skillet a quarter turn every 2 minutes. Slide rösti onto a wire rack set inside a rimmed baking sheet. Bake in preheated oven until crispy and browned and excess oil has pooled in baking sheet, 8 to 10 minutes.

6. Remove from oven, and let cool until slightly firm, about 5 minutes. Using a spatula, gently slide rösti onto a large plate. Top with crème fraîche, pastrami, chives, dill, mustard, and pickle slices.
— DANIEL HUMM

Bacony Potato Puree

ACTIVE 30 MIN; TOTAL 1 HR; SERVES 8

To make these next-level potatoes, F&W's Justin Chapple first steeps cubes of double-smoked bacon in half-and-half, then folds the strained bacon-scented cream into boiled and riced potatoes. Pressing the potatoes through a ricer makes a light and extra-creamy potato puree.

- ½ lb. double-smoked bacon or regular smoked bacon, cubed
- 2½ cups half-and-half
- 1 cup unsalted butter (8 oz.)
- 5 lb. russet potatoes, peeled and cut into 1-inch pieces
- 2 Tbsp. plus 1¾ tsp. kosher salt, divided
- ½ tsp. ground white pepper

1. Combine bacon, half-and-half, and butter in a medium saucepan. Cook over medium until butter is melted and half-and-half is just simmering, about 5 minutes. Remove from heat; cover and steep 30 minutes. Using a slotted spoon, remove bacon from saucepan, and reserve for another use.

2. While bacon steeps, place potatoes in a large pot. Add water to cover by 1 inch, and bring to a boil over medium-high. Add 2 tablespoons salt, reduce heat to medium, and simmer until tender, 20 to 25 minutes. Drain well. Press potatoes through a potato ricer back into pot. Slowly fold in bacon cream, ½ cup at a time.

Season with white pepper and remaining 1¾ teaspoons salt. — JUSTIN CHAPPLE

MAKE AHEAD The riced potatoes can be refrigerated overnight. Reheat gently before serving.

Chile-Infused Mashed Potatoes

ACTIVE 30 MIN; TOTAL 50 MIN; SERVES 10

For this creamy mash, fragrant dried guajillo and árbol chiles are steeped in half-and-half that gets folded into simmered and riced potatoes. Amp them up with a drizzle of cilantro oil, if you'd like.

- 3 dried guajillo chiles, stemmed, seeded, and torn into pieces
- 3 dried chiles de árbol, stemmed and crushed
- 2½ cups half-and-half
- 5 lb. Yukon Gold potatoes, peeled and cut into 1-inch chunks
- 7 tsp. kosher salt, divided
- 2 Tbsp. unsalted butter, cubed
- Cilantro Oil (optional) (recipe follows)

1. Place chiles in a medium saucepan over medium, and cook, stirring occasionally, until lightly toasted, about 5 minutes. Stir in half-and-half, and bring to a simmer. Reduce heat to very low, and let mixture stand, undisturbed, 30 minutes. Pour chile-infused half-and-half through a wire-mesh strainer over a bowl; discard solids.

2. Place potatoes in a large saucepan, and add cold water to cover by 1 inch; bring to a boil over high. Add 1 tablespoon salt; reduce heat to medium, and simmer until tender, about 25 minutes. Transfer potatoes to a colander to drain, shaking off any excess water.

3. Stir together butter and chile-infused half-and-half in a large saucepan over medium until butter is melted. Remove from heat. Press potatoes through a potato ricer into saucepan; stir mixture until combined. Season with remaining 4 teaspoons salt, and serve.
— JUSTIN CHAPPLE

CILANTRO OIL Puree 2 cups loosely packed fresh cilantro leaves, ½ cup canola oil, ½ cup extra-virgin olive oil, and 2 ice cubes in a blender until smooth. Season with salt to taste. Drizzle some oil on mashed potatoes just before serving; pass remaining oil at the table.

Herb-Scented Mashed Potatoes

ACTIVE 30 MIN; TOTAL 1 HR; SERVES 10

Fresh rosemary, sage, and garlic are steeped in a combination of milk and cream that is then folded into boiled and riced potatoes. To make them even more irresistible, the mashed potatoes are brushed with butter and broiled before serving, creating a deliciously light and crispy potato crust.

1¼ cups heavy cream

1¼ cups whole milk

2 sticks unsalted butter, plus melted butter for brushing

2 (4-inch) fresh rosemary sprigs

2 fresh sage sprigs

2 garlic cloves, crushed

5 lb. baking potatoes, peeled and cut into 2-inch pieces

Kosher salt and black pepper

1. Combine cream, milk, 2 sticks butter, rosemary, sage, and garlic in a medium saucepan; bring just to a simmer. Remove from heat and let steep for 15 minutes, then discard rosemary, sage, and garlic.

2. Meanwhile, place potatoes in a large pot, and add water to cover; bring to a boil. Add a generous pinch of salt, and simmer over medium until tender, about 20 minutes. Drain well, then pass potatoes through a ricer into pot. Fold in cream mixture and season generously with salt and pepper.

3. Light broiler and position a rack 8 inches from heat. Scrape potatoes into a 12-inch round heatproof pan or baking dish (2 inches deep) and, using a spoon, decoratively swirl top. Gently brush with melted butter. Broil until the top is browned in spots, about 8 minutes. Serve hot. — JUSTIN CHAPPLE & LAURA REGE

MAKE AHEAD The mashed potatoes can be prepared through Step 2 and refrigerated overnight. Reheat gently before scraping into the baking dish and broiling.

Crushed Potatoes with Spiced Olive Oil

ACTIVE 30 MIN; TOTAL 1 HR; SERVES 8

Pressing the boiled potatoes through a wire baking rack is a neat trick for easily peeling and coarsely crushing them all at once. A trio of toasted and ground seeds, caraway, fennel, and coriander mixed with extra-virgin olive oil gives these rustic potatoes a delicately fruity but warmly spiced flavor. Because of the generous amount of olive oil in this recipe, the potatoes are great served warm or at room temperature.

5 lb. medium-size Yukon Gold potatoes

3 Tbsp. kosher salt, divided

2 tsp. caraway seeds

2 tsp. coriander seeds

2 tsp. fennel seeds

1 cup extra-virgin olive oil

1 tsp. black pepper

1. Place potatoes in a large pot, and add water to cover by 1 inch. Bring to a boil over medium-high. Add 2 tablespoons salt, reduce heat to medium, and simmer until tender, 25 to 30 minutes.

2. Meanwhile, combine caraway seeds, coriander seeds, and fennel seeds in a small skillet. Cook over medium, stirring constantly, until spices are very fragrant, toasted, and seeds begin to pop, about 5 minutes. Transfer to a mortar, and crush with a pestle. Stir together crushed seeds and oil in a medium bowl until well combined.

3. Drain potatoes, and cut in half lengthwise. Place a wire rack over a large bowl. Working in batches, place potato halves, cut-side down, on rack, and press through until only skin remains; discard skins. Fold spiced oil into potatoes; gently stir in pepper and remaining 1 tablespoon salt. Serve warm or at room temperature. — JUSTIN CHAPPLE

MAKE AHEAD The crushed potatoes can be refrigerated overnight. Reheat gently before serving.

NOTE Press cooked potatoes through a wire baking rack to easily peel and coarsely crush them all at once.

Candied Sweet Potatoes with Bourbon

ACTIVE 20 MIN; TOTAL 1 HR 20 MIN; SERVES 8

At Thanksgiving, these are the sweet potatoes you would have found at the late Anthony Bourdain's table. Known not only for his entrancing storytelling but also his candid delivery, his commentary on this recipe? "Put those goddamn marshmallows away."

6 Tbsp. unsalted butter, divided

3 lb. sweet potatoes, peeled and cut into 1½-inch pieces

¾ cup packed dark brown sugar

¼ cup fresh apple cider

3 Tbsp. bourbon

Kosher salt

1. Preheat oven to 400°F. Grease a 13- × 9-inch glass or ceramic baking dish with 1 tablespoon butter. Blanch sweet potatoes in a large saucepan of salted boiling water until barely tender, 8 to 10 minutes. Drain well. Spread them in prepared baking dish in an even layer.

2. Melt remaining 5 tablespoons butter with brown sugar in a small saucepan. Whisk in cider and bourbon, season with salt, and bring to a boil. Cook over medium-high, stirring, until sugar dissolves, 1 to 2 minutes. Pour mixture over sweet potatoes and gently stir to coat.

3. Bake sweet potatoes until tender and sauce is syrupy, 35 to 40 minutes. — ANTHONY BOURDAIN

MAKE AHEAD The recipe can be prepared through Step 2 and refrigerated overnight. Bring to room temperature before baking.

**Crushed Potatoes with
Spiced Olive Oil**

Tartiflette

Tartiflette

ACTIVE 45 MIN; TOTAL 2 HR 5 MIN; SERVES 8

In this stunningly rich side from Angie Mar of New York's The Beatrice Inn, buttery and sweet Fromager d'Affinois is melted over tender potatoes and jammy caramelized onions; dry white wine cuts the richness and highlights the cheese's mild flavor. Substitute Brie, Camembert, or Taleggio if Fromager d'Affinois is unavailable.

- 4 medium russet potatoes (about 2¼ lb.), peeled
- 2 Tbsp. plus ½ tsp. kosher salt, divided
- ½ cup rendered beef fat or unsalted butter
- 2 medium yellow onions, thinly sliced (about 5 cups)
- 1½ tsp. granulated sugar
- ⅔ cup dry white wine, divided
- 1½ tsp. thinly sliced fresh sage
- ½ tsp. black pepper, divided
- ¼ cup crème fraîche
- 1 (1-lb.) Fromager d'Affinois round, at room temperature, halved crosswise, rind left on

1. Place potatoes in a large pot, and add water to cover. Add 2 teaspoons salt, and bring to a boil over high. Reduce heat to medium-low, and simmer until potatoes are fork-tender, about 20 minutes. Drain and let potatoes cool 30 minutes. Cut potatoes crosswise into ¼-inch-thick slices, and set aside.

2. Meanwhile, preheat oven to 400°F. Heat a large skillet over medium-high. Add rendered beef fat, and heat until shimmering, about 2 minutes. Add onions and 1½ teaspoons salt. Cook, stirring occasionally, until onions begin to brown, 10 to 12 minutes. Stir in sugar, and cook, stirring occasionally, until lightly browned, about 8 minutes. Add ⅓ cup wine. Cook, stirring and scraping bottom of skillet to loosen any browned bits, until wine has almost completely reduced and onions are golden and soft, about 6 minutes. Add remaining ⅓ cup wine, and cook, stirring occasionally, until onions are rich brown and jammy, 4 to 6 minutes. Stir in sage.

3. Arrange half the potato slices in an even layer in a 1½-quart oval soufflé dish or 10- × 7- × 1½-inch baking dish. Sprinkle with 1½ teaspoons salt and ¼ teaspoon pepper. Top with half the onion mixture (about ⅓ cup). Layer with remaining potatoes, remaining 1½ teaspoons salt, and remaining ¼ teaspoon pepper. Top with remaining onion mixture, and drizzle with any remaining drippings in skillet. Dot casserole with spoonfuls of crème fraîche, and arrange Fromager d'Affinois cheese halves (with rind) on top. Place soufflé dish on a rimmed baking sheet, and bake in preheated oven until bubbly and lightly browned, 20 to 30 minutes. Serve immediately. — ANGIE MAR

MAKE AHEAD Caramelized onions can be prepared up to 1 week ahead and stored in an airtight container in the refrigerator.

WINE Pair with a dry, intense Chablis.

◆━━━◆━━━◆

Mushroom-and-Chestnut Stuffing with Giblets

ACTIVE 1 HR 30 MIN; TOTAL 3 HR, PLUS OVERNIGHT REFRIGERATING; SERVES 8 TO 10

This rich and delicious make-ahead Mushroom-and-Chestnut Stuffing with Giblets from the late Anthony Bourdain gets flavor from fresh herbs.

- 1½ sticks unsalted butter, divided, plus more for greasing
- 1½ cups whole peeled chestnuts (8 oz.)
- 12 cups 2-day-old country or peasant bread, cut into ½-inch cubes
- 4 cups turkey stock
- ½ cup finely chopped shallots
- 1 large onion, finely chopped
- 2 celery ribs, finely chopped
  Kosher salt and black pepper
- 1 Tbsp. chopped fresh thyme, plus 6 thyme sprigs
- 3 Tbsp. finely chopped fresh sage, plus 2 sage sprigs
- 1 lb. mixed mushrooms, finely chopped
- ½ cup dry white wine
- ⅓ cup chopped fresh parsley
- 3 large eggs, beaten
  Reserved giblets from 2 turkeys, trimmed and cut into ¼-inch pieces
- 1 cup reserved turkey pan drippings

1. Preheat oven to 425°F. Butter a 4-quart baking dish. Spread chestnuts and bread on 2 separate baking sheets. Bake until the chestnuts are deep golden and the bread is crisp, about 10 minutes; let cool. Coarsely chop chestnuts and transfer to a large bowl.

2. In a medium saucepan, bring stock to a simmer; keep warm.

3. Melt 4 tablespoons butter in a large nonstick skillet. Add shallots, onion, and celery, and season with salt and pepper. Cook over medium, stirring occasionally, until softened, about 5 minutes. Stir in chopped thyme and sage, and cook until fragrant, about 2 minutes. Scrape mixture into large bowl.

4. Melt 2 tablespoons butter in skillet. Add half of the mushrooms and cook over medium-high, stirring occasionally, until golden, about 5 minutes. Season with salt and pepper; add ¼ cup wine. Cook, scraping up any browned bits on bottom of skillet, until almost all wine has evaporated, about 1 minute. Scrape mushrooms into large bowl. Repeat with another 2 tablespoons butter and remaining mushrooms and wine.

5. Add parsley, eggs, bread, and warm stock to bowl. Season with salt and pepper. Mix gently but thoroughly. Transfer stuffing to prepared baking dish and cover with foil. Bake for 45 minutes. Transfer stuffing to a rack, uncover, and let cool to room temperature. Cover and refrigerate overnight.

6. Meanwhile, place turkey gizzards and hearts (reserve livers) in a medium saucepan and cover with water; bring to a boil. Blanch for 5 minutes, then drain. Return giblets to saucepan. Add thyme and sage sprigs and enough water to cover, and bring to a simmer. Cover partially and cook over medium-low until tender, about 2 hours. Drain giblets and discard herbs.

7. Preheat oven to 425°F. Drizzle reserved pan juices evenly over stuffing, and bake until golden, crisp, and heated through, about 40 minutes.

8. Melt remaining 4 tablespoons butter in a medium nonstick skillet. Add turkey livers, cooked hearts, and gizzards, and cook over medium-high, turning, until golden and livers are cooked through, about 3 minutes. Spoon giblets over stuffing, and serve. — ANTHONY BOURDAIN

Sweet Potatoes with Toasted Marshmallow Swirls

ACTIVE 1 HR; TOTAL 2 HR; SERVES 10 TO 12

Chef Tyler Florence serves the traditional combination of sweet potatoes and marshmallows in a unique way, standing roasted potatoes upright and piping swirls of homemade marshmallow on top.

- 6 medium sweet potatoes (4 lb.), scrubbed but not peeled
- Extra-virgin olive oil
- Sea salt
- 1 cup pecans
- 1 cup fresh orange juice
- ¾ cup honey
- ¾ cup packed light brown sugar
- ¾ cup granulated sugar
- ½ cup light corn syrup
- 2 large egg whites
- ¼ tsp. cream of tartar

1. Preheat oven to 400°F. Prick potatoes all over with a fork and put them on a rimmed baking sheet. Brush with oil and season with salt. Bake potatoes until tender, about 1 hour.

2. Meanwhile, spread pecans in a pie plate and toast in oven until golden and fragrant, about 7 minutes. Let cool, then coarsely chop.

3. Combine orange juice, honey, and brown sugar in a medium saucepan. Bring just to a boil, stirring to dissolve the sugar. Let the honey syrup cool.

4. Combine granulated sugar, corn syrup, and ¼ cup water in another medium saucepan. Cook over medium, stirring occasionally, until sugar syrup registers 240°F on a candy thermometer.

5. Beat egg whites and cream of tartar with a stand mixer fitted with a whisk attachment on medium speed until soft peaks form. Increase speed to medium-high and drizzle hot sugar syrup into egg whites in a very thin stream down side of bowl; beat until stiff peaks form and marshmallow is cool. Scrape marshmallow into a pastry bag fitted with a medium straight tip.

6. Cut off and discard the ends of warm potatoes, then cut them crosswise into 2- to 3-inch sections. Arrange on a platter. Spoon some of the honey syrup over potatoes and on platter. Pipe marshmallow topping onto potatoes and, using a kitchen torch, lightly toast tops. Alternatively, you can pipe marshmallow onto a greased foiled-lined baking sheet and broil, then use a cake spatula to transfer onto each sweet potato section. Sprinkle the pecans over the top, and serve. — TYLER FLORENCE

MAKE AHEAD The honey syrup can be refrigerated overnight. Bring to room temperature before using. The roasted potatoes can be refrigerated overnight and reheated before proceeding.

◆ ◆ ◆

Cornbread Dressing with Buttery Sage Croutons

ACTIVE 50 MIN; TOTAL 1 HR 40 MIN; SERVES 8

This classic southern stuffing from Canadian MasterChef contestant Josh Miller has a custardlike texture that holds its shape on an overflowing Thanksgiving plate. White bread acts as a sponge absorbing all the flavorful liquid and aromatics. Toasting the bread in the skillet dries it out just enough to keep it from getting soggy.

- 10 cups 1-inch cubes savory cornbread, divided
- 4 cups torn (1-inch pieces) white Pullman bread slices
- ¾ cup unsalted butter (6 oz.), melted, divided
- 2 Tbsp. chopped fresh sage
- 1 lb. thick-cut bacon, chopped
- 2 cups chopped yellow onion
- 1½ cups chopped Gala apple
- 1 cup chopped celery
- ¼ cup chopped fresh flat-leaf parsley
- 2 Tbsp. fresh thyme leaves
- 1 tsp. kosher salt, divided
- ½ tsp. ground black pepper, divided
- 3½ cups lower-sodium chicken broth, divided
- 3 large eggs

1. Preheat oven to 350°F. Toss together 5 cups cornbread cubes, torn white bread, ½ cup butter, and sage in a large bowl. Heat a large skillet over medium-high. In 2 batches, add corn bread mixture to skillet; cook, stirring, until bread is toasted, 5 to 8 minutes. Transfer cornbread mixture to a large bowl, and set aside. Wipe skillet clean.

2. Add bacon to skillet; cook over medium, stirring often, until crisp, about 12 minutes. Using a slotted spoon, remove bacon; add to cornbread mixture. Reserve 2 tablespoons bacon drippings in skillet; discard remaining drippings or reserve for another use. Add onion, apple, celery, parsley, thyme, ½ teaspoon salt, and ¼ teaspoon black pepper, and cook, stirring occasionally, until softened, about 5 minutes. Add onion mixture to cornbread mixture. Crumble remaining 5 cups cubed cornbread into cornbread mixture.

3. Whisk together 3 cups broth, eggs, remaining ½ teaspoon salt, and remaining ¼ teaspoon pepper in a medium bowl until blended. Fold into cornbread mixture. Spoon mixture into a 13- × 9-inch baking dish. Drizzle with remaining ½ cup broth and remaining ¼ cup butter. Bake in preheated oven until lightly toasted, about 35 minutes. — JOSH MILLER

MAKE AHEAD Dressing may be assembled up to 1 day ahead; cover and chill until ready to bake.

◆ ◆ ◆

Spice-Rubbed Roasted Potatoes

ACTIVE 20 MIN; TOTAL 1 HR 15 MIN; SERVES 10 TO 12

Three types of potatoes—sweet potatoes, baking potatoes, and red potatoes—enliven these harissa-and-cumin-spiced potatoes from Food Network star Ayesha Curry.

- 2 lb. sweet potatoes, peeled and cut into 2-inch pieces
- 2 lb. baking potatoes, scrubbed and cut into 2-inch pieces
- 2 lb. red or purple potatoes, scrubbed and cut into 2-inch pieces
- 8 medium shallots, halved lengthwise
- 16 garlic cloves, halved if large
- ½ cup extra-virgin olive oil
- ¼ cup harissa seasoning
- 1 Tbsp. ground cumin
- Kosher salt and black pepper

1. Preheat oven to 425°F. Toss sweet potatoes, baking potatoes, red potatoes, shallots, garlic, oil, harissa, and cumin in a large bowl. Season generously with salt and pepper, and toss again.

2. Spread potatoes on 2 large rimmed baking sheets. Roast in upper and lower thirds of oven until tender and lightly browned, 40 to 45 minutes, rotating pans halfway through. Let stand for 10 minutes before serving. — AYESHA CURRY

Sweet Potatoes
with Toasted
Marshmallow Swirls

Sourdough Stuffing with Sausage, Red Onion, and Kale

Thousand-Layer Duck Fat Potatoes

ACTIVE 1 HR; TOTAL 12 HR; SERVES 10

Chef Shaun Searley prepares these crispy potatoes with King Edward potatoes, which have a fluffy texture. Start a day ahead so the cooled confited potatoes slice cleanly. The portioned potatoes can then be stored in the freezer for up to a month before frying.

- 4½ lb. King Edward, Kennebec, or Yukon Gold potatoes, peeled and cut lengthwise into ⅛-inch-thick slices
- ½ cup duck fat, melted
- 1 Tbsp. plus 1½ tsp. kosher salt, divided
- Vegetable oil, for frying

1. Preheat oven to 300°F. Line an 8-inch square baking pan with parchment paper, allowing 2 inches of overhang on all sides. Toss together potatoes, duck fat, and 1 tablespoon salt in a large bowl until well coated. Place a single layer of potatoes in prepared pan. Top with a second layer of potatoes, covering any gaps in first layer. Repeat layers with remaining potatoes. Drizzle any remaining duck fat in bowl over top. Cut an 8-inch square of parchment paper, and press directly onto surface of potatoes. Cover pan tightly with aluminum foil. Bake in preheated oven until potatoes are tender (removing foil to test with a wooden pick), 2 to 3 hours.

2. Transfer pan to a wire rack, and remove foil, leaving parchment sheet on potatoes. Set a second 8-inch square pan on top of potatoes in pan, and weigh it down with unopened canned goods. Let cool to room temperature, about 1 hour. Chill potatoes 8 hours or overnight with weighted pan on top.

3. Remove weighted pan and top parchment sheet; discard parchment sheet. Run a knife around edges of pan to loosen potato cake. Invert potato cake onto a cutting board; remove and discard parchment liner. Cut potato cake into 7 equal strips (about 1 inch wide). Cut each strip crosswise into 3 equal pieces. Using a knife, carefully split each piece in half to form 42 (about 2½- × 1-inch) pieces (about ¾ inch thick). Transfer potato pieces to a baking sheet lined with parchment paper, and freeze until solid, at least 30 minutes or up to 1 month. (If freezing to use at a later date, transfer frozen potato pieces to a large zip-top plastic freezer bag.)

4. While potatoes are freezing, heat 1½ inches of oil in a Dutch oven over medium-high to 375°F. Working in batches, fry frozen potato pieces (keeping remaining pieces frozen), turning occasionally, until golden brown and crispy, 5 to 6 minutes. Using a slotted spoon, transfer potato pieces to a brown paper-lined rimmed baking sheet. Sprinkle fried potatoes evenly with remaining 1½ teaspoons salt. Serve immediately. —SHAUN SEARLEY

Sausage and Fennel Stuffing

ACTIVE 35 MIN; TOTAL 2 HR 50 MIN; SERVES 10

Wedges of fennel and onion plus chunks of sweet Italian sausage give this stuffing a super-satisfying texture.

- 2 Tbsp. unsalted butter
- 1 lb. sweet Italian sausage, casings removed and meat crumbled
- 2 small fennel bulbs, cut into ¾-inch wedges, fronds reserved
- 2 medium red onions, cut into ¾-inch wedges
- 4 fresh thyme sprigs
- ¼ cup extra-virgin olive oil
- 2½ tsp. kosher salt, divided
- 1 tsp. black pepper, divided
- 1 (1¼-lb.) sourdough or other rustic boule, torn into 1½-inch pieces
- 4 large eggs
- 2½ cups unsalted chicken stock or turkey stock

1. Preheat oven to 375°F. Grease a 13- × 9-inch baking dish with butter, and set aside. Place sausage, fennel, onions, and thyme in a single layer on a large rimmed baking sheet. Drizzle with oil, and sprinkle with 1 teaspoon salt and ¾ teaspoon pepper. Bake in preheated oven until browned and softened, 20 to 25 minutes. Set aside.

2. Place bread in a single layer on a rimmed baking sheet, and bake at 375°F until very lightly toasted and dried out, 15 to 18 minutes. Let cool 5 minutes.

3. Whisk together eggs and chicken stock in a large bowl. Add bread, sausage mixture, remaining 1½ teaspoons salt, and remaining ¼ teaspoon pepper; stir well.

Scrape into prepared baking dish. Cover tightly with aluminum foil; let stand at room temperature 45 minutes.

4. Bake, covered, at 375°F until heated through, about 40 minutes. Uncover and bake until lightly browned, about 30 minutes. Let stand 10 minutes; garnish with fennel fronds. — JUSTIN CHAPPLE

Sourdough Stuffing with Sausage, Red Onion, and Kale

ACTIVE 1 HR; TOTAL 2 HR 20 MIN; SERVES 10

- ½ stick unsalted butter, cubed, plus more for greasing
- 1 lb. sweet Italian sausage, casings removed and meat crumbled
- 2 medium red onions, cut into 1-inch wedges through the core
- ¼ cup extra-virgin olive oil
- Kosher salt and black pepper
- 1 lb. curly kale, leaves torn
- 4 large eggs
- 2½ cups chicken stock or low-sodium broth
- 1¼ lb. sourdough bread, torn into 2-inch pieces
- ½ cup chopped fresh parsley
- 1 Tbsp. fresh thyme leaves
- 1 tsp. crushed red pepper

1. Preheat oven to 375°F. Butter a 13- × 9-inch baking dish. Toss sausage, onions, and oil on a large rimmed baking sheet. Season with salt and black pepper. Roast until browned and softened, about 20 minutes. Scatter kale on top of sausage and onions, and roast until just wilted, about 5 minutes. Transfer one-fourth of mixture to a plate and reserve. Let cool slightly.

2. Beat eggs with stock in a large bowl. Add bread, ½ stick butter, parsley, thyme, red pepper, 1½ teaspoons salt, and 1 teaspoon black pepper; mix well. Fold in three-fourths of sausage-kale mixture, then scrape into prepared baking dish. Decoratively scatter reserved sausage-kale mixture on top, gently pressing it into stuffing. Cover baking dish tightly with foil.

3. Bake stuffing until hot, 30 minutes. Uncover and bake until lightly browned, 30 minutes longer. Let stand for 10 minutes before serving. — JUSTIN CHAPPLE & LAURA REGE

Sweet Onion Challah Stuffing

ACTIVE 1 HR; TOTAL 2 HR 40 MIN; SERVES 8

Baked in a thin layer in a sheet pan, this nostalgic stuffing has plenty of deliciously crispy edges. When buying challah, look for a loaf that feels springy; when you poke it, the loaf should slowly bounce back to its original shape. The addition of orange juice adds a lightly sweet, floral flavor to this otherwise-traditional dish.

- ½ lb. crusty Italian bread, cut into 1-inch cubes (about 6 cups)
- ¼ cup extra-virgin olive oil
- 2½ tsp. kosher salt, divided
- ¾ tsp. ground white pepper, divided
- 1 lb. challah bread, cut into 1-inch cubes (about 16 cups)
- 2 large sweet onions, coarsely chopped
- 1 large green bell pepper, coarsely chopped
- 4 celery stalks, coarsely chopped
- ½ cup unsalted butter (4 oz.), cut into pieces
- ¼ cup chopped fresh flat-leaf parsley
- 2 tsp. chopped fresh sage
- ¼ tsp. poultry seasoning
- 1 cup unsalted vegetable stock, turkey stock, or chicken stock, plus more if needed
- ¾ cup fresh orange juice
- 4 large eggs, lightly beaten

1. Preheat oven to 325°F. Place Italian bread cubes in a large bowl; drizzle olive oil over bread while stirring constantly. Season with ½ teaspoon salt and ¼ teaspoon white pepper. Spread in a single layer on a parchment paper-lined rimmed baking sheet. Bake in preheated oven until toasted, about 30 minutes, stirring once halfway through cooking. Set 3 cups Italian bread croutons aside. (Bread will shrink during baking.) Reserve any remaining croutons for another use.

2. Spread challah bread cubes in a single layer on 2 parchment paper-lined rimmed baking sheets. Place 1 baking sheet on top oven rack and the other on bottom rack; bake at 325°F until challah is dry, about 15 minutes, rotating baking sheets top to bottom halfway through cooking. Set challah croutons aside.

3. Working in 2 batches, pulse onions, bell pepper, and celery in a food processor until finely chopped, about 3 times.

4. Melt butter in a large skillet over medium-high until sizzling. Add onion mixture, parsley, and sage, and cook, stirring often, until vegetables are just tender but not browned, about 15 minutes. Stir in poultry seasoning, remaining 2 teaspoons salt, and remaining ½ teaspoon pepper. Cook, stirring constantly, until fragrant, about 1 minute. Remove from heat.

5. Whisk together stock, orange juice, and eggs until thoroughly blended. Toss together Italian bread croutons, challah croutons, and onion mixture in a large bowl until combined. Gradually pour stock mixture into crouton mixture, stirring constantly, adding more stock if stuffing looks dry. Let stand 10 minutes.

6. Spread stuffing in an even layer on a parchment paper-lined rimmed baking sheet; cover tightly with aluminum foil. Bake at 325°F until hot, about 30 minutes. Uncover and bake until lightly browned, about 15 minutes. — NINA FRIEND

MAKE AHEAD Bake the challah and Italian bread croutons up to 1 day ahead.

NOTE You can substitute 3 cups store-bought seasoned croutons for homemade Italian bread croutons.

◆ ━━━ ◆ ━━━ ◆

Wild Rice with Mushrooms, Cranberries, and Chestnuts

ACTIVE 1 HR 10 MIN; TOTAL 1 HR 30 MIN; SERVES 6 TO 8

Nutty wild rice and meaty mushrooms anchor this effortless side dish. Delicious at room temperature, it's an ideal make-ahead dish for Thanksgiving Day.

- 1½ cups uncooked wild rice blend (about 9 oz.)
- 2¾ cups chicken broth, divided
- 2 bay leaves
- 1½ tsp. kosher salt, divided
- 3 Tbsp. olive oil, divided
- 2 leeks, trimmed, halved lengthwise, and finely chopped
- 2 carrots, finely chopped
- 2 celery stalks, finely chopped
- 2 shallots, finely chopped
- 3 garlic cloves, finely chopped
- 2 tsp. finely chopped fresh sage
- 1 tsp. fresh thyme leaves
- 1 lb. fresh wild mushrooms, cut into large pieces
- 1 cup unsweetened dried cranberries
- 1 cup roasted and peeled whole chestnuts, or toasted pecans, chopped
- 1 Tbsp. white truffle oil, optional
- Fresh sage leaves, for garnish

1. Stir together rice, 2½ cups chicken broth, bay leaves, and ¼ teaspoon salt in a medium saucepan. Bring to a boil over high. Reduce heat to low, cover, and simmer until liquid is absorbed, 40 to 45 minutes. Remove from heat, and let stand, covered, until rice is tender, about 10 minutes. Remove and discard bay leaves. Fluff with a fork, and set aside.

2. While rice cooks, heat 2 tablespoons oil in a large skillet over medium. Add leeks, carrots, celery, shallots, and garlic, and cook, stirring occasionally, until leeks are crisp-tender, about 8 minutes. Add chopped sage and thyme leaves, and cook, stirring constantly, until fragrant, about 1 minute. Add mushrooms and remaining 1 tablespoon oil, and cook, stirring often, until mushrooms are tender and lightly browned, 10 to 15 minutes. Transfer mushroom mixture to a large bowl; fold in wild rice, cranberries, chestnuts, remaining ¼ cup chicken broth, remaining 1¼ teaspoons salt, and, if using, truffle oil until well mixed. Transfer to a serving dish, and top with sage leaves. — ALECIA MOORE & ROBBY GRANTHAM-WISE

MAKE AHEAD This rice salad can be made 2 days ahead and refrigerated. Bring to room temperature and garnish with sage just before serving.

Sweet Onion
Challah Stuffing

Key Lime Macarons, RECIPE P. 227

Spiced Italian Pecan Meringues, RECIPE P. 227

Christmas Morning Biscotti, RECIPE P. 224

Cookies, Bars & Candies

Chocolate Peppermint Marshmallow Cookies,
RECIPE P. 226

Einkorn Shortbreads,
RECIPE P. 226

Triple Chocolate-
Peppermint Cookies

Triple Chocolate-Peppermint Cookies

ACTIVE 45 MIN; TOTAL 2 HR, PLUS 4 HR
CHILLING; MAKES 2 DOZEN

The peppermint bark in these cookies from Linda Levinson Friend of Chicago's Big Fat Cookie is simple to make and adds a beautiful pop of color and flavor in each cookie, though store-bought bark will work well here, too.

PEPPERMINT BARK

- 5 peppermint candy canes (about 2½ oz.)
- 15 red-and-white peppermint chocolate kisses (about 2½ oz.)
- 3 (4-oz.) white chocolate baking bars, chopped
- Pink food coloring gel

COOKIES

- 5 cups unbleached all-purpose flour (about 21¼ oz.)
- ½ cup red Dutch-process unsweetened cocoa
- ½ cup Dutch-process cocoa blend
- ½ cup crushed chocolate wafer cookies (2 oz.)
- 2 tsp. baking powder
- 1½ tsp. kosher salt
- 2 cups unsalted butter (16 oz.), chilled and cut into ½-inch pieces
- 3 cups granulated sugar
- 4 oz. semisweet chocolate chips, melted and cooled
- 4 large eggs
- 1 (12-oz.) pkg. semisweet chocolate chips

1. Make the peppermint bark Combine candy canes and chocolate kisses in a food processor; pulse until finely chopped, 10 to 14 times. Set aside. Bring 1 inch of water to a simmer in a medium saucepan over medium. Place chopped white chocolate in a medium heatproof bowl, and place over simmering water, ensuring base of bowl does not touch water. Heat, stirring often, until chocolate is melted and smooth, about 6 minutes.

2. Remove from heat; stir in candy cane mixture and 1 drop of food coloring gel until incorporated. Pour chocolate mixture onto a parchment paper-lined baking sheet; spread into a 12- × 10-inch rectangle. Freeze, uncovered, until firm and set, about 2 hours. Break or cut bark into ½-inch pieces. Store in an airtight container in freezer until ready to use, up to 1 week.

3. Make the cookies Stir together flour, red Dutch-process cocoa, cocoa blend, crushed wafer cookies, baking powder, and salt in a large bowl; set aside.

4. Beat butter and sugar with a stand mixer fitted with a paddle attachment on medium speed until light and fluffy, about 5 minutes. Add melted semisweet chocolate, and beat until combined. Add eggs, one at a time, beating until well combined after each addition. With mixer running on low speed, gradually add flour mixture, beating until just incorporated. Stir in chocolate chips. Wrap dough tightly in plastic wrap, and refrigerate at least 4 hours or up to 3 days.

5. Preheat oven to 375°F. Using your hands, roll dough into 24 balls (about 3 ounces each). Place 6 dough balls 2 inches apart on a parchment paper-lined baking sheet (keep remaining dough balls chilled). Bake in preheated oven until cookies are set but still soft, 12 to 16 minutes. Remove from oven, and immediately top cookies with 6 to 8 peppermint bark pieces, slightly inserting edges of bark into warm cookies to hold in place. Let cookies cool on baking sheet 5 minutes. Serve warm, or transfer to a cooling rack to let cool completely, about 30 minutes. Repeat with remaining cookie dough balls and peppermint bark.

— LINDA LEVINSON FRIEND

MAKE AHEAD Peppermint bark may be frozen for up to 1 week. Freeze any remaining dough balls for up to 6 months in an airtight container, or freeze baked cookies in an airtight container and reheat in a 350°F oven for 5 minutes.

Chocolate-Pretzel Crinkle Cookies

PHOTO P. 229

ACTIVE 30 MIN; TOTAL 3 HR;
MAKES 5 DOZEN

Chocolate crinkle cookies are often more cloying than satisfying. This version of the holiday staple is not only gluten-free but also perfectly salty-sweet with the best-ever chewy center.

- 8 oz. gluten-free pretzels
- ¾ cup unsweetened cocoa (about 2½ oz.)
- 1 Tbsp. baking powder
- 1½ cups granulated sugar
- ¾ cup canola oil
- 4 large eggs
- 1 Tbsp. vanilla extract
- 1½ cups powdered sugar (about 6 oz.)

1. Preheat oven to 350°F. Place pretzels in a food processor; process until very finely ground, about 1 minute and 30 seconds. (You should have about 2 cups ground pretzels.)

2. Whisk together ground pretzels, cocoa, and baking powder in a medium bowl until combined. Beat granulated sugar, oil, eggs, and vanilla in a large bowl with an electric mixer on high speed until combined. Stir in ground pretzel mixture until dough comes together. Cover with plastic wrap, and refrigerate just until firm, about 2 hours.

3. Shape dough into 60 (1-inch) balls; roll in powdered sugar until evenly and generously coated. Arrange balls 2 inches apart on large parchment paper-lined baking sheets. Bake in batches in preheated oven until tops look cracked, 13 to 15 minutes. Let cookies cool on baking sheets 2 minutes. Transfer cookies to wire racks, and let cool completely, 15 to 20 minutes. (If reusing baking sheets, make sure you let them cool completely before adding more cookie dough balls.)

— JUSTIN CHAPPLE

MAKE AHEAD Cookies can be stored in an airtight container at room temperature up to 3 days and in the freezer up to 3 months.

Jam-Filled Mezzaluna Cookies

ACTIVE 45 MIN; TOTAL 1 HR 30 MIN; MAKES 14 TO 16 COOKIES

While traveling in Italy, pastry chef Dahlia Narvaez was inspired by all the different forms of pasta. Using a recipe Nancy Silverton taught her for a super-buttery dough, she made vanilla-scented cookies shaped like mezzaluna ("half moon") pasta and filled them with a mixed-berry jam.

- 1½ cups pastry flour, plus more for dusting
- 2 Tbsp. granulated sugar, plus more for sprinkling
- 1½ sticks (12 Tbsp.) unsalted butter, cut into small pieces and chilled
- 1 Tbsp. pure vanilla extract
- 1 large egg white
- ½ cup seedless raspberry or blackberry jam
- ½ cup thinly sliced blanched almonds
- Sifted confectioners' sugar, for dusting

1. Whisk 1½ cups pastry flour with 2 tablespoons granulated sugar in a bowl. Add butter and, using a pastry blender, your fingers, or 2 dinner knives, blend the butter into the flour until the mixture resembles coarse meal. Sprinkle on the vanilla and knead gently until a dough forms. Pat the dough into a disk, wrap in plastic, and refrigerate until thoroughly chilled, at least 1 hour.

2. Preheat oven to 350°F. Line 2 large baking sheets with parchment paper and refrigerate. Cut dough into 4 pieces. Working with 1 piece at a time and leaving the rest in the refrigerator, roll out the dough ⅛ inch thick on a lightly floured work surface. Using a 4-inch round biscuit cutter, stamp out as many rounds as possible; gather and reserve the scraps.

3. Brush the edges of each round with some of the egg white. Spoon 1 rounded teaspoon of jam onto one half of each round, leaving a ¼-inch border; fold the other half over to enclose the jam. Using the tines of a fork, press the edges together to seal. Transfer the mezzaluna to one of the chilled baking sheets, spacing them 2 inches apart. Repeat with the remaining 3 pieces of dough and filling, then repeat with the gathered scraps. Refrigerate the mezzalune for at least 10 minutes.

4. Brush the mezzaluna with egg white, sprinkle with granulated sugar, and top with a generous sprinkling of sliced almonds. Bake in the upper and lower thirds of the oven until golden brown, about 40 minutes, switching the pans halfway through for even baking. Transfer the cookies to a rack to cool. Dust with confectioners' sugar and serve. —DAHLIA NARVAEZ

MAKE AHEAD Mezzaluna cookies can be stored at room temperature in an airtight container for up to 2 days or wrapped tightly in plastic and frozen for up to 2 weeks. Thaw at room temperature before serving.

Chocolate-Peppermint Brownies

ACTIVE 15 MIN; TOTAL 45 MIN, PLUS 2 HR COOLING; MAKES 2 DOZEN

Claire Ptak—an American baker and food writer who runs the Violet bakery-café in London's East End—stirs peppermint extract into her rich brownie batter and also tops the brownies with candy cane pieces. If you can't find candy canes, use striped peppermint candies.

- 2 sticks unsalted butter, cut into small pieces, plus more for greasing
- 1 lb. bittersweet chocolate, chopped
- 2 tsp. pure peppermint extract
- 4 large eggs
- 1¾ cups packed light brown sugar
- ¾ cup all-purpose flour
- 1 tsp. fine sea salt
- 4 candy canes, crushed (⅓ cup)

1. Preheat oven to 350°F. Butter a 9- × 13-inch baking pan and line with parchment paper; allow 2 inches of overhang on long sides.

2. Combine two-thirds of the chopped chocolate and 2 sticks butter in a heatproof bowl. Set bowl over a pot of simmering water and stir until melted. Scrape chocolate into another bowl and let cool slightly. Add remaining chopped chocolate and peppermint extract to heatproof bowl and melt over simmering water; remove from heat and cool slightly.

3. Whisk eggs and brown sugar in a medium bowl until combined. Whisk in chocolate-butter mixture until glossy and thick. Sprinkle flour and salt into bowl, and stir until just incorporated. Spread brownie batter in prepared baking pan. Dollop peppermint chocolate onto brownie batter and swirl in with a table knife.

4. Bake brownies in center of oven for 15 minutes. Sprinkle crushed candy canes on top, and bake until edges are set and a wooden pick inserted in center comes out with a few moist crumbs, 10 to 15 minutes longer. Let brownies cool in pan for at least 2 hours. Cut into squares, and serve. —CLAIRE PTAK

Chewy Black Licorice Chocolate Brownies

ACTIVE 30 MIN; TOTAL 1 HR 10 MIN, PLUS COOLING; MAKES 12

This deeply dark-chocolaty brownie is her homage to Top Chef judge Gail Simmons' father, Ivor. It has a sophisticated touch of salt, plus notes of molasses and anise from black licorice, and the combo makes a brilliant treat that is irresistibly chewy.

- 1½ sticks unsalted butter, melted, plus more for brushing
- 1 cup all-purpose flour
- ½ cup unsweetened cocoa powder
- 2 Tbsp. licorice root powder
- 2 tsp. ground anise seeds
- ½ tsp. kosher salt
- 1 cup granulated sugar
- 1 cup packed brown sugar
- 3 large eggs
- 1 tsp. pure vanilla extract
- 2 oz. bittersweet chocolate, chopped
- ½ cup chopped soft black licorice chews (3 oz.)

1. Preheat oven to 350°F. Line a 9-inch square baking pan with parchment paper or foil, leaving 2 inches of overhang on 2 sides. Brush paper with butter.

2. Whisk flour, cocoa powder, licorice root powder, anise, and salt in a medium bowl. Whisk 1½ sticks melted butter, granulated sugar, and brown sugar in a large bowl, then whisk in eggs and vanilla. Stir in flour mixture, then three-fourths of the chocolate and licorice chews. Scrape batter into prepared pan and smooth top. Gently press remaining chocolate and licorice chews into batter.

3. Bake brownies until a wooden pick inserted in the center comes out clean, with a few moist crumbs attached, about 40 minutes. Let brownies cool completely, then lift out of pan using the foil paper. Cut brownies into 12 rectangles, and serve. —GAIL SIMMONS

**Chewy Black Licorice
Chocolate Brownies**

Raspberry Linzer Bars

Raspberry Linzer Bars

ACTIVE 25 MIN; TOTAL 3 HR, PLUS
OVERNIGHT CHILLING; MAKES 2 DOZEN

Pastry chef Della Gossett's linzer bars are a sturdier version of her Austrian-born boss Wolfgang Puck's adored but delicate cookies. "I added rye flour for an earthy taste," she says, "and I turned them into bars so they hold up for a cookie swap."

- 1½ cups all-purpose flour
- ¾ cup rye flour
- 6 Tbsp. hazelnut flour
- 1½ tsp. baking powder
- 1 tsp. ground cinnamon
- ¾ tsp. kosher salt
- 2 sticks unsalted butter, at room temperature
- 1½ cups granulated sugar
- 4 tsp. grated lemon zest
- 1 tsp. pure vanilla extract
- 3 large egg yolks
  Nonstick cooking spray
- 1¼ cups raspberry jam
  Confectioners' sugar, for dusting

1. Whisk all-purpose flour, rye flour, hazelnut flour, baking powder, cinnamon, and salt in a medium bowl. Beat butter, granulated sugar, lemon zest, and vanilla with a stand mixer fitted a paddle attachment on medium speed until smooth, about 5 minutes. Beat in egg yolks, one at a time, scraping down side of bowl, until incorporated. Beat in flour mixture on low speed until dough just comes together. Press one-third of the dough and two-thirds of the dough into 2 disks and wrap in plastic. Refrigerate overnight until firm.

2. Preheat oven to 350°F. Coat a 13- × 9-inch metal baking pan with cooking spray. Line with parchment paper, leaving a 2-inch overhang on long sides, and coat with cooking spray. Using large holes of a box grater, shred larger disk of dough evenly in the pan.

3. Spread jam over shredded dough, leaving a ½-inch border. Shred smaller disk over jam. Bake until top is deep golden brown, 35 to 40 minutes, rotating pan halfway through. Transfer to a wire rack and let cool. Refrigerate in pan until firm, at least 2 hours.

4. Using the paper, transfer pastry to a work surface. Dust with confectioners' sugar, cut into 2-inch bars, and serve cold or at room temperature. — DELLA GOSSETT

MAKE AHEAD The bars can be stored in an airtight container for up to 4 days.

◆ ◆ ◆

Vanilla-Mint Marshmallows

TOTAL 1 HR, PLUS 3 HR SETTING;
MAKES ABOUT 50

Jami Curl of Quin Candy in Portland, Oregon, uses sheets of silver leaf gelatin to help give these delicately minty marshmallows their smooth, pillowy texture. While granulated gelatin is more accessible, it does not melt as evenly as sheet gelatin and can make for gritty marshmallows.

- Canola oil
- ¼ cup plus 1 Tbsp. light corn syrup
- 1 Tbsp. pure peppermint extract
- 1 vanilla bean, split lengthwise and seeds scraped
- 20 sheets silver leaf gelatin (see Note)
- ⅓ cup plus 2 Tbsp. ice water
- 3 cups granulated sugar
- 1 cup plus 1 Tbsp. water
- 15 drops natural red food coloring
- 1 cup plus 1 Tbsp. confectioners' sugar
- 1 cup cornstarch

1. Lightly grease a 13- × 9-inch metal baking pan with canola oil. Beat corn syrup, peppermint extract, and vanilla seeds with a stand mixer fitted with a whisk attachment on low speed until combined. Reserve vanilla bean pod for another use.

2. Place gelatin sheets in a heatproof medium bowl, cover with ⅓ cup plus 2 tablespoons ice water, and let stand, stirring occasionally, until gelatin is evenly moistened and water is absorbed, about 5 minutes. Bring 2 inches of water to a simmer in a medium saucepan. Set bowl with gelatin over simmering water and cook, stirring once or twice, until melted, about 5 minutes. Do not let bowl touch water. Carefully remove saucepan from heat.

3. Bring granulated sugar and 1 cup plus 1 tablespoon water to a boil in a small, heavy-bottom saucepan. Cook, without stirring, until sugar syrup registers 225°F on a candy thermometer, 8 to 10 minutes. Use a wet pastry brush to wash down side of pan.

4. With stand mixer on low speed, slowly stream hot sugar syrup into corn syrup. Add warm gelatin and continue beating until slightly thickened and opaque, about 2 minutes. Increase speed to medium-high and beat until marshmallow is thick and glossy and registers 105°F, about 12 minutes.

5. Lightly grease a rubber spatula. Scatter food coloring over marshmallow, then, using spatula, quickly scrape marshmallow into prepared pan, swirling food coloring as you go. Let stand at room temperature until set, at least 3 hours or overnight.

6. Sift confectioners' sugar and cornstarch into a shallow bowl. Invert marshmallows onto a work surface and cut into 2-inch squares. Toss in sugar mixture, shaking off any excess, then serve. — JAMI CURL

NOTE Silver leaf gelatin is available at most baking supply shops and on amazon.com.

MAKE AHEAD The marshmallows can be stored in an airtight container at room temperature for up to 1 month.

St. Nicholas Day Letters

ACTIVE 50 MIN; TOTAL 3 HR 15 MIN;
MAKES 16

California chef David LeFevre twists his flaky, buttery almond cream-filled cookies into the letter S in honor of his sister, Suzanne, but they can be adapted to make any letter. Whatever the shape, a hit of fleur de sel just before baking kicks up the flavor.

- 1½ cups all-purpose flour
- 2 sticks unsalted butter, cubed and chilled
- 4 oz. almond paste
- 1 large egg white
- ⅓ cup granulated sugar
- 2 Tbsp. packed light brown sugar
- ½ tsp. pure vanilla extract
- ¼ tsp. ground cardamom
- 1 large egg
- 2 Tbsp. whole milk
- Fleur de sel, for sprinkling

1. Combine flour and butter in a food processor. Pulse until mixture resembles coarse meal. Add ½ cup ice water, and pulse just until dough comes together. Divide in half and press into disks. Wrap in plastic and refrigerate until firm, at least 1 hour or overnight.

2. Meanwhile, beat almond paste, egg white, granulated sugar, brown sugar, vanilla, and cardamom in a stand mixer fitted with a paddle attachment on medium speed until smooth, about 4 minutes. Spoon spiced almond paste into a pastry bag fitted with a ½-inch tip, or use a sturdy, zip-top plastic bag and snip off a corner.

3. Line 2 baking sheets with parchment paper. Lightly beat egg with milk in a small bowl. On a lightly floured surface, roll out 1 disk of dough into a 14- × 8-inch rectangle. Cut dough crosswise into 8 (1¾-inch) strips.

4. Pipe a line of almond paste down center of each strip. Brush one side of each strip with beaten egg. Roll one side over filling and pinch seam closed. Transfer logs to prepared baking sheets, seam-side down. Form each log into an S shape. Repeat with remaining disk of dough, almond paste, and beaten egg. Freeze cookies until firm, about 1 hour.

5. Preheat oven to 375°F. Brush cookies with remaining beaten egg and sprinkle with fleur de sel. Bake until golden, 20 to 25 minutes. Transfer cookies to a wire rack and let cool slightly. Serve warm or at room temperature. — DAVID LEFEVRE

MAKE AHEAD The cookies can be stored in an airtight container for up to 3 days.

Vanilla-Brown Butter Sable Cookies

ACTIVE 45 MIN; TOTAL 6 HR 40 MIN, PLUS
8 HR CHILLING TIME; MAKES 2 DOZEN

Vanilla, a notoriously difficult product to grow and source, really shines in this recipe from New York pastry chef Natasha Pickowicz, making the quality especially important. To efficiently seed a vanilla bean, use a paring knife to split the bean in half, then use the full edge of the knife to scrape the seeds from the cut sides.

- 2½ cups unsalted butter (20 oz.)
- 1½ cups granulated sugar, divided
- ¾ cup unsifted powdered sugar (3 oz.)
- 5 large egg yolks
- 1 Tbsp. vanilla extract
- 4¼ cups all-purpose flour (18⅛ oz.), sifted
- 2 tsp. kosher salt
- 1 large egg white, beaten
- ¾ tsp. sel gris or other crunchy sea salt, divided

1. Prepare an ice bath in a large bowl; set aside. Melt butter in a medium-size deep saucepan over medium, swirling often, until butter bubbles and develops a heavy foam, foam subsides, and butter turns a deep golden color, about 14 minutes. Remove from heat; pour brown butter into a heatproof bowl, scraping milk solids from bottom of saucepan into bowl. Place bowl in prepared ice bath; let cool, stirring occasionally, 10 minutes. Remove bowl from ice bath; let stand at room temperature 2 hours. Cover and chill overnight or up to 3 days.

2. Remove brown butter from fridge; let stand at room temperature 1 to 2 hours to soften. Transfer butter to bowl of a heavy-duty electric stand mixer fitted with paddle attachment. Add 1 cup granulated sugar and powdered sugar. Beat on medium-low

speed until smooth and creamy but not yet light and fluffy, about 2 minutes. (Do not overbeat.) Add egg yolks, one at a time, beating after each addition, stopping to scrape down sides of bowl as needed. Add vanilla, and beat until just combined, about 5 seconds. Reduce speed to low; gradually add flour and kosher salt, beating until just combined, about 1 minute.

3. Form dough into a ball; transfer to a large sheet of parchment paper. Cover with a second sheet of parchment paper. Using a rolling pin, gently roll dough between parchment to ⅓-inch thickness. Transfer dough sandwiched between parchment paper onto a baking sheet. Chill until firm, 1 hour or overnight.

4. Remove top sheet of parchment paper from chilled dough. Cut dough into 24 (3-inch) circles. (Reroll dough scraps as needed; rechill dough if it becomes too soft to handle.) Transfer dough rounds to a baking sheet lined with parchment paper; freeze until solid, about 1 hour.

5. Preheat oven to 350°F. Remove 12 dough rounds from freezer. Place remaining ½ cup granulated sugar in a small bowl. Brush edges of the 12 dough rounds with half of the egg white; roll edges of dough rounds in granulated sugar to coat. Place dough rounds 3 inches apart on 2 baking sheets lined with parchment paper. Sprinkle tops evenly with half of the sel gris. Bake in preheated oven until centers of cookies are just set and edges are lightly browned, about 14 minutes. Remove from oven. Cool cookies on baking sheets 2 minutes; transfer to a wire rack to cool completely, about 30 minutes. Repeat procedure with remaining 12 dough rounds, remaining half of egg white, remaining granulated sugar (discard leftover granulated sugar once all 24 cookies have been rolled), and remaining half of sel gris. — NATASHA PICKOWICZ

MAKE AHEAD Unbaked dough rounds may be prepared through Step 4. Freeze until completely frozen, about 6 hours or up to overnight. Transfer frozen rounds to a zip-top plastic bag and keep frozen until ready to bake.

**Vanilla-Brown Butter
Sable Cookies**

Lemon-Tahini Cookies

ACTIVE 30 MIN; TOTAL 2 HR 30 MIN;
MAKES ABOUT 30 COOKIES

For the crispiest cookies, be sure to chill the dough; it helps reduce spreading during baking and concentrates the flavor by allowing the dough to dry slightly.

- ¾ cup unsalted butter (6 oz.), softened
- ¾ cup granulated sugar
- ½ cup well-stirred smooth tahini
- 1 large egg
- 3 Tbsp. lemon zest plus 2 tsp. fresh lemon juice
- 1 tsp. vanilla extract
- 2 cups all-purpose flour (about 8½ oz.)
- 1 tsp. kosher salt
- ½ cup cacao nibs (optional)
- ⅓ cup black sesame seeds
- ⅓ cup white sesame seeds

1. Line 2 baking sheets with parchment paper. Beat butter, sugar, and tahini in a medium bowl with an electric mixer on medium-high speed until light and fluffy, 3 to 5 minutes. Add egg, lemon zest and juice, and vanilla; beat until combined, about 1 minute, scraping down sides of bowl as needed. With mixer running on low speed, gradually add flour and salt; beat until dough comes together. If using, fold in cacao nibs until combined.

2. Divide dough in half; place each half on a large piece of plastic wrap. Fold plastic wrap over to cover dough, and, using your hands, roll each into a smooth log 1 inch in diameter. Refrigerate until firm, at least 1 hour and 30 minutes or up to 8 hours.

3. Preheat oven to 350°F. Combine sesame seeds on a small sheet pan or flat plate. Remove dough logs from plastic wrap, and roll in sesame seeds, pressing firmly so seeds adhere evenly. Slice dough logs into ¼-inch-thick rounds. Place 1 inch apart on prepared baking sheets.

4. Bake cookies in preheated oven until golden around edges, 8 to 10 minutes. Let cool on baking sheets 5 minutes; transfer to a wire rack and let cool completely, about 15 minutes. Store in an airtight container at room temperature up to 5 days. — GAIL SIMMONS

MAKE AHEAD Dough can be made and frozen up to 3 weeks ahead. Let thaw 30 minutes before rolling in sesame seeds.

Lebkuchen

ACTIVE 45 MIN; TOTAL 2 HR;
MAKES 18 COOKIES

Lebkuchen are traditional, delicately spiced German molasses-ginger cookies. This recipe, from mixologist Jeffrey Morgenthaler, was passed down from his great-grandmother to his grandmother to his uncle.

- 1 cup heavy cream
- 1 Tbsp. white vinegar
- 4 cups all-purpose flour
- ½ cup almond flour
- 2 Tbsp. minced candied orange peel
- 2 Tbsp. minced candied lemon peel
- 1 Tbsp. ground cinnamon
- 1 tsp. ground cloves
- 1 tsp. ground allspice
- 1 tsp. baking soda
- ½ tsp. freshly grated nutmeg
- ½ tsp. kosher salt
- 1 cup dark brown sugar
- ½ cup vegetable shortening, at room temperature
- ½ cup unsulfured molasses
- ⅓ cup blanched whole almonds
- 2½ cups confectioners' sugar, sifted
- 5 Tbsp. whole milk

1. Stir cream and vinegar together in a small bowl, and let stand until thickened, about 30 minutes.

2. Preheat oven to 325°F. Whisk all-purpose flour with almond flour, candied orange and lemon peels, cinnamon, cloves, allspice, baking soda, nutmeg, and salt in a medium bowl. In the bowl of a stand mixer fitted with the paddle, beat brown sugar with shortening and molasses on medium speed until light and fluffy, about 3 minutes. Add the thickened cream and beat until smooth. Add dry ingredients and beat on low speed just until combined.

3. Line 2 large rimmed baking sheets with parchment paper. Working in 2 batches, using a 2-ounce ice cream scoop or ¼-cup measure, scoop the dough into mounds on the prepared sheets, spacing them 3 inches apart. Place 3 whole almonds in a star pattern on top of each cookie and, with the palm of your hand, gently flatten each mound slightly.

4. Bake cookies in preheated oven until lightly browned, 15 minutes; rotate the baking sheets from top to bottom and front to back halfway through baking. Let cookies cool on baking sheets for 10 minutes. Transfer to a wire rack and let cool completely.

5. In a small, wide bowl, whisk confectioners' sugar with milk until smooth. Dip the top of each cookie in the glaze, letting excess drip back into the bowl. Transfer cookies to a rack and let stand until glaze hardens, about 10 minutes. —JEFFREY MORGENTHALER

MAKE AHEAD The lebkuchen can be stored in an airtight container for up to 5 days.

Bakewell Biscotti

ACTIVE 1 HR; TOTAL 2 HR, PLUS COOLING; MAKES ABOUT 30 BISCOTTI SANDWICHES

Dominique Ansel was inspired by the traditional Bakewell tart pie pastry filled with jam and almond cream to create these addictive sandwich cookies.

BISCOTTI

- 2½ cups bread flour, plus more for dusting
- ½ tsp. baking soda
- ¼ tsp. fine salt
- 1⅓ cups granulated sugar
- 4 Tbsp. unsalted butter, softened
- 1 tsp. finely grated lemon zest
- 3 large eggs
- ¾ cup dried sour cherries, chopped

FILLING

- 1 stick unsalted butter, softened
- ¾ cup confectioners' sugar
- 2 large eggs
- 1½ cups almond flour
- 2 Tbsp. cornstarch
- 1 Tbsp. dark rum
- Cherry jam, for spreading

1. Make the biscotti Preheat oven to 350°F. Line a large baking sheet with parchment paper. Whisk 2½ cups bread flour, baking soda, and salt in a medium bowl.

2. In a stand mixer fitted with a paddle, beat granulated sugar, butter, and lemon zest with a stand mixer on medium speed until pale and creamy, 2 minutes. Beat in eggs one at a time until incorporated. Beat in flour mixture on low speed until dough just comes together, then beat in cherries.

3. Scrape dough onto prepared baking sheet and, using lightly floured hands, shape it into a 15- × 5-inch log. Bake until golden and just firm, about 35 minutes, then let cool completely on baking sheet.

4. Make the filling Beat butter and confectioners' sugar with a stand mixer fitted with a paddle attachment on medium speed until smooth. Beat in eggs one at a time until incorporated; scrape down side and bottom of bowl as needed. Beat in almond flour and cornstarch until combined, then beat in rum. Transfer almond cream to a medium bowl and refrigerate until just set, about 20 minutes.

5. Transfer baked log to a cutting board. Using a serrated knife, cut it crosswise into ¼-inch-thick slices. Spread a scant tablespoon of almond cream on half the slices and arrange on 2 large parchment paper-lined baking sheets. Spread a teaspoon of jam on almond cream. Close sandwiches with remaining slices.

6. Bake biscotti sandwiches until lightly browned and nearly crisp, about 15 minutes. Let cool completely before serving. — DOMINIQUE ANSEL

MAKE AHEAD The biscotti sandwiches can be stored in an airtight container for up to 5 days.

Christmas Morning Biscotti

PHOTO P. 212

ACTIVE 25 MIN; TOTAL 1 HR 45 MIN; MAKES ABOUT 2 DOZEN

Los Angeles chef Merrin Mae Gray is Filipina, not Italian, but she really connects with Italy's soulful food: "These biscotti spiced with cocoa nibs and anise seeds are my Italian interpretation of biskotso, a twice-baked cookie I grew up eating with hot chocolate."

- Nonstick cooking spray
- 1¾ cups all-purpose flour
- 1 tsp. baking powder
- ½ tsp. baking soda
- Kosher salt
- 5 Tbsp. unsalted butter, softened
- ⅔ cup sugar
- 3 large eggs
- 1 Tbsp. plus 1 tsp. anisette liqueur
- ¼ cup cocoa nibs
- 1½ tsp. whole anise seeds

1. Preheat oven to 325°F. Coat a baking sheet with cooking spray. Line with parchment paper; coat with cooking spray.

2. Whisk flour, baking powder, baking soda, and a pinch of salt in a medium bowl. Beat butter and sugar in a stand mixer fitted with a paddle attachment on medium-high speed until fluffy, about 3 minutes. Beat in 2 eggs, one at a time. Beat in 1 tablespoon anisette. Beat flour mixture on low speed until just combined. Mix in cocoa nibs and anise seeds.

3. On prepared baking sheet, using lightly floured fingers, shape dough into a slightly flattened 12-inch log ¾ inch thick. Lightly whisk remaining egg and remaining 1 teaspoon anisette in a small bowl. Brush log with egg mixture. Bake until pale golden, 20 minutes. Transfer baking sheet to a wire rack and let log cool slightly.

4. Using a serrated knife, cut log into diagonal, ½-inch-thick slices. Arrange slices on baking sheet; bake until toasted, about 10 minutes, flipping halfway through. Transfer baking sheet to a wire rack; let biscotti cool. — MERRIN MAE GRAY

MAKE AHEAD The biscotti can be stored in an airtight container for up to 1 week.

Almond Crescents

ACTIVE 30 MIN; TOTAL 1 HR 15 MIN, PLUS COOLING; MAKES ABOUT 3 DOZEN

Dust these crowd pleasers from baking superstar Dorie Greenspan with colorful granulated sugar for more holiday pop.

- 2 sticks unsalted butter, softened
- ½ cup granulated sugar
- ½ tsp. fine sea salt
- 1½ tsp. pure vanilla extract
- ¼ tsp. pure almond extract
- 1¾ cups all-purpose flour
- 1⅓ cups almond flour
- 1½ cups confectioners' sugar, plus more for dusting

1. Preheat oven to 350°F. Line a large rimmed baking sheet with parchment paper. Beat butter, granulated sugar, and salt in a large bowl with an electric mixer on medium speed until light and fluffy, 3 minutes. Beat in vanilla extract and almond extract. Reduce speed to low and add all-purpose flour and almond flour, mixing until just combined. Refrigerate dough until firm, about 30 minutes.

2. Scoop 12 rounded tablespoonfuls of dough onto prepared baking sheet. Using your hands, roll each ball into a 4-inch rope, then shape into a crescent; return to baking sheet. If dough gets too soft, refrigerate until firm. Bake cookies until lightly browned around the edges, 13 to 15 minutes, rotating sheet halfway through baking. Transfer to a wire rack and let cool for 5 minutes.

3. Sift 1½ cups confectioners' sugar into a shallow bowl. Dredge warm cookies in confectioners' sugar; return to wire rack and let cool completely. Repeat baking and dredging with remaining dough. Dust cookies with additional confectioners' sugar before serving. — DORIE GREENSPAN

Bakewell Biscotti

Chocolate Peppermint Marshmallow Cookies

PHOTO P. 213

ACTIVE 1 HR 15 MIN; TOTAL 3 HR 30 MIN; MAKES 4 DOZEN

In this version of the holiday favorite from Los Angeles pastry chef Della Gossett, crunchy peppermint candy nicely balances the pillowy marshmallow filling.

MARSHMALLOWS

Nonstick cooking spray

¼ cup powdered gelatin

2 large egg whites, at room temperature

2¼ cups sugar

1 Tbsp. light corn syrup

2 tsp. pure vanilla extract

1 cup crushed peppermint candies (10 oz.), plus more for sprinkling

8 to 12 drops of red food coloring

COOKIES

1¼ cups bread flour

1 cup pastry flour

½ tsp. kosher salt

2 sticks unsalted butter, at room temperature

1 cup sugar

½ vanilla bean, split lengthwise and seeds scraped

1 large egg

1 large egg yolk

2 tsp. pure vanilla extract

Neutral oil, such as grapeseed, for brushing

GLAZE

28 oz. dark chocolate (65%–70% cacao), chopped

4 oz. cocoa butter

1. Make the marshmallows Coat a 18- × 13-inch rimmed baking sheet with cooking spray. Line with parchment paper and coat with cooking spray. Whisk gelatin and ¾ cup water in a small microwavable bowl. Microwave on HIGH in 10-second increments, stirring after each, until the gelatin is just melted, about 50 seconds.

2. Beat egg whites in a stand mixer fitted with a whisk on medium-low speed until very foamy. Meanwhile, combine sugar, corn syrup, and 1 cup water in a medium saucepan and bring to a boil, stirring occasionally. Cook over medium, without stirring, until the sugar syrup registers 260°F on a candy thermometer, about 10 minutes. Remove pan from heat and carefully stir in gelatin until melted.

3. Carefully drizzle hot syrup into egg whites down side of bowl, beating on medium speed. Add vanilla and beat on high speed until thick and glossy, about 10 minutes. Using a rubber spatula, fold in 1 cup peppermint candies. Sprinkle in food coloring, then quickly scrape marshmallow mixture onto prepared baking sheet, swirling food coloring, and smooth surface. Let stand at room temperature until set, at least 2 hours or overnight.

4. Make the cookies Whisk bread flour, pastry flour, and salt in a medium bowl. Beat butter, sugar, and vanilla bean seeds in a stand mixer fitted with a paddle attachment on medium speed until fluffy, about 5 minutes. Beat in egg, egg yolk, and vanilla extract. Beat in flour mixture on low speed until just combined. Divide dough in half and press into disks. Wrap in plastic and refrigerate until firm, at least 1 hour or overnight.

5. On a lightly floured sheet of parchment paper, roll out 1 disk of dough into a rectangle, ¼ inch thick. Transfer on parchment paper to a baking sheet and refrigerate until firm, about 30 minutes. Repeat with second disk of dough.

6. Preheat oven to 325°F. Using a square cookie cutter or a knife, cut 2-inch squares from dough and arrange on baking sheets 1 inch apart. Reroll scraps and cut more squares. Bake cookies until golden brown, 10 to 12 minutes. Transfer baking sheets to wire racks and let cookies cool.

7. Lightly brush cookie cutter or a knife with oil, repeating as needed. Cut out 48 (2-inch) marshmallows. Place 1 marshmallow on top of each cookie and transfer to baking sheets. Freeze until cold, at least 15 minutes.

8. Make the glaze Combine chocolate and cocoa butter in a large microwavable bowl. Microwave on HIGH in 20-second increments, stirring after each one, until mixture is melted and smooth.

9. Coat 2 rimmed baking sheets with cooking spray. Line with parchment paper and coat with cooking spray. Using a fork, dip each cookie in glaze, then set on a prepared baking sheet and sprinkle with some peppermint candy. Refrigerate until set, at least 15 minutes, and serve cold. — DELLA GOSSETT

MAKE AHEAD The cookies can be refrigerated in an airtight container for up to 4 days.

Einkorn Shortbreads

PHOTO P. 213

ACTIVE 25 MIN; TOTAL 2 HR 25 MIN; MAKES 20

In her quest to re-create the quintessential flavor of her grandmother's butter cookies, Roxana Jullapat, chef-owner of Friends & Family in East Hollywood, came up with these unique cookies that get nutty, caramel-like notes from the wheatlike grain einkorn.

6 Tbsp. confectioners' sugar

⅓ cup dark brown sugar

2 sticks unsalted butter, cubed, at room temperature

1¼ cups whole-grain einkorn flour (see Note)

1 cup all-purpose flour

1¾ tsp. kosher salt

1. Preheat oven to 300°F. Place confectioners' sugar and brown sugar in a food processor; pulse until combined. Add butter, and pulse to combine. Add einkorn flour, all-purpose flour, and salt, and pulse until dough comes together. Divide in half and press into disks. Wrap in plastic and refrigerate for 30 minutes.

2. Roll out each disk of dough between 2 sheets of parchment paper into a ¼-inch-thick round. Peel off the top layer of parchment. Using a 2½-inch round cookie cutter, stamp out cookies and transfer to 2 baking sheets, spaced ½ inch apart. Using a small star-shape cookie cutter, stamp out a star in upper right corner of each cookie. Transfer stars to a separate baking sheet. Reroll scraps and cut out more cookies.

3. Bake cookies and stars until deep golden brown, 25 to 30 minutes for cookies and 10 to 12 minutes for stars. Transfer baking sheets to wire racks and let cool completely. — ROXANA JULLAPAT

MAKE AHEAD The cookies can be stored in an airtight container for up to 3 days.

NOTE Einkorn flour is available from jovialfoods.com.

Key Lime Macarons

PHOTO P. 212

ACTIVE 1 HR; TOTAL 3 HR; MAKES 70

These tangy, one-bite sandwiched meringues from California pastry chef Uyen Nguyen get a surprise pop of flavor courtesy of fennel seeds.

FILLING

- 3 large eggs
- ½ tsp. powdered gelatin
- ¾ cup fresh Key lime juice
- ¾ cup granulated sugar
- 1½ sticks unsalted butter, cubed and chilled

MACARON SHELLS

- 2 cups almond flour
- 1⅔ cups confectioners' sugar
- 5 large egg whites, at room temperature
- 2 tsp. finely grated lime zest
- 30 drops of green food coloring or 5 drops of green food gel
- 1 cup granulated sugar
- 1½ tsp. fennel seeds

1. Make the filling Beat the eggs in a medium bowl to mix. Whisk gelatin with 1 tablespoon water in a small bowl. Combine Key lime juice and granulated sugar in a medium saucepan. Bring to a boil over medium-high, stirring occasionally. Slowly pour juice mixture into eggs, whisking constantly. Scrape egg mixture back into pan, and cook over medium, stirring, until bubbles appear and mixture thickens, about 3 minutes. Add gelatin mixture, and stir until melted.

2. Pour custard through a fine wire-mesh strainer over a small heatproof bowl; discard solids. Gradually whisk butter into custard until it is fully incorporated. Cover with plastic and refrigerate until cold, at least 2 hours. Spoon custard into a small pastry bag fitted with a ¼-inch tip, or use a sturdy zip-top plastic bag and snip off a corner.

3. Make the macaron shells Line 4 or 5 baking sheets with silicone mats or parchment paper. Sift almond flour and confectioners' sugar in a medium bowl. Stir in half the egg whites, lime zest, and food coloring until a smooth paste forms; color should be a shade or two darker than final desired color.

4. Combine granulated sugar and ¼ cup water in a small saucepan, and bring to a boil, stirring occasionally. Cook over medium, without stirring, until sugar syrup reaches 240°F on a candy thermometer, about 5 minutes.

5. Beat remaining egg whites with a stand mixer fitted with a whisk attachment on medium speed until medium peaks form, about 4 minutes. Carefully drizzle in hot syrup on medium speed. Increase speed to high and beat meringue until stiff and glossy, about 5 minutes.

6. Stir one-third of the meringue into almond mixture. Using a rubber spatula, fold in remaining meringue, then cut through it, pressing it against side of the bowl to slightly deflate to a thick, lavalike consistency.

7. Transfer meringue to a pastry bag fitted with a plain ½-inch tip; pipe onto prepared baking sheets in 1-inch mounds, 1 inch apart. Tap sheets on counter and top each macaron shell with a few fennel seeds. Let dry until a skin forms, 1 to 3 hours.

8. Preheat oven to 350°F. Bake meringues until crisp on the outside and slightly chewy on the inside, 9 to 12 minutes. Transfer baking sheets to wire racks and let cool completely. Using a thin metal spatula, peel meringues off baking sheets. Pipe custard onto flat sides of half the meringues. Top with remaining meringues. — UYEN NGUYEN

MAKE AHEAD The macarons can be refrigerated in an airtight container for up to 5 days.

Spiced Italian Pecan Meringues

PHOTO P. 212

ACTIVE 15 MIN; TOTAL 2 HR; MAKES ABOUT 1½ DOZEN

The pecans and potent grappa are unexpectedly elegant, and the crisp outsides and chewy centers make these meringues from Los Angeles chef Merrin Mae Gray seriously addictive.

- ¾ cup shelled pecans
- 3 large egg whites
- ¾ cup sugar
- 1½ tsp. grappa
- ¼ tsp. ground cinnamon
- ⅛ tsp. ground nutmeg
- ⅛ tsp. ground cloves

1. Preheat oven to 300°F. Spread pecans on a small rimmed baking sheet and toast until browned, about 20 minutes, tossing halfway through. Transfer to a work surface and let cool, then coarsely chop.

2. Line 2 rimmed baking sheets with parchment paper. Beat egg whites with a stand mixer fitted with a whisk attachment on medium-high speed until foamy, about 30 seconds. Beat in sugar, 1 tablespoon at a time, until whites are stiff and glossy, 5 to 7 minutes. Beat in grappa, cinnamon, nutmeg, and cloves. Using a rubber spatula, gently fold in the chopped pecans.

3. Spoon heaping tablespoons of meringue onto prepared baking sheets, spaced 1 inch apart. Bake for 15 minutes. Reduce oven temperature to 200°F and bake until meringues are firm on outside but still chewy in center, 1 hour and 15 minutes. Transfer baking sheets to wire racks and let cool completely. — MERRIN MAE GRAY

MAKE AHEAD The meringues can be stored in an airtight container for up to 1 week.

Molasses Thumbprints with Cajeta

ACTIVE 55 MIN; TOTAL 3 HR; MAKES ABOUT 3 DOZEN

"The cajeta filling for these cookies was a natural twist at a Mexican restaurant," says pastry chef Ivan Arturo Marquez of Broken Spanish. "I also like the play of the sweet goat-milk caramel, slightly bitter molasses, and sharp candied ginger."

CAJETA

- 4 cups goat milk
- 1 cup granulated sugar
- 1 tsp. finely grated lemon zest
- ½ tsp. baking soda
- ½ vanilla bean, split lengthwise and seeds scraped

COOKIES

- 1½ cups all-purpose flour
- 1 Tbsp. cornstarch
- 1½ tsp. ground ginger
- 1 tsp. ground cinnamon
- 1 tsp. ground cloves
- ¾ tsp. baking soda
- 6 Tbsp. unsalted butter, at room temperature
- ½ cup packed light brown sugar
- ¼ cup unsulfured molasses
- 1 large egg
- ½ tsp. pure vanilla paste
- ½ cup finely chopped candied ginger (2½ oz.)
- ½ cup turbinado sugar

1. Make the cajeta Combine goat milk, granulated sugar, and lemon zest in a medium saucepan. Bring to a boil over medium. Remove pan from heat, and whisk in baking soda and vanilla bean seeds. Return pan to medium-low and simmer, whisking occasionally, until caramel is amber and consistency of condensed milk, about 1 hour and 30 minutes. Set a fine-mesh strainer over a small heatproof bowl. Strain caramel into bowl; discard solids. Let cool slightly. Cover with plastic wrap and refrigerate until firm and cold, at least 1 hour.

2. Make the cookies Whisk flour, cornstarch, ground ginger, cinnamon, cloves, and baking soda in a medium bowl. Beat butter and brown sugar in a stand mixer fitted with a paddle attachment on medium speed until light and fluffy, about 2 minutes. Add molasses and beat until incorporated. Add egg and vanilla paste, and beat until smooth. Beat in flour mixture on low speed until just combined. Stir in candied ginger. Cover bowl with plastic wrap and refrigerate until cold, at least 1 hour.

3. Preheat oven to 325°F. Line 2 baking sheets with parchment paper. Spread turbinado sugar in a shallow bowl. Roll tablespoons of dough into balls, then coat in turbinado sugar; transfer to prepared baking sheets, spaced 1 inch apart. Freeze for 15 minutes.

4. Bake cookies until crisp on the outside but still tender on the inside, about 10 minutes, rotating the baking sheets halfway through. Remove baking sheets from oven. Using back of a ½-teaspoon measuring spoon, make an indentation in center of each warm cookie. Transfer baking sheets to wire racks and let cool completely.

5. Fill each cookie with about ½ teaspoon of cold caramel and refrigerate just until set, about 30 minutes.
— IVAN ARTURO MARQUEZ

MAKE AHEAD The caramel can be refrigerated in an airtight container for up to a week. The cookies can be refrigerated for up to 3 days.

S'mores Linzer Cookies

PHOTO P. 229

ACTIVE 1 HR; TOTAL 2 HR 45 MIN; MAKES 2 DOZEN

Linzer cookies are descendants of the linzertorte, named for the Austrian city of Linz. Hazelnut meal gives this twist on the classic a slightly nutty flavor.

- 1¼ cups all-purpose flour (about 5⅜ oz.), plus more
- ¾ cup graham flour (about 4 oz.)
- ½ cup hazelnut meal (about 1⅞ oz.)
- ¾ tsp. kosher salt
- 1 cup unsalted butter (8 oz.), at room temperature
- ⅔ cup granulated sugar
- 1 tsp. vanilla extract
- 2 cups marshmallow creme
- 1 (4-oz.) bittersweet chocolate baking bar, chopped

1. Whisk together all-purpose flour, graham flour, hazelnut meal, and salt in a medium bowl; set aside. Beat butter, granulated sugar, and vanilla with a stand mixer fitted with a paddle attachment (or a large bowl and electric mixer) on medium speed until creamy, about 2 minutes. With machine running on low speed, add flour mixture, beating until smooth. Divide dough in half, and pat each half into a disk. Wrap each disk in plastic wrap, and chill until cold, about 1 hour.

2. Preheat oven to 350°F. Line 2 large baking sheets with parchment paper. Unwrap dough disks, and discard plastic wrap. On a lightly floured work surface, carefully roll each dough disk to a scant ¼-inch thickness. (Press dough back together if it cracks.) From one rolled-out disk, using a 2-inch square cutter, cut out 24 dough squares as close together as possible. Using a smaller square cutter, cut out centers of dough squares, reserving smaller center squares. Place larger dough squares 2 inches apart on one prepared baking sheet.

3. From second rolled-out disk, cut out 24 (2-inch) dough squares, rerolling scraps (including reserved cut-out dough centers) as necessary. Place 2 inches apart on second prepared baking sheet. Refrigerate all dough squares until chilled, about 30 minutes.

4. Bake cookies in preheated oven on middle and upper oven racks until very lightly browned and just firm, 15 to 17 minutes, rotating pans from top to bottom and front to back halfway through baking. Let cool completely on baking sheets, about 20 minutes.

5. Spread about 2 teaspoons marshmallow creme on each whole square cookie; cover each with a square cut-out cookie. Place chocolate in a microwavable bowl, and microwave on HIGH until melted and smooth, about 2 minutes, stirring every 20 seconds. Transfer chocolate to a small zip-top plastic freezer bag. Snip 1 corner of bag to make a small hole; drizzle chocolate over cookies. Let cookies stand until chocolate is firm, about 2 minutes. — JUSTIN CHAPPLE

MAKE AHEAD Assembled cookies can be stored in an airtight container at room temperature up to 3 days. To freeze, prepare recipe through Step 4. Freeze baked cookie squares up to 3 months. Thaw cookies, and proceed with Step 5.

Chocolate-Pretzel Crinkle Cookies, RECIPE P. 215

S'mores Linzer Cookies, RECIPE P. 228

Triple-Ginger Rye Cookies, RECIPE P. 231

Gluten-Free Cacao
Nib Meringues

Triple-Ginger Rye Cookies

PHOTO P. 229

ACTIVE 40 MIN; TOTAL 6 HR;
MAKES 4 DOZEN

Hearty rye flour paired with three types of ginger—powdered, candied, and fresh—lends an earthy, lightly spicy flavor to these delicious holiday cookies.

- ¾ cup all-purpose flour (about 3¼ oz.)
- ¾ cup dark rye flour (about 3⅜ oz.)
- ⅓ cup crystallized ginger, finely chopped
- 2 tsp. baking powder
- 1 tsp. ground ginger
- Pinch of kosher salt
- 1¼ cups granulated sugar
- ½ cup unsalted butter, melted and slightly cooled
- 2 large eggs
- ¼ cup molasses
- 1 Tbsp. finely grated peeled fresh ginger (from 1 [3-inch] piece)
- 1 tsp. vanilla extract
- Turbinado sugar, for coating

1. Whisk together all-purpose flour, dark rye flour, crystallized ginger, baking powder, ground ginger, and salt in a medium bowl until combined; set aside. Beat granulated sugar and butter with a stand mixer fitted with a paddle attachment (or a large bowl and electric mixer) on medium speed until fluffy, about 2 minutes. Beat in eggs, one at a time, until incorporated; beat in molasses, fresh ginger, and vanilla. With machine running on low speed, beat in flour mixture until smooth. Cover with plastic wrap, and refrigerate until well chilled and firm, at least 4 hours or up to overnight.

2. Preheat oven to 350°F. Shape dough into 1-inch balls, and coat with turbinado sugar. Arrange balls 3 inches apart on large parchment paper-lined baking sheets. Bake in batches in preheated oven until crisp around the edges and slightly soft in center, 13 to 15 minutes. Let cool completely on baking sheets, about 30 minutes. (If reusing baking sheets, make sure you let them cool completely before adding more cookie dough balls.)
— JUSTIN CHAPPLE

NOTE Swapping out half of the all-purpose flour with rye flour gives these cookies a robust flavor and a chewy texture.

Gluten-Free Cacao Nib Meringues

ACTIVE 25 MIN; TOTAL 1 HR 10 MIN;
MAKES 18

Made with chocolate, cacao, and cocoa, these intensely flavored meringues from the late Chicago chef Charlie Trotter have a delicate, crispy exterior with a soft, chewy, marshmallow-like interior.

- 4 large egg whites
- 1 cup granulated sugar
- 3 oz. bittersweet baking chocolate, chopped (about ½ cup)
- 2 Tbsp. cacao nibs, plus more for sprinkling
- 1 Tbsp. unsweetened cocoa

1. Preheat oven to 300°F. Place oven rack in lower third of oven. Combine egg whites and sugar in bowl of a stand mixer. Bring 1½ inches of water to a simmer in a small saucepan over medium. Place bowl with egg white mixture over simmering water, ensuring base of bowl does not touch water. Cook, whisking constantly, until sugar is dissolved, 6 to 8 minutes.

2. Transfer bowl with egg white mixture to stand mixer fitted with a whisk attachment. Beat on medium-low speed, gradually increasing speed to high, until mixture is very thick, fluffy, and reaches room temperature, 6 to 8 minutes. (Mixture will resemble marshmallow fluff.) Using a rubber spatula, fold in chocolate, cacao nibs, and cocoa until incorporated.

3. Using a 1¾-inch scoop, drop small mounds (about 2 tablespoons each) onto 2 parchment paper-lined baking sheets, leaving 2 inches between mounds. Sprinkle mounds with cacao nibs. Bake in preheated oven until exteriors of meringues are dry and cookies can be lifted off of paper without sticking, 18 to 22 minutes, rotating baking sheets halfway through baking time. Let meringues cool completely on baking sheets, about 20 minutes. Store in an airtight container up to 1 week. — CHARLIE TROTTER

MAKE AHEAD These cookies are best eaten the same day, but they will keep in an airtight container at room temperature for up to 1 week.

Matcha Tea Marshmallow Crispy Treats

ACTIVE 15 MIN; TOTAL 1 HR 15 MIN;
MAKES 15

Ted Hopson, executive chef and co-owner of The Bellwether in Studio City, California, is generally not a cookie fan, but he loves Rice Krispies Treats. "And I especially like this nontraditional combo of tannic, floral green tea and subtly sweet white chocolate," he says.

- 5 Tbsp. unsalted butter, sliced, plus more at room temperature for brushing
- 1 lb. marshmallows
- 8½ cups crisped rice cereal (8 oz.)
- 1 cup white chocolate chips (6 oz.)
- 1 tsp. flaky sea salt
- 2 Tbsp. matcha tea powder

1. Brush a 13- × 9-inch baking dish with butter. Melt 5 tablespoons butter in a large pot over medium. Add marshmallows and cook, stirring with a wooden spoon, until completely melted, about 3 minutes. Remove pot from heat, add cereal, and stir to coat. Let mixture stand until cool to touch, about 2 minutes.

2. Working quickly, fold in white chocolate and salt until just combined. Scrape mixture into prepared baking dish and press into an even layer. Let stand at room temperature until cool, about 45 minutes. Using a fine wire-mesh strainer, dust with matcha powder. Cut into 3-inch squares, and serve. — TED HOPSON

MAKE AHEAD The treats can be stored in an airtight container for up to 2 days.

Armagnac Chocolate Truffles

ACTIVE 1 HR 15 MIN; TOTAL 7 HR 30 MIN;
MAKES ABOUT 50

*Dipped in melted dark chocolate and
rolled in cocoa powder, Dominique Ansel's
Armagnac-spiked beauties are exquisite
after a meal, with an espresso.*

GANACHE

- 1 cup heavy cream
- ½ cup sugar
- 9 oz. dark chocolate (66% cacao),
  finely chopped
- 2 tsp. Armagnac or Cognac

COATING

- 12 oz. dark chocolate (66% cacao),
  finely chopped
- ½ cup unsweetened cocoa powder

1. Make the ganache Bring heavy
cream and sugar just to a boil in a small
saucepan, stirring to dissolve sugar. Pour
hot cream over chopped chocolate in a
heatproof medium bowl. Let stand for
2 minutes, then add Armagnac and whisk
until smooth. Press a piece of plastic
directly onto surface of ganache and
refrigerate until firm, at least 4 hours.

2. Scoop 2-teaspoon-size mounds of
ganache onto a parchment paper-lined
baking sheet. Refrigerate mounds until
firm, about 30 minutes.

3. Using your hands, roll each mound of
ganache into a ball. Refrigerate balls until
very firm, about 1 hour.

4. Make the coating Heat chocolate in a
microwave-safe medium bowl at HIGH
in 20-second intervals, until nearly
melted; stir between intervals. Let stand
for 1 minute, then stir until smooth. Let
cool slightly.

5. Put cocoa powder in a medium bowl.
Using a fork, dip each ganache ball in
melted chocolate, letting excess drip
back into bowl, then coat in cocoa powder
and return to baking sheet. Refrigerate
truffles for 2 hours before serving.
— DOMINIQUE ANSEL

MAKE AHEAD The coated truffles can be
refrigerated in an airtight container for up
to 3 days.

Chai Caramels with Salted Pepitas

TOTAL 1 HR, PLUS OVERNIGHT SETTING;
MAKES ABOUT 115

*To achieve a perfectly smooth
caramel, Jami Curl of Quin Candy in
Portland, Oregon, suggests gradually
incorporating—in this case poking—the
granulated sugar into the corn syrup base
instead of stirring it in. Stirring sugar
encourages recrystallization, says Curl.
That will create a grainy texture that
nobody wants in your finished candy.*

- 2 sticks plus 5 Tbsp. room-
  temperature unsalted butter, cut
  into 1-inch pieces, plus more for
  greasing
- 1 cup heavy cream
- 3 chai tea bags
- 1 Tbsp. plus 1½ tsp. pure vanilla
  extract
- 1 Tbsp. kosher salt
- 1¼ cups plus 1 Tbsp. light corn syrup
- 4 cups sugar
- ¾ cup roasted salted pepitas (hulled
  pumpkin seeds)
- 5-inch squares of cellophane or wax
  paper, for wrapping

1. Lightly butter a 13- × 9-inch metal
baking pan and line with parchment paper,
leaving a 1-inch overhang on all 4 sides.

2. Bring cream to a boil in a small
saucepan; remove from heat. Add tea
bags, cover, and let stand for 12 minutes.
Gently squeeze tea bags to release any
cream, then discard. Stir in vanilla and salt;
keep warm.

3. Cook corn syrup in a medium, heavy-
bottom saucepan over medium-high,
swirling pan occasionally, until it begins
to bubble, 2 minutes. Sprinkle one-third

of the sugar over corn syrup and, using a
small heatproof spatula, poke sugar into
hot syrup until incorporated. Do not stir.
Repeat with remaining sugar in 2 batches,
using a wet pastry brush to wash down
any crystals on side of the pan. Continue
cooking over medium-high, swirling pan
occasionally, until a dark amber caramel
forms and temperature reaches 330°F on
a candy thermometer, about 15 minutes.

4. Remove saucepan from heat and
gradually add warm cream, whisking
constantly, until incorporated. Add 2 sticks
plus 5 tablespoons butter in 2 batches,
whisking until melted before adding more.
Continue whisking caramel vigorously
until it is glossy and registers 190°F on a
candy thermometer, about 5 minutes. Fold
in pepitas.

5. Scrape caramel into prepared pan,
then gently tap it on a work surface to
release any air bubbles. Let stand at room
temperature for at least 3 hours, cover
loosely with foil, and let stand overnight.

6. Invert caramel onto a work surface, peel
off parchment paper, and cut into 1-inch
squares. Wrap each caramel in a square
of cellophane and twist the ends to seal.
— JAMI CURL

MAKE AHEAD The wrapped caramels can
be stored in an airtight container at room
temperature for up to 6 months.

CARAMEL PERFECTION

ALL IN THE WRIST: Vigorously whisk
in the cream and butter to ensure
they emulsify so the caramel doesn't
get grainy.

ON THE MONEY: Your caramel will tell
you when it's done: It should be the
dark amber color of an old penny.

GOLDEN RULE: To cut perfectly sized
square caramels, use a ruler as your
guide and a long knife to slice.

Armagnac Chocolate Truffles

Desserts

**Pumpkin Cream
Pie in a Chocolate
Crust,** RECIPE P. 258

Chocolate-and-Citrus Cassata

ACTIVE 1 HR 30 MIN; TOTAL 7 HR 25 MIN;
SERVES 12

This spectacular holiday dessert comes from Rebecca Wilcomb's New Orleans restaurant Gianna. To decorate it, use an offset spatula, a bench scraper, and a cake turntable to spread the frosting evenly for the smoothest cake with straight sides. Prevent air bubbles from forming in the dark chocolate ganache glaze by using a spatula to stir the melting chocolate.

CAKE LAYERS

- Nonstick cooking spray
- 2 cups all-purpose flour (about 8½ oz.)
- ⅔ cup unsweetened cocoa
- 1 tsp. baking soda
- 1 tsp. baking powder
- 1 tsp. fine sea salt
- 1⅓ cups packed dark brown sugar
- ½ cup unsalted butter (4 oz.), softened
- ½ cup mayonnaise
- 4 large eggs
- 2 tsp. vanilla extract
- 1¼ cups buttermilk

BUTTERMILK-CHOCOLATE FROSTING

- 6 oz. 100% cacao unsweetened chocolate, chopped (1½ cups)
- 3 oz. 60–65% cacao bittersweet chocolate, chopped (¾ cup)
- ¾ cup unsalted butter (6 oz.)
- 3 cups powdered sugar (about 12 oz.)
- ½ cup buttermilk
- ½ tsp. vanilla extract

PISTACHIO PRALINE

- 1 cup shelled raw pistachios
- 1 cup granulated sugar

RICOTTA FILLING

- 32 oz. whole-milk ricotta cheese, weighted and drained overnight
- ¾ cup powdered sugar (about 3 oz.)
- ½ tsp. orange zest
- ½ vanilla bean pod, split, seeds scraped

DARK CHOCOLATE GANACHE GLAZE

- 8 oz. 60–65% cacao bittersweet baking chocolate, chopped (about 1½ cups)
- 1 Tbsp. unsalted butter
- 1¼ cups heavy cream
- 2 Tbsp. light corn syrup

ADDITIONAL INGREDIENTS

- Sliced fresh clementines and blood oranges, orange peel twists, and fresh or candied kumquats

1. Make the cake layers Preheat oven to 350°F. Lightly grease 3 (8-inch) round cake pans with cooking spray; line bottoms with parchment paper. Set aside. Sift together flour, cocoa, baking soda, and baking powder. Stir in salt.

2. Beat brown sugar, butter, and mayonnaise with stand mixer fitted with a paddle attachment on medium speed until light and fluffy, about 3 minutes. Add eggs, one at a time, beating until fully incorporated after each addition. Stir in vanilla. With machine running on low speed, add flour mixture alternately with buttermilk in 3 additions, beginning and ending with flour mixture. Beat until just incorporated after each addition. Divide batter evenly among prepared pans.

3. Bake in preheated oven until a wooden pick inserted in center comes out clean, 16 to 20 minutes. Let cakes cool in pans on wire racks 10 minutes. Remove cakes from pans, and let cool completely on wire racks, about 1 hour.

4. Make the buttermilk-chocolate frosting Bring 1 inch water to a simmer in a medium saucepan over medium. Combine unsweetened chocolate, bittersweet chocolate, and butter in a medium-size heatproof bowl. Place bowl over simmering water, ensuring base of bowl does not touch simmering water. Cook, stirring often, until mixture is melted and smooth, 8 to 10 minutes. Remove from heat, and let cool slightly, 10 to 15 minutes.

5. Beat sugar, buttermilk, and vanilla with a stand mixer fitted with a whisk attachment on low speed until smooth, about 1 minute. With machine running on low speed, gradually add cooled chocolate mixture, beating until just incorporated, about 30 seconds. Set frosting aside, uncovered, and let stand, stirring occasionally, until completely cool, 1 to 2 hours. (Frosting should thicken as it cools. Do not chill.)

6. Make the pistachio praline Place pistachios in a single layer centered on a parchment paper-lined rimmed baking sheet; set aside. Bring sugar and ¼ cup water to a boil in a small saucepan over medium-high. Cook, stirring often, until sugar dissolves, about 2 minutes. Cook, without stirring, until sugar turns amber in color and registers 350°F on a candy

thermometer, 8 to 10 minutes. Pour caramel over pistachios (do not stir). Let cool completely, about 20 minutes. Transfer hardened pistachio mixture to a cutting board; chop into pieces.

7. Make the ricotta filling Stir together ricotta, powdered sugar, orange zest, and vanilla bean seeds. (Mixture should be very thick and hold its shape when scooped.) Cover and chill until ready to use.

8. Assemble the cassata Place 1 cake layer on a cake board. Spoon half the ricotta filling (about 1½ cups) over top of cake layer, spreading to leave a ½-inch border around edges. Top with a second cake layer; spread remaining ricotta filling to leave a ½-inch border around edges. Top with remaining cake layer. Stir buttermilk-chocolate frosting until smooth; spread a thin layer (about 2½ cups) on top and sides of cake to seal in any crumbs and fill gaps between layers to encase filling. Chill cake, uncovered, until frosting is hardened, about 30 minutes. Spread top and sides of cake with a thick layer of remaining buttermilk-chocolate frosting, smoothing frosting with a bench scraper. Chill cake until frosting is firm and cold, at least 2 hours or up to overnight.

9. Make the dark chocolate ganache glaze Combine bittersweet chocolate and butter in a 4-cup glass measuring cup with a spout; set aside. Bring cream and corn syrup to a low simmer in a small saucepan over medium-low. Pour cream mixture over chocolate mixture, and let stand 2 minutes. Stir glaze with a spatula until completely smooth; let stand at room temperature, stirring occasionally, until cooled to 100°F to 105°F, 4 to 10 minutes. (It should be pourable and fluid.)

10. Remove chilled cake from refrigerator, and place on a wire rack or inverted bowl inside a rimmed baking sheet. Pour glaze over top of cake, allowing glaze to flow down sides, making sure cake is completely covered. Let stand 1 minute, allowing excess glaze to drip off sides. Run an offset spatula around bottom edge of cake to remove any drips. Chill cake until glaze is set, about 1 hour. Carefully transfer cake to a cake stand or serving plate. Garnish with sliced clementines, other citrus, and desired amount of pistachio praline. (Reserve any remaining

continued on page 239

Chocolate-and-Citrus Cassata

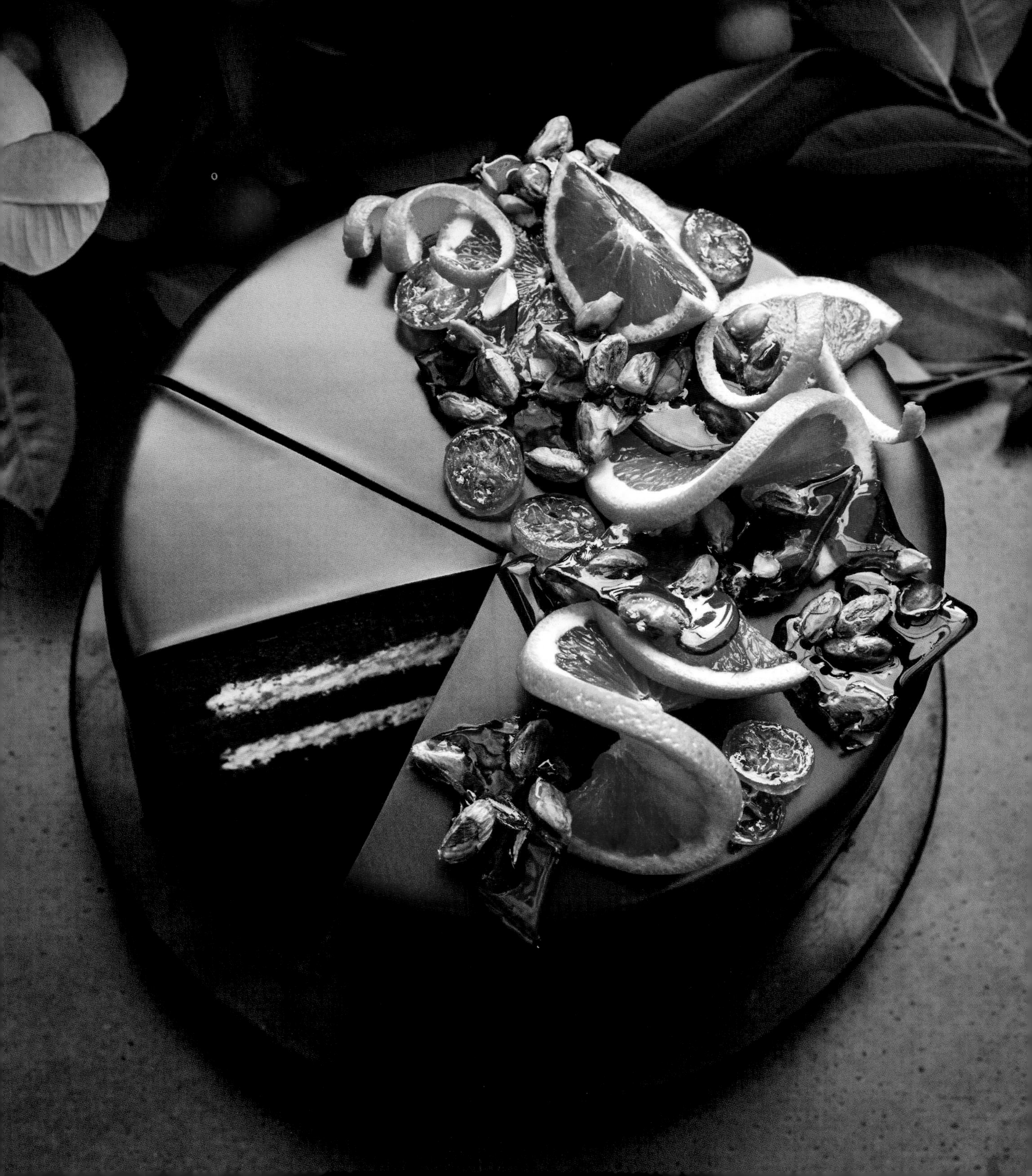

HOW TO MAKE CHOCOLATE-AND-CITRUS CASSATA

This Chocolate-and-Citrus Cassata is a stunner, (recipe, p. 236). With a bit of planning, the many delicious elements are easy to make and assemble. Here's how to do it.

GET A HEAD START

1. Weight and Drain the Ricotta
At least one day before you make the cassata, spoon ricotta into a cheesecloth-lined colander set inside a bowl. Wrap cheesecloth over ricotta; place 2 or 3 canned goods in a small bowl, and set on top of ricotta to extract moisture. Refrigerate; drain at least 24 hours or up to 3 days.

2. Bake the Cake Layers
The cake layers may be baked one day ahead. Cool cake in pans on wire rack 10 minutes; remove cakes from pans, and cool to room temperature, about 1 hour. Immediately wrap each cake layer in plastic wrap, and refrigerate until ready to assemble the cassata.

3. Make the Pistachio Praline
The pistachio praline may be made up to one week before serving the cassata, but it must be kept completely dry and stored in an airtight container until ready to assemble the cassata. (This type of hard candy will start to get sticky and melt if it's refrigerated or stored in a humid kitchen.)

ASSEMBLE THE CAKE!

1. Get Set Up
Place a 7½-inch cake board (or cardboard round) on a cake turntable or overturned large dinner plate. (The cake board will be slightly smaller than the cake layers so the cake can be glazed evenly.) Place one cake layer on cake board.

2. Fill the Cake
Add half of the ricotta filling to the center of the cake layer. Using an offset spatula, spread the ricotta, pushing from the center to the edge of the cake and leaving a ½-inch border. Repeat with remaining cake layers and ricotta filling.

3. Apply the Crumb Coat
Spread about 2½ cups of the buttermilk-chocolate frosting in a thin layer over the top and sides of cake to secure crumbs, making sure to work frosting into gaps between layers to encase ricotta filling. Chill cake until frosting is firm to the touch.

4. Frost Cake
Spread remaining frosting over the top and sides of the cake in an even layer. Using the edge of a bench scraper, smooth the frosting while rotating cake turntable. Chill cake at least 2 hours and up to overnight.

5. Glaze Cake
Transfer chilled cake to a wire rack set inside a rimmed baking sheet. In a continuous motion starting from middle of cake, pour glaze over cake, ensuring it coats the top and sides. Pour in a speedy, controlled manner; a rippled finish will result if poured too slowly.

6. Garnish the Cake
Just before serving, slice a mix of fresh citrus into wedges or wheels, and blot dry. Use a channel knife to remove long strands of orange peel for twists. Garnish glazed cake with pistachio praline pieces, fresh citrus, orange peel twists, and candied citrus. Serve cake immediately.

continued from page 236

pistachio praline for another use.) Serve chilled. — REBECCA WILCOMB

MAKE AHEAD Ricotta must be drained at least 24 and up to 72 hours ahead. Cake layers may be baked 1 day ahead, individually wrapped in plastic, and chilled. Pistachio praline may be made up to 1 week ahead and stored in an airtight container. Unglazed frosted cake may be assembled and chilled overnight.

Moody Tongue's Chocolate Cake

PHOTO P. 240

ACTIVE 2 HR 35 MIN; TOTAL 5 HR 15 MIN; MAKES 1 (10-INCH) CAKE

When Jared Rouben decided to open Moody Tongue brewery in Chicago, one of his first calls was to pastry chef Shannon Morrison, a friend from their time together in culinary school. "Jared said, 'Make me your perfect cake,'" she recounts. "His only other directive was that it be big enough to turn heads."

CHOCOLATE CAKES

- 1 cup canola oil, plus more for greasing
- 3½ cups all-purpose flour
- 4 cups granulated sugar
- 1½ cups Dutch-process cocoa powder
- 4 tsp. baking soda
- 2 tsp. baking powder
- 2 tsp. kosher salt
- 2 cups buttermilk
- 4 large eggs
- 2 tsp. pure vanilla extract
- 1 cup hot coffee mixed with 1 cup hot water

GERMAN CHOCOLATE FILLING

- 1 cup evaporated milk
- 1 cup granulated sugar
- 1 stick unsalted butter
- 3 large egg yolks
- 1 tsp. kosher salt
- 1½ cups shredded sweetened coconut
- 1 cup coarsely chopped toasted pecans
- 2 tsp. pure vanilla extract

CHEESECAKES

- Nonstick cooking spray
- 4 whole graham crackers, crushed
- ⅓ cup mini pretzels
- ⅓ cup chocolate cereal, such as Annie's Cocoa Bunnies or Cocoa Puffs
- ½ stick unsalted butter, melted
- 1 lb. cream cheese, at room temperature
- ⅔ cup granulated sugar
- 2 large eggs
- 1 Tbsp. espresso powder
- 1 tsp. pure vanilla extract

BUTTERCREAM

- 2 cups confectioners' sugar
- ½ cup Dutch process cocoa powder
- ½ tsp. kosher salt
- 6 large egg whites
- 1½ cups granulated sugar
- 1 Tbsp. pure vanilla extract
- 4 sticks unsalted butter, softened and cut into cubes
- ¾ cup vegetable shortening

GANACHE

- 2 cups heavy cream
- 3 Tbsp. light corn syrup
- 3 Tbsp. unsalted butter
- 1 lb. chopped dark chocolate (2¾ cups)

1. Make the chocolate cakes Preheat oven to 350°F. Grease 2 (10-inch) round cake pans, line with parchment, and grease parchment paper. Whisk flour, sugar, cocoa powder, baking soda, baking powder, and salt with a stand mixer fitted with a whisk attachment. Whisk buttermilk, 1 cup canola oil, eggs, and vanilla in a large bowl.

2. Beat buttermilk mixture into flour mixture with a stand mixer fitted with a paddle attachment on low speed. Add hot coffee, and beat until just combined.

3. Pour batter into prepared pans, and bake until a wooden pick inserted in center comes out clean, 35 to 45 minutes. Transfer cakes to a wire rack to cool for 15 minutes, then turn out onto wire rack, peel off parchment, and let cool completely. Wrap in plastic and refrigerate.

4. Make the German chocolate filling Combine evaporated milk, sugar, butter, egg yolks, and salt in a medium saucepan over medium. Cook, stirring, until mixture comes to a boil and thickens, 8 to 10 minutes. Remove from heat and stir in coconut, pecans, and vanilla. Scrape filling into a bowl. Refrigerate until cold.

5. Make the cheesecakes Preheat oven to 350°F. Spray 2 (10-inch) round cake pans with cooking spray, line with parchment paper, and spray parchment paper with cooking spray. Combine graham crackers, pretzels, and chocolate cereal in a food processor, and pulse until fine crumbs form. Add melted butter, and pulse to combine. Press crumbs evenly over bottom of one cake pan to form a very thin crust. Bake crust until fragrant and browned, about 5 minutes. Transfer to a wire rack and let cool completely.

6. Reduce oven temperature to 300°F. Beat cream cheese and sugar with a stand mixer fitted with a paddle attachment on medium speed until light and fluffy, about 2 minutes. Add eggs, espresso powder, and vanilla, and beat until combined. Divide batter into prepared pans (one with crust, one without) and spread batter evenly. Bake until cheesecake is set, about 15 minutes. Transfer to a wire rack to cool for 30 minutes, then wrap pans in plastic and refrigerate until completely cooled.

7. Make the buttercream Whisk confectioners' sugar, cocoa powder, and salt in a medium bowl. Whisk egg whites and granulated sugar in top of a double boiler over simmering water until sugar has dissolved, about 2 minutes. Beat egg whites with a stand mixer fitted with a whisk attachment on high speed until stiff, glossy, and cool, about 5 to 7 minutes. Whisk in cocoa mixture on medium speed until combined, then add vanilla. Beat in butter and shortening with a paddle attachment, adding a few tablespoons of each at a time, until buttercream is fluffy and firm, about 5 minutes.

8. Assemble the cake Using a serrated knife, trim domed tops of chocolate cakes to flatten them; reserve scraps for another use. Cut each chocolate cake horizontally into 2 even layers.

9. Place a small spoonful of buttercream in center of a large, flat plate. Invert crusted cheesecake onto another plate and remove parchment paper, then turn it crust-side down and center it on top of buttercream. Spread 1½ cups buttercream on top of cheesecake and top with 1 layer of chocolate cake. Spread half the German chocolate filling on top of chocolate cake and top with second layer of chocolate cake. Spread ½ cup buttercream over chocolate cake (a very thin layer) and top with crustless

continued on page 241

**Moody Tongue's
Chocolate Cake,**
RECIPE P. 239

continued from page 239

cheesecake. Remove parchment paper from cheesecake. Spread 1½ cups buttercream over cheesecake and top with third layer of chocolate cake. Spread remaining German chocolate filling over chocolate cake and cover with remaining fourth layer of cake. Spread remaining buttercream all over cake, using an offset spatula to ensure that top and side are smooth and even. Freeze cake for 20 minutes.

10. Make the ganache Bring cream, corn syrup, and butter to a boil in a small saucepan. Remove saucepan from heat. Add chocolate, and whisk until melted and mixture is smooth. (The ganache should be warm to the touch but not hot. If the ganache is too cold, microwave in 20-second increments.)

11. Set a cooling rack over a rimmed baking sheet. Very carefully transfer cake from plate to wire rack. Starting at center and working outward in circles, slowly pour ganache over cake until you reach edge, letting ganache drip over side to enrobe cake. Let set for a few minutes, then very carefully transfer cake to a platter. Refrigerate until ready to serve, at least 30 minutes. If cold, let cake come to room temperature before serving.

— SHANNON MORRISON

◆ ◆ ◆

Apple-Rum Compote

ACTIVE 25 MIN; TOTAL 1 HR 25 MIN;
MAKES ABOUT 1¼ CUPS

McIntosh apples have a sweet aroma, while Granny Smiths bring acidity and texture that holds up to cooking. The two apple varieties combine for a super-flavorful cake filling. This deeply flavored, smooth, and rich compote also makes a delicious topping for waffles or latkes.

- 1 medium McIntosh, Braeburn, or Fuji apple, peeled, cored, and cut into ½-inch pieces
- 1 medium Granny Smith apple, peeled, cored, and cut into ½-inch pieces
- 5 Tbsp. packed light brown sugar
- 1 Tbsp. all-purpose flour
- ¼ tsp. kosher salt
- ⅛ tsp. ground cinnamon
- ½ cup (4 oz.) gold rum
- 1 tsp. fresh lemon juice
- ½ tsp. vanilla extract

1. Stir together apples, sugar, flour, salt, and cinnamon in a large skillet. Let stand at room temperature, stirring occasionally, until sugar begins to dissolve, about 30 minutes.

2. Cook apple mixture in skillet over medium-high, stirring often, until tender, about 5 minutes.

3. Pour rum into a heatproof measuring cup with a pour spout. Remove skillet from heat; turn off burner. Pour rum into skillet. Carefully ignite the fumes just above the rum mixture with a long match. Gently shake skillet until flames extinguish, about 1 minute.

4. Return skillet to heat over medium-high; cook, stirring often, until liquid has almost completely evaporated, about 2 minutes. Remove from heat.

5. Break up apple mixture using a potato masher or fork until mostly smooth. Stir in lemon juice and vanilla. Set aside at room temperature to cool completely, about 30 minutes. — JOANNE CHANG

◆ ◆ ◆

Bibi's Coconut Cake

ACTIVE 1 HR 30 MIN; TOTAL 3 HR 45 MIN;
SERVES 12

Food blogger and recipe developer Julie Tanous uses coconut in every part of this festive dessert, from cake to filling to frosting. Bibi was her grandmother, and she inspired this deeply southern recipe.

FILLING

- 1¾ cups whole milk
- ¾ cup granulated sugar
- 1 Tbsp. plus ½ tsp. pure coconut extract
- Kosher salt
- 3 large egg yolks
- 2 Tbsp. cornstarch
- 1 cup sweetened shredded coconut
- 2 Tbsp. unsalted butter
- ¼ cup heavy cream

CAKE

- 2 sticks unsalted butter, at room temperature, plus more for greasing
- 3 cups cake flour, plus more for dusting
- 1 Tbsp. plus 1½ tsp. baking powder
- ½ tsp. kosher salt
- 1 cup unsweetened coconut milk
- ½ cup whole milk

- 1 Tbsp. pure coconut extract
- 2⅓ cups granulated sugar
- 5 large egg whites

FROSTING

- 8 oz. cream cheese, at room temperature
- 1 stick unsalted butter, at room temperature
- 4 cups confectioners' sugar
- 1 to 2 Tbsp. whole milk
- 1 tsp. pure coconut extract
- 3 cups unsweetened coconut flakes, toasted

1. Make the filling Combine milk, granulated sugar, coconut extract, and a pinch of salt in a medium saucepan over medium. Bring to a simmer, stirring, until sugar is dissolved, 3 minutes.

2. Beat egg yolks and cornstarch in a bowl. Gradually whisk ½ cup hot milk into yolks. Scrape mixture into saucepan and cook over medium-high, whisking, until thickened, 5 minutes. Remove from heat. Whisk in shredded coconut and butter. Scrape into a bowl; let cool.

3. Whisk cream until stiff in another medium bowl. Fold whipped cream into cooled coconut filling. Press a piece of plastic directly on surface and refrigerate until well chilled, about 1 hour.

4. Make the cake Preheat oven to 350°F. Butter two (8-inch) round cake pans and line with parchment paper. Butter parchment paper and dust pans with cake flour.

5. Whisk cake flour, baking powder, and salt in a medium bowl. Whisk coconut milk, whole milk, and coconut extract in another medium bowl. Beat 2 sticks butter and granulated sugar with a stand mixer fitted with a paddle attachment on medium speed until fluffy, about 2 minutes. At medium-high speed, beat in egg whites in 3 additions. On low speed, beat in half the flour mixture until nearly incorporated. Beat in wet ingredients, then beat in remaining flour mixture until just incorporated; scrape down side of bowl as needed.

6. Pour batter into prepared pans, and bake until cakes are golden and springy, 40 to 45 minutes. Transfer cakes to a wire rack to cool for 15 minutes, then turn out onto wire rack, peel off parchment, and let cool completely, about 45 minutes.

continued on page 243

**Pumpkin Layer Cake with
Mascarpone Frosting**

continued from page 241

7. Make the frosting Beat cream cheese and butter with a stand mixer fitted with a paddle until smooth. At low speed, beat in confectioners' sugar, 1 tablespoon milk, and coconut extract until just incorporated, then beat on medium speed until light and smooth, 1 to 2 minutes; add another tablespoon of milk if too thick.

8. Using a serrated knife, cut each cake in half horizontally to create 4 layers. Set 1 cake layer cut-side up on a cake plate. Spread one-third of the filling on top. Repeat with 2 more cake layers and remaining two-thirds filling. Cover with last cake layer. Freeze until well chilled, about 15 minutes. Frost cake with a thin layer of frosting, and freeze until set, about 15 minutes. Frost cake with remaining frosting and coat side with coconut flakes. Refrigerate until the frosting is set, about 1 hour, before serving. — JULIE TANOUS

WINE Pair with a lush, fruity Champagne.

Pumpkin Layer Cake with Mascarpone Frosting

ACTIVE 50 MIN; TOTAL 3 HR; SERVES 10 TO 12

This classic pumpkin cake from F&W's Justin Chapple is perfectly moist and delicately spiced. The simple vanilla buttercream frosting gets a lovely tang from the mascarpone that's blended in.

CAKE

　　Unsalted butter, for greasing
　3　cups all-purpose flour, plus more for dusting
　2　Tbsp. ground cinnamon
1½　Tbsp. ground ginger
1½　tsp. baking soda
　1　tsp. baking powder
1½　tsp. kosher salt
　4　large eggs
1½　cups packed light brown sugar
　1　(15-oz.) can pure pumpkin puree
　1　cup canola oil

FROSTING

1½　sticks unsalted butter, softened
　3　cups confectioners' sugar
1½　tsp. pure vanilla extract
　　Kosher salt
1½　cups mascarpone cheese

1. Make the cake Preheat oven to 350°F. Butter 2 (9-inch) round cake pans and line bottoms with parchment paper. Butter parchment paper and dust with flour, tapping out excess.

2. Whisk 3 cups all-purpose flour, cinnamon, ginger, baking soda, baking powder, and salt in a medium bowl.

3. Beat eggs, brown sugar, pumpkin puree, and canola oil in a large bowl with an electric mixer on medium-high speed until blended. Beat in flour mixture on low speed.

4. Scrape batter into prepared pans, and bake in center of oven until a wooden pick inserted in center of cakes comes out clean, about 40 minutes. Let cakes cool in pans for 30 minutes, then invert onto a wire rack to cool completely. Peel off parchment paper.

5. Make the frosting Beat butter, confectioners' sugar, vanilla, and a pinch of salt in a large bowl with an electric mixer until smooth. Add mascarpone, and beat on high speed just until smooth; do not overbeat. Refrigerate frosting until just set, about 30 minutes.

6. Set 1 cake layer on a platter. Spread ¾ cup frosting on top and cover with second cake layer. Spread a thin layer of frosting all over cake and refrigerate until set, about 15 minutes. Spread remaining frosting over top and side of cake. Refrigerate until firm, at least 30 minutes, before serving. — JUSTIN CHAPPLE

MAKE AHEAD The cake can be refrigerated for up to 3 days.

Vanilla Sponge Cake with Blackberry-Tarragon Jam

ACTIVE 40 MIN; TOTAL 1 HR 45 MIN; SERVES 8

Pastry genius Dominique Ansel bakes a delicate sponge, the foundation of France's intricate layer cakes, in a homey loaf pan like an English quick bread to create a new Anglo-French baking tradition. It's ethereal served with his easy, licorice-y jam.

CAKE

　2　Tbsp. unsalted butter, melted, plus more for brushing
½　cup all-purpose flour
¼　cup cake flour
¾　tsp. baking powder
½　tsp. fine salt
　1　Tbsp. plus 1 tsp. honey
　1　vanilla bean, split lengthwise and seeds scraped, or ½ tsp. pure vanilla extract
　3　large egg yolks
　1　cup granulated sugar, divided
　7　large egg whites
　　Confectioners' sugar, for dusting

JAM

　8　oz. blackberries
½　cup granulated sugar
　1　Tbsp. chopped fresh tarragon leaves
　1　tsp. gin
　1　tsp. fresh lemon juice
¼　tsp. black pepper

1. Make the cake Preheat oven to 375°F. Brush a 9- × 4-inch loaf pan with butter. Whisk all-purpose flour, cake flour, baking powder, and salt in a medium bowl. Mix 2 tablespoons melted butter, honey, and vanilla seeds in a small bowl.

2. Beat egg yolks and ½ cup granulated sugar with a stand mixer fitted with a whisk attachment on high speed until thick and pale, about 5 minutes. Scrape into a medium bowl. Clean mixer bowl and whisk.

3. Beat egg whites with stand mixer fitted with a whisk attachment on high speed until soft peaks form, about 2 minutes. With machine on high, gradually add remaining ½ cup granulated sugar, and beat until stiff, about 3 minutes more. Using a rubber spatula, fold a large scoop of beaten egg whites into egg yolk mixture to lighten it. Gently fold egg yolk mixture into egg whites until no streaks remain.

4. Sift flour mixture over eggs, then gently fold it in. Fold in butter mixture. Scrape batter into prepared pan and smooth top. Bake until springy and browned, about 25 minutes. Let cool completely, then unmold onto a platter and dust with confectioners' sugar.

5. Make the jam Using a mortar and pestle, lightly crush blackberries, granulated sugar, tarragon, gin, lemon juice, and pepper until a coarse jam forms. Transfer to a serving bowl. Cut cake into slices, and serve with jam. — DOMINIQUE ANSEL

MAKE AHEAD The cake can be stored in an airtight container for up to 3 days. The jam can be refrigerated for up to 3 days.

Concord Cake

ACTIVE 1 HR 30 MIN; TOTAL 2 HR 30 MIN,
PLUS 6 HR CHILLING; MAKES 1 (8-INCH) CAKE

*The Concord Cake is a deeply chocolaty,
crispy, creamy, chewy meringue-and-
mousse confection covered with crunchy
chocolate meringue sticks. Created by
French pâtissier Gaston Lenôtre in honor
of the Concorde, it became popular at
Manhattan's beloved (now-shuttered)
Soutine Bakery in the '80s. Somewhere
along the way the "e" in the name got lost,
but we think the cake is here to stay.*

CHOCOLATE MOUSSE

- 10 oz. semisweet chocolate (64% cacao), finely chopped
- 5 Tbsp. unsalted butter, cut into small pieces
- ½ cup plus 3 Tbsp. granulated sugar
- 2 large egg whites
- ½ vanilla bean, split
- 2 cups heavy cream, chilled

CHOCOLATE MERINGUE

- 2 cups confectioners' sugar, plus more for dusting
- 1 cup unsweetened cocoa powder
- 9 large egg whites
- 1⅓ cups granulated sugar

1. Make the chocolate mousse Place chocolate and butter in a large bowl set over a saucepan of simmering water, and melt, stirring occasionally, until smooth. Remove from heat and keep warm.

2. Combine sugar and ¼ cup water in a small saucepan and bring to a boil over medium-high, without stirring, until sugar syrup reaches 240°F on a candy thermometer, about 7 minutes.

3. Beat egg whites with a stand mixer fitted with a whisk attachment on medium-high speed until soft peaks form, about 3 minutes.

4. Gradually pour hot syrup into egg whites in a steady stream and beat at medium-high speed until whites are stiff and glossy, about 5 minutes. Using a large rubber spatula, fold in melted chocolate until no streaks of white remain. Scrape chocolate mixture into a large bowl. Wash and dry mixing bowl and whisk.

5. Scrape vanilla bean seeds into heavy cream, and beat cream in a stand mixer fitted with a whisk attachment on medium speed until firm. Using a rubber spatula, fold whipped cream into chocolate mixture until no streaks remain. Cover mousse with plastic wrap and refrigerate until firm, at least 2 hours or overnight.

6. Make the chocolate meringue Sift 2 cups confectioners' sugar with cocoa powder in a medium bowl. Line 4 rimmed baking sheets with parchment paper. Trace an 8-inch circle on 2 of the sheets.

7. Beat egg whites in a stand mixer fitted with a whisk attachment on low speed until foamy. Increase speed to medium-high and beat until soft peaks form. Beat in granulated sugar, 3 tablespoons at a time, beating well after each addition. Once all of sugar has been added, beat whites until stiff and glossy, about 3 minutes longer. Transfer meringue to a large bowl and, using a large rubber spatula, gradually fold in cocoa powder and confectioners' sugar until just a few streaks remain.

8. Scrape meringue into a piping bag fitted with a ½-inch tip. Pipe meringue into traced circles in a spiral, beginning at center; there should be no space between spirals. On other 2 prepared sheets, pipe remaining meringue in long sticks,

STEP-BY-STEP

1. MAKE THE MOUSSE Fold the melted chocolate mixture into beaten egg whites until no streaks of white remain.

2. FINISH THE MOUSSE Fold whipped cream into chocolate mixture until no streaks remain. Cover and refrigerate 2 hours.

3. MAKE THE MERINGUE Transfer the meringue to a large bowl; gradually fold in confectioners' sugar mixture.

4. SHAPE THE CAKE LAYERS Pipe a chocolate meringue spiral onto each of 2 parchment paper-lined baking sheets.

leaving about 1 inch between them. Let meringue rounds and sticks stand at room temperature for 30 minutes.

9. Preheat oven to 350°F. Bake meringue rounds until firm and can be lifted off parchment with an offset spatula, about 25 minutes. Transfer to wire racks to cool completely.

10. Bake meringue sticks until firm enough to be lifted off parchment, 12 to 14 minutes. Cut into 6-inch lengths and transfer to a wire rack to cool completely. Using a sharp knife, cut sticks into 1½- to 2-inch lengths.

11. Transfer a meringue round to a cake stand or platter. Spoon half the chilled chocolate mousse onto meringue and spread it in an even layer with a large offset spatula. Cover with second meringue round and spread remaining mousse on top, mounding it slightly in center. Cover cake entirely with meringue sticks. Refrigerate until mousse is firm, at least 6 hours or overnight. Dust cake with confectioners' sugar just before serving.
— GASTON LENÔTRE

MAKE AHEAD The cake can be refrigerated for 1 day.

5. FORM THE CRUNCHY TOPPING Pipe the remaining meringue onto parchment-lined sheets in long sticks, about an inch apart.

6. CUT THE MERINGUE STICKS Use a sharp knife to create 1½- to 2-inch pieces for decorating the cake.

7. FILL THE CAKE Using an offset spatula, spread half of the chilled chocolate mousse over one of the meringue spirals.

8. ADD ANOTHER LAYER Place the second round of meringue on top and cover with the remaining chocolate mousse.

Three-Layer
Thanksgiving Cake

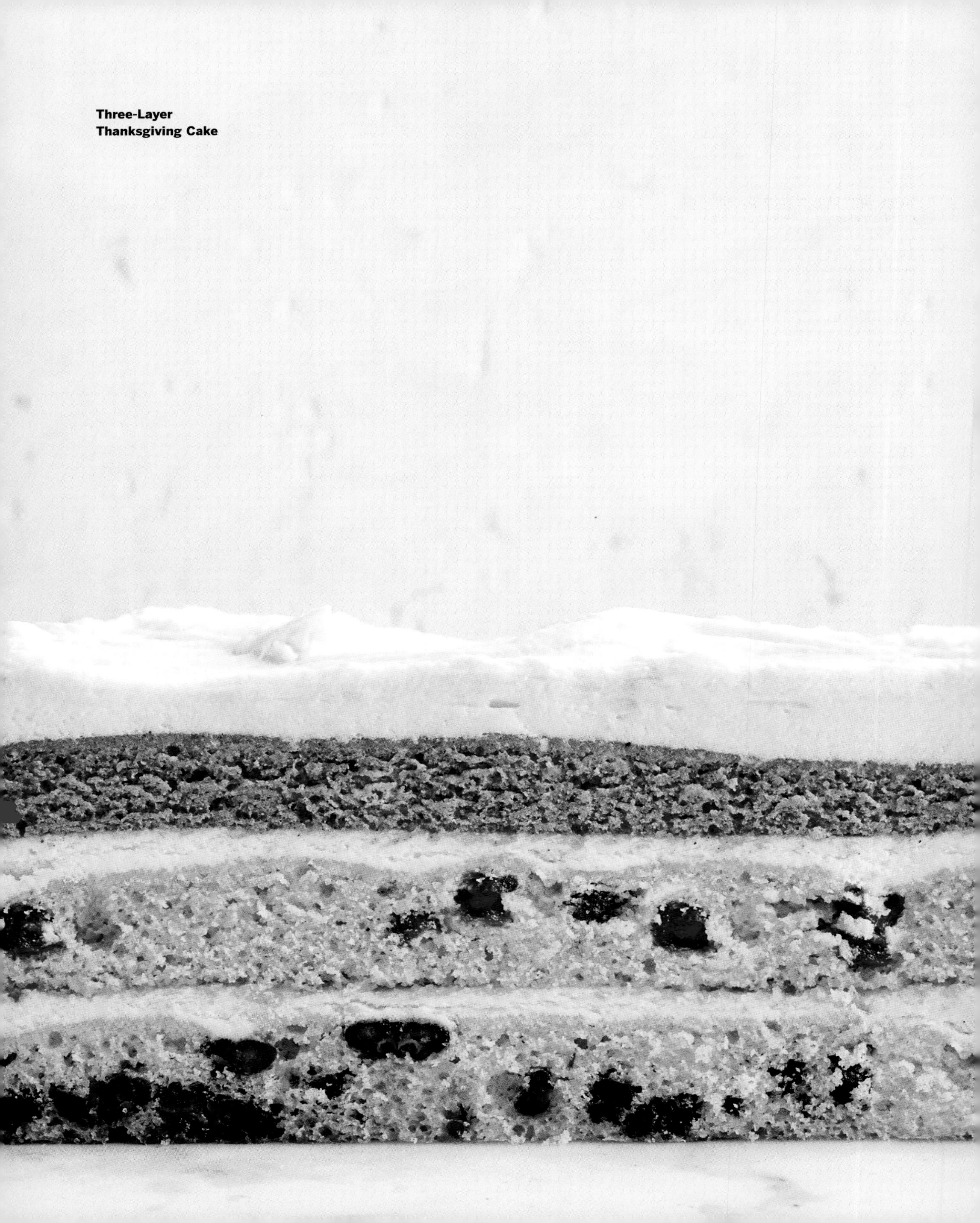

Three-Layer Thanksgiving Cake

ACTIVE 35 MIN; TOTAL 2 HR; SERVES 10

To celebrate the myriad flavors of fall, F&W's Laura Rege layers three separate cakes—pumpkin, candied pecan, and cranberry-cornmeal—into one giant cake, all finished with a luscious cream cheese frosting. It's got a little something for everyone at the Thanksgiving table.

CAKES

- 1½ sticks unsalted butter, melted and cooled, plus softened butter for greasing
- 2¼ cups plus 1 Tbsp. all-purpose flour
- 1⅛ tsp. baking soda
- ¾ tsp. baking powder
- ¾ tsp. kosher salt
- 1¼ cups granulated sugar
- 1 cup buttermilk, at room temperature
- 3 large eggs, at room temperature
- ⅓ cup pure pumpkin puree
- 1¼ tsp. pumpkin pie spice
- 1¼ cups fresh or frozen cranberries, thawed and drained if frozen
- ⅓ cup stone-ground yellow cornmeal
- 1¼ cups candied pecans, roughly chopped

FROSTING

- 1¼ lb. cream cheese, softened
- 2½ sticks unsalted butter, softened
- 5 cups confectioners' sugar
  Kosher salt

1. Make the cakes Preheat oven to 350°F with oven racks positioned in upper and lower thirds. Butter 3 (9-inch) square metal cake pans and line with parchment paper; allow 2 inches of overhang on 2 sides. Butter parchment paper.

2. Whisk 2¼ cups flour, baking soda, baking powder, and salt in a medium bowl. Whisk 1½ sticks melted butter, granulated sugar, buttermilk ,and eggs in a large bowl until well combined. Whisk in flour mixture until just combined.

3. Divide batter among 3 medium bowls (1½ cups per bowl). Whisk pumpkin puree, pumpkin pie spice, and remaining 1 tablespoon flour into one of the bowls, then scrape batter into one of the prepared pans. Fold cranberries and cornmeal into another bowl, and scrape into second prepared pan. Fold pecans into the final bowl and scrape batter into last prepared pan.

4. Transfer all 3 pans to oven, and bake until a wooden pick inserted in the center of each cake comes out clean, about 15 minutes, rotating halfway through. Let cakes cool in pans for 15 minutes, then invert onto wire racks to cool completely. Peel off parchment paper.

5. Make the frosting Beat cream cheese, butter, confectioners' sugar, and a pinch of salt with a stand mixer fitted with a paddle attachment until smooth.

6. Place pecan layer on a platter. Scrape ¾ cup frosting on top and spread to edge. Top with cranberry layer; scrape another ¾ cup frosting on top and spread to edge. Top with pumpkin layer. Spread a thin layer of frosting all over cake and refrigerate until set, 15 minutes. Spread remaining frosting all over cake. Refrigerate until firm, at least 30 minutes, before serving.
— JUSTIN CHAPPLE & LAURA REGE

Apple and Olive Oil Bundt Cake

ACTIVE 35 MIN; TOTAL 4 HR 5 MIN; SERVES 12

This adaptation of an Italian apple cake is moist and light, fragrant with freshly ground spices and studded with chunks of fruit. In the spring, substitute fresh rhubarb for the apples.

- Unsalted butter, for greasing
- 2⅓ cups all-purpose flour (about 10 oz.), plus more for dusting
- 2 green cardamom pods
- 1⅔ cups granulated sugar
- 4 large eggs
- 2 large egg yolks
- ½ tsp. kosher salt
- 1 Tbsp. orange zest
- 2 tsp. vanilla extract
- 1 cup extra-virgin olive oil
- 1 Tbsp. baking powder
- 1 lb. Granny Smith apples (about 2 large apples), peeled and cut into ½-inch pieces
- 2 Tbsp. powdered sugar
- 1½ cups lightly sweetened whipped cream, for serving

1. Preheat oven to 350°F. Generously grease and flour a 14-cup Bundt pan. Heat cardamom pods in a small skillet over medium, stirring often, until lightly toasted and fragrant, about 2 minutes. When cool enough to handle, crack open outer shells, and transfer small brown seeds to a mortar and pestle. Discard shells. Crush seeds until finely ground; set aside.

2. Place granulated sugar, eggs, egg yolks, and salt in bowl of a stand mixer fitted with a whisk attachment. Beat on medium speed until mixture is light and fluffy, about 2 minutes. Beat in orange zest, vanilla, and ground cardamom, stopping to scrape down sides of bowl as needed. With machine running on medium speed, gradually add oil in a slow, steady stream, slowing pour as necessary to ensure oil is fully incorporated.

3. Sift flour and baking powder over egg mixture. Using a rubber spatula, fold in flour mixture until almost completely incorporated; add apples, and fold just until combined. Spoon batter into prepared pan. Bake in preheated oven until golden brown and a long wooden pick inserted in center comes out clean, about 1 hour. Transfer cake in pan to a wire rack, and let cool 30 minutes. Invert cake onto wire rack, and cool completely, about 2 hours. Sprinkle with powdered sugar, and serve with whipped cream.
— RACHAEL COYLE

NOTE Cake may be wrapped in plastic wrap and stored at room temperature up to 2 days.

PASTRY TIP Olive oil emulsifies into a foamy batter to create a light, airy cake. Use a fruity olive oil for the best flavor.

Flambéed Candied Chestnut Cake

ACTIVE 35 MIN; TOTAL 3 HR 45 MIN;
SERVES 12

With a texture like pound cake and studded with candied chestnuts, this celebratory cake gets doused with flaming Cognac just before serving. Top slices with a dollop of crème fraîche.

- 3 cups (about 12¾ oz.) plus 2 Tbsp. all-purpose flour, divided, plus more for dusting
- 1 tsp. kosher salt
- 2 cups unsalted butter (16 oz.), at room temperature, plus more for greasing pan
- 2 cups granulated sugar
- 6 large eggs
- ½ cup heavy cream
- 1 Tbsp. crème fraîche, plus more for serving
- 2 tsp. vanilla extract
- 6½ oz. drained canned candied chestnuts in syrup (about 8 nuts), quartered
- 2 Tbsp. (1 oz.) Cognac

1. Preheat oven to 325°F. Stir together 3 cups flour and salt in a medium bowl. Grease and flour a 10-inch (10- to 15-cup) Bundt pan. Set both aside.

2. Beat sugar and butter with a stand mixer fitted with a paddle attachment on high speed until light and fluffy, 5 to 6 minutes. Reduce speed to medium, and add eggs, one at a time, beating until fully incorporated after each addition and stopping to scrape down sides of bowl after every 2 eggs. With machine running on low speed, add flour mixture in 3 additions alternately with heavy cream, beginning and ending with flour mixture. Stir in crème fraîche and vanilla.

3. Toss together chestnuts and remaining 2 tablespoons flour until well coated. Spoon half of batter into prepared pan; top with chestnuts. Add remaining batter, and smooth top. Tap cake pan on work surface to release any air bubbles. Bake in preheated oven until golden brown and a wooden pick inserted in center comes out clean, 1 hour to 1 hour and 20 minutes. Cool cake in pan on a wire rack 10 minutes. Invert cake onto wire rack, and let cool completely, about 2 hours.

4. To serve, transfer cake to a heatproof, rimmed serving platter. Place Cognac in a heatproof measuring cup with a spout. Heat a small saucepan over medium until warm, about 30 seconds. Remove saucepan from heat, turn off burner, and pour in Cognac. Using a long match or lighter, carefully ignite fumes just above surface of Cognac. Slowly and carefully pour flaming liquid over cake. Allow flames to extinguish before slicing and serving.
— ANGIE MAR

MAKE AHEAD Cake can be prepared 1 day ahead through Step 3 and stored, covered, at room temperature.

NOTE Clement Faugier canned whole candied chestnuts can be purchased from amazon.com.

◆ ━━━ ◆ ━━━ ◆

Pear Sticky Toffee Cakes with Miso-Caramel Sauce

ACTIVE 30 MIN; TOTAL 1 HR 5 MIN;
SERVES 12

Drenched in a salty-sweet miso caramel, these pear-studded, personal-size desserts are easy to bake in a muffin tin. Just before serving, gently reheat the remaining caramel sauce before spooning it over the finished cakes.

PEAR STICKY TOFFEE CAKES

- ¼ cup unsalted butter (2 oz.), plus softened butter for greasing tin
- 1 cup all-purpose flour (about 4¼ oz.), plus more for dusting tin
- 1 cup dried dates (about 6 oz.), pitted and coarsely chopped
- 1 cup water
- 1 tsp. ground cinnamon
- ¾ tsp. baking powder
- ¾ tsp. baking soda
- ½ tsp. kosher salt
- ¾ cup packed light brown sugar
- 2 large eggs
- 2 medium Bartlett or Anjou pears, peeled, cored, and cut into ⅓-inch pieces (about 2 cups)

MISO-CARAMEL SAUCE

- ¾ cup unsalted butter (6 oz.)
- 1 cup packed light brown sugar
- ½ cup white miso (organic, if possible)
- 1 cup heavy cream

WHIPPED CREAM

- 1 cup heavy cream

1. Make the pear sticky toffee cakes
Preheat oven to 350°F. Grease a 12-cup muffin tin with softened butter, and dust with flour; set aside. Stir together dates and 1 cup water in a small saucepan. Bring to a boil over medium, and cook, stirring occasionally, until dates are softened and liquid is mostly absorbed, about 5 minutes. Remove from heat, and let cool 5 minutes. Using a potato masher or fork, mash mixture until mostly smooth.

2. Stir together flour, cinnamon, baking powder, baking soda, and salt in a bowl. Set aside. Beat brown sugar and ¼ cup butter with a stand mixer fitted with a paddle attachment on medium-high speed until light and fluffy, 4 to 5 minutes. Add eggs, one at a time, beating well after each addition. With machine running on low speed, gradually add flour mixture, beating until just combined, 1 to 2 minutes, stopping to scrape down sides of bowl as needed. Stir in date mixture. Fold in pear pieces.

3. Spoon batter evenly into prepared muffin tin, filling each cup about ⅓ inch from top (about ⅓ cup each). (Discard any remaining batter, or reserve for another use.) Bake in preheated oven until a wooden pick inserted in centers of cakes comes out clean, 18 to 22 minutes.

4. Make the miso-caramel sauce Melt butter in a medium saucepan over medium-low. Add brown sugar and miso; whisk until dissolved, 1 to 2 minutes. Whisk in heavy cream. Let mixture come to a boil, and cook, whisking constantly, 1 minute. Remove from heat; set aside.

5. Once cakes are finished baking, remove from oven; immediately poke holes all over cakes with a wooden pick. Spoon about 1 tablespoon sauce over each cake. Let cakes cool in muffin tin 20 minutes, occasionally poking additional holes.

6. Make the whipped cream Beat heavy cream with a stand mixer fitted with a whisk attachment on medium-high speed until soft peaks form, 1 to 2 minutes.

7. Run a small offset spatula around each cake to help loosen from muffin tin. Invert cakes onto individual serving plates; top each with about 1½ tablespoons miso-caramel sauce. Serve with whipped cream and remaining miso-caramel sauce.
— GAIL SIMMONS

MAKE AHEAD Cakes can be made the night before and reheated for 10 minutes at 325°F before adding sauce.

**Pear Sticky Toffee Cakes
with Miso-Caramel Sauce**

Apple-Rum Spice Cake

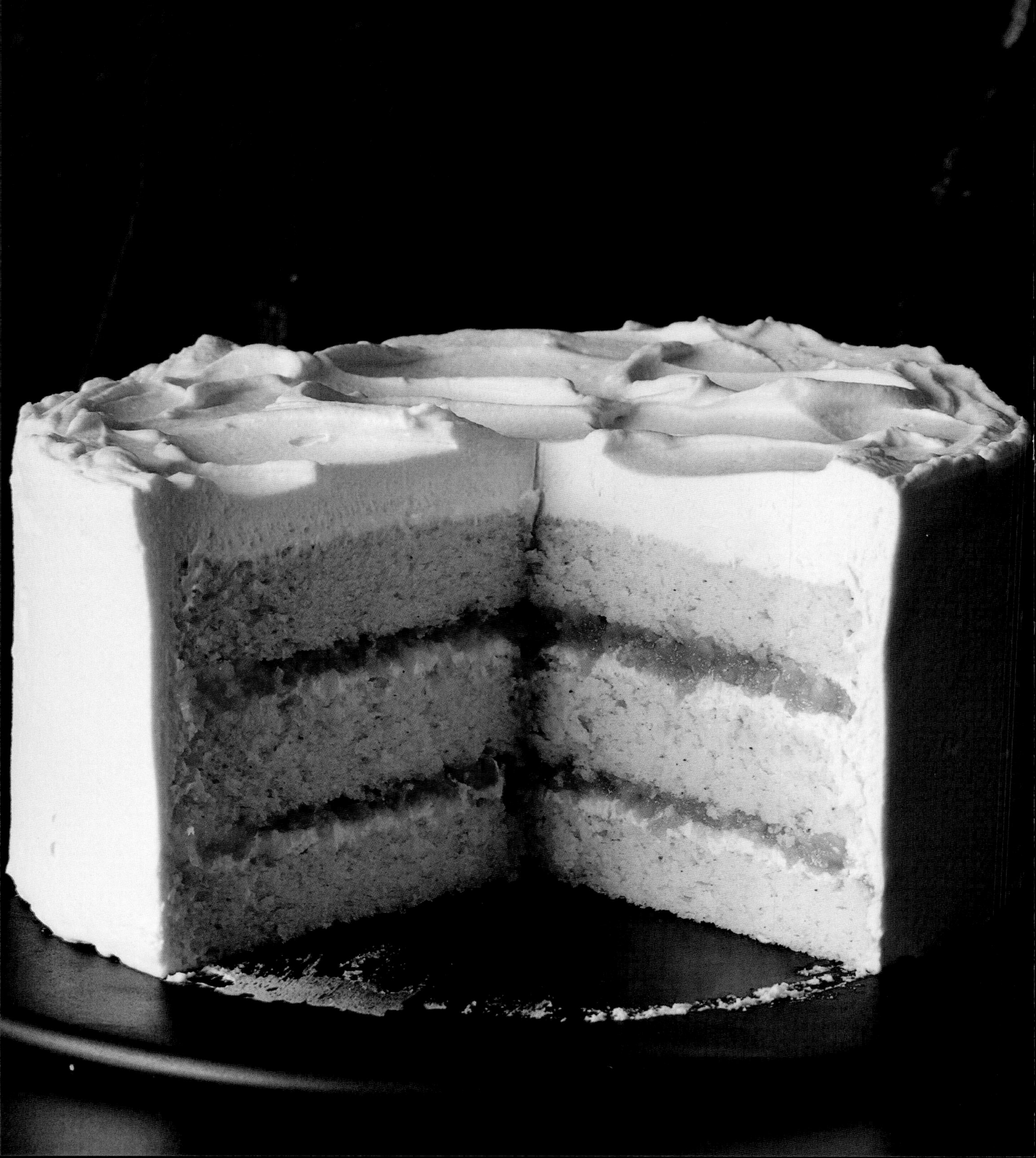

Apple-Rum Spice Cake

ACTIVE 1 HR; TOTAL 1 HR 40 MIN, PLUS 4 HR CHILLING; SERVES 10 TO 12

A stunning dessert for the grown-ups' table, warm spices and more than a shot of rum pair with tender chiffon cake and billowy ginger-cream cheese frosting.

CAKE LAYERS

Vegetable shortening

2¼ **cups sifted bleached cake flour (about 7½ oz.), plus more for dusting pans**

1¼ **cups granulated sugar**

1 **Tbsp. baking powder**

1 **tsp. ground cinnamon**

½ **tsp. freshly grated nutmeg**

½ **tsp. kosher salt**

5 **large eggs, separated**

⅔ **cup water**

½ **cup canola oil**

2 **Tbsp. fresh lemon juice**

1 **tsp. vanilla extract**

½ **tsp. cream of tartar**

GINGER-CREAM CHEESE FROSTING

1 **(4-inch) piece fresh ginger, unpeeled and grated on a Microplane (about 3 Tbsp.)**

8 **oz. cream cheese, softened**

⅓ **cup granulated sugar**

1½ **tsp. vanilla extract**

¼ **tsp. kosher salt**

2 **cups heavy cream**

ADDITIONAL INGREDIENT

Apple-Rum Compote (recipe, p. 241)

1. Make the cake layers Preheat oven to 350°F. Grease 3 (8-inch) round cake pans with shortening; dust with flour. Whisk together flour, sugar, baking powder, cinnamon, nutmeg, and salt in a large bowl. Whisk together egg yolks, ⅔ cup water, canola oil, lemon juice, and vanilla in a separate bowl until smooth. Whisk egg yolk mixture into flour mixture until batter is just combined.

2. Beat egg whites in a medium bowl with an electric mixer fitted with a whisk attachment on medium-high speed until foamy, about 1 minute. Add cream of tartar; beat until soft peaks form, 1 to 2 minutes. Fold one-third of egg white mixture into batter. Add remaining egg white mixture; gently fold until just combined. Divide batter evenly among prepared pans.

3. Bake in preheated oven until cakes are light golden brown and a wooden pick inserted in cake centers comes out clean, 16 to 20 minutes. Cool cakes in pans on a wire rack 10 minutes. Remove cakes from cake pans; transfer to wire racks, and let cool completely, about 30 minutes.

4. Make the ginger-cream cheese frosting Place grated ginger in center of a square of folded cheesecloth; gather edges of cheesecloth and squeeze ginger over a small bowl to equal 2 tablespoons juice. Discard solids; set aside ginger juice.

5. Beat cream cheese, sugar, vanilla, and salt in a medium bowl with an electric mixer fitted with a whisk attachment on medium-high speed until light and fluffy, about 3 minutes, stopping to scrape down sides of bowl as needed.

6. Stir together ginger juice and heavy cream in a small bowl. With machine running on medium-high speed, gradually drizzle ginger juice mixture into cream cheese mixture; beat until stiff peaks form, 2 to 3 minutes. Use immediately.

7. Assemble the cake Place 1 cake layer on a serving platter. Spread top with about ⅓ cup frosting. Spoon ¾ cup frosting into a zip-top plastic bag; cut a ⅓-inch hole in one corner. Pipe a ⅓-inch-tall ring of frosting just inside the top edge of frosted cake layer (to create a barrier). Spread half the cooled compote (about ⅔ cup) in an even layer inside piped ring. Top with second cake layer; repeat process with frosting, frosting ring, and remaining compote. Top with third cake layer; spread remaining frosting over top and sides of cake. Refrigerate assembled cake at least 4 hours or up to 1 day. Serve chilled.
— JOANNE CHANG

MAKE AHEAD Compote can be made up to 3 days ahead and stored in an airtight container in refrigerator. Cake layers can be made a day ahead, wrapped in plastic wrap, and stored at room temperature. Cake may be assembled and kept chilled up to 1 day.

Black Forest Mousse
Cake with Cherry-Chile-
Pomegranate Glaze

Black Forest Mousse Cake with Cherry-Chile-Pomegranate Glaze

ACTIVE 1 HR 45 MIN; TOTAL 8 HR 45 MIN; SERVES 18

In the hands of Renee Bolstad, former pastry chef at Joule in Seattle, black forest cake—traditionally chocolate cake layered with kirsch, cherries, and whipped cream—morphs into a modern layered mousse. To add texture and heat, Bolstad sandwiches it between a spicy pomegranate-chile glaze and crispy chocolate. If you can't find Thai chiles, swap in habanero, jalapeño, or cayenne. For the smoothest, silkiest mousse, be careful not to over-whip the cream. Just under soft peaks will result in the best final texture.

CAKE

- **Nonstick cooking spray**
- 6 oz. **70% cacao dark chocolate, chopped**
- 3 Tbsp. **unsalted butter**
- 1 large **egg white, at room temperature**
- ¼ cup **granulated sugar, divided**
- 2 large **eggs, at room temperature**

CHOCOLATE CRUNCH

- 2 oz. **70% cacao dark chocolate, chopped**
- 1 oz. **39% cacao milk chocolate, chopped**
- 2 Tbsp. **unsalted butter**
- 3 oz. **cornflakes cereal (about 3 cups), finely crushed**
- ½ tsp. **kosher salt**

MOUSSE

- 14 oz. **39% cacao milk chocolate, chopped**
- 6 oz. **70% cacao dark chocolate, chopped**
- 2½ cups **heavy cream**
- ¼ tsp. **kosher salt**

GLAZE

- 1 cup **frozen pitted dark sweet cherries, thawed, juice reserved**
- ⅓ cup **pomegranate juice**
- 1 medium **red Thai chile, stemmed**
- 1 (¼-oz.) envelope **unflavored gelatin**
- 3 Tbsp. **cold water**
- ½ cup **granulated sugar**
- 1 Tbsp. **pectin**
- 1 Tbsp. **light corn syrup**

1. Make the cake Preheat oven to 300°F. Line a 13- × 9-inch baking pan with heavy-duty aluminum foil, allowing 2 inches of overhang on all sides. Lightly grease foil with cooking spray. Combine chocolate and butter in top of a double boiler over simmering water, and cook over medium, stirring occasionally, until melted and smooth, about 6 minutes. Cool chocolate mixture 5 minutes. Beat egg white with a stand mixer fitted with a whisk attachment on medium speed until frothy, about 1 minute. Increase speed to medium-high, and gradually add 2 tablespoons sugar, beating until stiff peaks form, 2 to 3 minutes.

2. Whisk together eggs and remaining 2 tablespoons sugar in a separate medium bowl. Whisk vigorously until light, fluffy, tripled in volume, and mixture makes ribbons, 4 to 5 minutes. Fold in chocolate mixture until incorporated. Gently fold in egg white mixture just until combined. Pour batter into prepared pan; using an offset spatula, smooth into an even layer to completely cover bottom of pan. Bake in preheated oven until a wooden pick inserted in center comes out clean, about 15 minutes. Transfer pan to a wire rack, and let cool completely, about 45 minutes.

3. Make the chocolate crunch Line a 13- × 9-inch baking pan with parchment paper, allowing 2 inches of overhang on 2 long sides; set aside. Combine dark chocolate, milk chocolate, and butter in top of a double boiler over simmering water, and cook over medium, stirring occasionally, until melted and smooth, about 3 minutes. Remove from heat, and stir in cornflakes and salt until well combined. Spread mixture in a very thin layer (about ⅛ inch thick) to completely cover bottom of prepared pan. Freeze until set, at least 1 hour or up to 2 days. Using parchment paper as handles, lift chocolate crunch from pan in one piece. Carefully remove parchment, and place chocolate crunch sheet on top of cooled cake layer in baking pan. Freeze, uncovered, while preparing mousse.

4. Make the mousse Combine milk chocolate and dark chocolate in top of a double boiler over simmering water, and cook over medium, stirring occasionally, until melted and smooth, about 10 minutes. Let chocolate stand until slightly cool, about 15 minutes. Meanwhile, beat heavy cream and salt with a stand mixer fitted with a whisk attachment on medium speed until fluffy but still pourable (not quite soft peaks), about 3 minutes. Fold half the whipped cream into slightly cooled chocolate until combined. Gently fold in remaining whipped cream. Spread mousse on top of frozen chocolate crunch layer in baking pan. Using an offset spatula, smooth mousse to sides of pan in an even layer to completely cover surface. If needed, dip offset spatula in hot water, and dry with a towel to make top layer of mousse as level as possible. Chill, uncovered, until set, about 2 hours.

5. Make the glaze Combine cherries and juice, pomegranate juice, and chile in a blender. Process until smooth, about 45 seconds. Pour mixture through a fine wire-mesh strainer into a bowl; discard solids. Sprinkle gelatin over 3 tablespoons cold water in a small bowl; let stand 5 minutes. Meanwhile, whisk together sugar and pectin in a small saucepan. Add cherry mixture and corn syrup to sugar mixture. Bring to a boil over medium-high, whisking often. Boil, whisking constantly, 2 minutes. Remove from heat, and whisk in bloomed gelatin until dissolved. Transfer mixture to a medium bowl, and let cool completely, about 2 hours. Pour glaze over chilled mousse layer. Tilt pan to evenly cover surface. Chill, uncovered, until glaze is set, about 1 hour. Prepared cake can be chilled up to 2 days.

6. When ready to serve, use foil handles to carefully lift cake from pan. Run a hot offset spatula along edges to break seal between cake and foil. Carefully remove cake from foil, and transfer to a cutting board. Using a hot, thin knife (not serrated) and dipping in hot water and drying knife between each cut, trim edges of cake to form an 11½- × 8-inch rectangle. Cut rectangle in half lengthwise, and cut each half into 9 (about 4- × 1¼-inch) rectangles.

— RENEE BOLSTAD

PASTRY TIP Make the layers in stages, chilling each one well and ensuring it is fully set before adding the next.

No-Bake Bananas Foster Cheesecake

ACTIVE 2 HR; TOTAL 5 HR; SERVES 10 TO 12

This mousse-like cheesecake from star chef Tyler Florence has a delicious graham cracker crust and gets topped with sweet and boozy bananas.

CHEESECAKE

Nonstick cooking spray

1½ cups sugar, divided

1 packet unflavored powdered gelatin

1 cup hot water

3 cups fresh ricotta cheese (about 1½ lb.)

8 oz. cream cheese, at room temperature

1 tsp. finely grated lemon zest plus 3 Tbsp. fresh lemon juice

½ tsp. pure vanilla extract

24 whole graham crackers (1 lb.), broken up

¼ tsp. ground cinnamon

4 Tbsp. unsalted butter, softened

BANANAS FOSTER

4 Tbsp. unsalted butter

1 cup sugar

½ tsp. ground cinnamon

Pinch of ground allspice

Pinch of kosher salt

¼ cup amaretto

¼ cup dark rum

4 ripe bananas, sliced ¼ inch thick

1. Make the cheesecake Coat a 2½-quart glass bowl with cooking spray and line with plastic wrap, allowing 6 inches of overhang all around.

2. Whisk ½ cup sugar and gelatin in a medium bowl. Stir in 1 cup hot water and let stand for 3 minutes, then whisk to dissolve sugar and gelatin.

3. Beat ricotta and cream cheese with a stand mixer fitted with a paddle attachment on medium speed until smooth. With machine running, gradually beat in gelatin mixture, then beat in lemon zest, lemon juice, and vanilla. Scrape cheesecake mixture into prepared bowl and cover with overhanging plastic. Refrigerate until nearly set, about 1 hour.

4. Meanwhile, combine graham crackers and cinnamon in a food processor, and pulse until fine crumbs form. Transfer to a heatproof medium bowl.

5. Combine remaining 1 cup sugar and ½ cup water in a medium saucepan, and cook over medium until it reaches 330°F on a candy thermometer, 5 to 7 minutes. Remove from heat and whisk in butter. Immediately pour mixture over graham cracker crumbs, and stir quickly until evenly moistened; clumps will form.

6. Uncover cheesecake and sprinkle graham cracker mixture evenly on top, packing it gently onto surface of cake. Cover and refrigerate until cake is completely set, at least 2 hours or overnight.

7. Make the bananas Foster Melt butter and sugar in a large saucepan over medium. Cook, swirling pan, until a very light caramel forms, 5 to 7 minutes. Stir in cinnamon, allspice, and salt, and cook, swirling, for 30 seconds. Add amaretto and rum and, very carefully, using a long-handled match, ignite alcohol. When flame subsides, stir in bananas. Let cool.

8. Unwrap cake and carefully invert onto a rimmed serving plate. Spoon bananas Foster over top, and serve right away.

— TYLER FLORENCE

Master Pie Dough

ACTIVE 10 MIN; TOTAL 2 HR 40 MIN; MAKES 2 (12-OZ.) PIE SHELLS

This all-butter dough keeps well in the freezer—we like to have several disks on hand during the holidays. Use the shells for any of the pies in this story.

2¾ cups all-purpose flour (12 oz.), plus more for work surface

1 Tbsp. kosher salt

1 Tbsp. granulated sugar

1 cup unsalted butter, cut into ½-inch pieces and frozen

½ cup ice water

1. Combine flour, salt, and sugar in food processor; pulse to combine, about 5 times. Add butter; pulse until butter resembles peas, about 10 times. With machine running, drizzle in ice water; process until mixture just starts to clump, about 10 seconds. (Do not overmix; dough should not form a ball.) Turn mixture out onto a clean work surface; knead until dough just starts to come together, 4 to 5 times.

2. Divide dough into 2 equal portions. Flatten each portion into a 4-inch disk; wrap each tightly in plastic wrap. Chill at least 2 hours or up to 3 days.

3. Roll dough into a 12-inch circle on a lightly floured surface. Fit dough into a 9-inch pie plate or cast-iron skillet; trim excess dough, and crimp edges. Freeze pie shell, uncovered, until hard, at least 30 minutes or up to overnight. Dough can be frozen up to 1 month. — PAIGE GRANDJEAN

Black-Bottom Walnut Pie

ACTIVE 20 MIN; TOTAL 6 HR 20 MIN; SERVES 8

A layer of bittersweet chocolate anchors this rich nut pie from Jaynelle St. Jean of PieTisserie in Oakland, California. With a filling reminiscent of classic pecan pies, the walnuts in the pie float to the top of the custard and toast to golden brown perfection. Be sure to let the pie cool fully before slicing.

4 oz. bittersweet chocolate, finely chopped

¼ cup heavy cream

1 frozen Master Pie Dough pie shell (recipe at left)

1 cup light corn syrup

2 large eggs, beaten

¼ cup packed light brown sugar

2 Tbsp. all-purpose flour

2 Tbsp. unsalted butter, melted

1 Tbsp. molasses

1 tsp. vanilla extract

¼ tsp. kosher salt

2 cups walnut halves

1. Place chocolate in a small heatproof bowl. Place cream in a microwavable bowl; microwave on HIGH until hot, 30 to 45 seconds. Pour over chocolate; stir until smooth and melted. Spread chocolate mixture in an even layer on bottom of frozen pie shell. Freeze, uncovered, until hard, at least 1 hour or up to overnight.

2. Preheat oven to 350°F. Whisk together corn syrup, eggs, brown sugar, flour, butter, molasses, vanilla, and salt in a bowl. Sprinkle walnuts over chocolate layer in frozen pie shell; pour corn syrup mixture over walnuts. Bake in preheated oven until edges are set, about 1 hour. Transfer pie to a wire rack to cool completely, about 4 hours. — JAYNELLE ST. JEAN

Black-Bottom Walnut Pie

Honey-Flower Pie

Honey-Flower Pie

ACTIVE 25 MIN; TOTAL 5 HR 55 MIN;
SERVES 8

*Use a mild-tasting honey, such as clover,
to let the dried lavender in this pie from
Shauna Lott Harman of Long I Pie in Denver
really shine. Flaky sea salt adds crunch to
the silky chess pie texture.*

- ¾ cup granulated sugar
- 1 Tbsp. dried culinary lavender
- ½ cup unsalted butter (4 oz.), melted
- 2 Tbsp. fine yellow cornmeal
- ¼ tsp. kosher salt
- ¾ cup honey
- 2 tsp. white vinegar
- ¼ tsp. vanilla extract
- ½ cup heavy cream
- 3 large eggs, beaten
- 1 frozen Master Pie Dough pie shell
  (recipe, p. 254)
- ¼ tsp. coarse or flaky sea salt

1. Combine granulated sugar and lavender
in a food processor; process until lavender
is incorporated, about 20 seconds.
Transfer to a stand mixer fitted with a
paddle attachment. Add butter, cornmeal,
and kosher salt; beat on medium-low
speed until combined, about 10 seconds.
Stir in honey, vinegar, and vanilla. Add
cream and eggs; beat on medium-
low speed until just combined, about
15 seconds. Cover and chill 1 hour.

2. Preheat oven to 400°F. Pour chilled
honey filling into frozen pie shell. Bake in
preheated oven until top is dark brown
and filling is set around edges, 45 to
50 minutes, covering edges of crust with
aluminum foil after 35 minutes if crust
is getting too dark. Remove from oven;
sprinkle with sea salt. Transfer to a wire
rack to cool completely, about 4 hours.
— SHAUNA LOTT HARMAN

Brown Butter Pecan Pie with Espresso Dates

ACTIVE 1 HR; TOTAL 5 HR 15 MIN, PLUS
COOLING; MAKES 1 (9-INCH) PIE

*This not-too-sweet pie is a terrific
alternative to the cloying kind. The recipe
was adapted from* Soframiz: Vibrant
Middle Eastern Recipes from Sofra
Bakery and Cafe *by Ana Sortun and
Maura Kilpatrick.*

PIE CRUST

- 1¼ cups all-purpose flour
- 1½ tsp. granulated sugar
- ½ tsp. kosher salt
- 1 stick unsalted butter, cubed and
  frozen
- ¼ cup ice water

FILLING

- 2 cups pecan halves (7 oz.)
- ½ lb. Medjool dates, pitted and
  chopped (1 cup)
- 3 Tbsp. brewed espresso or strong
  coffee
- 1 stick unsalted butter
- 1 cup packed light brown sugar
- 1 cup Lyle's Golden Syrup or light
  corn syrup
- 1½ tsp. instant espresso powder
- 1½ tsp. kosher salt
- 3 large eggs
- Whipped cream, for serving

1. Make the pie crust Combine flour,
granulated sugar, and salt in a food
processor; pulse. Add butter, and pulse
until mixture resembles small peas. Add
¼ cup ice water and pulse until dough is
evenly moistened. Gradually add more
water if needed. Scrape dough onto a
work surface, and knead 2 to 3 times, just
until it comes together. Form into a disk,
wrap in plastic, and refrigerate until firm,
about 1 hour.

2. On a lightly floured work surface, roll
out dough to a 12-inch round; transfer to a
9-inch pie plate. Fold edge of dough under
itself and crimp edge. Freeze pie crust for
at least 2 hours or overnight.

3. Preheat oven to 375°F. Line pie crust
with parchment paper and fill with
pie weights or dried beans. Bake until
lightly browned around the edge, about
25 minutes. Remove parchment paper
and weights, and bake until the bottom is
lightly browned, about 10 minutes. Let cool
completely.

4. Make the filling Reduce oven
temperature to 350°F. Spread pecans
on a rimmed baking sheet and toast
until fragrant, 8 to 10 minutes. Let cool
completely.

5. Combine dates and brewed espresso
in a small skillet over medium, and cook,
stirring, until very soft, 3 to 5 minutes.
Scrape mixture into a small bowl and wipe
out skillet.

6. Put butter into skillet, and cook over
medium, swirling, until milk solids turn a
deep golden brown, about 5 minutes. Let
cool slightly.

7. Whisk brown sugar, golden syrup,
espresso powder, and salt in a large bowl.
Whisk in eggs, then gradually whisk in
brown butter until the filling is smooth.

8. Set pie plate on a rimmed baking sheet.
Spread espresso dates in crust and scatter
pecans on top. Pour filling over pecans.
Bake until filling is set around edge and
slightly jiggly in center, about 1 hour and
15 minutes. Transfer pie to a wire rack and
let cool completely. Serve with whipped
cream. — ANA SORTUN & MAURA KILPATRICK

MAKE AHEAD The pecan pie can be
covered and kept at room temperature
for 3 days. The unbaked pie crust can be
wrapped in plastic and frozen for 1 month.

WHISKEY Pair with a spice- and toffee-
scented small-batch bourbon.

Buttermilk Eggnog Pie

ACTIVE 30 MIN; TOTAL 3 HR 45 MIN, PLUS
COOLING; SERVES 12

*TV chef Carla Hall flavors her southern
buttermilk pie with rum and lots of nutmeg,
which evoke the flavors of eggnog.*

CRUST

- 1 cup all-purpose flour
- 1½ tsp. sugar
- ½ tsp. kosher salt
- 1 stick cold unsalted butter, cut into
  ½-inch cubes
- 2 Tbsp. ice water

FILLING

- 1½ cups sugar
- 1 Tbsp. all-purpose flour
- 2 tsp. freshly grated nutmeg
- ½ tsp. kosher salt
- 3 large eggs, at room temperature
- 5 Tbsp. unsalted butter, melted and
  cooled
- 1 cup buttermilk, at room
  temperature
- 1 Tbsp. dark rum
- 1 tsp. pure vanilla extract

1. Make the crust Whisk flour, sugar, and
salt in a medium bowl. Add butter and,
using your fingertips, rub butter into flour
mixture until mixture resembles coarse
meal with some pea-size pieces remaining.
Stir in 2 tablespoons ice water just until
dough comes together. Form dough into
a ball, then flatten into a 1-inch-thick disk.
Wrap in plastic and refrigerate until firm, at
least 1 hour or up to 1 day.

2. On a lightly floured work surface, using
a lightly floured rolling pin, roll out dough
to a 12-inch round. Ease dough into a
9-inch pie plate and tuck any overhang
under itself. Crimp decoratively. Freeze
until firm, about 30 minutes.

3. Preheat oven to 425°F. Line dough with
parchment paper, then fill with pie weights
or dried beans. Bake, just until the dough is
set, about 25 minutes. Remove parchment
paper and weights; bake, until light golden,
8 to 10 minutes longer. Transfer crust to a
wire rack to cool slightly, about 10 minutes.
Reduce oven temperature to 375°F.

4. Make the filling Whisk sugar, flour,
nutmeg, and salt in a large bowl. Whisk
in eggs, one at a time. While whisking
constantly, slowly drizzle in melted butter
followed by buttermilk, rum, and vanilla.
Pour filling into warm crust. Bake for
15 minutes, then reduce oven temperature
to 350°F and bake until custard is just set
at edge and slightly jiggly in center, about
40 minutes longer. Transfer pie to a wire
rack and let cool completely. Serve at
room temperature or chilled. — CARLA HALL

MAKE AHEAD The pie can be refrigerated
overnight.

Pumpkin Cream Pie in a Chocolate Crust

PHOTO P. 235

ACTIVE 30 MIN; TOTAL 2 HR 15 MIN, PLUS
COOLING; SERVES 8 TO 10

*At Thanksgiving, you can't get wildly
experimental with unfamiliar flavors.
Instead, you need recipes everyone is
going to love. This pumpkin pie? You might
want to make two.*

CRUST

- 8 oz. chocolate wafer cookies
  (33 cookies)
- 1 stick unsalted butter, melted
- 2 Tbsp. granulated sugar

FILLING

- 1 (15-oz.) can pure pumpkin puree
- ¾ cup heavy cream
- 2 large eggs
- 1 Tbsp. bourbon, brandy, or apple
  cider

- ½ cup packed light brown sugar
- 1 tsp. finely grated peeled fresh
  ginger
- 1½ tsp. ground ginger
- 1½ tsp. ground cinnamon
- ½ tsp. fine sea salt
- ¼ tsp. grated nutmeg
- ⅛ tsp. ground allspice

TOPPING

- 1 cup crème fraîche
- ½ cup heavy cream
- 2 Tbsp. confectioners' sugar
  Chocolate curls (see Note), for
  garnish

1. Make the crust Place cookies in a food
processor, and pulse until finely ground.
Transfer to a medium bowl and add
butter and granulated sugar. Mix until well
combined, then press into a 9-inch metal
pie plate. Refrigerate for 30 minutes.

2. Preheat oven to 350°F. Bake crust until
set, 8 to 10 minutes. Transfer to a wire rack
and let cool.

3. Make the filling Whisk pumpkin puree,
cream, eggs, bourbon, brown sugar,
grated ginger, ground ginger, cinnamon,
salt, nutmeg, and allspice in a large bowl
until smooth. Scrape filling into pie crust
and bake until filling is set but slightly
jiggly in the center, 50 minutes to 1 hour.
Transfer to a wire rack and let cool
completely.

4. Make the topping Beat crème fraîche,
cream, and confectioners' sugar in a
medium bowl using an electric mixer until
soft peaks form. Spoon topping over pie,
garnish with chocolate curls, and serve.
— MELISSA CLARK

MAKE AHEAD The pie can be refrigerated
overnight. Garnish with chocolate curls
before serving.

NOTE To make chocolate curls, use a
vegetable peeler to shave them right off of
a large block of chocolate.

Buttermilk Eggnog Pie

Pecan Pumpkin Cream Pie

Pecan-Pumpkin Cream Pie

ACTIVE 55 MIN; TOTAL 3 HR 40 MIN, PLUS
6 HR REFRIGERATION; SERVES 8

This pie slices beautifully to reveal not one but two classic Thanksgiving pie fillings: a richly spiced pumpkin custard layered atop toasty, sweet pecan. Bake the pie up to one day ahead and keep refrigerated so it slices cleanly. Top with the whipped cream just before serving.

PECAN FILLING

- ⅓ cup granulated sugar
- ½ cup light corn syrup
- 1 Tbsp. unsalted butter
- 2 large eggs
- ½ tsp. vanilla extract
- ¼ tsp. kosher salt
- 1¼ cups pecan halves (about 5 oz.), toasted
- All-Butter Pie Shell (recipe follows)

PUMPKIN FILLING

- 1 cup canned pumpkin
- ½ tsp. vanilla extract
- ¼ tsp. ground ginger
- ¼ tsp. ground cinnamon
- ¼ tsp. kosher salt
- ⅛ tsp. ground nutmeg
- ⅔ cup heavy cream
- ¼ cup granulated sugar
- 2 large eggs

WHIPPED CREAM

- 1 cup heavy cream
- 2 Tbsp. powdered sugar

1. Make the pecan filling Preheat oven to 350°F. Stir together granulated sugar and ¼ cup water in a medium saucepan. Using a pastry brush dipped in water, brush off any sugar clinging to sides of pan. Bring mixture to a boil over high, taking care not to jostle pan. Continue boiling, undisturbed, until syrup starts to turn a slightly pale brown, 6 to 8 minutes; gently swirl pan to even out caramelization. Continue boiling over high, swirling pan often, until syrup turns golden brown, about 2 minutes. Reduce heat to medium; carefully pour in corn syrup. (Mixture will sputter a bit and turn clumpy.) Cook, whisking occasionally, until clumps have completely melted, 1 to 2 minutes. Remove from heat; whisk in butter until melted.

2. Whisk together eggs, vanilla, and salt in a medium-size heatproof bowl. Gradually pour hot sugar mixture into egg mixture, whisking constantly, until completely combined. Add pecans; stir well to coat.

3. Pour pecan mixture into cooled pie shell. Bake pie in preheated oven until top is starting to set but filling is still jiggly, 15 to 20 minutes. Remove from oven; let cool 5 minutes.

4. Make the pumpkin filling Whisk together pumpkin, vanilla, ginger, cinnamon, salt, and nutmeg in a small saucepan. Cook over high, whisking constantly, until mixture reduces slightly and starts to darken in color, 3 to 4 minutes. Remove from heat; whisk in cream and sugar. Whisk in eggs until well combined.

5. Pour pumpkin filling over warm pecan filling in pie shell; smooth top. (Cover edges of pie with aluminum foil to prevent overbrowning if crust is getting too dark.) Bake at 350°F until pumpkin filling puffs up and is set, 30 to 40 minutes. Remove from oven; let cool completely on a wire rack, about 2 hours. Gently press plastic wrap onto surface of pie; chill until cold, at least 6 hours or up to overnight.

6. Make the whipped cream Beat cream and powdered sugar with an electric mixer fitted with a whisk attachment on medium speed until stiff peaks form, 2 to 3 minutes. Transfer whipped cream to a piping bag fitted with a star tip. Pipe large stars over surface of chilled pie. Serve immediately, or chill, uncovered, up to 6 hours. Serve chilled. — JOANNE CHANG

MAKE AHEAD Pie shell can be prepared and baked up to 4 hours in advance. Pie can be baked up to 1 day ahead; keep chilled until ready to serve.

ALL-BUTTER PIE SHELL Stir together 1 cup all-purpose flour, 2 tablespoons granulated sugar, and ½ teaspoon kosher salt in bowl of a stand mixer fitted with a paddle attachment. Add ½ cup plus 1 tablespoon cold unsalted butter cut into ½-inch pieces; beat on low speed until flour holds together when pinched and there are pecan-size lumps of butter throughout, about 45 seconds. Whisk together ¼ cup cold milk and 1 large egg yolk in a small bowl; add to flour mixture. Beat on low speed just until mixture barely comes together, about 30 seconds. (Dough will be very shaggy.)

Dump dough onto a clean work surface, and gather it into a tight mound. Using palm of hand, smear dough on work surface, piece by piece, until most butter chunks are smeared into dough and dough comes together. Gather dough into a tight mound. Wrap with plastic wrap; press down to shape into a 1-inch-thick disk. Refrigerate dough disk at least 1 hour or up to 4 days.

Unwrap dough; roll out into a 12-inch circle on a well-floured work surface. Place dough inside a 9-inch pie plate, and trim edges to leave a ½-inch overhang. Crimp edges. Refrigerate pie shell, uncovered, at least 30 minutes or up to 4 hours.

Preheat oven to 350°F. Line pie shell with parchment paper, and fill with pie weights or dried beans. Bake in preheated oven until pie shell sides are light brown, 35 to 40 minutes. Transfer pie shell to a wire rack; let cool completely with pie weights still in shell, about 1 hour. Once cool, remove weights and parchment. Pie shell can be stored, uncovered, at room temperature up to 4 hours. — JOANNE CHANG

MAKE AHEAD Pie dough may be prepared through Step 2, wrapped in an additional layer of plastic, and frozen up to 1 month. Defrost in refrigerator before using.

Purple Sweet Potato Pie with Coconut and Five-Spice

ACTIVE 35 MIN; TOTAL 8 HR 35 MIN;
SERVES 8

Interdisciplinary artist Krystal Mack draws inspiration from the communities nearby. The purple ube, or sweet potato, comes from the Filipino-Americans who make up a vital part of Baltimore's culture. The Taiwanese and Southeast Asian populations introduced Mack to five-spice and inspired the addition of coconut. Toasted marshmallows brings in the Americana of a Black Thanksgiving. Ube flavoring, a liquid extract, amps up the radiant purple color of the yams.

- 1¾ lb. purple sweet potatoes or yams
- 1 cup plus 2 Tbsp. packed light brown sugar, divided
- 1 cup evaporated milk
- ½ cup plus 2 Tbsp. unsalted butter, melted, divided
- 3 large eggs, beaten
- 1 tsp. vanilla extract
- 1 tsp. ube flavoring
- ¾ tsp. ground cinnamon, divided
- ½ tsp. five-spice powder
- ¼ tsp. kosher salt
- ¼ tsp. ground nutmeg
- 1 frozen Master Pie Dough pie shell (recipe, p. 254)
- ¼ cup uncooked regular rolled oats
- ¼ cup chopped pecans
- 2 Tbsp. sweetened shredded coconut
- 2 Tbsp. miniature marshmallows

1. Preheat oven to 350°F. Pierce yams several times with a fork, and wrap each in aluminum foil. Bake in preheated oven until tender, 1 hour to 1 hour and 30 minutes. Remove from oven; cool completely, about 2 hours.

2. Preheat oven to 350°F. Peel cooled yams and discard skins. Process yams in a food processor until mixture is smooth and forms a ball, about 1 minute. Place 1½ cups yam puree in a large bowl; reserve remaining puree for another use. Whisk in 1 cup brown sugar, milk, ½ cup butter, eggs, vanilla, ube flavoring, ½ teaspoon cinnamon, five-spice, salt, and nutmeg until smooth and combined. Pour mixture into frozen pie shell. Bake in preheated oven until filling is set, about 50 minutes.

3. Meanwhile, stir together oats, pecans, coconut, remaining 2 tablespoons brown sugar, remaining 2 tablespoons butter, and remaining ¼ teaspoon cinnamon in a bowl. Set aside.

4. Remove pie from oven; sprinkle center of pie with oat mixture. Return to oven; bake at 350°F until topping is lightly browned, about 10 minutes. Sprinkle marshmallows over topping, and bake until lightly browned, about 5 minutes. Transfer pie to a wire rack to cool completely, about 4 hours. — KRYSTAL MACK

◆ ◆ ◆

Pear-and-Cranberry Slab Pie

ACTIVE 50 MIN; TOTAL 3 HR, PLUS COOLING;
SERVES 8 TO 10

Instead of making a traditional two-crust pie in a pie plate, F&W's Justin Chapple makes this freeform, fruit-filled, ginger-laced pie on a baking sheet.

- 2¾ cups all-purpose flour, divided
- ½ cup plus 1 Tbsp. granulated sugar
- 1½ tsp. kosher salt, divided
- 2 sticks unsalted butter, cubed and chilled
- ½ cup ice water
- 4 firm Bartlett or Anjou pears, peeled, cored, and cut into ¾-inch wedges
- 1½ cups frozen cranberries
- 1 tsp. ground fresh ginger
- 1 large egg beaten with 1 Tbsp. water
- Turbinado sugar, for sprinkling
- Vanilla ice cream, for serving

1. Combine 2½ cups flour, 1 tablespoon granulated sugar, and 1 teaspoon salt in a food processor; pulse to mix. Add butter, and pulse in 1-second bursts until mixture resembles coarse meal. Drizzle ½ cup ice water over mixture and pulse in 1-second bursts until dough just comes together. Turn dough out onto a work surface, gather any crumbs, and pat into 2 squares. Wrap squares in plastic and refrigerate until chilled, about 45 minutes.

2. Preheat oven to 400°F. On a floured work surface, roll out 1 piece of dough to a 12-inch square. Slide dough onto a large sheet of parchment paper, then slide onto a large baking sheet. Repeat with second piece of dough. Refrigerate for 15 minutes.

3. Slide 1 square of dough onto a work surface. Toss pears, cranberries, ginger, ½ teaspoon salt, remaining ½ cup granulated sugar, and remaining ¼ cup flour in a large bowl. Spread fruit evenly on dough square on baking sheet, leaving a 1-inch border. Ease other square of dough on top of fruit. Fold over edge and crimp decoratively all around to seal. Brush pie with egg wash and sprinkle with turbinado sugar. Cut 16 small slits in the top and freeze for 15 minutes.

4. Bake pie until golden and pears are tender, about 50 minutes, rotating halfway through baking. Let cool. Cut pie into squares, and serve with vanilla ice cream. — JUSTIN CHAPPLE

MAKE AHEAD The pie can be stored at room temperature for up to 2 days.

Pear-and-Cranberry Slab Pie

Dark-Cherry Crumble Pie

ACTIVE 35 MIN; TOTAL 5 HR 50 MIN;
SERVES 8

Whole sweet cherries mingle with amaretto and toasted oats in this pie from Maya-Camille Broussard's Justice of the Pies in Chicago.

- 12 cups pitted fresh or thawed frozen dark sweet cherries (about 4 lb.)
- 2 cups granulated sugar
- 2 Tbsp. fresh lemon juice
- 2 Tbsp. amaretto
- 1 tsp. almond extract
- ½ tsp. kosher salt
- 1 Tbsp. fine yellow cornmeal
- 1 frozen Master Pie Dough pie shell (recipe, p. 254)
- ½ cup uncooked regular rolled oats
- ⅓ cup unbleached all-purpose flour (about 1½ oz.)
- ¼ cup packed light brown sugar
- ¼ cup cold unsalted butter, cut into ½-inch pieces

1. Preheat oven to 350°F. Stir together cherries, granulated sugar, and lemon juice in a large saucepan. Cook over medium-high, stirring often, until cherries soften and release liquid, about 15 minutes. Pour mixture into a colander set over a bowl; let drain 20 minutes.

2. Transfer drained cherries to a large bowl; reserve strained juice for another use. Stir in amaretto, almond extract, and salt. Sprinkle cornmeal in an even layer over bottom of frozen pie shell; pour cherry mixture evenly into prepared pie shell. Bake in preheated oven until crust is light golden brown, about 35 minutes.

3. While pie bakes, stir together oats, flour, and brown sugar in a bowl. Add butter; using your hands, incorporate butter until mixture resembles small peas.

4. Remove pie from oven; sprinkle with oat mixture. Return to oven; bake at 350°F until topping and crust are golden brown, about 20 minutes. Transfer to a wire rack to cool completely, at least 4 hours or up to overnight. — MAYA-CAMILLE BROUSSARD

Cranberry-Walnut Tart with Buckwheat Crust

ACTIVE 30 MIN; TOTAL 2 HR 30 MIN;
MAKES 1 (14-INCH) TART

This gorgeous tart has a wheaty, cookie-like crust, a creamy walnut filling, and a topping of glistening cranberries. The recipe is from Claire Ptak of London's cult-favorite Violet Bakery.

DOUGH
- 1 cup buckwheat flour
- 1 Tbsp. tapioca flour
- 1 stick plus 2 Tbsp. cold unsalted butter, cubed, plus more for greasing
- 1 tsp. kosher salt
- 2 large egg yolks
- 1 large egg, lightly beaten

FRANGIPANE
- ½ cup walnut halves
- ¼ cup sugar
- ½ stick unsalted butter, softened
- 1 large egg
- 1 Tbsp. tapioca flour
- 1 Tbsp. heavy cream
- 1 Tbsp. Grand Marnier
- Finely grated zest of 1 clementine or small orange
- Pinch of kosher salt

TOPPING
- 2 cups fresh or thawed frozen cranberries
- ¼ cup sugar
- 3 Tbsp. fresh clementine or orange juice
- Greek yogurt, for serving

1. Make the dough Combine buckwheat flour, tapioca flour, butter, and salt in a food processor. Pulse until mixture is texture of wet sand. Add egg yolks and 1 tablespoon water, and pulse until dough just comes together in a ball. Transfer to a work surface and pat into a 3- × 6-inch rectangle. Wrap in plastic and refrigerate until firm, at least 30 minutes.

2. Butter a 4- × 14-inch fluted rectangular tart pan with a removable bottom. Set the dough between 2 sheets of plastic wrap; roll out to a 6- × 16-inch rectangle. Discard top sheet of plastic wrap and invert dough into prepared pan. Gently press into corners and up sides of pan. Discard plastic wrap and trim overhanging dough flush with rim. Refrigerate until firm, at least 15 minutes.

3. Preheat oven to 375°F. Line tart shell with parchment paper and fill with pie weights or dried beans. Bake for 15 minutes. Remove parchment and pie weights, and brush tart shell with beaten egg. Bake until set, about 5 minutes more. Let cool slightly. Reduce oven temperature to 350°F.

4. Make the frangipane Combine walnuts and sugar in a food processor, and process until finely chopped. Add butter, egg, tapioca flour, cream, Grand Marnier, clementine zest, and salt, and pulse until smooth. Scrape frangipane into a bowl; chill until firm, 30 minutes.

5. Make the topping Combine cranberries, sugar, and clementine juice in a food processor, and pulse just until cranberries begin to break up.

6. Spread frangipane in tart shell and top with cranberries. Set tart on a rimmed baking sheet and bake, rotating once, until frangipane is puffed and lightly browned at edges, 30 to 35 minutes. Transfer to a wire rack and let cool. Unmold, and serve with Greek yogurt. — CLAIRE PTAK

Sweet Potato and Coffee Cream Pie

ACTIVE 1 HR 25 MIN; TOTAL 9 HR;
SERVES 8 TO 10

Want some coffee with that slice? Espresso flavors the cookie crust and the whipped pastry cream atop an orange-infused sweet potato filling.

COOKIE SHELL

- ¾ cup all-purpose flour
- 2½ tsp. espresso powder
- ¼ tsp. baking soda
- ¾ tsp. kosher salt, divided
- 5 Tbsp. unsalted butter, softened, plus 6 Tbsp. melted and cooled
- ¼ cup plus 2 Tbsp. granulated sugar
- ¼ cup packed light brown sugar
- 1 large egg
- 1 cup shelled pecans
- 1 Tbsp. finely grated orange zest

FILLINGS

- 3 large sweet potatoes
- ⅓ cup honey
- 1 Tbsp. fresh orange juice
- 2½ cups whole milk, divided
- ¾ cup roasted coffee beans
- 6 tsp. powdered gelatin (from 2 packets)
- ⅔ cup granulated sugar
- 1 large egg plus 2 large egg yolks
- 2½ tsp. espresso powder
- ¼ cup cornstarch
- 5 Tbsp. unsalted butter, softened
- 1 cup heavy cream
- Julienned candied citrus peel (see Note), for garnish

1. Make the cookie shell Preheat oven to 325°F. Line a baking sheet with parchment paper. Whisk flour, espresso powder, baking soda, and ½ teaspoon salt in a medium bowl. Beat 5 tablespoons softened butter, ¼ cup granulated sugar, and brown sugar with a stand mixer fitted with a paddle attachment at medium-high speed until light and fluffy, about 2 minutes. Beat in egg. At low speed, beat in flour mixture until combined.

2. Scrape soft dough into center of prepared baking sheet. Top with another sheet of parchment paper and roll into a thin sheet. Refrigerate until firm, about 15 minutes. Remove top paper, and bake until golden, about 15 minutes. Transfer to a wire rack and let cool completely.

3. Increase oven temperature to 350°F. Break cookie into pieces and transfer to a food processor. Add pecans, remaining 2 tablespoons granulated sugar, orange zest, and ¼ teaspoon salt, and pulse until fine crumbs form. Add 6 tablespoons melted butter, and pulse to incorporate. Press crumbs evenly over bottom and up side of a 9-inch metal pie plate. Bake until fragrant and browned, about 20 minutes. Transfer to a wire rack and let cool completely.

4. Make the fillings Increase oven temperature to 400°F. Prick sweet potatoes with a fork, wrap each in foil, and transfer to a baking sheet. Roast until tender, about 1 hour. Let cool slightly.

5. Split sweet potatoes lengthwise and scrape flesh into a medium saucepan. Add honey, and cook over medium, stirring often, until thickened to a paste, about 20 minutes. Blend sweet potatoes and orange juice in a food processor until smooth. Spread in cookie shell and refrigerate until cold, 1 hour.

6. Meanwhile, bring 2 cups milk to a bare simmer in a medium saucepan over medium. Remove from heat and add coffee beans. Let stand for 30 minutes. Strain; discard coffee beans. Bring coffee milk to a bare simmer in same pan over medium.

7. Whisk gelatin and remaining ½ cup milk in a small bowl. Whisk granulated sugar, whole egg, egg yolks, espresso powder, and cornstarch in a large heatproof bowl. Gradually whisk in half the hot coffee milk. Scrape mixture into same saucepan, and bring to a boil over medium, stirring constantly. Cook, whisking constantly, until pastry cream is thickened, about 2 minutes. Remove saucepan from heat, and whisk in gelatin and softened butter.

8. Scrape pastry cream into bowl of a stand mixer. Press plastic wrap directly on surface and refrigerate until chilled, at least 4 hours.

9. Beat pastry cream with stand mixer fitted with a paddle attachment on medium-high speed until smooth. Switch to whisk attachment and whip in cream until fluffy and stiff peaks form, about 1 minute. Mound pastry cream over sweet potatoes and smooth top. Refrigerate until cold, at least 4 hours or overnight. Garnish pie with candied citrus peel, and serve cold. —ANGELA PINKERTON

NOTE Excellent small-batch candied citrus peel is available from junetaylorjams.com.

Knafeh (Shredded
Phyllo-and-Cheese Pie)

Knafeh (Shredded Phyllo- and-Cheese Pie)

ACTIVE 20 MIN; TOTAL 30 MIN; SERVES 8

The sweet, cheese-filled dessert from Palestinian food writer Reem Kassis is encased in shredded phyllo pastry (kataifi) and soaked in a fragrant syrup laced with rose and orange blossom.

- 2 cups superfine sugar
- 1 Tbsp. fresh lemon juice
- ½ tsp. orange blossom water
- ½ tsp. rose blossom water
- ¾ cup ghee or unsalted butter, melted, plus more for greasing
- 16 oz. low-moisture part-skim mozzarella cheese, shredded (about 4 cups)
- 9 oz. ricotta cheese (about 1 cup)
- 1 lb. frozen kataifi (shredded phyllo pastry), broken into ¾-inch pieces and thawed
- ¼ cup finely chopped salted roasted pistachios

1. Bring sugar, 1½ cups water, and lemon juice to a boil in a small saucepan over medium-high. Reduce heat to medium, and simmer, stirring occasionally, until sugar is dissolved, about 5 minutes. Let syrup cool completely, about 30 minutes; stir in blossom waters.

2. Preheat oven to 400°F with oven rack in bottom third of oven. Generously grease a 13- × 9-inch pan with ghee or butter. Stir together mozzarella and ricotta in a medium bowl until combined; cover and refrigerate until ready to use.

3. Using your hands, mix together kataifi and ghee in a large bowl until combined. Scatter half the kataifi mixture into prepared pan, pressing firmly to evenly cover bottom. Dollop spoonfuls of cheese mixture evenly over top, and, using damp hands or an offset spatula, spread in an even layer. Scatter remaining kataifi mixture over filling, and press firmly.

4. Bake in preheated oven on lower rack until cheese has melted and crust is golden brown, 25 to 35 minutes. Let cool in pan on a wire rack 5 minutes. Invert pie onto a serving platter. Immediately drizzle with enough of the cooled syrup to soak the cake (about 1½ cups). Sprinkle with pistachios, and serve with remaining syrup. — REEM KASSIS

Orange-Anise Croquembouche with White Chocolate

ACTIVE 1 HR; TOTAL 7 HR 45 MIN; SERVES 20

The classic croquembouche—a decadent tower of cream-filled choux pastry puffs encased in ribbons of hard caramel—is showing up on menus once again. In this fresh, bright update from Victoria Dearmond, pastry chef at Georgia James in Houston, the puffs are filled with orange- and anise-infused cream.

ORANGE-ANISE CREAM

- 2 cups heavy cream
- 2 whole star anise, lightly crushed
- ½ cup powdered sugar (about 2 oz.)
- ¼ tsp. kosher salt
- ⅛ tsp. black pepper
- 1 tsp. orange zest plus 2 Tbsp. fresh orange juice

PÂTE À CHOUX

- ¾ cup unsalted butter (6 oz.)
- 1 Tbsp. granulated sugar
- ¾ tsp. kosher salt
- 1½ cups all-purpose flour (about 6½ oz.)
- 7 large eggs

ADDITIONAL INGREDIENTS

- 8 oz. white baking chocolate, melted
- Edible gold luster dust, for garnish (optional)
- Whole star anise, for garnish
- Candied orange peel, for garnish

1. Make the orange-anise cream Stir together heavy cream and star anise in a medium bowl. Cover and chill at least 6 hours or up to overnight.

2. Make the pâte à choux Stir together 1½ cups water, butter, granulated sugar, and salt in a medium saucepan. Bring to a simmer over medium-high, stirring occasionally. Add flour all at once, and stir vigorously with a wooden spoon until combined. Reduce heat to medium-low, and cook, stirring constantly, until a film develops on bottom of pan and dough pulls away from sides, 2 to 3 minutes. Transfer dough to bowl of a stand mixer fitted with a paddle attachment, and beat on medium-low speed until slightly cooled, about 2 minutes. Add eggs, one at a time, beating until mixture comes back together as a smooth dough after each addition. Press plastic wrap directly on surface

of dough, and chill at least 2 hours or up to 6 hours.

3. Preheat oven to 375°F. Transfer one-third of the dough to a large pastry bag fitted with a ½-inch round tip. Keep remaining dough in refrigerator. Pipe about 26 (1¼-inch) mounds 1 inch apart on a large parchment paper-lined baking sheet. (To help make a perfect circle, pipe mounds without moving the tip. Pipe as smoothly and evenly as possible, pulling tip quickly to one side when finished with each mound to prevent a Hershey's Kiss look.) Using a wet finger, gently smooth any "beaks" on tops of mounds. Using a spray bottle filled with water, mist mounds, and place in preheated oven. Immediately reduce oven temperature to 350°F, and bake until golden brown and puffed, 35 to 40 minutes. Remove puffs from oven, and let stand on baking sheet until completely cool, about 30 minutes. Increase oven temperature to 375°F, and repeat process 2 times with remaining dough. (Make sure you use cool baking sheets each time.) Using a ⅓-inch round piping tip, poke a ¼-inch-deep hole into bottom of each puff.

4. Pour chilled cream-anise mixture through a strainer lined with cheesecloth into a bowl; discard solids. Transfer strained cream mixture to bowl of a heavy-duty stand mixer fitted with a whisk attachment. Beat strained cream mixture on medium-high speed, gradually adding powdered sugar, salt, and pepper. Beat until soft peaks form, about 1 minute and 30 seconds. Add orange zest and juice, and beat until stiff peaks form, 30 seconds to 1 minute. Transfer orange-anise cream to a piping bag fitted with a ⅓-inch round tip.

5. Insert tip of piping bag into premade hole of each puff, and fill with orange-anise cream. Dip top of puff in white chocolate. Stack filled cream puffs on a platter in a conical tower. Sprinkle with luster dust, if desired, and decorate with whole star anise and candied orange peel. — VICTORIA DEARMOND

PASTRY TIP Build the tower in layers, setting the cream puffs on freshly dipped white chocolate to secure the shape.

Sour Cherry-Cheesecake Trifle with Black Pepper and Saba

ACTIVE 1 HR 30 MIN; TOTAL 5 HR 30 MIN; SERVES 16

At Brothers and Sisters in Washington, D.C., pastry director Pichet Ong's riff on a proper British trifle retains the classic form while reinventing the components. Cheesecake stands in for egg custard; pound cake replaces ladyfingers. Rather than sherry, Ong's trifle uses saba, a syrup made from cooking down grape must, which has a flavor similar to balsamic vinegar.

SOUR CHERRIES IN SABA

1½ lb. frozen pitted sour cherries

½ cup granulated sugar

¼ cup saba

1 Tbsp. vanilla extract

1 tsp. lemon zest plus 2 Tbsp. fresh lemon juice (from 1 lemon)

⅛ tsp. kosher salt

POUND CAKE

1½ cups unsalted butter (12 oz.), softened, plus more for greasing

2¼ cups granulated sugar

½ tsp. kosher salt

4 large eggs, at room temperature

3 cups all-purpose flour (about 12¾ oz.), plus more for pan

½ cup whole milk

1 tsp. vanilla extract cheesecake filling

CHEESECAKE FILLING

3 cups heavy cream

¾ cup powdered sugar (about 3 oz.), divided

12 oz. cream cheese, softened

1 Tbsp. honey

1 tsp. lemon zest

¼ tsp. kosher salt

4 oz. goat cheese, softened

½ cup crème fraîche

ADDITIONAL INGREDIENTS

2 Tbsp. unsalted butter, melted

½ tsp. black pepper, plus more for garnish

Edible flowers and fresh fruit, for garnish (optional)

1. Make the sour cherries in saba Stir together cherries, sugar, saba, vanilla, lemon zest and juice, and salt in a large saucepan. Cook over medium, stirring occasionally, until warmed through, about 10 minutes. Remove from heat, and cool completely, about 1 hour.

2. Make the pound cake Preheat oven to 300°F. Grease and flour a 13- × 9-inch baking pan. Beat butter with a stand mixer on medium speed until light and creamy, about 5 minutes. Gradually add sugar and salt, beating on medium speed until pale and fluffy, about 4 minutes. Add eggs, one at a time, beating until combined after each addition. Add flour in 3 additions alternately with milk, beating on low speed until combined after each addition. Stir in vanilla. Pour batter into prepared pan, and smooth top with an offset spatula. Bake in preheated oven until golden brown and a wooden pick inserted in center comes out clean, about 1 hour. Cool in pan on a wire rack 20 minutes. Invert cake onto wire rack, and cool completely, about 1 hour. Cut cake into 1-inch pieces.

3. Make the cheesecake filling Beat cream with an electric mixer fitted with a whisk attachment on medium speed, gradually beating in ½ cup powdered sugar until soft peaks form, 3 to 4 minutes. Cover and chill. Combine cream cheese, honey, lemon zest, salt, and remaining ¼ cup powdered sugar in bowl of stand mixer fitted with a paddle attachment. Beat on medium speed until light and smooth,

about 6 minutes, stopping to scrape down sides of bowl as needed. Add goat cheese, and beat on medium speed until smooth, about 1 minute. Add crème fraîche, and beat until incorporated, about 30 seconds. Fold 2 cups whipped cream into cream cheese mixture just until incorporated. Fold in another 2 cups whipped cream just until incorporated. Chill and reserve remaining 2 cups whipped cream.

4. Preheat oven to 300°F. Crumble 2 cups cake pieces over a rimmed baking sheet. Add butter and pepper; toss to coat. Bake, stirring occasionally, until golden brown and dry, 25 to 30 minutes.

5. Drain cherries in saba, reserving juice. Reserve ¼ cup drained cherries and 1 tablespoon juice for garnish. Layer one-third of untoasted cake pieces (about 4 cups) in a 4-quart trifle dish. Top with one-third of drained cherries (about 1 cup), and drizzle with one-third of juice (about ½ cup). Spread half of cheesecake filling (about 2½ cups) over top. Sprinkle with ½ cup toasted cake crumbs. Layer with half of remaining untoasted cake pieces and half the remaining drained cherries; drizzle with half the remaining juice (about ½ cup). Spread remaining half of cheesecake filling over top. Top with remaining untoasted cake pieces and remaining drained cherries, and drizzle with remaining ½ cup juice. Spread reserved 2 cups whipped cream over top. Chill, uncovered, until cake has softened, about 2 hours. Garnish with reserved ¼ cup drained cherries, black pepper, and, if desired, edible flowers and fresh fruit. Garnish with a sprinkle of the toasted cake crumbs, reserving remaining crumbs to garnish individual servings. — PICHET ONG

Sour Cherry-Cheesecake Trifle
with Black Pepper and Saba

**Butterscotch Pudding Parfait
with Gingersnap Crumble**

Caramel Falafel

ACTIVE 2 HR; TOTAL 3 HR 30 MIN, PLUS
OVERNIGHT FREEZING; MAKES ABOUT 20

*Pastry chef Dominique Ansel has improved
the ethereal cream puff with a genius
crunchy coating of chocolaty panko. The
puff is then fried like a falafel.*

CHOUX

- ¼ cup whole milk
- 5½ Tbsp. unsalted butter, cubed and softened
- 1 tsp. granulated sugar
- 1 tsp. kosher salt
- ⅔ cup all-purpose flour
- 3 large eggs
- 1 large egg beaten with 1 large egg yolk

FILLING

- 1½ cups heavy cream
- ⅔ cup light corn syrup
- ¼ cup packed dark brown sugar
- ½ cup granulated sugar, divided
- ½ tsp. fleur de sel

COATING

- 1 cup panko
- 1 Tbsp. unsweetened cocoa powder
- 1 large egg beaten with 1 large egg yolk
- Grapeseed or canola oil, for frying
- Confectioners' sugar, for dusting

1. Make the choux Preheat oven to
375°F. Line a large baking sheet with
parchment paper.

2. Combine ⅓ cup water, milk, butter,
sugar, and salt in a medium saucepan;
bring to a boil over medium. When butter
melts, add flour all at once and beat
with a wooden spoon until a tight dough
pulls away from side of the pan, about
2 minutes.

3. Scrape dough into a medium bowl. Using
a wooden spoon, beat in eggs, one at a
time, until smooth. (The dough should be
glossy and fall slowly from the spoon in thick
ribbons.) Scoop dough into a pastry bag
fitted with a ½-inch plain tip. Pipe 1½-inch
mounds onto prepared baking sheet,
spacing them 1 inch apart. Brush mounds
with beaten egg. Bake choux until browned
and puffed, about 30 minutes, rotating sheet
halfway through baking. Let cool completely.

4. Make the filling Combine cream,
corn syrup, and brown sugar in a

medium saucepan; bring just to a boil,
stirring occasionally. Keep warm over
very low heat.

5. Cook ¼ cup granulated sugar in another
medium saucepan over high, without
stirring, until it starts to caramelize, about
3 minutes. Gradually whisk in remaining
¼ cup granulated sugar, letting it start
to caramelize before adding more. Cook,
swirling pan occasionally, until a deep
amber caramel forms, about 3 minutes.
Remove from heat and carefully whisk in
warm cream mixture.

6. Bring caramel to a boil over high and
cook, whisking occasionally, until it
reaches 228°F on a candy thermometer,
about 12 minutes. Remove from heat and
stir in fleur de sel. Let cool completely.
Transfer to a pastry bag fitted with a
¼-inch plain tip. Refrigerate until just
chilled, about 45 minutes.

7. Insert piping tip in bottom of each choux
and pipe in caramel filling.

8. Make the coating Whisk panko and
cocoa powder in a medium bowl. Brush
each choux with some beaten egg, then
dredge in panko and return to baking
sheet. Freeze overnight.

9. Heat 3 inches grapeseed oil to 350°F
in a large saucepan. In batches, fry choux
over medium, turning, until browned and
crisp, about 4 minutes per batch. Using
a slotted spoon, transfer falafel to paper
towels to drain. Let stand for 10 minutes,
then dust with confectioners' sugar, and
serve. — DOMINIQUE ANSEL

Butterscotch Pudding Parfait with Gingersnap Crumble

TOTAL 50 MIN, PLUS 6 HR REFRIGERATION;
SERVES 8

*Pastry chef Joanne Chang bakes her own
gingersnaps to sprinkle over the top of the
parfaits; use your favorite store-bought
cookies for a shortcut.*

BUTTERSCOTCH PUDDING

- 1½ cups heavy cream
- 2 cups whole milk, divided
- 1 cup packed dark brown sugar
- 1¼ tsp. kosher salt
- 4 large egg yolks
- ¼ cup cornstarch (about 1⅛ oz.)
- 2 Tbsp. (1 oz.) dark rum or Scotch whiskey

- 2 tsp. vanilla extract
- ½ cup cold unsalted butter (4 oz.), cut into ½-inch pieces

WHIPPED CRÈME FRAÎCHE

- 1 cup heavy cream
- ½ cup crème fraîche or sour cream
- 3 Tbsp. powdered sugar
- ¼ tsp. vanilla extract

ADDITIONAL INGREDIENT

- 2 cups gingersnaps (about 6¾ oz.), crushed (about 1¾ cups)

1. Make the butterscotch pudding Stir
together cream, 1½ cups milk, brown
sugar, and salt in a large saucepan.
Bring mixture to a simmer over medium,
whisking often to dissolve sugar.

2. Meanwhile, whisk together egg
yolks, cornstarch, rum, vanilla, and
remaining ½ cup milk in a heatproof bowl
until smooth.

3. Gradually ladle about half the hot cream
mixture into egg yolk mixture, whisking
constantly. Once half the hot cream
mixture is whisked into egg yolk mixture,
scrape all egg yolk mixture into remaining
hot cream in pan.

4. Cook pudding over medium-low,
whisking constantly, until bubbly and
thickened, 2 to 3 minutes. Pour mixture
through a fine wire-mesh strainer into a
medium-size heatproof bowl. Gradually
add butter pieces, whisking until butter
is completely incorporated before next
addition. Press plastic wrap directly on
surface of pudding; chill until set, at least
6 hours or up to 3 days.

5. Remove chilled butterscotch pudding
from refrigerator; peel off and discard
plastic. Set pudding aside.

6. Make the whipped crème fraîche Beat
cream, crème fraîche, powdered sugar,
and vanilla with a stand mixer fitted with a
whisk attachment on medium speed until
soft peaks form, 1 to 2 minutes.

7. Spoon about ½ cup pudding into each of
8 glasses. Sprinkle each pudding evenly with
about 3 tablespoons crushed gingersnaps.
Top each with about ⅓ cup whipped crème
fraîche. Garnish with remaining crushed
gingersnaps (about ½ tablespoon each).
Serve immediately, or chill, uncovered, up to
8 hours. — JOANNE CHANG

MAKE AHEAD Butterscotch pudding can
be made up to 3 days in advance, covered
with plastic wrap, and stored in the
refrigerator.

Rum-Caramel Bread Pudding with No-Churn Pumpkin Ice Cream and Candied Pepitas

ACTIVE 45 MIN; TOTAL 2 HR 40 MIN; SERVES 10 TO 12

This ridiculously good dessert from cookbook author and TV cook Ayesha Curry is best when you get a bite of each component at the same time.

CARAMEL

- 1½ cups granulated sugar
- 1½ tsp. fresh lemon juice
- 1 vanilla bean, split lengthwise and seeds scraped
- ¾ cup heavy cream
- 3 Tbsp. cold unsalted butter, cubed
- Pinch of kosher salt
- 3 Tbsp. dark rum

BREAD PUDDING

- Unsalted butter, for greasing
- 2 cups whole milk
- 2 Tbsp. packed light brown sugar
- 2 cinnamon sticks
- 2 tsp. pure vanilla extract
- Pinch of kosher salt
- 4 large eggs
- 2 (14-oz.) brioche loaves, torn into 2-inch pieces
- No-Churn Pumpkin Ice Cream and Candied Pepitas (recipes follow), for serving

1. Make the caramel Mix sugar, ¼ cup water, lemon juice, and vanilla bean and seeds in a medium saucepan. Cook over medium-high until sugar is dissolved. Using a wet pastry brush, wash down any crystals from side of pan. Continue to cook, gently swirling pan occasionally, until an amber caramel forms, about 10 minutes.

2. Remove pan from heat and carefully whisk in cream, butter, and salt until smooth; caramel will bubble up. Transfer to a bowl and let cool to warm, about 1 hour. Discard vanilla pod, then stir in rum.

3. Make the bread pudding Preheat oven to 400°F. Butter a 13- × 9-inch baking dish. Combine milk, brown sugar, cinnamon sticks, vanilla, and salt in a small saucepan. Bring just to a boil, then remove from heat and let steep for 10 minutes; discard cinnamon sticks.

4. Beat eggs in a large bowl. Add brioche and steeped milk; mix well. Scrape mixture into prepared baking dish and drizzle 1 cup warm caramel on top. Bake until puffed and top is golden, 25 to 30 minutes. Serve warm with No-Churn Pumpkin Ice Cream, Candied Pepitas, and the remaining caramel. — AYESHA CURRY

MAKE AHEAD The unbaked bread pudding and caramel sauce can be refrigerated separately overnight. Bring the bread pudding to room temperature and drizzle with warmed caramel before baking.

— ◆ ◆ ◆ —

No-Churn Pumpkin Ice Cream

TOTAL 30 MIN, PLUS OVERNIGHT FREEZING; SERVES 10 TO 12

- 1 cup heavy cream
- 1 (14-oz.) can sweetened condensed milk
- ¾ cup pure pumpkin puree
- 1 tsp. pure vanilla extract
- ½ tsp. ground cinnamon
- Kosher salt

1. Beat cream until stiff peaks form in a large chilled bowl. Whisk condensed milk, pumpkin puree, vanilla, cinnamon, and a pinch of salt in another large bowl. Fold one-third of the whipped cream into pumpkin mixture to lighten it, then gently fold in the rest until no streaks remain.

2. Scrape ice cream into a chilled 9- × 5-inch loaf pan. Press a piece of plastic wrap directly on surface and freeze overnight before serving. — AYESHA CURRY

— ◆ ◆ ◆ —

Candied Pepitas

TOTAL 20 MIN; MAKES 1 CUP

- 1 cup pepitas
- 2 Tbsp. sugar
- ¼ tsp. freshly grated nutmeg
- ¼ tsp. ground cinnamon
- ⅛ tsp. cayenne pepper
- Pinch of kosher salt

Mix pepitas, sugar, nutmeg, cinnamon, cayenne, and salt in a large skillet. Cook over medium, stirring and tossing occasionally, until pepitas are lightly browned and coated in a very light caramel, about 7 minutes. Transfer to a plate to cool completely before serving. — AYESHA CURRY

Mhalabiyeh (Fragrant Milk Pudding with Cranberries)

ACTIVE 20 MIN; TOTAL 2 HR 40 MIN; SERVES 12

Mhalabiyeh—a Middle Eastern milk pudding—is commonly flavored with mastic, which has a pleasant flavor reminiscent of licorice or pine. Purchase mastic gum at amazon.com. Alternatively, Reem Kassis suggests substituting 1 teaspoon of rose or orange blossom water.

- 4 mastic gum pieces
- 1¼ cups plus 1 pinch granulated sugar, divided
- 4 cups whole milk, divided
- ½ cup cornstarch
- 1 cup heavy cream
- 2 cups fresh or frozen cranberries

1. Grind mastic gum pieces and a pinch of sugar in a mortar and pestle until finely ground. Whisk together ground mastic gum mixture, 1 cup milk, and cornstarch in a small bowl until dissolved.

2. Whisk together cream, ¾ cup sugar, and remaining 3 cups milk in a large, heavy saucepan. Bring to a simmer over medium. When milk mixture is about to boil, add mastic mixture, and cook, whisking constantly, until thickened, about 1 minute. Remove from heat.

3. Carefully ladle hot pudding into 12 (6- to 8-ounce) heatproof dessert bowls or glasses. Press plastic wrap or wax paper directly onto surface of each pudding to prevent a skin from forming. Let cool slightly, about 20 minutes; refrigerate until set and chilled, at least 2 hours or up to 24 hours.

4. Meanwhile, combine cranberries, ¼ cup water, and remaining ½ cup sugar in a small saucepan. Cook over low, stirring occasionally, until cranberries burst and release their juices, 8 to 10 minutes. Remove from heat, and let cool. Cover and chill until ready to serve.

5. Serve puddings cold, topped with cranberry sauce. — REEM KASSIS

MAKE AHEAD Pudding may be made up to a day in advance.

**Mhalabiyeh (Fragrant Milk
Pudding with Cranberries)**

Tropical Ambrosia

Tropical Ambrosia

ACTIVE 45 MIN; TOTAL 13 HR 30 MIN;
SERVES 8

Chef Ryan Ratino of Bresca in Washington, D.C., was inspired by memories of his grandmother's ambrosia, a marshmallow-studded fruit salad. Pink peppercorns add a fruity, peppery bite to the meringue; lightly crush them to release their fragrant oils.

COCONUT TAPIOCA

- ½ cup uncooked large pearl tapioca
- 1 cup coconut water
- 1 cup granulated sugar
- ¼ cup well-shaken and stirred unsweetened canned coconut milk
- ½ tsp. coconut extract
- ½ tsp. kosher salt

MERINGUE

- 2 large egg whites, at room temperature
- ¼ tsp. cream of tartar
- ⅛ tsp. kosher salt
- ½ cup superfine sugar
- 2 tsp. pink peppercorns, crushed

ADDITIONAL INGREDIENTS

- 4 cups mango sorbet
- ¾ cup finely diced mango
- ¾ cup finely diced pineapple
- ½ cup passion fruit pulp (from 8 passion fruit)
- 2 Tbsp. fresh lemon balm leaves or mint leaves, for garnish

1. Make the coconut tapioca Stir together 4 cups water and tapioca in a bowl. Cover and chill 8 hours or overnight.

2. Drain soaked tapioca, and transfer to a medium saucepan. Add coconut water, and cook over low, stirring often, until heated through, about 5 minutes. Add granulated sugar, coconut milk, coconut extract, and salt, and cook, stirring often, until mixture has thickened and tapioca pearls are tender, about 25 minutes. Transfer to a medium bowl, and cool completely, about 2 hours.

3. Make the meringue While coconut tapioca cools, preheat oven to 200°F. Beat egg whites with a stand mixer fitted with a whisk attachment on medium speed until frothy, about 1 minute. Add cream of tartar and salt, and beat until soft peaks form, 1 to 2 minutes. With machine running, gradually add superfine sugar, 1 tablespoon at a time, beating until completely incorporated. Increase speed to high, and beat until stiff, glossy peaks form, 2 to 3 minutes.

4. Using an offset spatula, spread meringue in a ¼-inch-thick rectangle on a parchment paper-lined baking sheet. Sprinkle with crushed pink peppercorns. Bake in preheated oven until firm and dry to the touch, 2 to 4 hours. Turn oven off, and leave meringue inside oven until completely dry, about 2 hours. Remove from oven, and let cool completely, about 30 minutes. Break meringue into small pieces.

5. To serve, place ¼ cup sorbet in each of 8 (8-ounce) serving glasses. Top each with ¼ cup coconut tapioca, 1½ tablespoons diced mango, 1½ tablespoons diced pineapple, and 1 tablespoon passion fruit pulp. Top each with ¼ cup sorbet, and garnish with meringue shards and lemon balm. Serve immediately. — RYAN RATINO

PASTRY TIP For the lightest, snappiest meringue, bake it until completely firm and dry to the touch.

Sticky Drunken Pears

ACTIVE 10 MIN; TOTAL 1 HR 20 MIN;
SERVES 8

These elegant pears, from Claire Ptak at London's cult-favorite Violet Bakery, are baked in a sweet wine syrup that becomes a wonderful glaze.

- 8 firm Bosc pears, stems attached
- 2 Tbsp. fresh lemon juice
- 3 cups sweet wine, such as Muscat de Beaumes-de-Venise
  Strips of zest from 1 lemon
- 1 vanilla bean, split and seeds scraped
- 1 medium cinnamon stick
- 1 cup turbinado sugar
  Whipped crème fraîche, for serving

1. Preheat oven to 400°F. In a 9-inch square baking dish, arrange pears stem-end up, leaving space between them. Mix lemon juice and sweet wine, and pour over pears. Add lemon zest, vanilla bean and seeds, and cinnamon stick to baking dish, and sprinkle sugar over pears. Bake, basting every 15 minutes, until pears are softened and starting to burst slightly, about 45 minutes. Let cool for 10 minutes.

2. Using a slotted spoon, transfer pears to a serving dish. Pour syrup into a small saucepan. Cook over medium-high until reduced by one-third, 12 to 15 minutes. Pour syrup over pears; serve with whipped crème fraîche. — CLAIRE PTAK

Whipped Vanilla Ganache Toasts with Pear and Pomegranate

ACTIVE 45 MIN; TOTAL 3 HR 15 MIN; MAKES ABOUT 24

San Francisco pastry chef William Werner whips a rich and delicious white chocolate ganache until it's light and fluffy, then spreads on pain de mie bread toasts.

POACHED PEARS

- 1 vanilla bean, halved lengthwise, seeds scraped and pod reserved
- 2 cups sugar
- 5 (3-inch-long) pieces of lemon zest, divided
- 4 Forelle pears (1 lb.), peeled, halved lengthwise, and cored

WHIPPED VANILLA GANACHE

- 3 oz. white chocolate, chopped
- 1¼ cups heavy cream, divided
- ½ Tbsp. light corn syrup
- ¼ tsp. vanilla bean paste or ½ vanilla bean, halved lengthwise and seeds scraped
  Pain de mie bread toasts, for serving (see Note)
  Pomegranate seeds, for garnish

1. Make the poached pears Combine vanilla seeds and pod, sugar, 2½ cups water, and 3 pieces lemon zest in a medium saucepan. Bring to a simmer, stirring to dissolve sugar. Remove pan from heat and let steep for 30 minutes. Pour syrup through a fine wire-mesh strainer. Return syrup to saucepan and let cool completely.

2. Add pears and remaining 2 pieces lemon zest to syrup, and bring to a bare simmer. Cook over medium-low, turning occasionally, until pears are just tender, about 20 minutes. Remove saucepan from heat and let cool to room temperature. Cover and refrigerate until chilled, about 2 hours.

3. Make the whipped vanilla ganache Place white chocolate in a heatproof medium bowl. Combine ½ cup cream, corn syrup, and vanilla bean paste in a small saucepan, and bring to a boil. Pour hot cream over chocolate and let stand for 1 minute, then whisk until smooth; transfer to a blender. With machine running, slowly drizzle in remaining ¾ cup cream until smooth. Scrape vanilla ganache into a large bowl and chill until it is very cold, about 2 hours.

4. Beat chilled ganache using an electric mixer on medium speed until soft peaks form, about 2 minutes. Spread whipped ganache on toasts. Slice pears into thin wedges; arrange on top. Garnish with pomegranate seeds, and serve. — WILLIAM WERNER

NOTE Pain de mie is packaged sliced white bread that's available at bakeries.

MAKE AHEAD The poached pears can be stored in their syrup overnight. The ganache can be refrigerated overnight.

---◆◆◆---

Lemon Curd Toasts with Coconut

ACTIVE 45 MIN; TOTAL 3 HR; MAKES ABOUT 24

Olive oil and cocoa butter make this lemony curd from pastry chef William Werner extraordinarily creamy and luscious. Spread on baguette toasts, it becomes a fantastic dessert.

- 3 large eggs
- 1½ cups sugar, divided
- 3 Tbsp. finely grated lemon zest plus ⅔ cup fresh lemon juice
- ¼ cup extra-virgin olive oil
- ¼ cup chopped cocoa butter (see Note)
  Baguette toasts, for serving
  Fresh blackberries and toasted coconut flakes or chips, for garnish

1. Whisk eggs and ¾ cup sugar in a medium bowl until combined. Warm lemon zest, lemon juice, oil, cocoa butter, and remaining ¾ cup sugar in a small saucepan over medium, stirring to dissolve sugar. While whisking constantly, slowly drizzle half the lemon juice mixture into eggs. Add egg mixture to saucepan and cook curd over medium-low, stirring constantly, until thickened and a candy thermometer inserted in the curd registers 186°F, about 12 minutes.

2. Pour curd through a fine wire-mesh strainer into a blender. Puree until lightened, about 1 minute. Scrape into a bowl. Press a sheet of plastic wrap directly on the curd and let cool to room temperature. Refrigerate until cold and set, about 2 hours.

3. Spread lemon curd on toasts and top with blackberries. Garnish with toasted coconut, and serve. — WILLIAM WERNER

NOTE Solid cocoa butter is available at natural food shops, Whole Foods, and amazon.com.

MAKE AHEAD The lemon curd can be refrigerated for 1 week.

Yuzu Kosho Cashew Butter Toasts

ACTIVE 1 HR 30 MIN; TOTAL 3 HR; MAKES ABOUT 24

San Francisco pastry chef William Werner turns out contemporary pastries like this cashew butter spiked with citrusy red yuzu kosho spread on pumpernickel toasts.

CANDIED MANDARINS

- 1 cup sugar
- 4 mandarins (10 oz.), scrubbed and sliced crosswise ⅛ inch thick
- 1 vanilla bean, halved lengthwise, seeds scraped and pod reserved

YUZU KOSHO CASHEW BUTTER

- 2½ cups cashews (about 1 lb.)
- 3 Tbsp. sugar
- 2 tsp. kosher salt
- 1 Tbsp. red yuzu kosho (see Note)
- ⅓ cup canola oil
  Pumpernickel bread toasts, for serving
  Pure grade B maple syrup, for drizzling

1. Make the candied mandarins Combine sugar and 1½ cups water in a medium saucepan and bring to a bare simmer, stirring to dissolve sugar. Add mandarins and vanilla seeds and pod, and cook over low, stirring occasionally, until mandarins are softened and slightly translucent, about 1 hour and 15 minutes. Remove pan from heat; discard vanilla pod. Let mandarins cool in syrup about 1 hour.

2. Make the yuzu kosho cashew butter Preheat oven to 350°F. Spread cashews on a baking sheet, and toast until deep golden, about 20 minutes. Transfer sheet to a wire rack and let cashews cool completely.

3. Place cashews in a food processor, and pulse until finely chopped. Add sugar, salt, and yuzu kosho. With machine running, slowly drizzle in canola oil until well blended. Scrape into a medium bowl.

4. Spread yuzu kosho cashew butter on toasts and drizzle lightly with maple syrup. Top with drained candied mandarins, and serve. — WILLIAM WERNER

NOTE Red yuzu kosho is made with yuzu zest (from the sour citrus fruit), green chiles, and salt. Look for it at Asian markets.

MAKE AHEAD The yuzu kosho cashew butter can be refrigerated for 2 weeks. The candied mandarins can be refrigerated for 1 week; bring to room temperature before serving.

Whipped Vanilla Ganache Toasts with Pear and Pomegranate

Lemon Curd Toasts with Coconut

Yuzu Kosho Cashew Butter Toasts

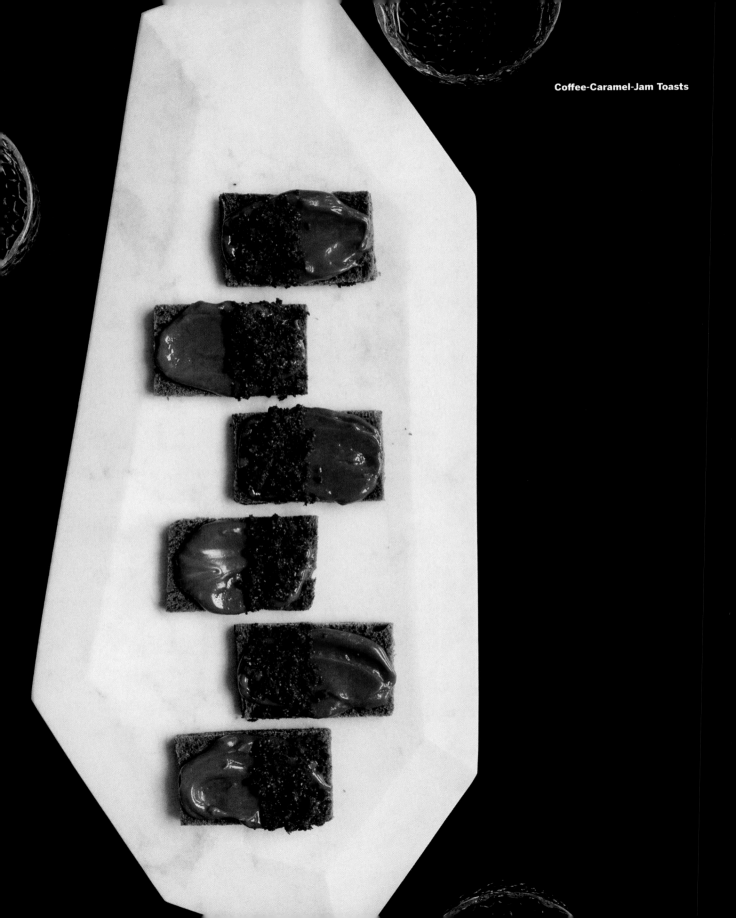

Zabaglione

TOTAL 10 MIN; MAKES 4 CUPS

There are as many variations on zabaglione, the boozy Italian custard sauce, as there are ways to enjoy it. The dead-simple recipe—in which egg yolks, sugar, and wine are beaten vigorously over low heat—can be made with any wine you like, depending on what you plan to pair it with. Use Marsala for the most classic flavor, then experiment with other wines to your taste. Here are three variations we love—and delicious ways to serve them.

6 large egg yolks

½ cup granulated sugar

Pinch of kosher salt

½ cup sweet wine, such as Marsala, Moscato, or Vin Santo

1. Beat yolks in a heatproof bowl (preferably copper) until combined. Add sugar and salt, whisking constantly until combined.

2. Pour wine into yolk mixture, and whisk until sugar is dissolved, about 30 seconds.

3. Heat mixture over a saucepan of barely simmering water, whisking vigorously to incorporate air into mixture.

4. Whisk until custard is warm and tripled in volume, and dragging the whisk across it leaves a ribbon on the surface, 8 to 9 minutes. Remove from heat. Serve immediately, or whisk over an ice bath until cooled. —MARY-FRANCES HECK

STRACCIATELLA SEMIFREDDO Coat a 9-inch loaf pan with cooking spray, and line with plastic wrap. Sprinkle bottom of pan with ⅓ cup toasted sliced almonds. Fold cooled Marsala zabaglione with 3 cups whipped heavy cream and ½ cup chocolate shavings; scrape into loaf pan, cover, and freeze until firm, at least 3 hours. To serve, invert onto a plate, and slice. —MARY-FRANCES HECK

CHAMPAGNE-GLAZED STRAWBERRIES Make a Champagne zabaglione, increasing the granulated sugar, if desired. Arrange a single layer of macerated strawberries in a crème brûlée dish, and top with enough zabaglione to cover (about ⅓ cup). Broil on high 3 to 4 inches from heat until zabaglione is bubbly and browned, 2 to 3 minutes. —MARY-FRANCES HECK

READY TO SERVE Drizzle warm zabaglione over ripe seasonal fruit.

◆ ◆ ◆

Coffee-Caramel-Jam Toasts

ACTIVE 1 HR; TOTAL 2 HR 15 MIN, PLUS OVERNIGHT STEEPING; MAKES ABOUT 24

Instead of using fruit jam, pastry chef William Werner spreads a rich, thick, and silky coffee-caramel jam over rye toasts to create this elegant dessert.

COFFEE-CARAMEL JAM

½ cup crushed coffee beans

1¼ cups heavy cream

1 cup whole milk

1 cup sugar

1 Tbsp. light corn syrup

2 tsp. instant espresso

⅛ tsp. fine sea salt

CHOCOLATE CRUMBLE

¾ cup all-purpose flour

¾ cup almond flour

½ cup sugar

¼ cup unsweetened cocoa powder

¼ tsp. fine sea salt

1 stick cold unsalted butter, cubed

Dark rye toasts, for serving

1. Make the coffee-caramel jam Preheat oven to 350°F. Spread coffee beans on a baking sheet and toast, until fragrant, 10 minutes. Transfer to a large bowl. Stir in cream and milk, cover, and let steep in the refrigerator overnight.

2. Pour coffee cream through a fine wire-mesh strainer, pressing on solids; you should have 2 cups. Cook sugar in a large saucepan over medium, stirring occasionally, until a light amber caramel forms, about 5 minutes. Slowly add coffee cream; be careful, as it will boil vigorously. Add corn syrup, espresso, and sea salt, and bring to a simmer; caramel will harden but will dissolve as it simmers. Cook over medium-low, stirring, until a candy thermometer inserted in the caramel jam registers 210°F, about 12 minutes. Carefully transfer jam to a blender, and puree until smooth and shiny. Scrape into a medium bowl and let cool to room temperature.

3. Make the chocolate crumble Whisk all-purpose flour, almond flour, sugar, cocoa powder, and sea salt in a medium bowl. Using your fingers, rub in butter until coarse crumbs form. Spread crumbs in an even layer on a parchment paper-lined baking sheet and refrigerate until firm, about 1 hour.

4. Preheat oven to 350°F. Bake crumble for about 18 minutes, until golden. Transfer to a wire rack to cool completely.

5. Spread some coffee-caramel jam on toasts. Sprinkle chocolate crumbles on one half of each toast; press gently to help them adhere. — WILLIAM WERNER

MAKE AHEAD The jam can be refrigerated for up to 1 week. Serve at room temperature. The baked crumble can be stored in an airtight container for 1 week or frozen for 1 month.

INDEX

PHOTO CREDITS

CONVERSION CHART

BASIC MEASUREMENTS

GALLON	QUART	PINT	CUP	OUNCE	TBSP	TSP	DROPS
1 gal	4 qt	8 pt	16 c	128 fl oz			
½ gal	2 qt	4 pt	8 c	64 fl oz			
¼ gal	1 qt	2 pt	4 c	32 fl oz			
	½ qt	1 pt	2 c	16 fl oz			
	¼ qt	½ pt	1 c	8 fl oz	16 Tbsp		
			⅞ c	7 fl oz	14 Tbsp		
			¾ c	6 fl oz	12 Tbsp		
			⅔ c	5 ⅓ fl oz	10 ⅔ Tbsp		
			⅝ c	5 fl oz	10 Tbsp		
			½ c	4 fl oz	8 Tbsp		
			⅜ c	3 fl oz	6 Tbsp		
			⅓ c	2 ⅔ fl oz	5 ⅓ Tbsp	16 tsp	
			¼ c	2 fl oz	4 Tbsp	12 tsp	
			⅛ c	1 fl oz	2 Tbsp	6 tsp	
				½ fl oz	1 Tbsp	3 tsp	
					½ Tbsp	1½ tsp	
						1 tsp	60 drops
						½ tsp	30 drops

U.S. TO METRIC CONVERSIONS

The conversions shown here are approximations. For more-precise conversions, use the formulas to the right.

VOLUME			WEIGHT			TEMPERATURE			CONVERSION FORMULAS
1 tsp	=	5 mL	1 oz	=	28 g	475°F	=	246°C	tsp × 4.929 = mL
1 Tbsp	=	15 mL	¼ lb (4 oz)	=	113 g	450°F	=	232°C	Tbsp × 14.787 = mL
1 fl oz	=	30 mL	½ lb (8 oz)	=	227 g	425°F	=	218°C	fl oz × 29.574 = mL
¼ c	=	59 mL	¾ lb (12 oz)	=	340 g	400°F	=	204°C	c × 236.588 = mL
½ c	=	118 mL	1 lb (16 oz)	=	½ kg	375°F	=	191°C	pt × 0.473 = L
¾ c	=	177 mL				350°F	=	177°C	qt × 0.946 = L
1 c	=	237 mL	**LENGTH**			325°F	=	163°C	oz × 28.35 = g
1 pt	=	½ L	1 in	=	2.5 cm	300°F	=	149°C	lb × 0.453 = kg
1 qt	=	1 L	5 in	=	12.7 cm	275°F	=	135°C	in × 2.54 = cm
1 gal	=	4.4 L	9 in	=	23 cm	250°F	=	121°C	(°F − 32) × 0.556 = °C

More books from
FOOD & WINE

Perfect Pairings

With chapters arranged by the most popular grape varieties, this collection of classic recipes takes the guesswork out of what dish to serve with your favorite wines. The easy-to-follow wine primers break down the nuances of grape varieties and regions so you can shop for bottles like a pro.

Cocktails

This book features more than 150 of our best recipes for cocktails and mocktails from innovative bartenders across the country. A must-have collection for the home bartender, inside you'll find essential tips, tools, and techniques, and 24 menu ideas for drinks and bites. Join the editors of *Food & Wine* as they showcase the art of mixing a proper cocktail and offering hospitality with the finest in food and drink. Cheers!

Grilling

This must-have grilling book features luscious recipes with full color photographs to inspire you, grilling basics to guide you, and essential tools, plus tips and practical advice from all-star chefs. It's the definitive book for grilling enthusiasts that goes beyond the basics to get the most out of every fire.